PIVOT POINT.

PIVOT POINT FUNDAMENTALS: COSMETOLOGY

STUDY GUIDE

© 1980-2021 Pivot Point International, Inc.
All rights reserved.
ISBN 978-1-940593-52-4

1st Edition
8th Printing, October 2021
Printed in China

Pivot Point International, Inc.
Global Headquarters
8725 West Higgins Road, Suite 700
Chicago, IL 60631 USA

847-866-0500
pivot-point.com

D1288452

STUDY GUIDE //
CONTENTS

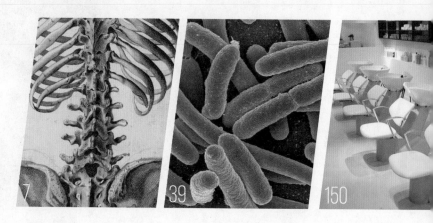

7   39   150

269   319   460   504   552

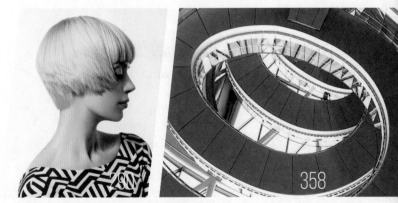

358

Workshop lessons are not included in study guide.

MINDFRAME OVERVIEW //

This course has been written by mindful professionals. It includes learning strategies that are found online, in your coursebooks/digital books, and within your study guide. These learning strategies are designed to boost your learning potential as you prepare for the future.

Because everyone learns in different ways, some parts of your course will be easier than other parts. You'll gain confidence as you put the different pieces of the puzzle together, because each piece involves a special way of learning.

These strategies can be grouped in a category called MINDFRAMES. Each MINDFRAME is a specific way of using your brainpower. The seven different MINDFRAMES include: Previewing, Naming, Connecting, Self-Checking, Applying, Self-Testing and Journaling. These MINDFRAMES overlap in rich and rewarding ways just the way your mind itself does—one MINDFRAME flows into another.

There is a MINDFRAME TOOLBAR at the bottom of every study guide page. The MINDFRAME used on each page is highlighted. On some pages, more than one MINDFRAME may be used.

This overview of the 7 MINDFRAMES offers a definition of what each MINDFRAME is, why it is important to you and how the MINDFRAME is used within the course. All "how" statements indicate a study guide, or other course location.

PREVIEWING 1	NAMING 2	CONNECTING 3	SELF-CHECKING 4	APPLYING 5	SELF-TESTING 6	JOURNALING/ TRANSFER 7
1	2	3	4	5	6	7

PREVIEWING 1

What: Helps you set the stage for meaningful learning

Why: To cue your attention and activate your interest

How: Achieve: Learning outcomes
Focus: Lesson overview

NAMING 2

What: Helps you put what you are learning into your own words; note-taking

Why: Helps you manage and organize information and see differences

How: SMARTNOTES

CONNECTING 3

What: Helps you sort things into groups that are related

Why: To highlight how things fit together and see similarities

How: Thinking Maps, Matching
Drawing, Learning Connections (online)

SELF-CHECKING 4

What: Provides a recap; summarizes

Why: To determine if you are ready to move forward

How: Check What You Know (Study Slides, online)
Design Decisions charts (coursebook, online)

APPLYING 5

What: Puts knowledge into action

Why: To practice and solve problems

How: Talking Points (online)
Show You Know (online)
Show You Can (online)

SELF-TESTING 6

What: Sends the signal to the brain that the coast is clear to take on new challenges

Why: To help you take responsibility for your learning

How: Lesson Challenges
Exam Prep
Exam Ace (online)

JOURNALING/TRANSFER 7

What: Makes true learning a deeply personal experience

Why: Because learning transfers to the future

How: Grow What You Know
Join the Conversation (online)

101ᶜ.1 // HEALTHY BODY & MIND

ACHIEVE //

Following this lesson on *Healthy Body and Mind*, you'll be able to:

» State the recommended number of hours to sleep per night

» Identify the effects of regular exercise

» Describe the value of a balanced diet

» Explain the differences between personal and public hygiene

» Summarize the elements involved in presenting a professional image

FOCUS //

HEALTHY BODY AND MIND

Rest and Relaxation

Exercise

Nutrition

Hygiene

Image

REST AND RELAXATION

BENEFITS

Necessary for:

Helps relieve:

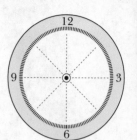

The number of sleep hours necessary to prevent fatique

EXERCISE

Regular exercise routine will help you _____and _____better

Exercise is a proven method through which you can:

-
-
-
-

NUTRITION

A balanced diet is essential for:

- Personal and professional _____ - _____

- Providing energy for the body to use and helping with prevention of

  certain _____

Almost all foods contain a mixture of these 3 things:

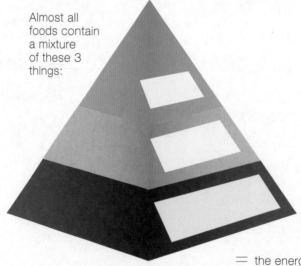

= the energy they contain is measured in calories.

The body uses this energy to:
- Heat itself
- Build its _____
- Move its parts during exercise and activities
- Energy may also be stored as _____

RECORD YOUR WEEK

	Monday	Tuesday	Wednesday	Thursday	Friday	Saturday	Sunday
Hours of sleep per night							
How much exercise							
Calories burned							

HYGIENE

Hygiene is the science that deals with _____ _____.

DIFFERENCES

Public Hygiene	Personal Hygiene

PUBLIC HYGIENE

Primary Health Hazards

- Impure air ventilation

- Improper disinfection practices

- Inadequate _____

- Improper _____ or use of food

PERSONAL HYGIENE

Oral Hygiene

Maintaining healthy teeth and keeping breath fresh.

Bad breath = _____

Guidelines for preventing unpleasant body odor include:

- Bathing regularly using _____

- Applying deodorant following _____

- Avoiding excessive use of perfume or cologne

- Washing clothing when _____

IMAGE

The salon business is a service business; therefore, close attention to personal grooming is a _____.

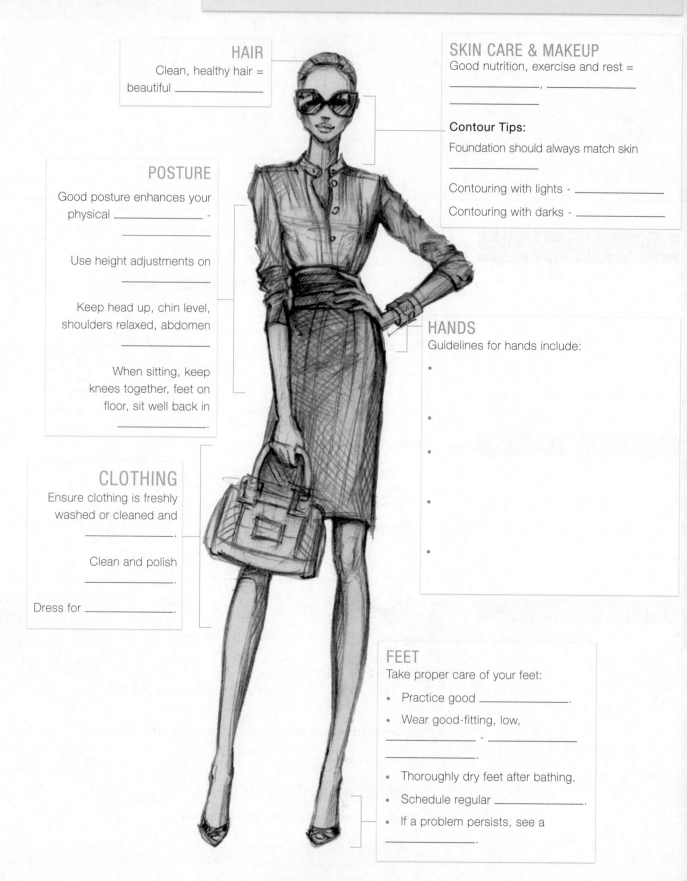

HAIR

Clean, healthy hair = beautiful _____

SKIN CARE & MAKEUP

Good nutrition, exercise and rest = _____, _____ _____

Contour Tips:

Foundation should always match skin _____

Contouring with lights - _____

Contouring with darks - _____

POSTURE

Good posture enhances your physical _____ - _____

Use height adjustments on _____

Keep head up, chin level, shoulders relaxed, abdomen _____

When sitting, keep knees together, feet on floor, sit well back in _____.

HANDS

Guidelines for hands include:

-
-
-
-
-

CLOTHING

Ensure clothing is freshly washed or cleaned and _____.

Clean and polish _____.

Dress for _____.

FEET

Take proper care of your feet:

- Practice good _____.
- Wear good-fitting, low, _____ - _____ _____.
- Thoroughly dry feet after bathing.
- Schedule regular _____.
- If a problem persists, see a _____

THINKING MAP

Create a Thinking Map to help yourself make sense of how your notes fit together. Use words in the Jump Start Box as well as your own words and pictures to make a visual that will help you connect the important ideas of this lesson. Be creative!

HEALTHY BODY & MIND

JUMP START BOX

REST	VENTILATION	HYGIENE
CALORIES	EXERCISE	CONTOURING
PERSONAL HYGIENE	GROOMING	ENERGY
DARK	POSTURE	LIGHT
ETHICS	NUTRITION	PUBLIC HYGIENE
		LIGHTING

LESSON CHALLENGE *Multiple choice. Indicate one correct answer for each question.*

1. **Which of the following terms defines the art and science of beauty care?**
   a. onychology
   b. cosmetology
   c. ethical conduct
   d. personal hygiene

2. **How many hours of sleep are required for most people to function properly and avoid fatigue?**
   a. 1-2 hours
   b. 3-4 hours
   c. 6-8 hours
   d. 9-12 hours

3. **Which of the following activities helps stimulate blood circulation in the body?**
   a. exercise
   b. watching TV
   c. reading a book
   d. listening to music

4. **The energy contained in food is measured in:**
   a. calories
   b. degrees
   c. fat content
   d. protein content

5. **An individual's system for maintaining cleanliness and health is known as:**
   a. nutrition
   b. public hygiene
   c. public sanitation
   d. personal hygiene

6. **Healthy, glowing skin is equally dependent on all of the following EXCEPT:**
   a. rest
   b. exercise
   c. good nutrition
   d. lack of sleep

7. **When applying makeup, contouring with light colors will always have what effect on the face?**
   a. narrowing
   b. broadening
   c. highlighting
   d. moisturizing

8. **An overly wide jaw can be visually narrowed by applying:**
   a. lighter contour cream to the inner areas of the jawline
   b. lighter contour cream to the outer areas of the jawline
   c. darker contour cream to the outer areas of the jawline
   d. darker contour cream to the inner areas of the jawline

9. **When performing chemical services, a salon professional should always wear:**
   a. makeup
   b. head bands
   c. comfortable shoes
   d. protective gloves

10. **Keeping the abdomen flat, the chin level and the head up are key points in having:**
    a. bad posture
    b. good posture
    c. potential injuries
    d. a poor standing position

LESSON CHALLENGE REFERENCES

Check your answers. Place a check mark next to the page number for any incorrect answer. On the lines, jot down topics that you still need to review.

1. PAGE 4 _____
2. PAGE 4 _____
3. PAGE 4 _____
4. PAGE 6 _____
5. PAGE 7 _____
6. PAGE 9 _____
7. PAGE 9 _____
8. PAGE 9 _____
9. PAGE 10 _____
10. PAGE 11 _____

▶ GROW WHAT YOU KNOW

Reflect on what you have learned and predict how this information will be useful in the future.

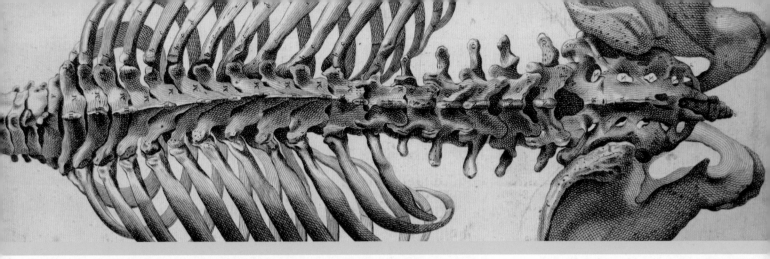

101ᶜ.2 // ERGONOMICS

ACHIEVE //

Following this lesson on *Ergonomics*, you'll be able to:

» Explain the importance of ergonomics and how it affects a salon professional's job performance

» Identify common causes of neck and back pain and ways to prevent it

» State common causes of foot and leg problems and ways to prevent them

» Compare common causes of hand and wrist problems and ways to prevent them

» Cite common causes of shoulder strain and ways to prevent it

FOCUS //

ERGONOMICS

Neck and Back

Foot and Leg

Hands and Wrists

Shoulders

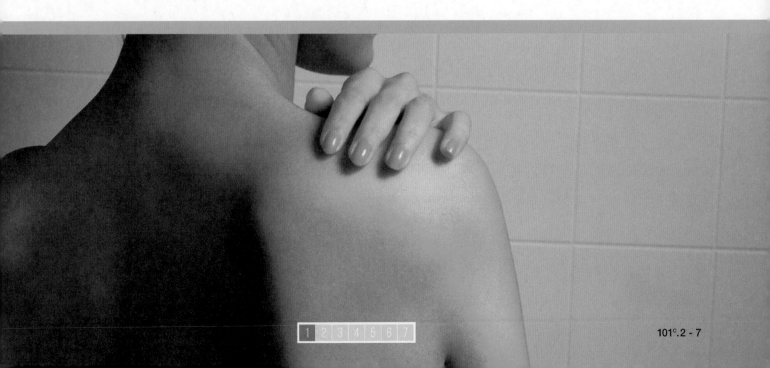

Ergonomics: *noun* | er·go·nom·ics | **Science that looks at how you do your work, what body movements, positions, tools, etc., you use and the effect it has on your body**

NECK AND BACK

Recommendations to Prevent Neck and Back Problems

General

-
-

-

-

-

-

Service-Specific

- Use freestanding _____.
- Adjust height of client's chair.
- Tilt client's _____.
- Have clients with very long hair stand up.
- Use a chair with tilted seat when doing a _____.
- Place one foot on a stool or rung of client's chair.
- Position facial chair or bed close to avoid unnecessary _____.

FOOT AND LEG

Recommendations to Prevent Foot and Leg Problems

General

-
-
-
-
-

Service-Specific

- Hydraulic chairs should adjust up and down at least 5".
- Use a stool or movable seat, if necessary, to rest your _____.
- Raise your feet on a stool when you take a _____.
- Adjust facial stool and facial chair or bed up or _____.

HANDS AND WRISTS

| Tendonitis | Carpal Tunnel Syndrome |

Main Causes:

1.

2.

3.

Recommendations to Prevent Hand and Wrist Problems

General

-
-
-
-
-

Service-Specific

- Adjust chair _____ .
- Try to position yourself next to client so you don't have to raise your_____.
- Tilt client's head so you don't have to bend arm, hand and wrist as much.
- Use sharp shears that fit your hand and are correctly adjusted/lubricated.
- Twirl the handle of round brush between thumb and _____ _____.
- Use armrests for both you and client at manicure stations.
- Use strength of arms, not hands and wrists, during _____.

SHOULDERS

Recommendations to Prevent Shoulder Problems

General

-
-
-

Service-Specific

- Adjust chair height and swivel chair so your arms are close to your _____.
- Tilt client's head to a position that is comfortable for you.
- Hold tools so you don't have to raise your _____.
- Have client extend a hand toward you when you're doing a _____ _____.
- Use an armrest when you do a manicure, or support arms on folded _____.
- Position facial chair or bed and facial machines to be close to you.
- Be sure not to tense shoulders while performing facial treatments and _____.

SCRAMBLE

Unscramble these important terms from the lesson.

GOESRNOCIM

TSITNEODNI

TIBSURIS

VIPELC TTIL

LAPCRA NNLETU SEYNDMOR

1 2 3 4 5 6 7

LESSON CHALLENGE *Multiple choice. Indicate one correct answer for each question.*

1. The science that looks at how individuals perform work and what body movements, tools and equipment benefit the health and comfort of the salon professional and client is called:
   a. economics
   b. ergonomics
   c. public hygiene
   d. personal hygiene

2. Prevent neck and back strain by:
   a. bending forward when performing a service
   b. not reaching overhead for supplies
   c. standing for a long time in high heels
   d. twisting your body to get closer to a client

3. All of the following can help prevent neck and back strain EXCEPT:
   a. working with the back straight
   b. reaching overhead for supplies
   c. using freestanding shampoo bowls
   d. adjusting the height of the client's chair

4. Which type of shoes should be worn to reduce fatigue caused by standing for long periods of time?
   a. high-heeled shoes
   b. shoes with pointed toes
   c. low, broad-heeled shoes
   d. shoes without arch support

5. Rotating footwear has all of the following effects EXCEPT:
   a. reduces fatigue
   b. strengthens your arch
   c. makes them last longer
   d. shortens how long they last

6. Which of the following preventative measures will help alleviate foot and leg problems?
   a. wearing high heels
   b. standing for long periods of time
   c. wearing shoes with poor arch support
   d. raising your feet on a stool during breaks

7. What condition occurs when tendons become inflamed?
   a. bursitis
   b. sore feet
   c. tendonitis
   d. varicose veins

8. All of the following movements cause Carpal Tunnel Syndrome EXCEPT:
   a. using sharp shears
   b. gripping with force
   c. bending your wrist a lot
   d. repeating a motion over and over

9. Which of the following will help prevent shoulder problems?
   a. holding heavy clippers
   b. reaching across a table to manicure
   c. reaching for supplies on a high shelf
   d. adjusting the height of the chair when you work on a client

10. An inflammation of the fluid sac that lies between a tendon and skin or bone is called:
    a. bursitis
    b. tendonitis
    c. dermatitis
    d. carpal tunnel

LESSON CHALLENGE REFERENCES

Check your answers. Place a check mark next to the page number for any incorrect answer. On the lines, jot down topics that you still need to review.

1. PAGE 15 _____
2. PAGE 15 _____
3. PAGE 16 _____
4. PAGE 17 _____
5. PAGE 17 _____

6. PAGE 17 _____
7. PAGE 18 _____
8. PAGE 18 _____
9. PAGE 20 _____
10. PAGE 20 _____

▶ GROW WHAT YOU KNOW

Reflect on what you have learned and predict how this information will be useful in the future.

101ᶜ.3 //

BASIC COMMUNICATION

ACHIEVE //

Following this lesson on *Basic Communication*, you'll be able to:

>> Identify, monitor and use forms of nonverbal communication to your advantage

>> Express clear and concise verbal messages

>> Explain the elements of effective communication

>> Compare the key points of two-way communication

>> Examine strategies that result in good listening habits

FOCUS //

BASIC COMMUNICATION

Nonverbal Communication

Verbal Communication

Listening

NONVERBAL COMMUNICATION

Communication: _____
_____

Body Language

- Smiling

- Standing straight, shoulders squared, head high, extending hand

- Bowed shoulders, sloping body posture

- Eye contact

Message

-
-
-
-

KEY ELEMENTS OF NONVERBAL COMMUNICATION

Facial Expression

Eye Contact

Gesture

Posture

Proximity

A 3-step approach to speaking with clarity

1.

2.

3.

VERBAL COMMUNICATION

Verbal Communication: _____
_____
_____

KEY ELEMENTS OF VERBAL COMMUNICATION

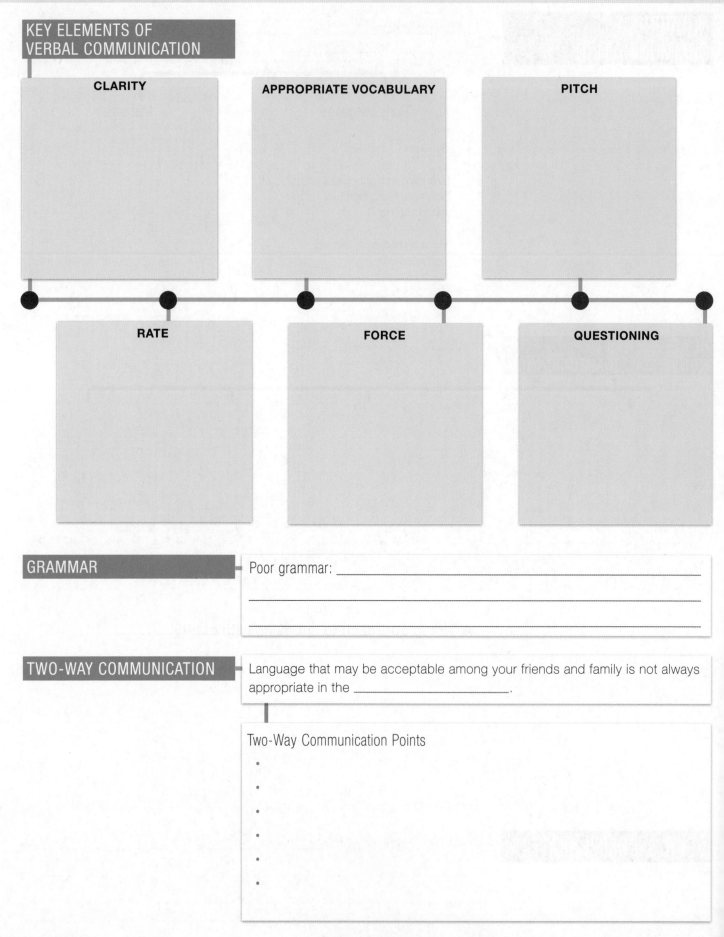

CLARITY

APPROPRIATE VOCABULARY

PITCH

RATE

FORCE

QUESTIONING

GRAMMAR

Poor grammar: _____

_____

_____

TWO-WAY COMMUNICATION

Language that may be acceptable among your friends and family is not always appropriate in the _____.

Two-Way Communication Points

-
-
-
-
-
-

LISTENING

KEY ELEMENTS OF GOOD LISTENING HABITS

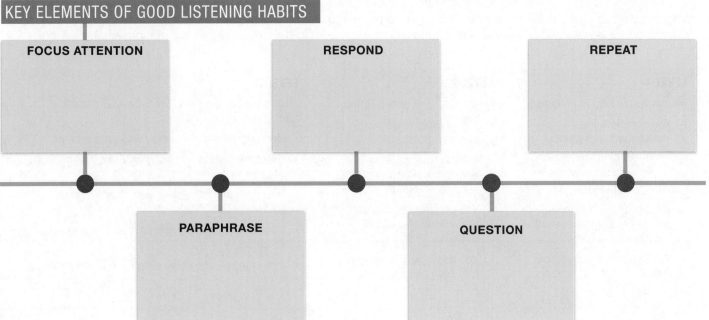

FOCUS ATTENTION

RESPOND

REPEAT

PARAPHRASE

QUESTION

WEB

From the Jump Start Box select the phrase(s) that describe the terms found in the outer boxes of the WEB.

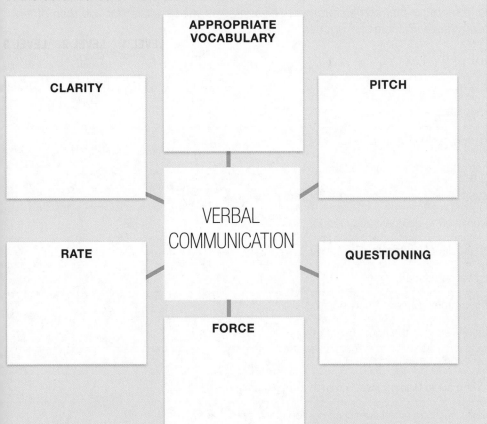

APPROPRIATE VOCABULARY

CLARITY

PITCH

VERBAL COMMUNICATION

RATE

QUESTIONING

FORCE

JUMP START BOX

Match your tone of voice to what you want to convey.

Be specific with word choices.

Speak slowly when explaining difficult concepts.

Speak loud enough to be heard, but not too loud.

Vary your tone of voice.

Avoid chewing gum.

Recognize and avoid common grammar mistakes.

Pay attention to environmental factors.

Used to encourage a response from another person.

Use words that create a clear mental picture.

Vary the rate you speak to maintain attention.

▶ PRACTICE MAKES PERFECT

On the following Communication Rubric, you see a list of statements on the left that describe behaviors assigned to each major section of communication. To the right of each statement you see the numbers 1, 2 and 3. These numbers represent various levels of performance. You can rate yourself using these levels of performance as your guide to see how you are doing along the way. Here is a summary of each level to help you assign your personal rating.

LEVEL 1

Means you're still "In Progress."

- You complete the strategy with assistance and/or prompting.
- You complete the strategy with inconsistent quality.
- You perform the strategy with several errors evident in technique.
- You describe the strategy with vague understanding.

LEVEL 2

Means you're "Getting Better."

- You complete the strategy alone.
- You complete the strategy approaching the industry standard.
- You perform the strategy with occasional errors evident in technique.
- You describe the strategy with prompting.

LEVEL 3

Means you've reached "Entry-Level Proficiency" for the beginning professional.

- You complete the strategy without a prompt.
- You complete the strategy and meet the industry standard described in the text.
- You perform the strategy with very few errors evident in technique.
- You communicate and reflect upon the strategy to others.
- You complete the entire strategy in a timely manner.

▶ COMMUNICATION RUBRIC

As you use the Communication Rubric, remember that some statements or strategies will be easier for you than others. On these strategies you will achieve "Entry-Level Proficiency" sooner.

BODY LANGUAGE	LEVEL 1 In progress	LEVEL 2 Getting better	LEVEL 3 Entry-level proficiency
• I offer a genuine smile to all I meet and greet.	☐	☐	☐
• I pay attention to what my facial expression communicates.	☐	☐	☐
• I avoid negative facial expressions when communicating with others.	☐	☐	☐
• I make eye contact early on to gain attention or as soon as I start a conversation.	☐	☐	☐
• I use eye contact throughout the conversation to demonstrate interest.	☐	☐	☐
• I avoid looking over the other person's shoulders when communicating.	☐	☐	☐
• I use a firm, steady handshake when greeting others.	☐	☐	☐
• I nod my head occasionally to affirm I am listening when in conversation.	☐	☐	☐
• I avoid gestures that may display negativity when in the company of others.	☐	☐	☐
• I carry and position myself using the appropriate posture guidelines.	☐	☐	☐
• I lean forward to communicate interest and avoid leaning away when in communication.	☐	☐	☐
• I position myself at a comfortable proximity to others when speaking; not too close or too far away.	☐	☐	☐
• I make a positive impression when first meeting others.	☐	☐	☐

	LEVEL 1 *In progress*	LEVEL 2 *Getting better*	LEVEL 3 *Entry-level proficiency*

SPEAKING

• I enunciate clearly when speaking.	☐	☐	☐
• I am specific with word choices and refrain from using words that cause confusion.	☐	☐	☐
• I am prepared to speak and avoid muffled and/or hesitant speech.	☐	☐	☐
• I enhance clarity by avoiding behaviors, such as chewing gum, that might get in the way.	☐	☐	☐
• I use words that create a clear mental picture.	☐	☐	☐
• I use positive rather than negative wording.	☐	☐	☐
• I recognize and avoid common grammar and vocabulary mistakes.	☐	☐	☐
• I refrain from using derogatory, profane and politically motivated expressions.	☐	☐	☐
• I refrain from using slang and jargon.	☐	☐	☐
• I use inflection when speaking and avoid extremes such as monotone or high pitch.	☐	☐	☐
• I match the tone of my voice to what I want to convey.	☐	☐	☐
• I vary the rate at which I speak to maintain attention.	☐	☐	☐
• I speak slowly when explaining difficult concepts.	☐	☐	☐
• I speak loudly enough to be easily heard, but not so loudly that others feel I am shouting.	☐	☐	☐
• I pay attention to factors such as the size of the room and background noise when speaking.	☐	☐	☐
• I use open-ended questions to gain information.	☐	☐	☐
• I ask close-ended questions to gain agreement or non-agreement.	☐	☐	☐

LISTENING

• I maintain an open listening channel and avoid prejudging others.	☐	☐	☐
• I am authentic and ask questions to show sincere interest.	☐	☐	☐
• I pay attention to nonverbal messages while listening to see possible body language signals.	☐	☐	☐
• I listen all the way to the end and don't assume I know the ending.	☐	☐	☐
• I understand that listening is not waiting for my turn to speak.	☐	☐	☐
• I recognize listening requires intention and energy, so I am present in the moment.	☐	☐	☐
• I respond or reply to the speaker to affirm I am listening.	☐	☐	☐
• I respond by using periodic comments to prompt the speaker to continue when I am listening.	☐	☐	☐
• I remain silent to give the speaker a chance to breathe, think and continue before I respond.	☐	☐	☐
• I restate what I heard to verify the message.	☐	☐	☐
• I listen for details and repeat factual information to gain accuracy.	☐	☐	☐
• I translate and summarize the meaning of what has been communicated by paraphrasing.	☐	☐	☐
• I use questions to expand and clarify my understanding.	☐	☐	☐
• I use questions to verify that I have understood accurately.	☐	☐	☐

LESSON CHALLENGE *Multiple choice. Indicate one correct answer for each question.*

1. Eye contact, smiling and posture are all examples of:
   - a. inflection
   - b. personality
   - c. verbal communication
   - d. nonverbal communication

2. Which of the following statements describes an appropriate technique to use when making eye contact?
   - a. stare directly into the other person's eyes
   - b. avoid making eye contact as soon as you start a conversation
   - c. use eye contact throughout the conversation to demonstrate interest
   - d. look over the other person's shoulders as though you find something more interesting

3. Leaning forward during a conversation might communicate:
   - a. "I'm very bored."
   - b. "I've had enough."
   - c. "I'm interested in what you are saying."
   - d. "I'm not interested in what you are saying."

4. The nearness of another to one's personal space is known as:
   - a. gesture
   - b. posture
   - c. carriage
   - d. proximity

5. The tone or inflection of your voice, level and rate of speech all play a role in:
   - a. listening
   - b. body language
   - c. verbal communication
   - d. nonverbal communication

6. Which of the following statements does NOT reflect proper grammar?
   - a. How may I help you?
   - b. May I shampoo you now?
   - c. This oil works well on a normal skin type.
   - d. This oil works good on a normal skin type.

7. Which of the following descriptions is true of speaking with clarity?
   - a. less is more
   - b. change the subject often
   - c. the more words the better
   - d. focus on unimportant details

8. Pronouncing words clearly, precisely and accurately is referred to as:
   - a. rate
   - b. tempo
   - c. inflection
   - d. enunciation

9. Changing the pitch of your voice while speaking is called:
   - a. rate
   - b. pitch
   - c. inflection
   - d. enunciation

10. The tempo used during a verbal exchange is called the:
    - a. rate
    - b. pitch
    - c. force
    - d. grammar

11. The strength of volume during a verbal exchange is called:
    - a. rate
    - b. pitch
    - c. force
    - d. inflection

12. Which of the following statements is NOT true about closed-ended questions?
    - a. begin with "Did"
    - b. begin with "Why"
    - c. begin with "Could"
    - d. begin with "Would"

13. How should a salon professional respond to a client insisting on a certain hair color that would not be flattering to their complexion?
    - a. by tactfully suggesting otherwise
    - b. by using overtones
    - c. by displaying a negative attitude
    - d. sharing her unflattering request with other clients

14. Use of a prompting comment such as "go on" is an example of a listening strategy called:
    - a. repeat
    - b. respond
    - c. question
    - d. paraphrase

15. Translating what you heard into your own words is referred to as:
    - a. repeating
    - b. responding
    - c. questioning
    - d. paraphrasing

LESSON CHALLENGE REFERENCES

Check your answers. Place a check mark next to the page number for any incorrect answer. On the lines, jot down topics that you still need to review.

1. PAGE 25 _____

2. PAGE 27 _____

3. PAGE 27 _____

4. PAGE 27 _____

5. PAGE 28 _____

6. PAGE 28 _____

7. PAGE 28 _____

8. PAGE 29 _____

9. PAGE 29 _____

10. PAGE 29 _____

11. PAGE 29 _____

12. PAGE 29 _____

13. PAGE 30 _____

14. PAGE 31 _____

15. PAGE 31 _____

GROW WHAT YOU KNOW

Reflect on what you have learned and predict how this information will be useful in the future.

101ᶜ.4 //
COMMUNICATE WITH CONFIDENCE

ACHIEVE //

Following this lesson on *Communicate With Confidence*, you'll be able to:

» List flexing strategies that will ensure others understand you

» Apply professional etiquette to show respect, integrity and commitment to personal excellence

» Practice guidelines for communication challenges

» Offer ways to solve scheduling issues while maintaining good client relationships

FOCUS //

COMMUNICATE WITH CONFIDENCE

Communication Essentials

Interacting With Clients

COMMUNICATION ESSENTIALS

Clearly understanding and interpreting client requests will help you provide the exact service they desire.

FLEXING Adjusting your _____.

Ensure that your messages are being _____.

Adapt your approach as needed.

FLEXING STRATEGIES

1.

2.

3.

4.

DISCUSSION TOPICS

AVOID

FOCUS

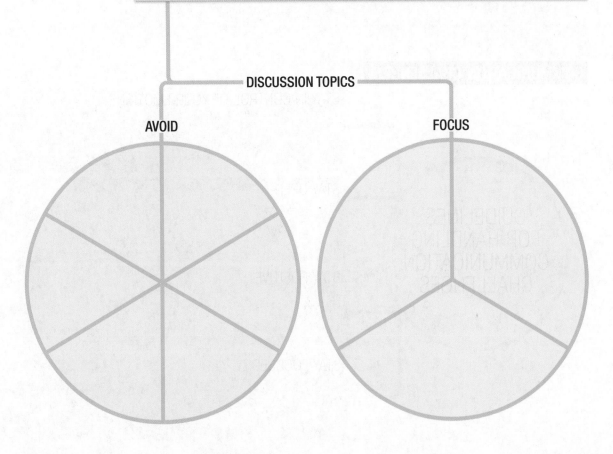

INTERACTING WITH CLIENTS

PROFESSIONAL ETIQUETTE

Professional Etiquette helps define your character and confirms a certain level of respect, integrity and commitment.

respect

integrity

commitment

COMMUNICATION CHALLENGES

GUIDELINES FOR HANDLING COMMUNICATION CHALLENGES

STAY IN CONTROL OF YOUR EMOTIONS

STAY OPEN

STAY POSITIVE

STAY FOCUSED

SCHEDULING CONCERNS

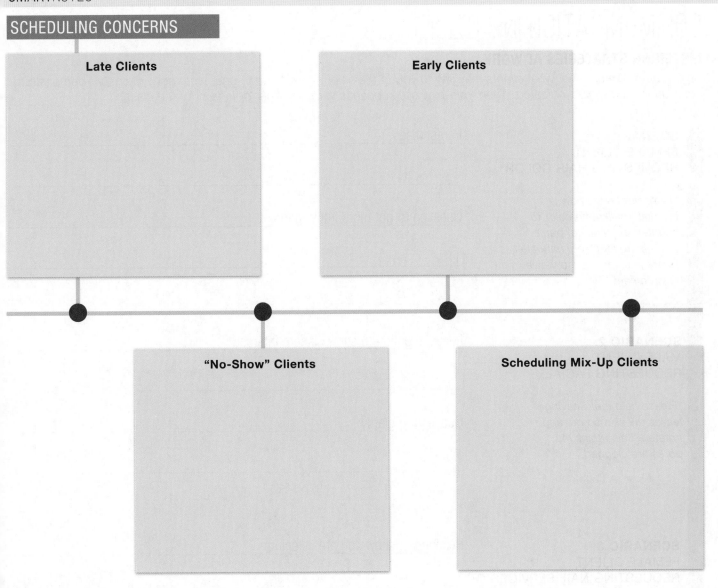

Late Clients

Early Clients

"No-Show" Clients

Scheduling Mix-Up Clients

MATCHING

Identify if the following statements are related to Respect, Integrity or Commitment. If the statement is about Respect, write "R" next to the corresponding number. If the statement is about Integrity, write "I" and if it is about Commitment, write "C."

_____ Be helpful; open doors regardless of gender

_____ Display a professional appearance

_____ Say "no" in a tactful way when responding to a request

_____ Apologize when you make a mistake or inconvenience others

_____ Persevere through difficult times

_____ Do what you say you will—match your actions with your words

_____ Take responsibility for your own actions

_____ Stay informed about industry trends

_____ Avoid stereotyping

_____ Support the success of others

COMMUNICATION IN ACTION

LISTENING STRATEGIES AT WORK

Below are 4 examples of what clients may say to you in the salon. Next to each one, write how you might demonstrate the listening strategies indicated. Then, role-play the scenarios with a partner or in front of the class.

SCENARIO 1:
FEMALE CLIENT
REQUESTING HAIR COLOR

"The color I have now is too dull. I'd like the color to brighten up my face, but it also has to look very natural— I work in a very conservative environment."

Paraphrase: _____

_____

Question to get more information: _____

_____

SCENARIO 2:
MALE CLIENT
REQUESTING FACIAL

"Please help me! Shaving leaves my skin so dry and irritated. I also think my pores are clogged."

Focus attention to show sincere interest: _____

_____

Question to clarify: _____

_____

SCENARIO 3:
FEMALE CLIENT
REQUESTING NAIL SERVICES

"I usually keep my nails fairly short because they break easily. I also tend to stick with pale shades of polish. I'm going to a party this weekend and would like to do something a little more daring."

Respond to show you are listening: _____

_____

Repeat: _____

_____

_____

SCENARIO 4:
MALE CLIENT
REQUESTING MASSAGE

"I'm in sales and am constantly traveling. My back and legs ache. I really like deep pressure massage, especially on my back."

Paraphrase: _____

_____

Respond to prompt client to continue: _____

_____

PRACTICE MAKES PERFECT

On the *Professional Etiquette Rubric* found below, you see a list of statements on the left that describe behaviors assigned to each major section of professional etiquette. To the right of each statement you see the numbers 1, 2 and 3. These numbers represent various levels of performance. You can rate yourself using these levels of performance as your guide to see how you are doing along the way. Here is a summary of each level to help you assign your personal rating.

LEVEL 1

Means you're still "In Progress."

- You complete the strategy with assistance and/or prompting.
- You complete the strategy with inconsistent quality.
- You perform the strategy with several errors evident in technique.
- You describe the strategy with vague understanding.

LEVEL 2

Means you're "Getting Better."

- You complete the strategy alone.
- You complete the strategy approaching the industry standard.
- You perform the strategy with occasional errors evident in technique.
- You describe the strategy with prompting.

LEVEL 3

Means you've reached "Entry-Level Proficiency" for the beginning professional.

- You complete the strategy without a prompt.
- You complete the strategy and meet the industry standard described in the text.
- You perform the strategy with very few errors evident in technique.
- You communicate and reflect upon the strategy to others.
- You complete the entire strategy in a timely manner.

PROFESSIONAL ETIQUETTE RUBRIC

As you use the *Professional Etiquette Rubric*, remember that some statements or strategies will be easier for you than others. On these strategies you will achieve "Entry-Level Proficiency" sooner.

	LEVEL 1 In progress	LEVEL 2 Getting better	LEVEL 3 Entry-level proficiency
FLEXING			
• I tune in to how the other person will be most comfortable interacting and communicating.	☐	☐	☐
• I adapt my approach to meet the needs of others.	☐	☐	☐
• I use questions to demonstrate interest while speaking with others.	☐	☐	☐
• I find things in common with others when conversing.	☐	☐	☐
• I show concern and compassion for others during conversation.	☐	☐	☐
• I recognize that communication is a two-way street.	☐	☐	☐
• I use appropriate ice-breakers to initiate conversations.	☐	☐	☐
RESPECT			
• I show common courtesy and consideration to others.	☐	☐	☐
• I smile and look interested in others.	☐	☐	☐
• I introduce myself and others, if appropriate.	☐	☐	☐
• I am helpful and offer assistance when possible.	☐	☐	☐
• I display decorum in public spaces.	☐	☐	☐
• I offer praise and compliments generously, but sincerely.	☐	☐	☐

	LEVEL 1 *In progress*	LEVEL 2 *Getting better*	LEVEL 3 *Entry-level proficiency*
• I receive praise and compliments graciously.	☐	☐	☐
• I respond to emails and phone messages promptly.	☐	☐	☐
• I avoid stereotyping and making assumptions about others.	☐	☐	☐

INTEGRITY

	LEVEL 1	LEVEL 2	LEVEL 3
• I consider apologies an important way to build rapport and express regret for accidental mistakes.	☐	☐	☐
• I avoid exaggerating or inflating the truth.	☐	☐	☐
• I choose the right time and place to discuss business matters.	☐	☐	☐
• I say "no" in a tactful way when responding to a request I cannot perform.	☐	☐	☐
• I communicate in open, honest ways and discuss only appropriate topics.	☐	☐	☐
• I do what I say I will do and take pride in matching my actions to my words.	☐	☐	☐
• I support the success of others.	☐	☐	☐
• I do the right thing regardless of the personal inconvenience.	☐	☐	☐
• I take responsibility for my actions.	☐	☐	☐

COMMITMENT

	LEVEL 1	LEVEL 2	LEVEL 3
• I show my passion for the profession through my appearance and enthusiastic personality.	☐	☐	☐
• I honor time schedules and arrive prepared and on-time for work, seminars and meetings.	☐	☐	☐
• I am dedicated to helping clients achieve the results they want.	☐	☐	☐
• I establish professional goals.	☐	☐	☐
• I stay informed about industry trends.	☐	☐	☐
• I engage in lifelong learning.	☐	☐	☐
• I represent my profession through involvement in the community.	☐	☐	☐
• I persevere through difficult times.	☐	☐	☐

COMMUNICATION CHALLENGES

	LEVEL 1	LEVEL 2	LEVEL 3
• I stay in control of my emotions and do not take derogatory comments personally.	☐	☐	☐
• I stay open-minded and do not prejudge the situation.	☐	☐	☐
• I maintain a positive attitude that reflects my confidence in reaching an agreeable solution.	☐	☐	☐
• I focus on 1 issue at a time and keep the discussion on-track.	☐	☐	☐
• I thank clients for bringing issues to my attention.	☐	☐	☐
• I apply a step-by-step, problem-solving process to manage communication challenges.	☐	☐	☐

LESSON CHALLENGE

Multiple choice. Indicate one correct answer for each question.

1. Paraphrasing to summarize the meaning of what has been communicated is known as:
   a. using tact
   b. reflective listening
   c. using overtones
   d. one-way communication

2. Adjusting your behavior to ensure your messages are being understood, and adapting your approach is referred to as:
   a. flexing
   b. reflecting
   c. fixing
   d. interacting

3. All of the following topics are considered to be controversial for discussion with the client EXCEPT:
   a. religion
   b. politics
   c. personal problems
   d. hair care products

4. Practicing good manners in the workplace is referred to as:
   a. flexing
   b. conflict resolution
   c. reflective listening
   d. professional etiquette

5. Not making assumptions about people based on appearances reflects use of:
   a. respect
   b. integrity
   c. etiquette
   d. commitment

6. If a person matches their actions with their words, it is an example of:
   a. respect
   b. integrity
   c. etiquette
   d. commitment

7. Persevering through difficult times is an example of:
   a. respect
   b. integrity
   c. etiquette
   d. commitment

8. As soon as you notice a discussion is getting off-track, you should:
   a. talk louder
   b. remain silent
   c. try harder to make your point
   d. bring it back to the main issue

9. The scheduling concern of a client arriving early can be addressed by:
   a. telling client how long before the service will begin
   b. welcoming client with a cool dismissiveness
   c. avoiding offering reading material
   d. letting client get their own beverage

10. "No-Show" clients can be handled with all of the following strategies EXCEPT:
    a. making reminder calls ahead of time
    b. offering other available appointment times
    c. informing client of cancellation policy
    d. never discussing the missed appointment

LESSON CHALLENGE REFERENCES

Check your answers. Place a check mark next to the page number for any incorrect answer. On the lines, jot down topics that you still need to review.

1. PAGE 34 _____
2. PAGE 34 _____
3. PAGE 34 _____
4. PAGE 36 _____
5. PAGE 36 _____
6. PAGE 36 _____
7. PAGE 37 _____
8. PAGE 38 _____
9. PAGE 38 _____
10. PAGE 38 _____

▶ GROW WHAT YOU KNOW

Reflect on what you have learned and predict how this information will be useful in the future.

101^c.5 //
HUMAN RELATIONS

ACHIEVE //

Following this lesson on *Human Relations*, you'll be able to:

» Point out the role personality, attitude and habits play in human relations

» Compare respect, self-respect, self-esteem and mutual respect

» Explain the meaning of professional ethics

FOCUS //

HUMAN RELATIONS

Personality

Respect

Ethics

Human relations is the psychology of getting along with others.

PERSONALITY

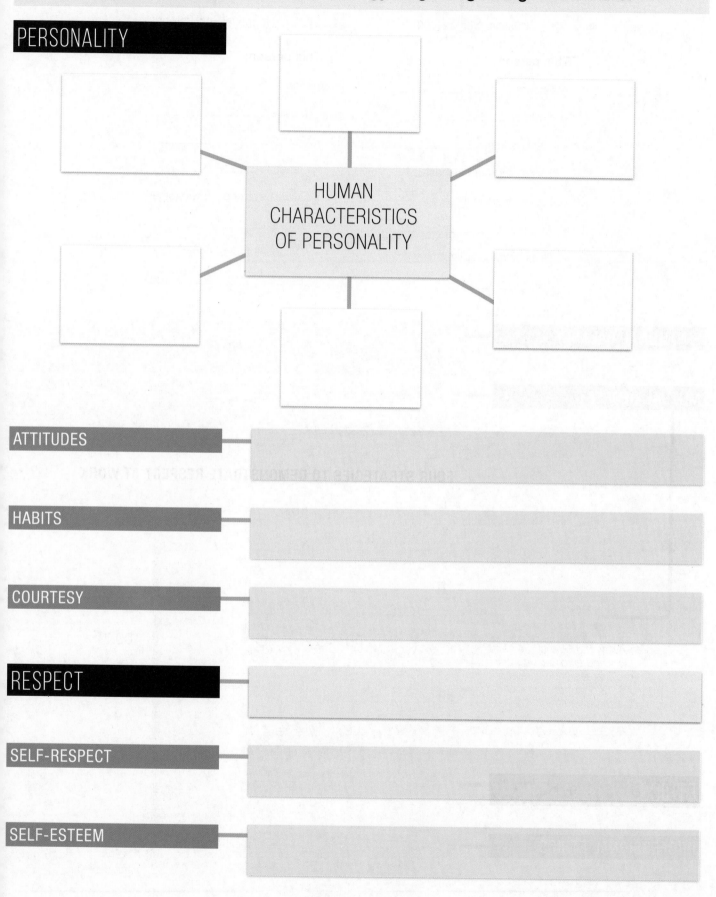

HUMAN CHARACTERISTICS OF PERSONALITY

ATTITUDES

HABITS

COURTESY

RESPECT

SELF-RESPECT

SELF-ESTEEM

SELF-ESTEEM IN ACTION

Positive Self-Esteem

This person:

- Shows _____
- Smiles _____
- Displays lots of _____
- Forms long-term friendships
- Looks others in the eye
- Accepts _____
- Demonstrates optimism
- Tells the _____

Negative Self-Esteem

This person:

- Fears _____
- Smiles _____
- Tires _____
- Tends to _____
- Avoids eye contact with others
- Avoids _____
- Demonstrates pessimism
- Bends _____

EMOTIONAL BALANCE

MUTUAL RESPECT

FOUR STRATEGIES TO DEMONSTRATE RESPECT AT WORK

1.

2.

3.

4.

Review the Mutual Respect Do's and Don'ts chart. List the 3 areas you think you will carry out the most and the three you think you will struggle with.

DO

DON'T

ETHICS

PROFESSIONAL ETHICS

ORGANIZER

Using the Jump Start Box below place the terms in the boxes under the correct category.

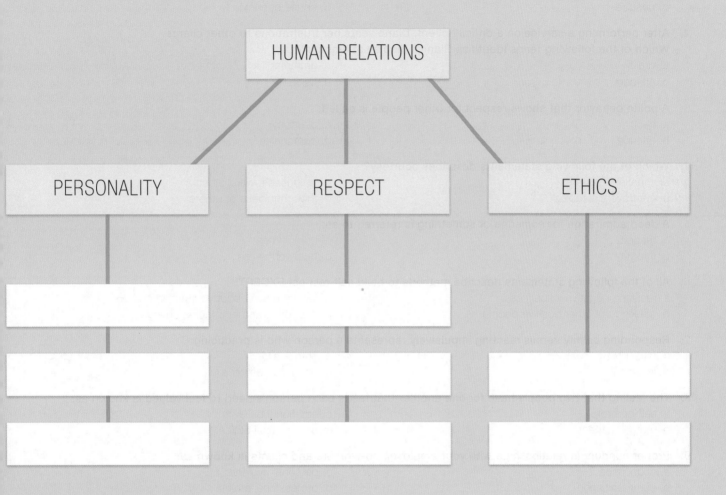

HUMAN RELATIONS

PERSONALITY · RESPECT · ETHICS

JUMP START BOX

Personal Ethics	Professional Ethics	Attitudes
Emotions	Self-Esteem	Mutual Respect
Self-Respect	Habits	

LESSON CHALLENGE

Multiple choice. Indicate the correct answer for each question.

1. An outward reflection of your inner feelings, thoughts, attitudes and values defines your:
    a. hygiene
    b. posture
    c. personality
    d. sense of humor

2. After performing a service on a difficult client, Diane vents her frustrations to other clients. Which of the following terms identifies Diane's display of emotion?
    a. vitality
    b. attitude
    c. grammar
    d. flexibility

3. A polite behavior that shows respect for other people is called:
    a. habit
    b. attitude
    c. courtesy
    d. personality

4. Which of the following statements describes courtesy?
    a. impatient gestures
    b. controversial topics
    c. rudeness toward others
    d. thoughtfulness of others

5. A deep admiration for someone or something is referred to as:
    a. respect
    b. integrity
    c. commitment
    d. trustworthiness

6. All of the following statements describe methods to build self-respect EXCEPT:
    a. resisting negative influences
    b. seeking out other positive people
    c. feeling down about yourself and others
    d. accepting and embracing change

7. Responding calmly versus reacting impulsively represents a person who is practicing:
    a. reliability
    b. insincerity
    c. enthusiasm
    d. emotional balance

8. The feeling that two people have for one another that feeds each person's need to feel valued is known as:
    a. self-control
    b. mutual respect
    c. emotional balance
    d. professional ethics

9. Proper conduct in relationships with your employer, co-workers and clients is known as:
    a. economics
    b. communication
    c. personal hygiene
    d. professional ethics

10. Which of the following responsibilities is NOT found in the professional code of ethics?
    a. failure to fulfill obligations
    b. being loyal to employer and co-workers
    c. being fair and courteous to your co-workers
    d. showing respect for the feelings and rights of others

LESSON CHALLENGE REFERENCES

Check your answers. Place a check mark next to the page number for any incorrect answer. On the lines, jot down topics that you still need to review.

1. PAGE 44 _____
2. PAGE 44 _____
3. PAGE 45 _____
4. PAGE 45 _____
5. PAGE 46 _____

6. PAGE 46 _____
7. PAGE 48 _____
8. PAGE 49 _____
9. PAGE 51 _____
10. PAGE 51 _____

GROW WHAT YOU KNOW

Reflect on what you have learned and predict how this information will be useful in the future.

101ᶜ.6 // RESILIENCE

ACHIEVE //

Following this lesson on *Resilience*, you'll be able to:

>> Express what it means to have integrity

>> List behaviors that destroy trust in work relationships

>> Describe the value of making good life choices

>> Explain how resilience plays a role in your professional career

FOCUS //

RESILIENCE

Integrity

Commitment

Resilience: *noun* | re·sil·ience | **the capacity to recover quickly from difficulties; toughness.**

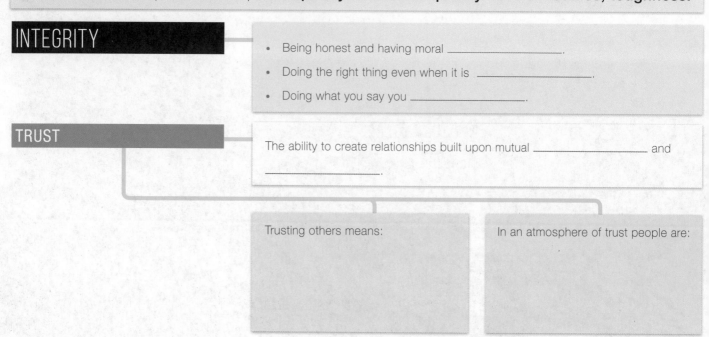

INTEGRITY

- Being honest and having moral _____.
- Doing the right thing even when it is _____.
- Doing what you say you _____.

TRUST

The ability to create relationships built upon mutual _____ and _____.

Trusting others means:

In an atmosphere of trust people are:

FIVE MOST EFFECTIVE WAYS TO BUILD OR LOSE TRUST AT WORK

Build Trust

- Stick to standards of ethical behavior
- Communicate in open, honest ways
- Show respect for ideas and beliefs of others
- Focus on shared, mutually beneficial goals
- Do the right thing regardless of personal risk

Lose Trust

-
-
-
-
-

GIVE EXAMPLES OF RESPONSES TO THE FOLLOWING TRUST BUSTERS

GOSSIP

INSINCERITY

INCONSISTENCY

POOR WORK ETHIC

SELF-ABSORBED BEHAVIOR

LACK OF COURAGE

LIFE CHOICES

Our choices shape the events of our lives, show our character and create our

_____.

Choosing trust and integrity =

_____

Choosing insincerity and poor work ethic =

_____

BLIND SPOTS

Negative aspects of ourselves we are unaware of, but others can _____.

Blind spots that go uncorrected can create problems and limit _____.

COMMITMENT

A pledge to a course of _____.

Passion and commitment bring meaning and _____.

NEW CHALLENGES

A person who lives life fully:

- Directs energy and focused attention to their _____
- Strives to learn new ways to handle _____
- Uses what's inside to lead a productive life _____

DECIDE FOR YOURSELF

- What are my personal strengths, talents and gifts?

- When am I at my best?

- Who is my best source of inspiration?

- What are my most important goals right now?

STAYING THE COURSE

Resilience:

Flexibility:

Persistence:

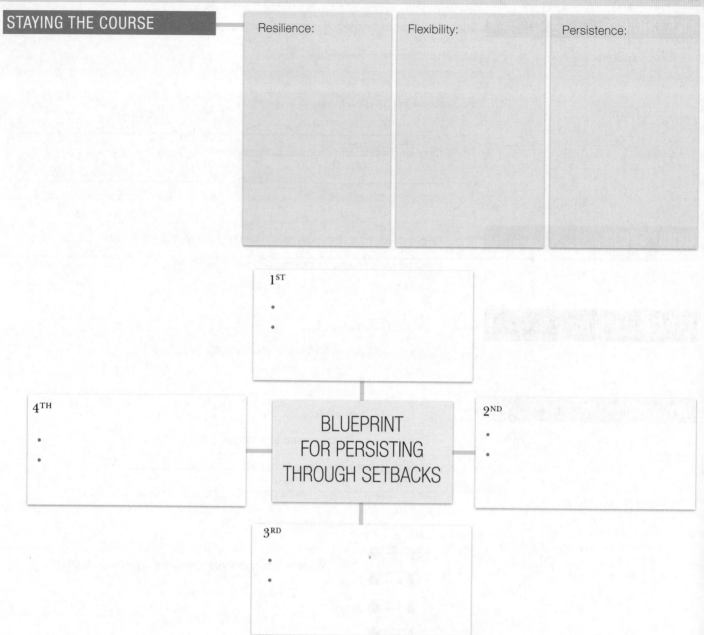

1ˢᵀ
-
-

4ᵀᴴ
-
-

BLUEPRINT
FOR PERSISTING
THROUGH SETBACKS

2ᴺᴰ
-
-

3ᴿᴰ
-
-

RESILIENCE IN ACTION

RATE YOURSELF ON PERSONAL KEYS TO SUCCESS

Rate yourself on personal keys to success by placing the number 1, 2 or 3 next to each of the 10 items shown using the following key:

3 ALWAYS   **2 OFTEN**   **1 SOMETIMES**

_____ I like myself.

_____ I am a student of life, always learning something new.

_____ I am aware of what I want in life.

_____ I make the best use of my talents.

_____ I treat others with respect.

_____ I get things done.

_____ I walk my talk.

_____ I behave ethically.

_____ I am grateful for the good things in my life.

_____ I am prepared to handle life's problems.

LIST AREAS WHERE YOU WOULD LIKE TO IMPROVE:

_____

_____

_____

LIFE CHOICES SELF-ASSESSMENT

Listed below are seven positive life choices. Where are you in relation to them? Shade in the spaces below each choice to indicate your degree of satisfaction at this point in your life.

1 Deal with others in an honest and straightforward way
dissatisfied   *satisfied*

2 Practice generosity and kindness
dissatisfied   *satisfied*

3 Treat others with respect
dissatisfied   *satisfied*

4 Do what I say I will do
dissatisfied   *satisfied*

5 Take conscious steps toward achieving my goals
dissatisfied   *satisfied*

6 Inspire others to be their best
dissatisfied   *satisfied*

7 Live life to the fullest by making the most of my talents
dissatisfied   *satisfied*

LESSON CHALLENGE
Multiple choice. Indicate one correct answer for each question.

1. **Integrity in simple terms could be described as:**
   a. inconsistency of character
   b. doing the right thing
   c. possessing a genius level of intellect
   d. deciding to act ethically only when it suits you

2. **An effective way to build trust is to:**
   a. tell half-truths
   b. communicate in open, honest ways
   c. be closed to the ideas of others
   d. seek personal gain above shared gain

3. **Which of the following actions would diminish trust within a work environment?**
   a. gossip
   b. respect
   c. sincerity
   d. consistency

4. **All of the following are trust-busters in a work environment EXCEPT:**
   a. integrity
   b. insincerity
   c. poor work ethic
   d. self-absorbed behavior

5. **Negative aspects of our personal character that we are unaware of but others can see are referred to as:**
   a. setbacks
   b. blind spots
   c. positive traits
   d. self-esteem

6. **Which of the following terms describes a pledge to a course of action?**
   a. trust
   b. integrity
   c. insincerity
   d. commitment

7. **Meeting life's new challenges can be assisted by:**
   a. acting before thinking
   b. focusing attention on goals
   c. focusing on fears versus opportunities
   d. choosing insincerity and shoddiness in work

8. **Resilience is developed by solving problems and:**
   a. reducing stress
   b. avoiding mistakes
   c. learning from mistakes
   d. choosing the most popular decision

9. **The ability to adapt or respond to change is called:**
   a. trust
   b. gossip
   c. sincerity
   d. flexibility

10. **Being persistent means:**
    a. changing all the time
    b. seeing yourself in positive ways
    c. holding others in high regard
    d. staying the course, not giving up

LESSON CHALLENGE REFERENCES

Check your answers. Place a check mark next to the page number for any incorrect answer. On the lines, jot down topics that you still need to review.

1. PAGE 58 _____
2. PAGE 60 _____
3. PAGE 60 _____
4. PAGE 61 _____
5. PAGE 62 _____

6. PAGE 63 _____
7. PAGE 63 _____
8. PAGE 64 _____
9. PAGE 64 _____
10. PAGE 64 _____

▶ GROW WHAT YOU KNOW

Reflect on what you have learned and predict how this information will be useful in the future.

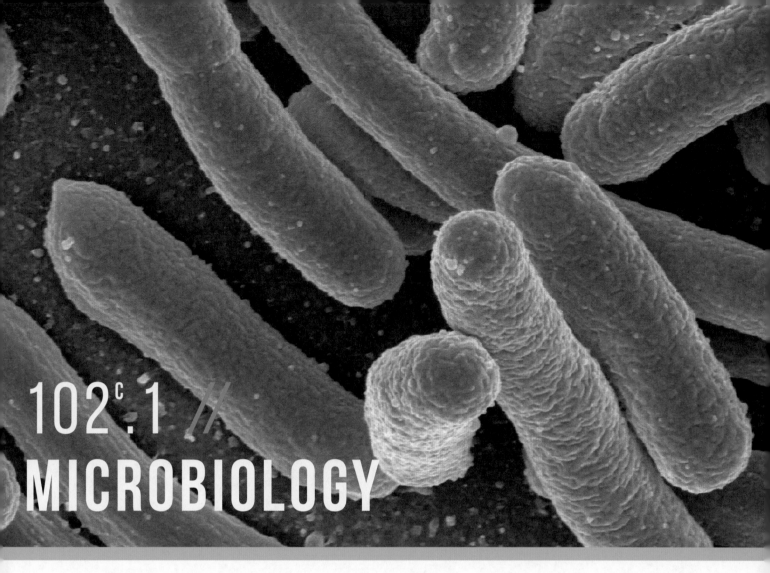

102ᶜ.1 //
MICROBIOLOGY

ACHIEVE //

Following this lesson on *Microbiology*, you'll be able to:

>> Define the types and classifications of bacteria and viruses

>> Identify the growth and reproduction patterns of bacteria and viruses

>> Explain the difference between bacteria and viruses

>> Give examples of external parasites that would prevent offering salon services

>> Describe the reason behind using universal precautions in the salon

>> Classify the two basic ways the body fights infections

FOCUS //

MICROBIOLOGY

Bacteria

Viruses

External Parasites

Infection

Immunity

Microbiology: *noun* | mi·cro·bi·ol·o·gy | micro (small) + bio (living) + ology (study)

BACTERIA

Bacteria: _____

The two general classifications of bacteria

1. _____   2. _____

NONPATHOGENIC BACTERIA

DIFFERENCES

Nonpathogenic Bacteria	Pathogenic Bacteria
•	•
•	•
•	•
•	

PATHOGENIC BACTERIA

1. COCCI

Round-shaped cells that appear in _____

or _____

Staphylococci

Streptococci

Diplococci

2. BACILLI

3. SPIRILLA

GROWTH OF BACTERIA

Two stages of growth cycle: _____ and _____

DIFFERENCES

Active
- •
- •
- •

Inactive
- •
- •
- •

MOVEMENT OF BACTERIA

Cocci travel via_____ or_____movement

Bacilli and spirilla use _____ and _____ to propel themselves through liquids

VIRUSES

Smaller than: _____

Cause: _____

Require: _____

Treatable: _____

EXAMPLE VIRUSES

Hepatitis B Virus (HBV)

Bloodborne pathogen that causes:

Vaccine-preventable disease:

Human Immunodeficiency Virus (HIV)

Virus can lead to:

Interferes with:

Causes:

Spreads when:

Human Papilloma Virus (HPV)

Virus can lead to:

EXTERNAL PARASITES

Live on or obtain nutrients from a _____

Prevent spread of contagions (fungi, bacteria and mites) through proper disinfection procedures

PARASITIC FUNGI

PARASITIC MITES

HEAD LICE   Transmitted person to person by contact with infested articles, like _____ and _____

Usually accompanied by head scratching, redness and/or small _____ _____

Easy to control with _____ _____

INFECTION

Caused by pathogenic bacteria or viruses entering the body and multiplying to the point of interfering with the body's normal state

Direct Transmission

Indirect Transmission

Contagious Infection
(Communicable Disease)

Micro-Organisms

Bloodborne Pathogens

If you have a contagious disease, it is important that you practice infection control procedures in order to not spread the infection.

Common ways of spreading infection in the salon

-
-
-
-
-
-

Local Infection

General Infection

Asymptomatic Carrier

Universal Precautions

IMMUNITY

Two basic types of immunity:

1. _____   2. _____

DIFFERENCES

Active

-
-
-
-

Passive

-
-
-

MATCHING

Identify which category each of the following phrases describes. Place the corresponding letter on the line in front of the appropriate phrase.

A – **Nonpathogenic** or B – **Pathogenic**

- [ ] 70% of all bacteria
- [ ] Produce disease
- [ ] Have 3 basic shapes
- [ ] Can be beneficial

A – **Active Bacteria** or B – **Inactive Bacteria**

- [ ] Grow rapidly
- [ ] Absorb food
- [ ] Form spores
- [ ] Stop growing

Draw a line to connect each type of bacteria with its matching description.

Bacilli	Grow in pairs and can cause pneumonia
Spirilla	Most common form of bacteria
Staphylococci	Pus-forming cells that form long chains; cause strep throat
Diplococci	Pus-forming cells that form bunches; found in boils
Streptococci	Spiral-shaped cells that cause syphilis and Lyme disease

LESSON CHALLENGE *Multiple choice. Indicate one correct answer for each question.*

1. Bacteriology is the study of:
   - a. toxins
   - b. disease
   - c. bacteria
   - d. personal hygiene

2. Bacteria that are harmless and can even be beneficial are called:
   - a. viruses
   - b. microbes
   - c. pathogenic
   - d. nonpathogenic

3. Pathogenic bacteria are responsible for all of the following, EXCEPT:
   - a. causing disease
   - b. producing toxins
   - c. causing infection
   - d. benefitting the environment

4. A communicable disease refers to a disease that is:
   - a. passive
   - b. dormant
   - c. spread from one person to another
   - d. not spread from one person to another

5. Rod-shaped bacterial cells are known as:
   - a. cocci
   - b. bacilli
   - c. spirilla
   - d. staphylococci

6. What bacteria, when viewed through a microscope, would appear to be spiraled, coiled, corkscrew-shaped bacterial cells?
   - a. spirilla
   - b. flagella
   - c. saprophytes
   - d. staphylococci

7. Pus-forming bacterial cells that form grapelike bunches or clusters and are present in abscesses are called:
   - a. spirilla
   - b. diplococci
   - c. streptococci
   - d. staphylococci

8. Bacterial cells that grow in pairs and are the cause of certain infections, such as pneumonia, are known as:
   a. spirilla
   b. bacilli
   c. diplococci
   d. staphylococci

9. During which stage of growth do bacteria reproduce and grow rapidly?
   a. active stage
   b. growth stage
   c. dormant stage
   d. inactive stage

10. Human Immunodeficiency Virus (HIV) causes the immune system to:
    a. speed up
    b. break down
    c. work efficiently
    d. continue working properly

11. Organisms that live on or obtain their nutrients from another organism are known as:
    a. viruses
    b. bacteria
    c. internal parasites
    d. external parasites

12. Disease-causing bacteria or viruses that are carried through the blood or body fluids are known as:
    a. cocci
    b. mites
    c. fungi
    d. bloodborne pathogens

13. Which of the following actions would be considered a universal precaution?
    a. arriving at work on time
    b. unsanitary salon conditions
    c. common use of drinking cup
    d. disinfecting salon equipment

14. Which of the following occurs when the circulatory system carries bacteria and their toxins to all parts of the body?
    a. local infection
    b. active immunity
    c. passive immunity
    d. general infection

15. What type of immunity is provided when a person is given antibodies to a disease rather than producing them through his or her own immune system?
    a. passive immunity
    b. active immunity
    c. natural immunity
    d. personal immunity

LESSON CHALLENGE REFERENCES

Check your answers. Place a check mark next to the page number for any incorrect answer. On the lines, jot down topics that you still need to review.

1. PAGE 6 _____
2. PAGE 6 _____
3. PAGE 6 _____
4. PAGE 6 _____
5. PAGE 7 _____
6. PAGE 7 _____
7. PAGE 7 _____
8. PAGE 7 _____

9. PAGE 8 _____
10. PAGE 10 _____
11. PAGE 11 _____
12. PAGE 12 _____
13. PAGE 13 _____
14. PAGE 13 _____
15. PAGE 14 _____

▶ GROW WHAT YOU KNOW

Reflect on what you have learned and predict how this information will be used in the future.

102^c.2 // INFECTION CONTROL

ACHIEVE //

Following this lesson on *Infection Control*, you'll be able to:

>> State the difference between cleaning, disinfection and sterilization

>> Explain the disinfection method for tools and multi-use supplies that have been in contact with blood or body fluids and those that haven't

>> Identify infection control procedures used in the salon

FOCUS //

INFECTION CONTROL

Cleaning

Disinfection

Efficacy

Sterilization

Infection Control Procedures

INFECTION CONTROL: Term used to describe efforts to prevent the spread of communicable diseases

3 INFECTION CONTROL CATEGORIES

Cleaning | Disinfection | Sterilization

CLEANING

Cleaning: Process of scrubbing to remove dirt and debris to aid in preventing the growth of _____

Level of Infection Control = _____

- Does not kill _____
- Reduces the future growth of microbes
- Requires a mechanical or scrubbing process that causes microbes to _____

Antiseptic: Sanitizer product that can reduce microbes when applied to the

_____

- Can't replace _____ _____
- Can't be used to clean _____ or _____

Antiseptics are appropriate for use only after proper hand washing or cleansing has occurred.

CLEANING GUIDELINES

Wash hands with soap and _____ _____

Wear clean, freshly laundered clothing

Avoid touching your face, mouth or _____

Never place tools, combs, rollers or bobby pins, etc., in your _____

or _____

Dispense all semi-fluids and powders with a shaker, dispenser pump, spray-type container, spatula or disposable applicator

Launder all client gowns and headbands properly before _____

CLEANING GUIDELINES (CONT'D)

Use a new or laundered cape on each client; cape should never touch client's _____

Use disposable towels or freshly laundered towels

Store soiled towels in a covered receptacle until laundered

Clean and remove hair and debris from all tools before _____

Sweep or vacuum all hair clippings from the floor after each service

Discard or _____

Clean shampoo bowls before and after each use

Empty waste receptacles _____

Provide well-lit _____ _____

Provide hot and cold running water

Provide disposable drinking cups

Clean sinks and water fountains _____

Provide clean restrooms, well-stocked with toilet tissue and disposable

_____

Never use restroom areas for storage of _____

Never allow pets or animals in service area (except for _____

_____)

Never use the salon for cooking or living quarters

Keep salon free from insects and rodents

Allow smoking only in _____ _____

VENTILATION GUIDELINES

Maintain an average room temperature of about _____

Supply air through vents and air returns and/or by opening windows and

_____

Vent so that the air does not have a stale, musty odor or odor of

_____ _____

Change air conditioner and forced-air filters, as _____

Provide exhaust ventilation where chemicals are mixed or where applying artificial

_____

Ensure fan in unit is powerful enough to draw or blow away chemical vapor or

_____

DISINFECTION

Disinfection: Disinfection standards require products to destroy or kill certain microbes on surfaces that are _____

Level of Infection Control = _____

Disinfectants: Chemical products used to destroy or kill most bacteria (except bacterial spores), fungi and viruses on nonporous surfaces.

Bactericidals	Kill:	_____ _____
Tuberculocidals	Kill:	_____
Fungicidals	Destroy:	_____
Virucidals	Kill:	_____
Pseudomonacidals	Kill:	_____

Disinfection products are toxic; follow manufacturer's directions.

OSHA = _____
_____

Enforces safety and health standards in the _____

•

•

•

SDS = _____

Designed to provide the key information on a specific _____

Circle the SDS information you think you will refer to most often.

1. Product identification

2. Hazard identification

3. Composition information

4. First-aid measures

5. Fire-fighting measures

6. Accidental release measures

7. Handling and storage

8. Exposure controls and personal protection

9. Physical and chemical properties

10. Stability and reactivity

11. Toxicology information

12. Ecological information

13. Disposal consideration

14. Transport information

15. Regulatory information

16. Revision date

EFFICACY

Efficacy: _____

EPA = _____

• Approves efficacy of products used for _____

_____

• Manufacturers submit a product for verification of _____

EPA Registration Number

• Given to a product along with approval of the efficacy claims on the

_____

• Ensures the product is both _____ and _____

EPA-Registered Disinfectant

• Effective to control spread of disease on surfaces that are

_____

• Efficacy demonstrated against both *Salmonella choleraesuis* and

_____

• Also called _____

EPA-Registered Hospital Disinfectant

• Effective to work in a hospital setting on nonporous surfaces

• Like approved EPA-registered, but also effective against

_____

• Most regulatory agencies require an approved EPA-registered hospital

disinfectant for incidents involving exposure to blood or _____

_____

OSHA Bloodborne Pathogens Standard

•

ALERT!

Bloodborne pathogens are infectious micro-organisms in human blood that can cause disease in humans.

DIFFERENCES

OSHA (REGULATING AGENCY)

Enforces safety and health standards in

the _____

Provides product Safety _____

_____

Enforces the labeling of products to include:

•

•

•

•

Requires the use of an approved

EPA-registered hospital disinfectant

for tools that come into contact with

_____

EPA

Approves efficacy of _____

Provides EPA registration number to

_____

_____

Informs user about product's effectiveness

against such things as:

•

•

TYPES OF DISINFECTANTS

EPA-Approved Forms of Salon Disinfectants:

• _____

• _____

• _____

Look for EPA-registered number along with efficacy label stating that product is an effective:

• _____

• _____

• _____

• _____

BRUSH OR COMB DISINFECTION PROCEDURE

①

②

③

④

⑤

⑥

Disinfectant Types:

• Quaternary Ammonium Compounds – Also known as _____

• Sodium Hypochlorite 5.25% Concentrate – Also known as _____

• Tuberculocidal Disinfectants

TYPES OF DISINFECTANTS (CONT'D)

Remember, when working with disinfectants:

*

*

*

*

SINGLE-USE (DISPOSABLE)

* Porous items
* Discarded after each use

Examples:

MULTI-USE (REUSABLE)

* Nonporous items
* Can be disinfected

Examples:

DISINFECTION GUIDELINES

Overview of Disinfection Practices:

Disinfect metal tools and nonporous supplies _____

Follow complete immersion and contact time listed on _____

Disinfect unplugged electrical appliances

Launder towels/linens in a timely manner

DISINFECTION PRECAUTIONS

Disinfection Precautions and Disposal of Related Items

Ensure proper storage and _____

Follow manufacturer's directions on:

*

*

*

For all chemicals being used keep this on file: _____

_____   _____

STERILIZATION

Sterilization: Sterilization procedures kill or destroy all _____

Level of Infection Control = 3rd and _____ _____

* Usually does not apply to cosmetology services
* Costly, time-consuming and requires a high degree of _____

  _____
* Requires use of a liquid sterilant and/or moist or dry _____

IN SUMMARY...

METHOD	ITEMS	PROCEDURE
Sterilization Kills: _____ _____	Tools used to puncture or invade the _____	Liquid sterilant and/or moist or dry _____
Disinfection Kills: _____ _____	Tools and multi-use supplies that HAVE come in contact with blood or _____	EPA-registered hospital _____
	Tools and multi-use supplies that have NOT come in contact with blood or body fluids	EPA-_____ _____
Cleaning Removes: _____ _____	Countertops, sinks, floors, toilets	EPA-registered _____ _____
	Towels, linens	Use laundry detergent unless a disinfectant detergent is required by your _____ _____
	Your hands before each _____	Soap and _____ _____
	Your hands and client's hands and/or feet prior to manicuring or pedicure service	Soap and warm water; antiseptic, if desired

INFECTION CONTROL PROCEDURES

Review Cleaning and Disinfecting Tools Procedure in the Coursebook

Review Basic Hand Washing Procedure in the Coursebook

Review Blood Exposure Incident Procedure in the Coursebook

DISCARD OR DISINFECT?

Using the Jump Start Box, place the items under the correct category of Discard or Disinfect.

DISCARD

DISINFECT

JUMP START BOX

NECK STRIPS	COLOR BOWLS	METAL PUSHERS
SHEARS	GAUZE	ROLLERS USED FOR WET HAIRSTYLING
BOBBY PINS	PUMICE STONES	SPONGES
EMERY BOARDS	WOODEN STICKS	COTTON BALLS
PAPER TOWELS	COMBS	

LESSON CHALLENGE *Multiple choice. Indicate one correct answer for each question.*

1. **Removing dirt and debris to aid in preventing the growth of microbes is:**
   a. cleaning
   b. calibration
   c. disinfection
   d. sterilization

2. **To destroy or kill most bacteria (except bacterial spores), fungi and viruses on nonporous surfaces is referred to as:**
   a. cleaning
   b. cleansing
   c. disinfection
   d. sterilization

3. **Virucidals are disinfectants used to kill:**
   a. viruses
   b. tuberculosis
   c. pseudomonas
   d. harmful bacteria

4. The regulating agency under the Department of Labor that enforces safety and health standards in the workplace is:
    a. DNR
    b. SDS
    c. USDA
    d. OSHA

5. Key information on a specific product regarding ingredients, associated hazards, combustion levels and storage requirements is provided by:
    a. SDS
    b. EPA
    c. the cap
    d. the efficacy label

6. What information is assigned to a product, along with the approval of the efficacy claims on the label to ensure the product is safe and effective?
    a. bar code
    b. toll-free number
    c. retail number
    d. EPA registration number

7. An approved EPA-registered disinfectant is effective on what type of surface?
    a. porous
    b. passable
    c. absorbent
    d. nonporous

8. Which of the following is the next step after removing all hair from a brush during a disinfection procedure?
    a. dry brush thoroughly
    b. wash brush with soap and water
    c. store brush in a dry, covered container
    d. immerse brush in a disinfecting solution

9. When disinfecting, tools must be precleaned before:
    a. lending
    b. disposal
    c. tightening
    d. immersion

10. What should you do with a porous item such as a neck strip, sponge or emery board once it has been used on a client?
    a. wash it
    b. spray it
    c. discard it
    d. disinfect it

11. Any tools or supplies that come in contact with the client during a service must be discarded or:
    a. sanitized
    b. ventilated
    c. sterilized
    d. disinfected

12. All of the following statements are precautions regarding disinfectants, EXCEPT:
    a. store in a cool, dry area
    b. tightly cover and label all containers
    c. purchase chemicals in small quantities
    d. use hands to remove objects from disinfectant

13. Dispose of sharp objects, such as razor blades in a(n):
    a. open container
    b. disposable bag
    c. closed container
    d. puncture-proof container

14. Destroying or killing all microbes is:
    a. cleaning
    b. sanitation
    c. disinfection
    d. sterilization

15. Tools and instruments used to puncture or invade the skin must be sterilized or designed to be:
    a. dull
    b. dirty
    c. porous
    d. disposable

LESSON CHALLENGE REFERENCES

Check your answers. Place a check mark next to the page number for any incorrect answer.
On the lines, jot down topics that you still need to review.

1. PAGE 20 _____

2. PAGE 22 _____

3. PAGE 22 _____

4. PAGE 22 _____

5. PAGE 23 _____

6. PAGE 24 _____

7. PAGE 24 _____

8. PAGE 26 _____

9. PAGE 26 _____

10. PAGE 27 _____

11. PAGE 27 _____

12. PAGE 29 _____

13. PAGE 29 _____

14. PAGE 30 _____

15. PAGE 30 _____

GROW WHAT YOU KNOW

Reflect on what you have learned, and predict how this information will be used in the future.

102^C.3 //
FIRST AID

ACHIEVE //

Following this lesson on *First Aid*, you'll be able to:

>> State first-aid techniques for bleeding and wounds

>> Identify first-aid techniques for chemical and heat or electrical burns

>> Describe first-aid techniques for choking

>> Explain first-aid techniques for fainting

>> Express first-aid techniques for eye injury

FOCUS //

FIRST AID

Bleeding and Wounds

Burns

Choking

Fainting

Eye Injury

Good Samaritan Laws:

-
-
-

BLEEDING AND WOUNDS

WRITE THE CORRECT FIRST-AID TECHNIQUES IN SEQUENTIAL ORDER

STEP 1:

STEP 2:

STEP 3:

STEP 4:

! IMPORTANT ! Never use a tourniquet unless you cannot control the bleeding. Have emergency personnel check victim for shock, if necessary.

BURNS

FIRST-AID TECHNIQUES

Chemical

1

2

3

Heat or Electrical

1

2

3

CHOKING

STEP 1: Determine if victim can talk or _____. If not, have someone call 9-1-1 while you give victim _____ _____.

STEP 2: Stand behind victim; wrap arms around their _____.

STEP 3: Make a thumbless fist with one hand and place that fist just above navel and well below the ribs, with thumb and forefinger side toward the _____.

STEP 4: Perform upward abdominal thrust by grasping fist with other hand and pulling it _____ _____ _____

FAINTING

STEP 1: Lay victim down on _____; allow plenty of fresh air.

STEP 2: Reassure victim and apply cold compress to _____.

STEP 3: If victim vomits, roll them onto their side, keep windpipe _____.

Call 9-1-1 if victim does not regain consciousness.

EYE INJURY

FIRST-AID TECHNIQUES

Chemical

1. Hold eyelids apart and flush eyeball with lukewarm water for _____ to _____ minutes; don't let runoff flow into other eye

2. Place gauze pad or cloth over both _____ ; secure with bandage

3. Get to eye specialist or emergency room immediately

Cut, Scratch or Embedded Object

1. Place gauze pad or cloth over both eyes and secure with a _____

2. Do not try to remove embedded _____

3. Get to an eye specialist or emergency room immediately

SAFETY DATA SHEET (SDS)

MATCHING

Match a first-aid technique on the left to a related phrase on the right.

Bleeding and Wounds	Do not try to removed embedded object
Chemical Burns	Apply firm steady pressure for 5 minutes
Heat or Electrical Burns	Remove any contaminated clothing from affected area
Choking	Immerse area in cool water or apply cool compress
Fainting	Determine if victim can talk or cough
Eye Injury	Make sure the victim has plenty of fresh air

LESSON CHALLENGE *Multiple choice. Indicate one correct answer for each question.*

1. When performing first aid for bleeding wounds, what is the next step after bleeding stops?
   a. apply pressure
   b. apply bandage
   c. apply tourniquet
   d. elevate injured limb

2. Chemical burns should be treated by:
   a. applying pressure
   b. applying a lotion or cream
   c. scrubbing with soap and hot water
   d. rinsing away all traces of chemicals

3. Which of the following steps should be taken FIRST when it is believed a person may be choking?
   a. make a thumbless fist
   b. perform abdominal thrusts
   c. apply a cold compress to face
   d. determine if the victim can speak or cough

4. If the skin is not broken following a heat or electrical burn, which of the following actions is recommended to treat the burn area?
   a. apply ointment
   b. immerse in cool water
   c. immerse in warm water
   d. apply warm compress

5. Which of the following steps should be taken if a person has fainted?
   a. stand the person up
   b. apply a cold compress
   c. apply a warm compress
   d. force the person to walk

6. In the case of a chemical injury to the eye, which of the following steps is recommended?
   a. flush eyeball with lukewarm water for 15 to 30 minutes
   b. flush eyeball with cold water for 45 minutes
   c. flush eyeball with hot water for 45 minutes
   d. flush eyeball with hot water for 3 to 5 minutes

7. If a victim appears to be having an allergic reaction, where could you locate information about product usage?
   a. SDS
   b. MDS
   c. DMS
   d. SMD

LESSON CHALLENGE REFERENCES

Check your answers as you did before. Place a check mark next to the page number for any incorrect answer. On the lines, jot down topics that you still need to review.

1. PAGE 41 _____
2. PAGE 42 _____
3. PAGE 42 _____
4. PAGE 42 _____
5. PAGE 43 _____
6. PAGE 43 _____
7. PAGE 43 _____

▶ GROW WHAT YOU KNOW

Reflect on what you have learned and predict how this information will be used in the future.

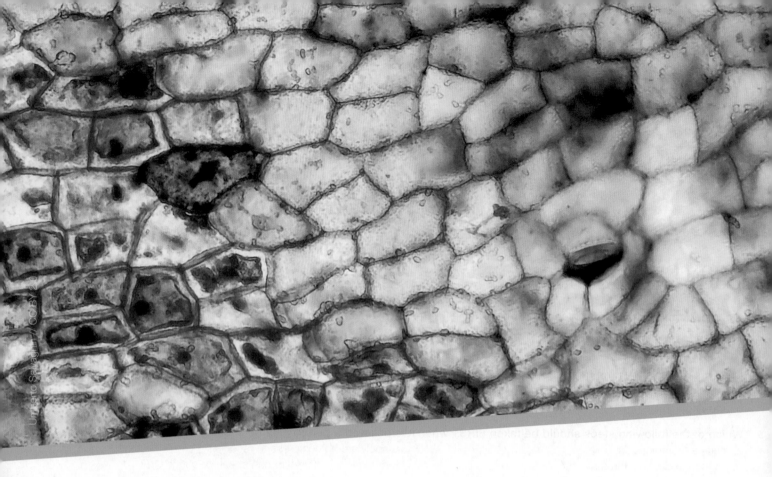

102^c.4 //
BUILDING BLOCKS OF THE HUMAN BODY

ACHIEVE //

Following this lesson on *Building Blocks of the Human Body*, you'll be able to:

>> Identify the structure of cells

>> State the structure and function of five types of tissue

>> Explain the function of the primary organs of the human body

>> Express the names of 10 body systems and their relationship to cells, tissues and organs

FOCUS //

BUILDING BLOCKS OF THE HUMAN BODY

Cells

Tissues

Organs

Body Systems

ANATOMY:

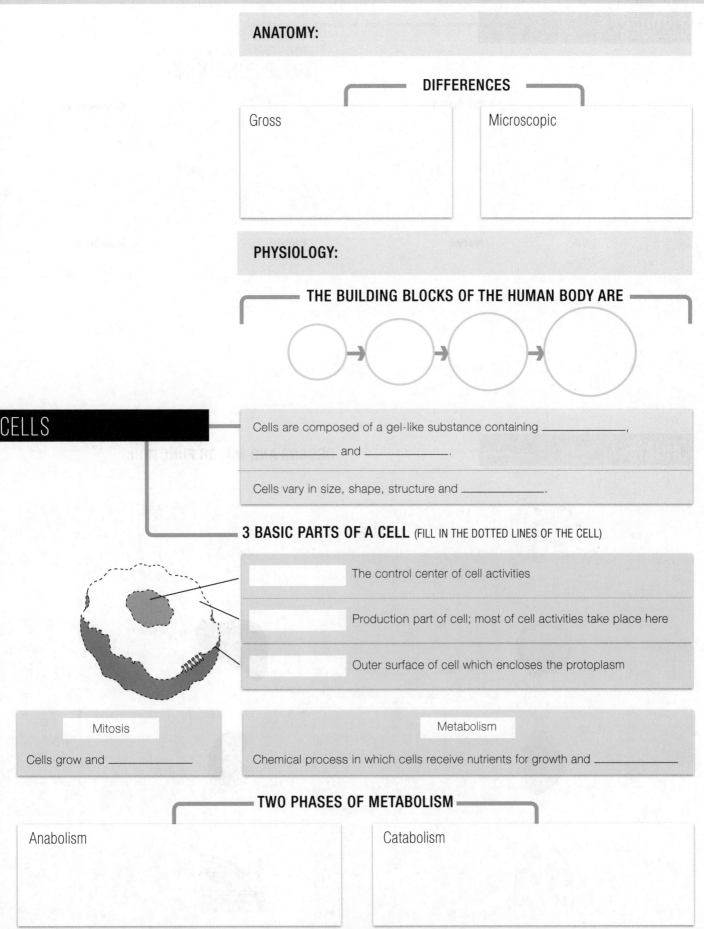

DIFFERENCES

Gross

Microscopic

PHYSIOLOGY:

THE BUILDING BLOCKS OF THE HUMAN BODY ARE

CELLS

Cells are composed of a gel-like substance containing _____,

_____ and _____.

Cells vary in size, shape, structure and _____.

3 BASIC PARTS OF A CELL (FILL IN THE DOTTED LINES OF THE CELL)

The control center of cell activities

Production part of cell; most of cell activities take place here

Outer surface of cell which encloses the protoplasm

Mitosis

Cells grow and _____

Metabolism

Chemical process in which cells receive nutrients for growth and _____

TWO PHASES OF METABOLISM

Anabolism

Catabolism

TISSUES

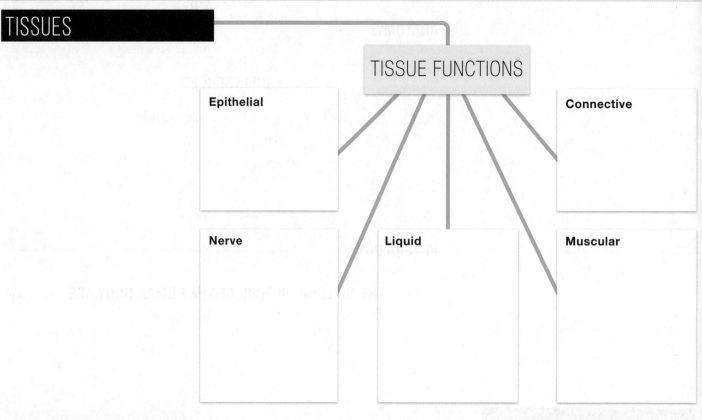

TISSUE FUNCTIONS

Epithelial

Connective

Nerve

Liquid

Muscular

ORGANS

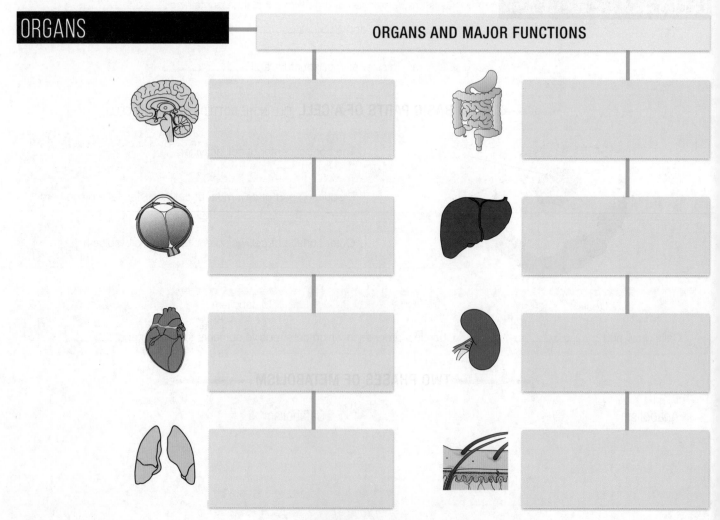

ORGANS AND MAJOR FUNCTIONS

BODY SYSTEMS

SYSTEM: _____

SYSTEM	FUNCTION
Skeletal	
Muscular	
Circulatory	
Nervous	
Digestive	
Excretory	
Respiratory	
Endocrine	
Reproductive	
Integumentary	

MINI REVIEW

CELLS: _____

TISSUES: _____

ORGANS: _____

SYSTEMS: _____

THINKING MAP

Draw a sketch to illustrate how cells make up tissues, how tissues make up organs and how organs make up systems.

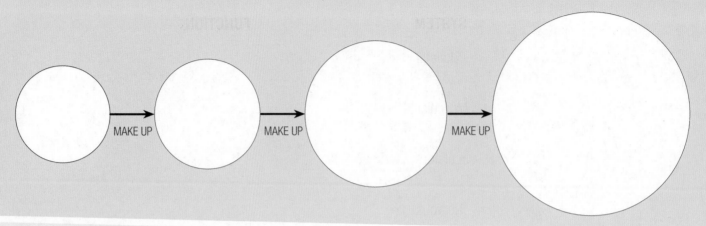

▶ MATCHING

Match a term on the left to its definition on the right.

a. Anatomy   _____ Study of the functions that organs and systems perform

b. Physiology   _____ Separate body structures that are composed of 2 or more different tissues that perform specific functions

c. Cells   _____ Group of body structures and/or organs that, together, perform functions for the body

d. Metabolism   _____ Study of organs and systems of the body

e. Tissues   _____ Cells receive nutrients for growth and reproduction

f. Organs   _____ Groups of cells of the same kind

g. Body Systems   _____ Basic units of living matter

LESSON CHALLENGE *Multiple choice. Indicate one correct answer for each question.*

1. Which area of science involves the study of the organs and systems of the body?
   a. myology
   b. histology
   c. anatomy
   d. physiology

2. The study of the functions of the organs and systems of the body is known as:
   a. biology
   b. anatomy
   c. physiology
   d. gross anatomy

3. What three basic parts are found in most human cells?
   a. muscle, cytoplasm, cell membrane
   b. nucleus, cytoplasm, cell membrane
   c. muscle, protoplasm, cell membrane
   d. nucleus, cytoplasm, connective tissue

4. The control center of cell activities is called the:
   a. nucleus
   b. cytoplasm
   c. protoplasm
   d. body system

5. Most of the activities of the cell take place in the:
   a. nucleus
   b. stomach
   c. cytoplasm
   d. cell membrane

6. The process of building up larger molecules from smaller ones is:
   a. anabolism
   b. catabolism
   c. physiology
   d. cell division

7. The release of energy within a cell necessary for the performance of specific body functions is caused by:
   a. sleep
   b. osteology
   c. anabolism
   d. catabolism

8. Groups of cells of the same kind make up:
   a. lungs
   b. tissues
   c. organs
   d. systems

9. What is the role of epithelial tissue?
   a. coordinate body functions
   b. contract to produce motion
   c. support, protect and hold the body together
   d. cover and protect body surfaces and internal organs

10. Which type of tissue supports, protects and holds the body together?
    a. nerve tissue
    b. connective tissue
    c. muscular tissue
    d. epithelial tissue

11. The tissue that contracts, when stimulated, to produce motion is known as:
    a. nerve tissue
    b. liquid tissue
    c. muscular tissue
    d. epithelial tissue

12. A separate body structure that is composed of two or more different tissues is a(n):
    a. organ
    b. tissue
    c. system
    d. muscle

13. The organ that controls all body functions is the:
    a. skin
    b. liver
    c. brain
    d. kidneys

14. The organ responsible for removing toxic byproducts of digestion is the:
    a. liver
    b. stomach
    c. kidneys
    d. intestines

15. The primary function of the excretory system is to:
    a. circulate blood throughout the body
    b. intake oxygen to be absorbed into the blood
    c. regulate and control the growth and reproduction of the body
    d. eliminate waste products from the body

LESSON CHALLENGE REFERENCES

Check your answers. Place a check mark next to the page number for any incorrect answer. On the lines, jot down topics that you still need to review.

1. PAGE 49 _____
2. PAGE 49 _____
3. PAGE 50 _____
4. PAGE 50 _____
5. PAGE 50 _____
6. PAGE 50 _____
7. PAGE 50 _____
8. PAGE 51 _____
9. PAGE 51 _____
10. PAGE 51 _____
11. PAGE 51 _____
12. PAGE 52 _____
13. PAGE 52 _____
14. PAGE 52 _____
15. PAGE 52 _____

▶ GROW WHAT YOU KNOW

Reflect on what you have learned and predict how this information will be used in the future.

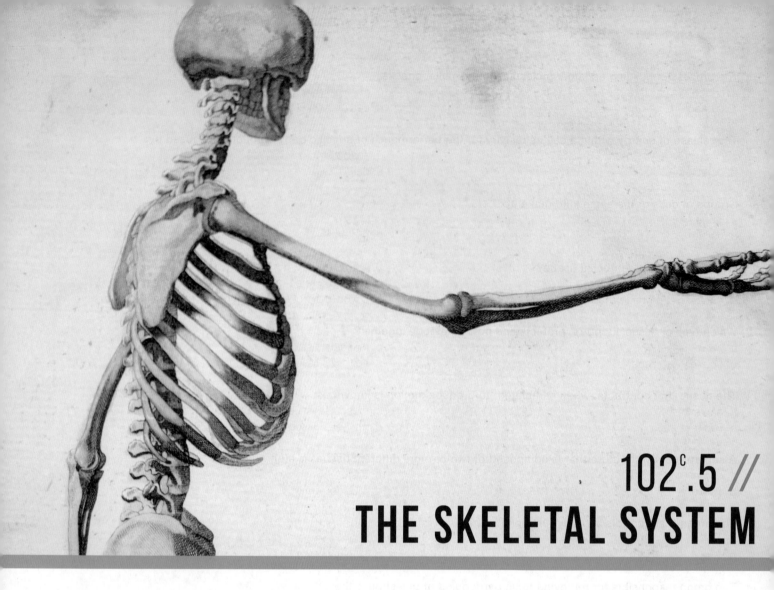

102ᶜ.5 //
THE SKELETAL SYSTEM

ACHIEVE //

Following this lesson on *The Skeletal System*, you'll be able to:

>> Identify the structure and function of the skeletal system

>> Recap the name and location of bones of the skull affected by massage

>> Offer examples of the name and location of bones of the neck, back, chest and shoulder

>> Go over the name and location of bones of the arm, wrist and hand

>> Summarize the name and location of bones of the leg, ankle and foot

FOCUS //

THE SKELETAL SYSTEM

Structure and Function of the Skeletal System

Study of the Bones

STRUCTURE AND FUNCTION OF THE SKELETAL SYSTEM

The physical foundation of the body

206: _____

JOINT: _____

OSTEOLOGY: _____

TWO TYPES OF JOINTS: _____ and _____

BONE

Long bones are found in the _____ and _____

Flat bones are found in the _____, _____ and _____

Irregular bones are found in the _____, _____ and _____ _____

Composed of: _____

Produces: white and red _____ _____

Stores: _____

FUNCTIONS OF THE SKELETAL SYSTEM

1.

2.

3.

4.

STUDY OF THE BONES

THE SKULL

Skeleton of head; encloses and protects the _____ and

_____ _____ _____

CRANIUM

Number of bones: _____

FACIAL SKELETON

Number of bones: _____

CRANIUM

DESCRIBE IN YOUR OWN WORDS

6 of 8 cranium bones affected by massage

Frontal

Parietal

Occipital

Temporal

LABEL THE CRANIUM

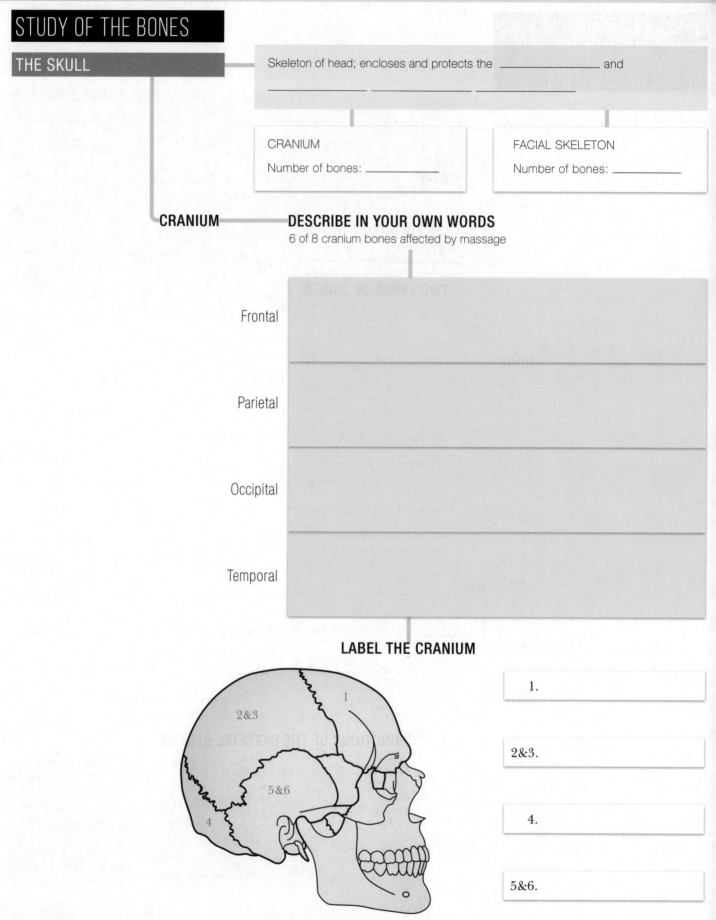

1.

2&3.

4.

5&6.

FACIAL SKELETON

Number of bones = _____

Number of bones involved in facial massage = _____

DESCRIBE IN YOUR OWN WORDS

Mandible

Maxillae

Nasal

Zygomatic (Malar)

Lacrimal

LABEL THE FACIAL SKELETON

1.

2-3.

4-5.

6-7.

8-9.

NECK BONES

Top part of the _____ _____

LABEL THE NECK BONES

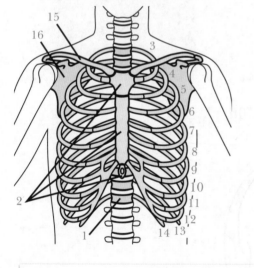

DESCRIBE IN YOUR OWN WORDS

Cervical Vertebrae

Hyoid

1-7.

8.

BACK, CHEST AND SHOULDER BONES

LABEL THE BACK, CHEST AND SHOULDER BONES

DESCRIBE IN YOUR OWN WORDS

Chest, or thorax: bony cage that protects the heart, lungs and other internal organs.

Thoracic Vertebrae

Sternum

Ribs

Clavicle

Scapula

1.

2.

3-14.

15.

16.

ARM, WRIST AND HAND BONES

LABEL THE ARM, WRIST AND HAND BONES

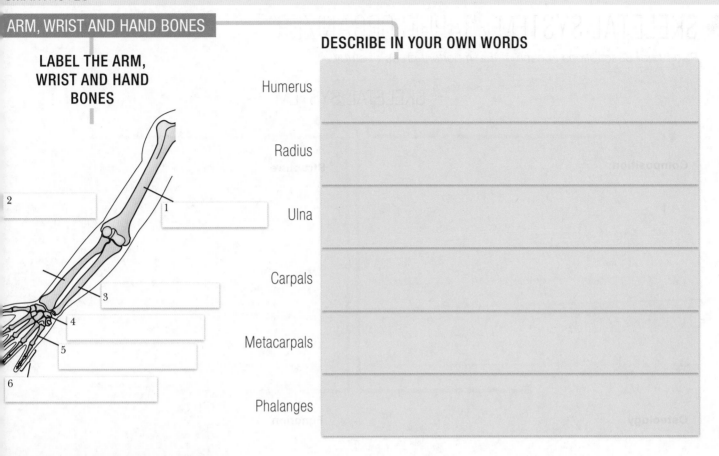

DESCRIBE IN YOUR OWN WORDS

Humerus

Radius

Ulna

Carpals

Metacarpals

Phalanges

LEG, ANKLE AND FOOT BONES

LABEL THE LEG, ANKLE AND FOOT BONES

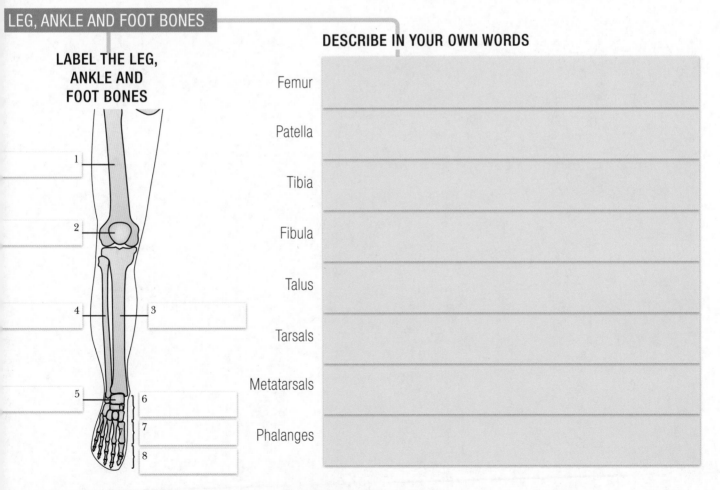

DESCRIBE IN YOUR OWN WORDS

Femur

Patella

Tibia

Fibula

Talus

Tarsals

Metatarsals

Phalanges

▶ SKELETAL SYSTEM GRAPHIC ORGANIZER

Place brief descriptions in each of the important areas of study.

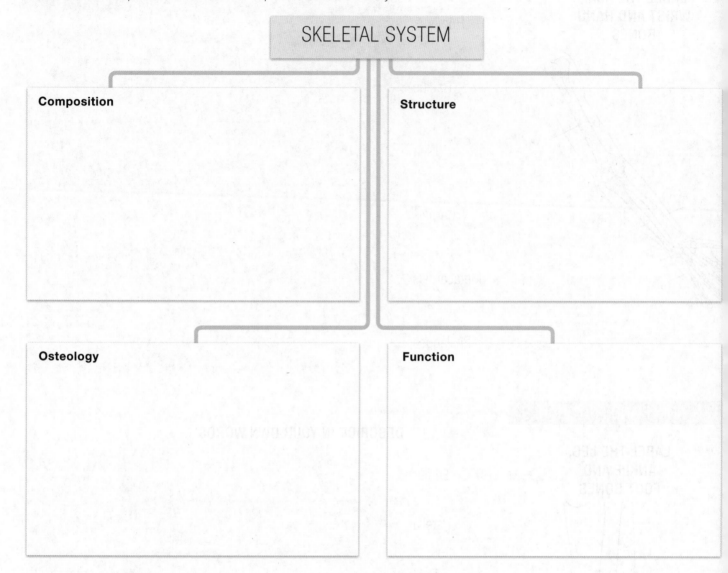

SKELETAL SYSTEM

Composition

Structure

Osteology

Function

1 2 **3** 4 5 6 7

LESSON CHALLENGE
Multiple choice. Indicate one correct answer for each question.

1. The point at which two or more bones are joined together is called a:
   a. joint
   b. tendon
   c. synapse
   d. ligament

2. Which system has the function of surrounding and protecting internal organs?
   a. skeletal system
   b. endocrine system
   c. circulatory system
   d. respiratory system

3. Long bones are found in the:
   a. legs
   b. back
   c. chest
   d. skull

4. All of the following are bones of the cranium, EXCEPT:
   a. frontal
   b. occipital
   c. temporal
   d. metacarpal

5. The parietal bones form the:
   a. cheek
   b. upper jaw
   c. bridge of the nose
   d. crown and upper sides of the head

6. The bone that forms the back of the skull, indenting above the nape area, is the:
   a. temporal
   b. parietal
   c. frontal
   d. occipital

7. The bone that makes up the lower jaw and is the largest bone of the facial skeleton is the:
   a. nasal
   b. lacrimal
   c. maxillae
   d. mandible

8. The 8 carpals held together with ligaments make up the:
   a. knee
   b. wrist
   c. hand
   d. elbow

9. The 5 long, thin bones that form the palm of the hand are the:
   a. carpals
   b. maxillae
   c. phalanges
   d. metacarpals

10. The outer and narrower of the 2 lower leg bones, extending from the knee to the ankle, is known as the:
    a. femur
    b. fibula
    c. patella
    d. metatarsals

LESSON CHALLENGE REFERENCES

Check your answers. Place a check mark next to the page number for any incorrect answer. On the lines, jot down topics that you still need to review.

1. PAGE 58 _____
2. PAGE 58 _____
3. PAGE 58 _____
4. PAGE 59 _____
5. PAGE 59 _____
6. PAGE 59 _____
7. PAGE 60 _____
8. PAGE 63 _____
9. PAGE 63 _____
10. PAGE 64 _____

▶ GROW WHAT YOU KNOW

Reflect on what you have learned and predict how this information will be used in the future.

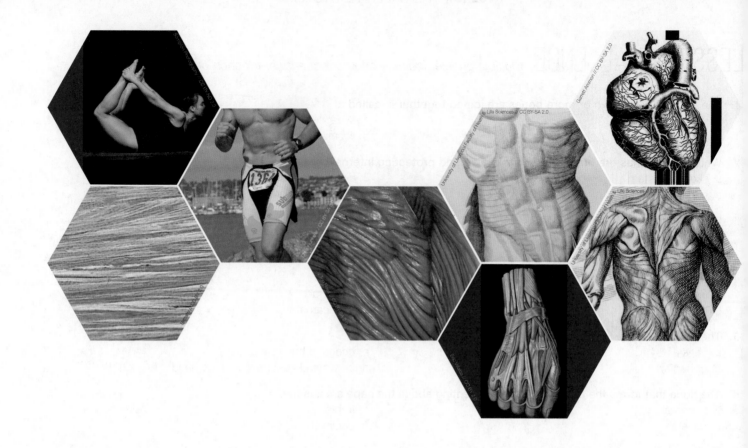

102ᶜ.6 // THE MUSCULAR SYSTEM

ACHIEVE //

Following this lesson on *The Muscular System*, you'll be able to:

>> Identify the structure and function of the muscular system

>> State the direction of massage movements used to affect muscles during massage

>> Describe the methods used to stimulate muscular tissue

>> Label the name, location and function of scalp and face muscles affected by massage

>> Call out the name, location and function of muscles of the neck and back

>> List the name, location and function of the muscles of the shoulder, chest, arm and hand

>> State the name, location and function of muscles of the leg and foot

FOCUS //

THE MUSCULAR SYSTEM

Structure and Function of the Muscular System

Study of the Muscles

STRUCTURE AND FUNCTION OF THE MUSCULAR SYSTEM

MYOLOGY:

Muscles: compose _____% to _____% of the body's _____

Produce movement when _____

MAJOR FUNCTIONS OF THE MUSCULAR SYSTEM

-
-
-
-

TWO TYPES OF MUSCLE TISSUE

DIFFERENCES

Striated	Non-Striated

CARDIAC (HEART) MUSCLE:

_____

_____

_____

SPECIAL TERMINOLOGY	MUSCLE LOCATION OR FUNCTION
Anterior	
Posterior	
Superioris	
Inferioris	
Levator	
Depressor	
Dilator	

THREE PARTS OF THE MUSCLE

1. Origin:

2. Belly:

3. Insertion:

How the Muscle Produces Movement: _____

_____

METHODS TO STIMULATE MUSCLES

MUSCULAR
STIMULATION

STUDY OF THE MUSCLES

Of primary interest to salon professional when performing scalp and neck massages and/or facials; massaged from the insertion attachment to the origin attachment

SCALP & FACE MUSCLES

LABEL THE SCALP MUSCLES

Epicranium

Epicranius

SCALP MUSCLES

Frontalis

Occipitalis

1.

2.

SCALP & FACE MUSCLES (CONT'D)

LABEL THE EAR MUSCLES

EAR MUSCLES: The three muscles of the ear are used to move the visible part of the ear.

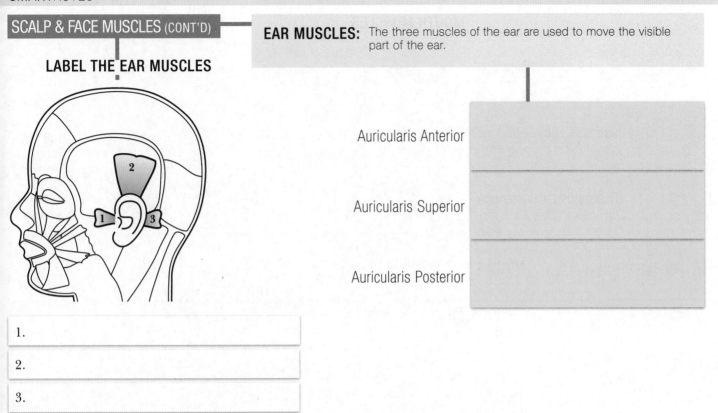

Auricularis Anterior

Auricularis Superior

Auricularis Posterior

1.

2.

3.

LABEL THE EYE AND NOSE MUSCLES

EYE AND NOSE MUSCLES

Corrugator

Levator Palpebrae Superioris

Orbicularis Oculi

Procerus

Four muscles located inside the nose, called the nasalis, dilator naris posterior, dilator naris anterior and depressor septi, control contraction and expansion of the nostrils.

1.

2.

3.

4.

MOUTH MUSCLES

Orbicularis Oris

Quadratus Labii Superioris
(Levator Labii Superioris)

Quadratus Labii Inferioris
(Depressor Labii Inferioris)

Mentalis

Risorius

Caninus
(Levator Anguli Oris)

Triangularis
(Depressor Anguli)

Zygomaticus
Major and Minor

Buccinator

LABEL THE
MOUTH MUSCLES

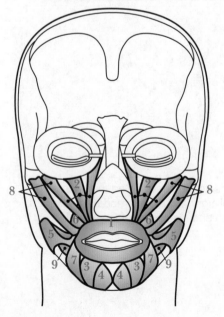

1.

2.

3.

4.

5.

6.

7.

8.

9.

LABEL THE MASTICATION MUSCLES

MASTICATION MUSCLES:

Temporalis

Masseter

1.

2.

NECK AND BACK MUSCLES

LABEL THE NECK AND BACK MUSCLES

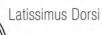

Platysma

Sternocleidomastoideus

Trapezius

Latissimus Dorsi

3.

4.

5.

6.

1 2 3 4 5 6 7

SHOULDER, CHEST, ARM AND HAND MUSCLES

SHOULDER, CHEST AND ARM MUSCLES

Pectoralis

Serratus Anterior

Deltoid

Biceps

Triceps

Supinator

Pronator

Flexor

Extensor

LABEL THE SHOULDER, CHEST AND ARM MUSCLES

1a.
1b.
2.
3.
4.
5.
6.
7.
8.
9.

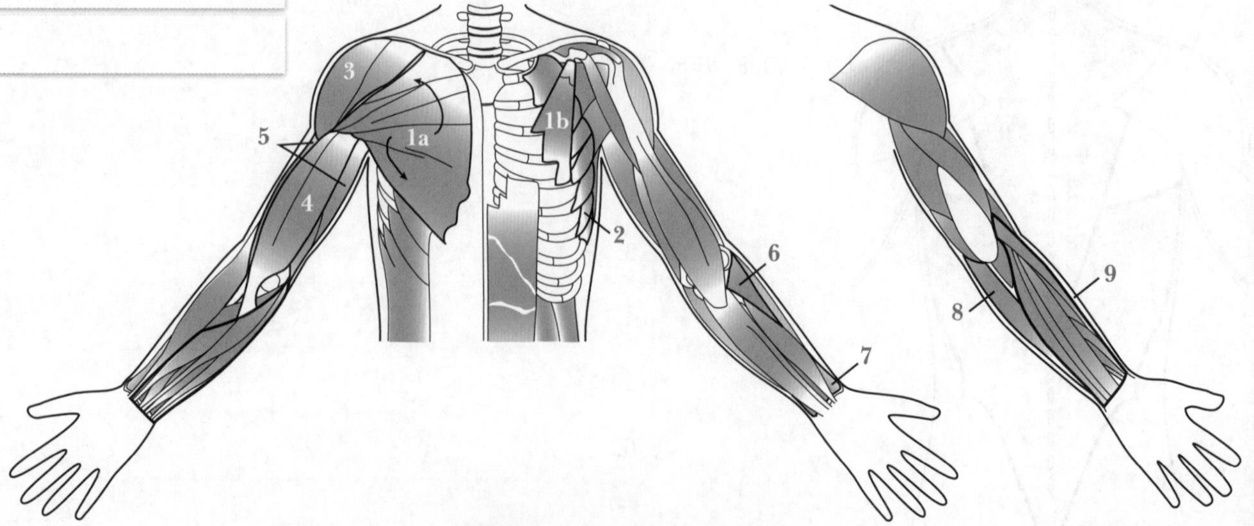

SMART NOTES

LABEL THE HAND MUSCLES

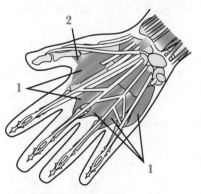

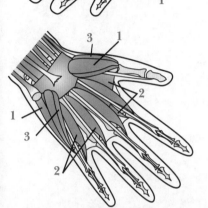

HAND MUSCLES:

Abductor

Adductor

Opponens

1.

2.

3.

LEG AND FOOT MUSCLES

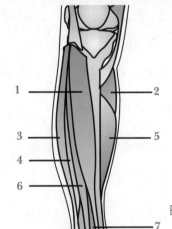

LEG MUSCLES:

Tibialis Anterior

Gastrocnemius

Peroneus Longus

Peroneus Brevis

Soleus

Extensor Digitorum Longus

Extensor Hallucis Longus

1. Bends the foot upward and _____

2. Pulls the foot _____

3. Causes the foot to invert and turn _____

4. Bends the foot down and _____

5. Bends the foot _____

6. Bends foot up and _____

7. Extends the big toe and _____

FOOT MUSCLES:

Flexor Digiti Minimi Brevis

Flexor Digitorum Brevis

Abductor Hallucis

Abductor Digiti Minimi

8. Flexes the joint of the _____ _____

9. Flexes the _____

10. Moves the big toe _____

11. Moves the smallest toe _____

MATCHING

Match the term with the best description by placing the number of the description in the space to the left of the term.

1. Close eyelids

2. Opens and closes jaw

3. Separates fingers

4. Bends the foot upward and inward

5. Raise nostrils (distaste)

6. Draws fingers together

7. Raise eyebrows

8. Draws mouth up (grin)

9. Causes the foot to invert and turn outward

10. Thumb movement

11. Wrinkles chin (doubt)

12. Chewing

13. Controls swinging of arms

14. Bends the foot down

15. Assists in breathing

16. Raise eyelids

17. Contracting, puckering and wrinkling the lips

18. Flexes the toes

19. Draws corners of mouth up (laugh)

20. Wrinkles nose

21. Pulls lip down (sarcasm)

22. Moves the big toe away from the other toes

23. Controls eyebrows

_____ Frontalis

_____ Corrugator

_____ Levator palpebrae superioris

_____ Orbicularis oculi

_____ Soleus

_____ Procerus

_____ Orbicularis oris

_____ Quadratus labii superioris

_____ Quadratus labii inferioris

_____ Mentalis

_____ Flexor digitorum brevis

_____ Risorius

_____ Zygomaticus

_____ Temporalis

_____ Peroneus longus

_____ Masseter

_____ Latissimus dorsi

_____ Serratus anterior

_____ Abductor

_____ Abductor hallucis

_____ Adductor

_____ Opponens

_____ Tibialis anterior

LESSON CHALLENGE
Multiple choice. Indicate one correct answer for each question.

1. Myology is the study of the structure, function and diseases of the:
   a. cells
   b. organs
   c. muscles
   d. skeleton

2. The salon professional is primarily concerned with which type of muscles found in the head, face, neck, hands and arms?
   a. autonomic
   b. voluntary
   c. involuntary
   d. non-striated

3. Which type of muscle responds automatically to control various body functions?
   a. cardiac
   b. striated
   c. voluntary
   d. non-striated

4. Muscles affected by massage are generally massaged from the:
   a. insertion attachment to belly attachment
   b. belly attachment to insertion attachment
   c. insertion attachment to origin attachment
   d. origin attachment to insertion attachment

5. The occipitalis muscle is located at the nape of the neck and draws the scalp:
   a. back
   b. forward
   c. to the left
   d. to the right

6. The muscle that circles the mouth and is responsible for contracting, puckering and wrinkling the lips, as in kissing or whistling, is known as:
   a. caninus
   b. mentalis
   c. orbicularis oris
   d. quadratus labii inferioris

7. The coordination of which two muscles enables the body to perform chewing (mastication)?
   a. risorius and corrugator
   b. temporalis and masseter
   c. procerus and latissimus dorsi
   d. auricularis and latissimus dorsi

8. The muscle that aids in drawing the head back and elevating the shoulder blades is known as the:
   a. trapezius
   b. platysma
   c. pectoralis
   d. sternocleidomastoideus

9. The muscle that turns the palm of the hand up is the:
   a. deltoid
   b. tricep
   c. pronator
   d. supinator

10. Which muscle straightens the fingers and wrist?
    a. tricep
    b. bicep
    c. flexor
    d. extensor

LESSON CHALLENGE REFERENCES

Check your answers. Place a check mark next to the page number for any incorrect answer. On the lines, jot down topics that you still need to review.

1. PAGE 69_____

2. PAGE 69_____

3. PAGE 69_____

4. PAGE 71_____

5. PAGE 71_____

6. PAGE 73_____

7. PAGE 74_____

8. PAGE 74_____

9. PAGE 76_____

10. PAGE 76_____

▶ GROW WHAT YOU KNOW

Reflect on what you have learned and predict how this information will be used in the future.

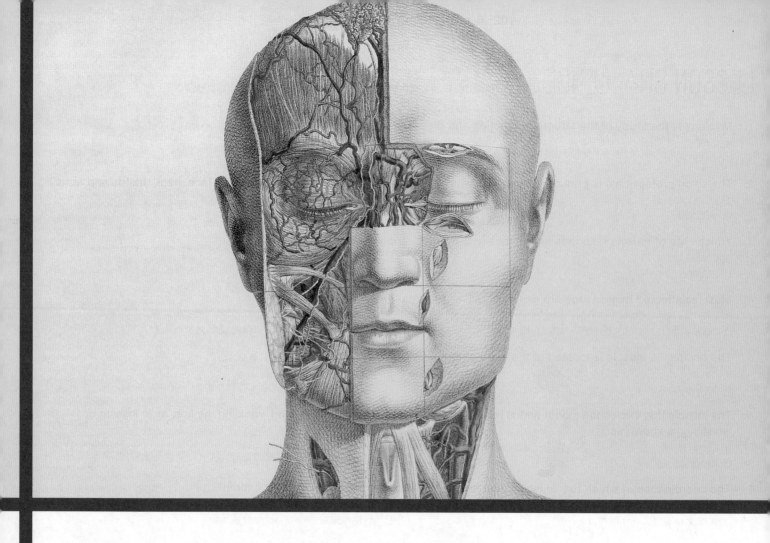

102ᶜ.7 // THE CIRCULATORY SYSTEM

ACHIEVE //

Following this lesson on *The Circulatory System*, you'll be able to:

» State the structure and function of the cardiovascular system

» Express how the heart forces blood to move through the circulatory system

» Identify the purpose of the blood within the human body

» Describe the blood vessels that circulate blood through the human body

» Offer examples of names of arteries and veins in the human body

» Explain the main function of the lymph-vascular system

FOCUS //

THE CIRCULATORY SYSTEM

The Cardiovascular System

The Lymph-Vascular System

CIRCULATORY (VASCULAR) SYSTEM:

**TWO INTERRELATED
SUBSYSTEMS OF THE
CIRCULATORY SYSTEM**

Cardiovascular System

-
-
-

Lymph-Vascular System

-
-
-

THE CARDIOVASCULAR SYSTEM

THE HEART

THE HEART:

PERICARDIUM:

LABEL THE HEART AND CHAMBERS

THE AVERAGE HEART RATE

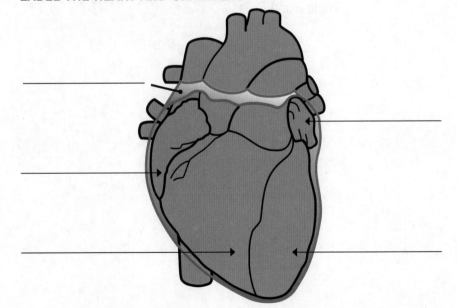

THE BLOOD

BLOOD:

Average adult blood supply: _____ to _____ _____.

FUNCTIONS OF THE BLOOD

-
-
-

FOUR COMPONENTS OF BLOOD (BLOOD CELLS)

Red Blood Cells
(RBCs)

White Blood Cells
(WBCs)

Blood Platelets

Plasma

BLOOD VESSELS

Arteries

Veins

Capillaries take nutrients and oxygen from arteries to cells

Capillaries take waste from cells to veins

BLOOD FLOW THROUGH THE HEART

1 **SYSTEMIC CIRCULATION** TO THE HEART

Oxygen-poor blood enters the right atrium of the heart through the _____

_____ _____ and _____

_____ _____ . Then it is pumped through the tricuspid

valve into the _____ _____.

2 **PULMONARY CIRCULATION** TO THE LUNGS

From the right ventricle, blood is pumped through the _____

_____ for _____.

3 **SYSTEMIC CIRCULATION** BACK TO THE HEART

Oxygenated blood returns to the heart from the lungs via the pulmonary vein and

enters the left _____. From the left atrium it goes to the left ventricle by

way of the _____ _____. From the left ventricle it goes to

the _____.

4 **SYSTEMIC CIRCULATION** TO THE BODY

Blood then flows throughout the body and returns to the heart to start the
process again.

ARTERIES AND VEINS OF THE FACE, HEAD AND NECK

COMMON CAROTID (CCA)

Supplies blood to:

Located:

Splits into:

ARTERIES AND VEINS OF THE FACE, HEAD AND NECK (CONT'D)

INTERNAL CAROTID ARTERY

Supplies blood to:

BRANCHES

Supraorbital | Supplies blood to:

Infraorbital | Supplies blood to:

EXTERNAL CAROTID ARTERY

Supplies blood to:

BRANCHES

Occipital

Posterior Auricular

Superficial Temporal

BRANCHES

Frontal

Parietal

Middle Temporal

Transverse

Anterior Auricular

EXTERNAL MAXILLARY (FACIAL)

BRANCHES

Submental

Inferior Labial

Angular

Superior Labial

Blood Returns to the Heart

All blood for the head, face and neck returns through two veins:

_____   _____

_____   _____

LABEL THE VEINS AND ARTERIES OF THE FACE, HEAD AND NECK

1.

2.

3.

4.

5.

6.

7.

8.

9.

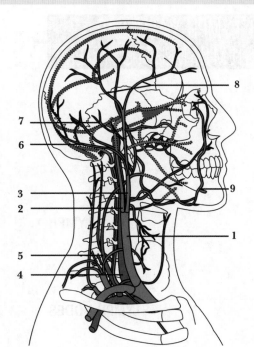

ARTERIES OF THE HAND AND ARM

Ulnar | 1. Supplies blood to:

Radial | 2. Supplies blood to:

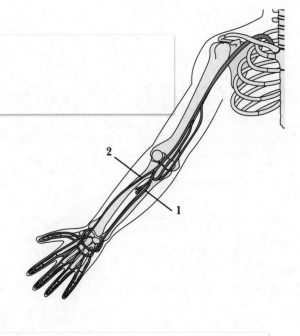

ARTERIES OF THE LOWER LEG AND FOOT

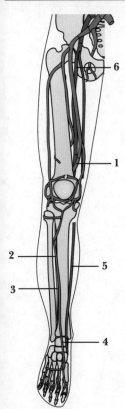

Popliteal | 1. Supplies blood to:

Anterior Tibial | 2. Supplies blood to:

Posterior Tibial | 3. Supplies blood to:

Dorsalis Pedis | 4. Carries blood to:

Saphenous Vein | 5. Transports blood from:

Femoral Vein | 6. Transports blood to:

THE LYMPH-VASCULAR SYSTEM (LYMPHATIC SYSTEM)

LYMPH

LYMPH NODES

MATCHING

Place the number of the common name in the space next to the corresponding Also Known As name found on the right.

Common Name

1. White blood cells

2. Red blood cells

3. Blood platelets

4. Vascular system

5. Lymphatic system

6. Facial artery

7. General circulation

8. IJV

9. Bicuspid valve

Also Known As

_____ Circulatory system

_____ Leukocytes

_____ Erythrocytes

_____ Mitral valve

_____ Thrombocytes

_____ Systemic circulation

_____ Internal jugular vein

_____ Lymph-vascular system

_____ External maxillary artery

LESSON CHALLENGE. *Multiple choice. Indicate one correct answer for each question.*

1. The body system responsible for circulation of the blood, including the heart, arteries, veins and capillaries, is called the:
   a. nervous system
   b. lymph-vascular system
   c. cardiovascular system
   d. integumentary system

2. What is the sticky, salty fluid that circulates through the body, bringing nourishment and oxygen to all parts of the body?
   a. blood
   b. lymph
   c. platelets
   d. thrombocytes

3. What is another name for red blood cells?
   a. plasma
   b. leukocytes
   c. hemoglobin
   d. erythrocytes

4. Cells that fight bacteria and other foreign substances are called leukocytes or:
   a. plasma
   b. hemoglobin
   c. red blood cells
   d. white blood cells

5. Thick-walled vessels that carry pure blood from the heart through the body are:
   a. veins
   b. arteries
   c. capillaries
   d. lymph vessels

6. The process of blood traveling from the heart, throughout the body and back to the heart is called:
   a. vein circulation
   b. local circulation
   c. arterial circulation
   d. general circulation

7. The occipital artery supplies blood to the:
   a. back of the head
   b. center of the forehead
   c. lower portion of the face
   d. sides and top of the head

8. Which artery supplies blood to the lower portion of the face, including the mouth and nose?
   a. occipital
   b. external maxillary
   c. posterior auricular
   d. superficial temporal

9. Which artery supplies blood to the crown and sides of the head?
   a. angular
   b. parietal
   c. submental
   d. inferior labial

10. A subsystem of the circulatory system responsible for distributing white blood cells to help develop immunity is known as the:
    a. nervous system
    b. lymph-vascular system
    c. cardiovascular system
    d. integumentary system

LESSON CHALLENGE REFERENCES

Check your answers. Place a check mark next to the page number for any incorrect answer. On the lines, jot down topics that you still need to review.

1. PAGE 83 _____
2. PAGE 84 _____
3. PAGE 86 _____
4. PAGE 86 _____
5. PAGE 86 _____

6. PAGE 87 _____
7. PAGE 88 _____
8. PAGE 88 _____
9. PAGE 88 _____
10. PAGE 91 _____

▶ GROW WHAT YOU KNOW

Reflect on what you have learned and predict how this information will be used in the future.

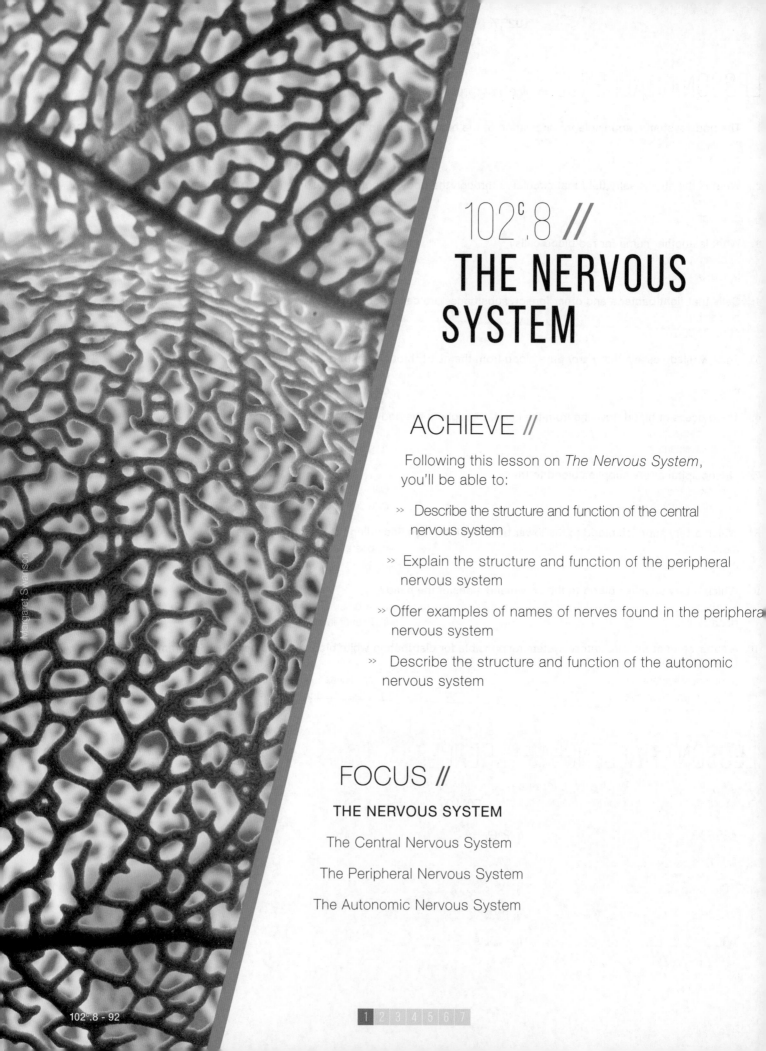

102ᶜ.8 //
THE NERVOUS SYSTEM

ACHIEVE //

Following this lesson on *The Nervous System*, you'll be able to:

>> Describe the structure and function of the central nervous system

>> Explain the structure and function of the peripheral nervous system

>> Offer examples of names of nerves found in the peripheral nervous system

>> Describe the structure and function of the autonomic nervous system

FOCUS //

THE NERVOUS SYSTEM

The Central Nervous System

The Peripheral Nervous System

The Autonomic Nervous System

THE NERVOUS SYSTEM ——— NEUROSCIENCE:

3 parts of nervous system:

1.

2.

3.

Primary components of nervous system:

1.

2.

3.

THE CENTRAL NERVOUS SYSTEM

THE BRAIN AND SPINAL CORD ——— BRAIN:

THE SPINAL CORD ———

Originates in base of

_____

Extends to base of

_____

Pairs of spinal nerves =

_____

THE PERIPHERAL NERVOUS SYSTEM

NERVE CELLS ———

TYPES OF NERVES

Sensory (a.k.a. Afferent)

·

·

Motor (a.k.a. Efferent)

·

·

·

The interaction of sensory and motor nerves is called a

_____ _____

FACE, HEAD AND NECK NERVES

TRIFACIAL NERVE:
(Trigeminal or 5th Cranial)

DIVIDES INTO 3 BRAIN BRANCHES AND 8 SMALLER BRANCHES

Ophthalmic	Maxillary	Mandibular
Nerve branch to: _____	Nerve branch to: _____	Nerve branch to: _____
Divides into:	Divides into:	Divides into:
•	•	•
•	•	•
•		
•		

FACIAL NERVE:
(7th Cranial)

6 Important Facial Nerve Branches
- •   •
- •   •
- •   •

LABEL THE NERVES OF THE FACE, HEAD AND NECK

1.	10.
2.	11.
2a.	12.
3.	13.
4.	14.
5.	15.
6.	16.
7.	17.
8.	18.
9.	

ARM AND HAND NERVES

LABEL THE NERVES OF THE ARM AND HAND

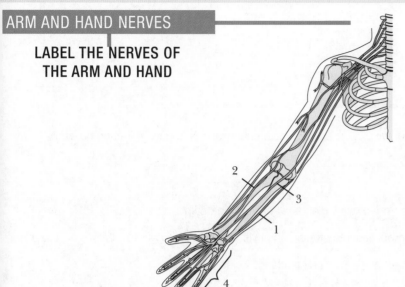

1.

2.

3.

4.

LOWER LEG AND FOOT NERVES

LABEL THE NERVES OF THE LOWER LEG AND FOOT

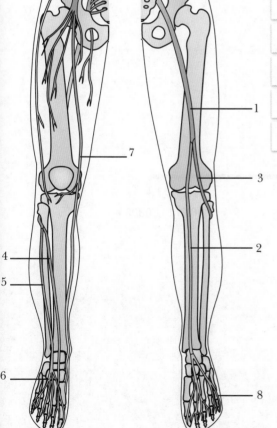

Anterior   **Posterior**

1.

2.

3.

4.

5.

6.

7.

8.

THE AUTONOMIC NERVOUS SYSTEM

THE DIGESTIVE SYSTEM

Breaks down _____; chemical compounds can then be easily

_____.

Enzymes from salivary glands start breaking down _____.

Food is propelled into stomach by twisting and turning of _____.

Food is broken down by hydrochloric acid and _____.

Partially digested food passes from stomach into _____

_____.

Undigested food passes into _____ _____.

Entire process takes _____ _____.

THE EXCRETORY SYSTEM

Skin

Liver

Kidneys

THE RESPIRATORY SYSTEM

Primary Functions

Primary Organs

THE ENDOCRINE SYSTEM

THE REPRODUCTIVE SYSTEM

FORM FOLLOWS FUNCTION

In this lesson, several important terms describe major functions. Can you describe the functions?

Central Nervous System _____

Peripheral Nervous System _____

Trifacial Nerve _____

Autonomic Nervous System _____

Digestive System _____

Enzymes _____

Excretory System _____

Skin _____

Liver _____

Kidneys _____

Respiratory System _____

Lungs _____

Diaphragm _____

Endocrine System _____

LESSON CHALLENGE

Multiple choice. Indicate one correct answer for each question.

1. The nervous system is made up of the central nervous system, the peripheral nervous system and the:
   a. axons
   b. dendrites
   c. autonomic nervous system
   d. cerebrospinal nervous system

2. The brain, spinal cord and spinal and cranial nerves make up the:
   a. involuntary system
   b. central nervous system
   c. peripheral nervous system
   d. autonomic nervous system

3. Which crucial part of the central nervous system is composed of long nerve fibers and originates in the base of the brain and extends to the base of the spine?
   a. spinal cord
   b. facial nerve
   c. trifacial nerve
   d. trigeminal nerve

4. What system is composed of sensory and motor nerves that extend from the spinal cord and brain to other parts of the body?
   a. central nervous system
   b. autonomic nervous system
   c. cerebrospinal nervous system
   d. peripheral nervous system

5. Motor nerves carry messages from the brain to the muscles and are called:
   a. sensory
   b. afferent
   c. efferent
   d. receptor

6. The primary motor nerve of the face is the:
   a. facial nerve
   b. trifacial nerve
   c. maxillary nerve
   d. mandibular nerve

7. The digestive, respiratory and circulatory systems are controlled by the:
   a. skeletal system
   b. ophthalmic branch
   c. voluntary nervous system
   d. autonomic nervous system

8. The system that breaks food down to be easily absorbed by cells or to become waste products is the:
   a. digestive system
   b. nervous system
   c. excretory system
   d. respiratory system

9. The primary function of the excretory system is to:
   a. circulate blood throughout the body
   b. intake oxygen to be absorbed into the blood
   c. eliminate solid, liquid and gaseous waste products
   d. regulate and control the growth and reproduction of the body

10. Hair growth, skin conditions and energy levels are all controlled by the:
    a. digestive system
    b. excretory system
    c. endocrine system
    d. circulatory system

LESSON CHALLENGE REFERENCES

Check your answers. Place a check mark next to the page number for any incorrect answer. On the lines, jot down topics that you still need to review.

1. PAGE 95 _____

2. PAGE 95 _____

3. PAGE 95 _____

4. PAGE 96 _____

5. PAGE 96 _____

6. PAGE 98 _____

7. PAGE 101 _____

8. PAGE 101 _____

9. PAGE 102 _____

10. PAGE 103 _____

▶ GROW WHAT YOU KNOW

Reflect on what you have learned and predict how this information will be used in the future.

ACHIEVE //

Following this lesson on *Principles of Electricity*, you'll be able to:

» Define major terms related to principles in electricity

» Describe direct current and alternating current

» Compare an electrical overload with an electrical short circuit

» Explain safety measures that are related to electricity

FOCUS //

PRINCIPLES OF ELECTRICITY

Vocabulary of Electricity

Electric Current

Safety Measures

VOCABULARY OF ELECTRICITY

ELECTRICITY AND ELECTRIC CURRENT

ELECTRICITY:

ELECTRIC CURRENT:

LOADS, CONDUCTORS AND INSULATORS

LOADS

CONDUCTORS

INSULATORS

CORD SAFETY

MEASURES OF ELECTRICITY

AMP	VOLT	OHM	WATT

APPLIANCE NAMEPLATE The nameplate of an appliance tells:

ELECTRIC CURRENT

ELECTRIC CURRENT EXISTS IN 2 FORMS

DC
AC

SPECIAL INSTRUMENTS USED TO CHANGE CURRENT

Inverter
Rectifier

DC

AC

Draw arrows in the dots to show which direction the electrons flow.

SOURCES OF ELECTRIC CURRENT

differences

Battery
-
-

Generator
-
-
-

HOW ELECTRIC CURRENT IS PRODUCED

TWO CONDITIONS NECESSARY FOR AN ELECTRIC CURRENT

SOURCE:

CIRCUIT:

CLOSED VS. OPEN CIRCUIT

GENERATOR (SOURCE)   CIRCUIT IS _____   OUTLET

SWITCH IS ON

Path of electron flow to _____

GENERATOR (SOURCE)   CIRCUIT IS _____   OUTLET

SWITCH IS OFF

Electron flow is _____

PARALLEL WIRING

SERIES WIRING

OVERLOAD AND SHORT CIRCUIT

OVERLOAD

SHORT CIRCUIT

SAFETY MEASURES

Because of the possibility of overloads and short circuits, safety devices are installed in many appliances and buildings

SAFETY DEVICES

FUSE

-
-
-

CIRCUIT BREAKER

-
-
-

GROUNDING

2-plug or prong system	3-plug or prong system	GFCI

SAFETY GUIDELINES FOR USING ELECTRICAL EQUIPMENT, CORDS, PLUGS AND OUTLETS
Review guidelines located in coursebook.

FIRE SAFETY GUIDELINES
Review guidelines located in coursebook.

FIRE

FIRE EXTINGUISHERS

For fire extinguisher use, remember **PASS**:

P =

A =

S =

S =

THINKING MAP

Create a Thinking Map to help yourself make sense of how your notes fit together. Use words in the Jump Start Box as well as your own words and pictures to make a visual that will help you connect the important ideas of this lesson. **Be creative!**

JUMP START BOX

CIRCUIT	OVERLOADING	AMP	INSULATORS
FUSE	SHORT CIRCUIT	LOAD	GENERATOR
ELECTRICITY	SOURCE	OPEN CIRCUIT	CONDUCTORS
VOLT	OHM	CURRENT	
WATT	CIRCUIT BREAKER	BATTERY	

LIGHT UP YOUR CREATIVITY

Here is an activity to help you remember the meaning of the terms you have read about so far. Draw a picture of the following "electric" words. A sample is provided to jump-start your creativity.

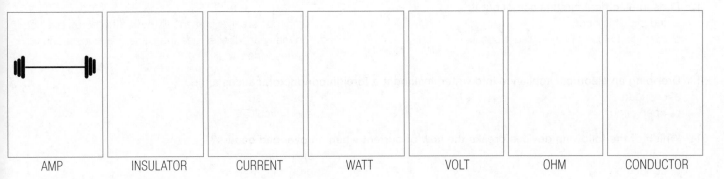

| AMP | INSULATOR | CURRENT | WATT | VOLT | OHM | CONDUCTOR |

LESSON CHALLENGE *Multiple choice. Indicate one correct answer for each question.*

1. Light, heat, chemical and magnetic changes are all produced by:
   a. force
   b. electricity
   c. conductors
   d. a short circuit

2. Most of the electricity you use daily consists of a flow of tiny, negatively charged particles called:
   a. atoms
   b. protons
   c. neutrons
   d. electrons

3. The movement of electricity along a path called a conductor is a(n):
   a. load
   b. conductor
   c. insulator
   d. electric current

4. Materials that best transport electricity are called:
   a. watts
   b. prisms
   c. insulators
   d. conductors

5. Which of the following materials does NOT allow a current to pass through it?
   a. metal
   b. water
   c. carbon
   d. alcohol

6. An ampere is a unit of electric:
   a. strength
   b. pressure
   c. frequency
   d. resistance

7. A volt is a unit of electric:
   a. strength
   b. pressure
   c. frequency
   d. resistance

8. A measure of how much electrical energy is being used is known as a:
   a. volt
   b. watt
   c. load
   d. conductor

9. A current in which electrons move at an even rate and flow in only one direction is called:
   a. EMS
   b. microcurrent
   c. direct current
   d. alternating current

10. When a blow dryer is on and air begins to flow, you have an example of a(n):
    a. open circuit
    b. series wiring
    c. closed circuit
    d. parallel wiring

11. When too many appliances are put on one circuit and are operated at the same time, more current flows than the line is designed to carry. This is known as:
    a. overload
    b. short circuit
    c. series wiring
    d. parallel wiring

12. Fires in electrical circuits can occur if:
    a. the circuit is open
    b. there is a closed path, called a circuit
    c. the circuit breaker is manually turned to the off position
    d. too many appliances use the same wall socket and overload the circuit

13. Dropping an electrical appliance into water, making it a foreign conductor, causes a(n):
    a. overload
    b. open circuit
    c. closed circuit
    d. short circuit

14. Which of the following devices breaks the flow of current when an overload occurs?
    a. insulator
    b. conductor
    c. circuit breaker
    d. grounding wire

15. Which of the following actions should NOT be done if a fire results from an overload of an electric circuit?
    a. put water on it
    b. turn off the circuit
    c. use a fire extinguisher
    d. smother it with a rug or heavy towel

LESSON CHALLENGE REFERENCES

Check your answers. Place a check mark next to the page number for any incorrect answer. On the lines, jot down topics that you still need to review.

1. PAGE 106 _____
2. PAGE 106 _____
3. PAGE 106 _____
4. PAGE 106 _____
5. PAGE 107 _____
6. PAGE 107 _____
7. PAGE 107 _____
8. PAGE 108 _____
9. PAGE 109 _____
10. PAGE 110 _____
11. PAGE 111 _____
12. PAGE 111 _____
13. PAGE 113 _____
14. PAGE 115 _____
15. PAGE 117 _____

▶ GROW WHAT YOU KNOW

Reflect on what you have learned and predict how this information will be used in the future.

102^c.10 //
ELECTRICITY
IN COSMETOLOGY

ACHIEVE //

Following this lesson on *Electricity in Cosmetology*, you'll be able to:

>> Explain the three kinds of effects that can be produced by electric current

>> Describe the benefits that can be created by special electric current used during electrotherapy and light therapy treatments

>> State the four types of electric current available for the salon professional's use

>> Compare the use of visible and invisible light

FOCUS //

ELECTRICITY IN COSMETOLOGY

Effects of Electric Current

Electrotherapy

Light Therapy

KNOW YOUR EQUIPMENT

THERMAL/HEAT EXAMPLES	MECHANICAL EXAMPLES	COMBINATION EXAMPLES
•	•	•

EFFECTS OF ELECTRIC CURRENT

HEATING	MECHANICAL OR MAGNETIC	ELECTROCHEMICAL

ELECTROTHERAPY

ALERT!

A person with any potentially restrictive medical condition should always consult a physician before receiving electrotherapy treatment.

BENEFITS

FOUR TYPES OF ELECTROTHERAPY

ELECTRODE

MOST COMMON TYPES

CONTRAINDICATION

Certain condition that suggests it is inadvisable to perform a procedure

ELECTROTHERAPY CONTRAINDICATIONS

- •
- •
- •
- •

- •
- •
- •
- •

GALVANIC CURRENT

Direct current (DC) that has electrochemical effect

-
-
-

ELECTROTHERAPY APPLICATORS

CATHODE =

ANODE =

PHORESIS
(BLEACHING)

differences

ANAPHORESIS
negative (-) pole

CATAPHORESIS
positive (+) pole

GALVANIC CURRENT ELECTROTHERAPY

ALERT!   DO NOT USE THE GALVANIC CURRENT OVER AN AREA THAT HAS MANY BROKEN CAPILLARIES.

EMS, ELECTRIC MUSCLE STIMULATION (FARADIC CURRENT)

TWO METHODS

Indirect =

Direct =

MICROCURRENT (SINUSOIDAL CURRENT)

ALERT!
Microcurrent should not be used on unhealthy and/or broken skin.

HIGH-FREQUENCY CURRENT (TESLA)

THREE METHODS

COSMETOLOGY USES FOR HIGH- FREQUENCY CURRENT

1. _____ _____

   Electrode applied directly to client's

   _____ or _____

2. _____ _____

   Glass electrode handed to client before activating current; client holds electrode; professional stimulates area

   _____

3. _____ _____

   Electrode handed to client before activating current; client experiences generalized _____ or _____

WEB

Heat Energy

General Precautions

Galvanic/EMS/Microcurrent Precautions

High-Frequency (Tesla) Current Precautions

ELECTROTHERAPY

Ultraviolet Light

Benefits of Light Therapy

Types of Medical Devices

LIGHT THERAPY

Infrared Light

Invisible Light

Visible Light

LESSON CHALLENGE *Multiple choice. Indicate one correct answer for each question.*

1. The application of special currents that have a variety of effects on the skin is called:
   a. light therapy
   b. electrotherapy
   c. chemical therapy
   d. mechanical therapy

2. When using galvanic current on clients in a salon, what precaution must a salon professional take to prevent injury to the client?
   a. do not wrap electrodes in moist cotton
   b. do not use over an area having broken capillaries
   c. do not apply the active electrode to the client's skin
   d. do not allow the client to hold the inactive electrode

3. Which of the following currents has chemical effects that are caused by passing the currents through particular acid or alkali solutions, then through body tissues and fluids?
   a. EMS
   b. galvanic
   c. microcurrent
   d. high-frequency

4. The electrode that is negatively charged during an electrotherapy treatment is known as a(n):
   a. anode
   b. cathode
   c. insulator
   d. grounding wire

5. What temporary effect will a negative pole produce when applying galvanic current during an electrotherapy treatment?
   a. increase in blood flow
   b. expansion of nerve tissues
   c. contraction of blood vessels
   d. production of an acid reaction

6. During scalp and facial massage, EMS current is used chiefly to cause:
   a. soothing effects
   b. chemical effects
   c. the transfer of heat
   d. muscle contractions

7. If a cream is used during scalp or other high-frequency treatments, be sure the cream contains no:
   a. oils
   b. water
   c. alcohol
   d. fragrance

8. A salon owner wants to balance the tones of light in the salon. Which type of light would likely be incorporated?
   a. infrared
   b. ultraviolet
   c. fluorescent
   d. incandescent

9. Which of the following is a benefit of using infrared light during a facial?
   a. kills bacteria
   b. produces vitamin D
   c. increases circulation
   d. helps control dandruff

10. Which of the following benefits is derived from UV light?
    a. it burns the skin
    b. it causes skin infections
    c. small doses tan the skin
    d. it photochemically damages hair

LESSON CHALLENGE REFERENCES

Check your answers. Place a check mark next to the page number for any incorrect answer. On the lines, jot down topics that you still need to review.

1. PAGE 123 _____

2. PAGE 124 _____

3. PAGE 125 _____

4. PAGE 125 _____

5. PAGE 125 _____

6. PAGE 126 _____

7. PAGE 129 _____

8. PAGE 131 _____

9. PAGE 133 _____

10. PAGE 134 _____

▶ # GROW WHAT YOU KNOW

Reflect on what you have learned and predict how this information will be used in the future.

102ᶜ.11 //
MATTER

ACHIEVE //

Following this lesson on *Matter*, you'll be able to:

» Define matter and its forms

» Compare physical changes with chemical changes of substances

» List the five elements of hair

» Describe the effects of side bonds when performing physical and chemical services in the salon

» Construct a chart to illustrate the hair's chemical structure

FOCUS //

MATTER

Properties of Matter

Physical and Chemical Changes

Elements

Chemical Bonds

PROPERTIES OF MATTER

CHEMISTRY

ORGANIC CHEMISTRY

INORGANIC CHEMISTRY

MATTER

PROPERTIES	BASIC FORMS
1.	1.
2.	2.
3.	3.
4.	
5.	

PHYSICAL AND CHEMICAL CHANGE

PHYSICAL

CHEMICAL

ELEMENTS

NUMBER	ELEMENT	SYMBOL	FORM
1			Gas
6			Solid
7			Gas
8			Gas
16			Solid

COHNS

ATOMS

3 PARTS OF AN ATOM

PROTON:

NEUTRON:

ELECTRON:

LABEL THE 5 ELEMENTS IMPORTANT TO SALON PROFESSIONALS

Positive Proton

Negative Electron

7 Neutral Neutrons

7 Negative Electrons

7 Positive Protons

6 Neutral Neutrons

6 Negative Electrons

6 Positive Protons

8 Negative Electrons

8 Positive Protons

8 Neutral Neutrons

16 Neutral Neutrons

16 Negative Electrons

16 Positive Protons

Hydrogen has the simplest atomic structure.

Hydrogen = 1 proton and 1_____.

Chemical behavior of atoms depends mostly on number of electrons in the

_____ _____

STABLE ATOM

UNSTABLE ATOM

MOLECULE

Substance = _____

_____

Mixture = _____

_____

With an **element**, the atoms are the _____.

With a **compound**, the atoms are _____.

CHEMICAL BONDS

AMINO ACIDS

Compounds of C, O, H, N; join together in chains to become _____.

Hair is made up of protein called _____.

Hair is 97% keratin and 3% trace materials.

Hair contains 19 common amino acids.

**PEPTIDE BONDS
(END BONDS)**

SIDE BONDS

SMARTNOTES

SIDE BONDS (CONT'D)

FOUR SIDE BONDS

HYDROGEN	SALT	DISULFIDE	van der WAALS FORCES
•	•	•	•
•	•	•	•
•		•	

LABEL THE BONDS

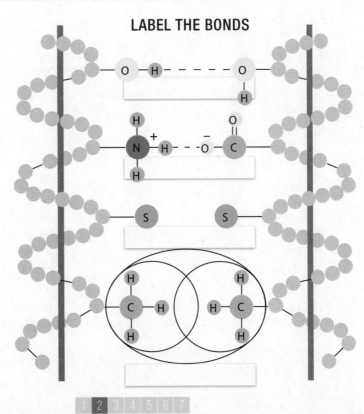

THINKING MAP

Create a Thinking Map to help yourself make sense of how your notes fit together. Use words in the Jump Start Box, as well as your own words and pictures to make a visual that will help you connect the important ideas of this lesson. Be creative!

MATTER

JUMP START BOX

NITROGEN	ELECTRON	HAIR	SIDE BOND	SALT BONDS
HYDROGEN	8	SOLID	BONDS	OXYGEN
CARBON	PHYSICAL CHANGE	LIQUID	ATOMS	16
CHEMICAL CHANGE	MOLECULES	GAS	SULFUR	van der WAALS FORCES
1	AMINO ACID	6	7	
PROTON	PROTEIN	PEPTIDE BOND	DISULFIDE	
NEUTRON	KERATIN	POLYPEPTIDE BOND	HYDROGEN BONDS	

MATCHING

Match the term with the best description by placing the number of the description in the space to the left of the term.

Change in a substance's characteristics without making a new substance

Negative electrical charge

Change in a substance that creates a new substance, new characteristics

Anything that occupies space

Smallest complete unit of an element

_____ Atom

_____ Matter

_____ Physical Change

_____ Electron

_____ Chemical Change

LESSON CHALLENGE *Multiple choice. Indicate one correct answer for each question.*

. The term used to identify anything that occupies space and has weight is called:
a. a gas
b. matter
c. a solid
d. organic

. Matter with definite weight and volume but no definite shape is called:
a. organic
b. a gas
c. a solid
d. a liquid

. Which of the following conditions is an example of chemical change?
a. water to ice
b. water to steam
c. raindrops turning to snow
d. oxygen and hydrogen combining to form water

. Basic substances that cannot be broken down into simpler substances are called:
a. solids
b. elements
c. molecules
d. compounds

. Atoms that are the same form a(n):
a. mixture
b. element
c. emulsion
d. compound

. Neutrons have which type of electrical charge?
a. none
b. chemical
c. positive
d. negative

. When two hydrogen atoms combine with one oxygen atom, the result is water, which is called a(n):
a. atom
b. mixture
c. element
d. compound

. Atoms that are different form a(n):
a. mixture
b. element
c. emulsion
d. compound

. Carbon, nitrogen, oxygen and hydrogen form the basis of:
a. mixtures
b. elements
c. compounds
d. amino acids

0. What makes up the primary composition of hair?
a. keratin
b. protons
c. electrons
d. trace minerals

11. Which bond is the backbone of all protein molecules?
   a. salt
   b. keratin
   c. peptide
   d. hydrogen

12. Putting a sodium hydroxide relaxer under a hair dryer:
   a. will link together all protein groups
   b. could turn into van der Waals forces
   c. will increase the hair's amino acid content
   d. could break the critical peptide bonds and destroy the protein structure

13. When amino acids combine to form the protein of the hair:
   a. they take on a spiraling configuration
   b. they form a new amino acid group
   c. the hair's amino acid content will decrease
   d. the hair's amino acid content will increase

14. What is the side bond that is of the greatest concern to the salon professional?
   a. salt bond
   b. disulfide bond
   c. hydrogen bond
   d. van der Waals forces

15. Which of the following statements describes how human hair is formed?
   a. salt bonds connect to amino acids
   b. hydrogen bonds create a chemical change
   c. amino acids cause a simple physical change
   d. bonding of protein chains to other protein chains

LESSON CHALLENGE REFERENCES

Check your answers. Place a check mark next to the page number for any incorrect answer. On the lines, jot down topics that you still need to review.

▶ GROW WHAT YOU KNOW

Reflect on what you have learned and predict how this information will be used in the future.

102ᶜ.12 // pH

ACHIEVE //

Following this lesson on *pH*, you'll be able to:

» Identify why it is important for salon professionals to be knowledgeable about pH

» Explain the effects of acids and alkalis in water in relation to pH

» Describe the pH scale and its three main categories

» State the three ways to measure pH

» Identify the importance of pH-balanced products

FOCUS //

pH

pH Starts with Water

The pH Scale

pH STARTS WITH WATER

pH:

NUMERICAL MEASUREMENT:

Draw in the molecules/ions to match the labels

→   +

Water Molecule
[H₂0]

Hydroxide
[OH-]

Hydrogen Ion
[H+]

H₂0

H₂0

OH-   H+

PURE WATER

-
-

ACIDS AND ALKALIS

differences

ACID
-
-

ALKALI
-
-

Add appropriate symbols and descriptive labels for each container.

Solution is acidic if it has:

Solution is neutral when it has:

Solution is alkaline if it has:

THE pH SCALE

Label the pH Scale

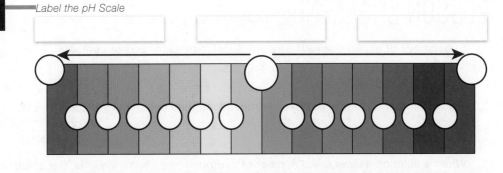

Fill in the numbers to identify the logarithm of the pH scale from Neutral 7 to Alkaline 14. The first two are completed.

7	8	9	10	11	12	13	14

_0_ x _10_ x _____ x _____ x _____ x _____ x _____ x _____

MEASURING pH

pH METER	INDICATOR LIQUID	INDICATOR PAPER

pH BALANCED

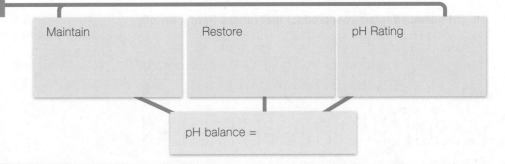

MATCHING

Match the term with the best description by placing the number of the description in the space to the left of the term.

1. Substance with a pH value of 4.5-5.5   _____ 0-6.99

2. Alkali pH range   _____ Neutral

3. Acid pH range   _____ 7.01-14

4. Water   _____ Logarithm

5. Change in value along the scale is a change of 10 times _____ pH balanced

LESSON CHALLENGE
Multiple choice. Indicate one correct answer for each question.

1. Substances of acidic or alkaline nature dissolve in water and/or contain:
   a. salt
   b. water
   c. carbon
   d. hydrogen

2. A solution that has more positive hydrogen ions than negative hydroxide ions is:
   a. acidic
   b. neutral
   c. alkaline
   d. slightly alkaline

3. When a solution has an equal number of hydrogen and hydroxide ions, the solution is considered:
   a. acidic
   b. neutral
   c. positive
   d. negative

4. Distilled water with a pH of 7 is considered:
   a. a salt
   b. neutral
   c. an acid
   d. an alkali

5. On the pH scale, numbers less than 7 indicate a(n):
   a. acidic solution
   b. neutral solution
   c. chemical solution
   d. alkaline solution

6. On the pH scale, numbers greater than 7 indicate a(n):
   a. acidic solution
   b. neutral solution
   c. chemical solution
   d. alkaline solution

7. A pH of 5 is how many more times acidic than a pH of 6?
   a. 1.5
   b. 10
   c. 100
   d. 1,000

8. The most accurate method of measuring pH is with:
   a. a pH meter
   b. pH paper
   c. indicator paper
   d. indicator liquid

9. What is the pH range of hair, skin and nails?
   a. 4.5 to 5.5
   b. 6.5 to 7.0
   c. 7.5 to 10.5
   d. 11.5 to 12.0

10. pH balanced refers to a product that ranges from a pH of:
    a. 4.5 to 5.5
    b. 6.5 to 7.0
    c. 7.5 to 10.5
    d. 11.5 to 12.0

LESSON CHALLENGE REFERENCES

Check your answers. Place a check mark next to the page number for any incorrect answer. On the lines, jot down topics that you still need to review.

1. PAGE 151 _____
2. PAGE 152 _____
3. PAGE 152 _____
4. PAGE 154 _____
5. PAGE 154 _____

6. PAGE 154 _____
7. PAGE 154 _____
8. PAGE 155 _____
9. PAGE 155 _____
10. PAGE 155 _____

GROW WHAT YOU KNOW

Reflect on what you have learned and predict how this information will be used in the future.

102ᶜ.13 //
HAIR CARE PRODUCT KNOWLEDGE

ACHIEVE //

Following this lesson on *Hair Care Product Knowledge*, you'll be able to:

» Identify the six general cosmetic classifications

» Classify the differences between various shampoo, rinse and conditioner products

» Describe the precautions that are necessary when working with various professional products and cosmetics

FOCUS //

HAIR CARE PRODUCT KNOWLEDGE

Cosmetic Classifications

Shampoos

Rinses and Conditioners

Product Information

COSMETIC CLASSIFICATIONS

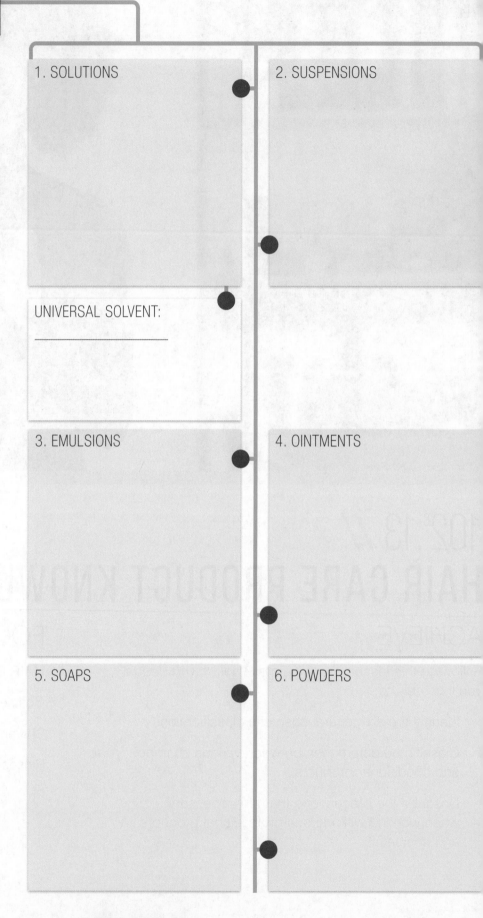

1. SOLUTIONS

2. SUSPENSIONS

UNIVERSAL SOLVENT:
_____

3. EMULSIONS

4. OINTMENTS

5. SOAPS

6. POWDERS

SHAMPOOS

Surfactants: _____

_____

HOW SHAMPOO WORKS

1. Water-loving (_____)

    •

2. Oil-loving (_____)

    •

THE ROLE OF WATER

HARD WATER   **SOFT WATER**

•

•

•

•

•

•

The primary ingredient in shampoo is usually _____

WATER PURIFICATION

Sedimentation   →   Filtration   →   Chlorine added

•   •   •

                                                           •

WEB

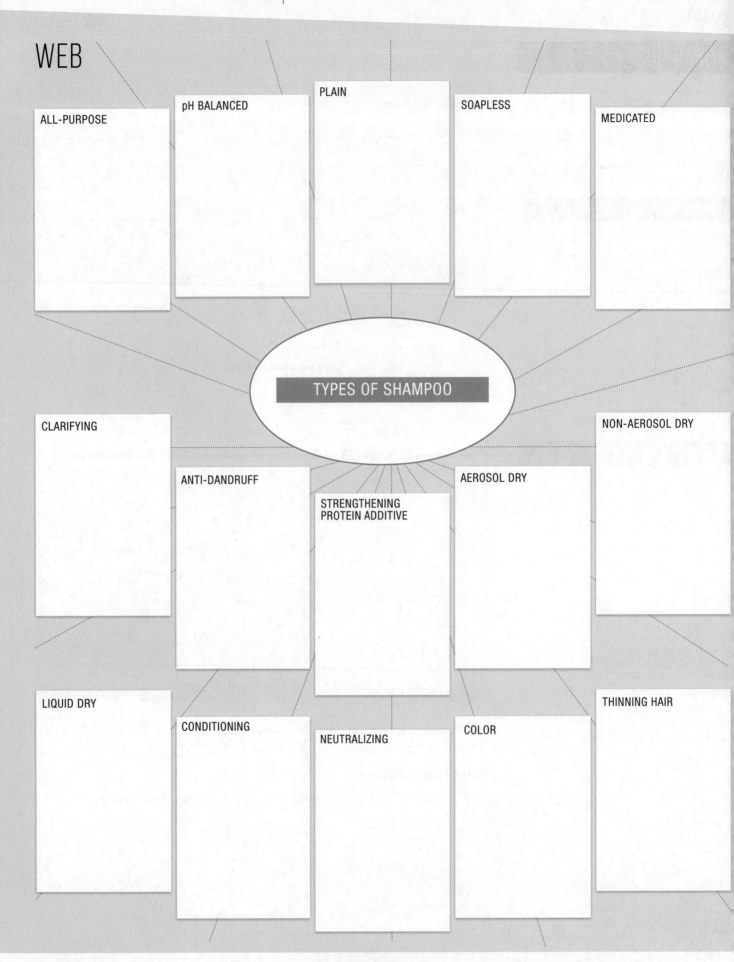

ALL-PURPOSE

pH BALANCED

PLAIN

SOAPLESS

MEDICATED

CLARIFYING

ANTI-DANDRUFF

TYPES OF SHAMPOO

STRENGTHENING PROTEIN ADDITIVE

AEROSOL DRY

NON-AEROSOL DRY

LIQUID DRY

CONDITIONING

NEUTRALIZING

COLOR

THINNING HAIR

HEALTHY HAIR

-
-
-
-

COSMETIC APPEARANCE

-

POROSITY

-

MANAGEABILITY

-

ELASTICITY

-

RINSES AND CONDITIONERS

RINSES

Affect mostly the surface of the hair

1. Vinegar and lemon (acid) – _____

2. Crème – _____

3. Medicated – _____

CONDITIONERS

Penetrate deep into the hair

1. Instant – _____

2. Normalizing – _____

3. Body-building – _____
   _____

4. Moisturizing – _____
   _____

5. Customized – _____

Example ingredients for conditioners:

-
-
-
-
-

Fine Hair
- Use _____

Thick or Curly Hair
- Use _____

Control Curl or Waves
- Use _____

PRODUCT INFORMATION

Safety Data Chart = _____

Additional Resources:

FDA = _____

U.S.P. = _____

International Cosmetic Ingredient Dictionary and Handbook published by the Personal Care Products Council

COSMETIC INGREDIENTS

-
-
-
-

LESSON CHALLENGE *Multiple choice. Indicate one correct answer for each question.*

1. A mixture of two or more kinds of molecules, evenly dispersed, would be a(n):
   a. solution
   b. emulsion
   c. suspension
   d. combination

2. Mixtures of two or more kinds of molecules, having a tendency to separate when left standing, are known as:
   a. solutions
   b. ointments
   c. emulsions
   d. suspensions

3. Which of the following terms means liquids not able to be mixed?
   a. solvent
   b. solution
   c. miscible
   d. immiscible

4. Which of the following statements about surfactants is NOT true?
   a. contains a lipophilic part
   b. contains a hydrophilic part
   c. used to remove oil from the hair
   d. prevents shampoo from lathering

5. The oil-loving part of a surface active agent is called:
   a. lipophilic
   b. emulsifier
   c. surfactant
   d. hydrophilic

6. The ability of hair to absorb moisture, liquids or chemicals refers to the hair's:
   a. texture
   b. porosity
   c. elasticity
   d. manageability

7. How far can healthy hair be stretched without breaking when wet?
   a. 10%
   b. 30%
   c. 50%
   d. 75%

8. Rinses, which affect mostly the surface of the hair:
   a. repair broken bonds of the hair
   b. usually penetrate deep into the hair
   c. can be detrimental if allowed to build up on the hair
   d. are usually left on hair for 30 minutes before removing

9. Which conditioner will penetrate into the damaged hair shaft and deposit proteins into the cortex?
   a. instant conditioner
   b. normalizing conditioner
   c. moisturizing conditioner
   d. body-building conditioner

10. If a product label lists the following ingredients: "water, cetyl alcohol, tocopherol and panthenol," which ingredient would be found to have the largest amount?
    a. water
    b. panthenol
    c. tocopherol
    d. cetyl alcohol

LESSON CHALLENGE REFERENCES

Check your answers. Place a check mark next to the page number for any incorrect answer. On the lines, jot down topics that you still need to review.

1. PAGE 160 _____
2. PAGE 160 _____
3. PAGE 159 _____
4. PAGE 162 _____
5. PAGE 162 _____

6. PAGE 166 _____
7. PAGE 166 _____
8. PAGE 167 _____
9. PAGE 169 _____
10. PAGE 170 _____

▶ GROW WHAT YOU KNOW

Reflect on what you have learned and predict how this information will be used in the future.

HAIR THEORY

ACHIEVE //

Following this lesson on *Hair Theory*, you'll be able to:

>> State how the hair bulb is formed

>> Identify the three stages of hair growth

>> Illustrate the three major layers of the hair

>> Explain the three factors that affect the behavior of hair

>> Describe the process of how hair gains its color

FOCUS //

HAIR THEORY

Hair Bulb Formation

Hair Growth

Hair Structure and Behavior

Natural Hair Color

Trichology: _____

Only cells of the hair bulb are alive; hair itself is _____ _____

MAIN PURPOSES OF HAIR

- •
- Protection from: • • •

HAIR BULB FORMATION

Primitive Hair Germ

Basal Layer

Start of Sebaceous Gland and Arrector Pili Muscle

Hair Follicle

Papilla

- •
- •
- •
- •

The shape of the follicle will determine the shape of the

_____ _____.

Draw the shape of the follicle for each hair type.

STRAIGHT HAIR   WAVY TO CURLY HAIR   TIGHTLY CURLED HAIR

TWO PRIMARY PARTS OF THE HAIR

- • _____
- • _____

HAIR GROWTH

Papilla	Germinal Matrix Cells	Hair pulled out from the roots will grow again unless the papilla is _____

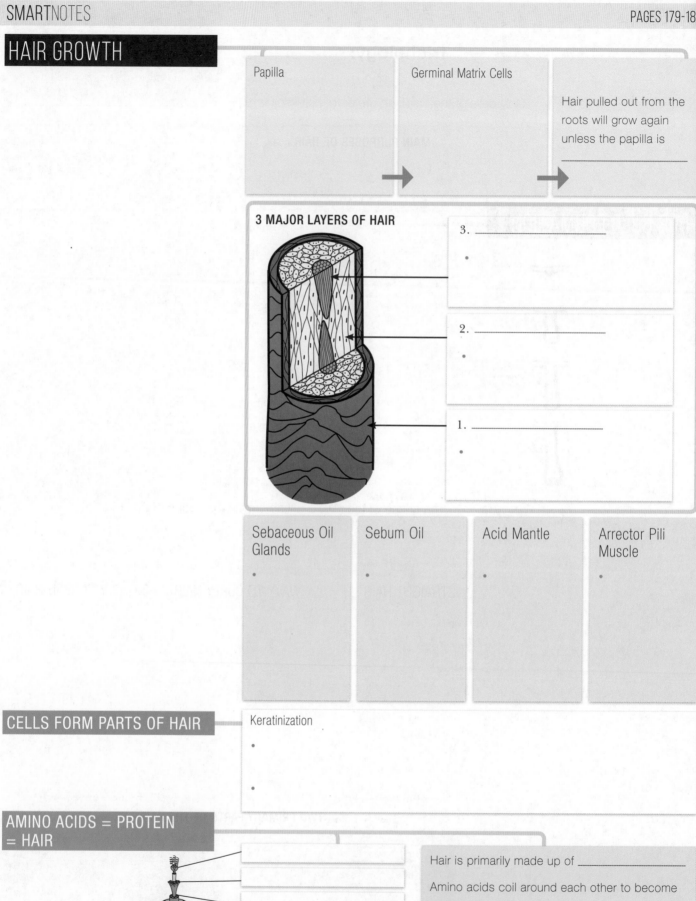

3 MAJOR LAYERS OF HAIR

3. _____
•

2. _____
•

1. _____
•

Sebaceous Oil Glands	Sebum Oil	Acid Mantle	Arrector Pili Muscle
•	•	•	•

CELLS FORM PARTS OF HAIR

Keratinization
•

•

AMINO ACIDS = PROTEIN = HAIR

Hair is primarily made up of _____

Amino acids coil around each other to become

protein chains that form the _____

Twisting gives hair ability to _____

STAGES OF HAIR GROWTH

1._____   2._____   3._____

Active _____   Brief _____   _____

Attached _____   Cell division _____   No attached _____

_____   _____

Hair growth can be affected by:

•

•

•

•

HAIR STRUCTURE AND BEHAVIOR

3 FACTORS AFFECTING THE BEHAVIOR OF HAIR

Heredity: _____

Environment: _____

Products or Appliances: _____

STRUCTURAL ORGANIZATION OF HAIR

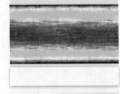

Label the illustration.

Cuticle = _____ , _____

Cortex = _____ , _____

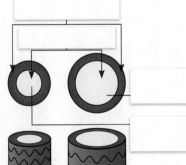

• Higher cuticle/cortex ratio =

_____

• Lower cuticle/cortex ratio =

_____

NATURAL HAIR COLOR

Melanocytes produce melanosomes, which contain the pigment _____

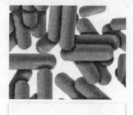

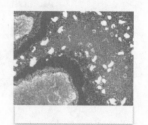

TWO TYPES OF MELANIN

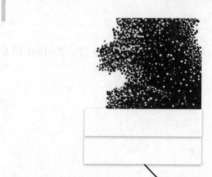

Melanins influence the resulting hair colors by: _____
_____

When there is a total lack of pigmentation in the hair and skin, the resulting condition is called albinism.

Gray Hair

-
-
-
-
-

Melanin in the Skin

-

-

MATCHING

Match the definition in the left column to its matching term in the right column.

A. The outer covering of the hair shaft made up of overlapping layers of transparent scales

B. The second layer of hair that gives hair most of its pigment and strength (elasticity)

C. The central core of the hair shaft; also called the pith or marrow

D. The active growing stage of hair growth

E. A brief transitional stage of hair growth, when all cell division stops

F. The resting stage of hair growth

G. Melanin that is brown/black in color

H. Melanin that is red/yellow in color

_____ Cuticle

_____ Anagen Stage

_____ Cortex

_____ Eumelanin

_____ Catagen Stage

_____ Medulla

_____ Pheomelanin

_____ Telogen Stage

LESSON CHALLENGE *Multiple choice. Indicate one correct answer for each question.*

1. When looking through a microscope, which portion of the hair would display living cells?
   a. hair bulb
   b. hair fiber
   c. hair shaft
   d. hairstrand

2. Hair grows from a tube-like "pocket" called a root sheath or a(n):
   a. bulb
   b. follicle
   c. papilla
   d. arrector pili

3. The follicle in straight hair is typically:
   a. round
   b. elliptical
   c. oval or elliptical
   d. round or elliptical

4. The hair follicle that produces tightly curled hair is typically:
   a. wavy
   b. round
   c. square
   d. elliptical

5. Located at the bottom of the follicle and supplying nourishment to the germinal matrix is the:
   a. tube
   b. base
   c. papilla
   d. medulla

6. The outer covering of the hair shaft made up of overlapping layers of transparent scales is called the:
   a. cortex
   b. cuticle
   c. papilla
   d. medulla

7. The layer of hair consisting of unique protein structures that give the hair most of its pigment and strength (elasticity) is called the:
   a. cortex
   b. cuticle
   c. follicle
   d. medulla

8. Hair that has been pulled out from the roots will grow back under which of the following circumstances?
   a. the cortex has not been destroyed
   b. the cuticle has not been destroyed
   c. the papilla has not been destroyed
   d. the medulla has not been destroyed

9. What helps prevent the hair and skin from becoming too dry?
   a. sebum
   b. hair fiber
   c. protofibrils
   d. primitive hair germ

10. What is formed when sebum produced by the oil glands mixes with the body's perspiration?
    a. medulla
    b. acid mantle
    c. arrector pili
    d. sebaceous glands

11. The muscle that causes the hair to stand on end when a person is scared or cold is known as the:
    a. cuticle
    b. papilla
    c. medulla
    d. arrector pili

12. Which of the following terms is known as the active growing stage of hair?
    a. resting stage
    b. anagen stage
    c. catagen stage
    d. transitional stage

13. Catagen, a brief transitional stage, lasts for what amount of time?
    a. only a few weeks
    b. 1-2 years
    c. 2-6 years
    d. up to 10 years

14. The resting stage of hair growth when the hair bulb has no attached root sheath is referred to as the:
    a. active stage
    b. telogen stage
    c. anagen stage
    d. catagen stage

15. The lips, soles of the feet, palms of the hands and eyelids do not have:
    a. hair
    b. cells
    c. nerves
    d. muscles

16. Hair that is 90% cortex and 10% cuticle when compared to hair that is 40% cuticle would be considered to be:
    a. less elastic
    b. more elastic
    c. resistant to holding a set
    d. resistant to holding a perm

17. What is the total lack of pigmentation in the hair and skin called?
    a. lanugo
    b. anagen
    c. albinism
    d. alopecia

18. Gray hair is caused by a(n):
    a. reduced pigment in the medulla layer of the hair
    b. reduced color pigment, melanin, in the cortex layer of the hair
    c. excessive color pigment in the cuticle layer of the hair
    d. excessive color pigment in the cortex layer of the hair

19. Eumelanin is the type of melanin that produces:
    a. red hair color
    b. red/orange hair color
    c. brown/black hair color
    d. brown/orange hair color

20. People with lighter colored hair have melanin in the:
    a. cortex only
    b. cuticle only
    c. medulla only
    d. cuticle and cortex

LESSON CHALLENGE REFERENCES

Check your answers. Place a check mark next to the page number for any incorrect answer. On the lines, jot down topics that you still need to review.

1. PAGE 177 _____
2. PAGE 178 _____
3. PAGE 178 _____
4. PAGE 178 _____
5. PAGE 179 _____
6. PAGE 179 _____
7. PAGE 179 _____

8. PAGE 179 _____
9. PAGE 179 _____
10. PAGE 179 _____
11. PAGE 179 _____
12. PAGE 182 _____
13. PAGE 182 _____
14. PAGE 182 _____

15. PAGE 182 _____
16. PAGE 184 _____
17. PAGE 185 _____
18. PAGE 185 _____
19. PAGE 185 _____
20. PAGE 185 _____

▶ GROW WHAT YOU KNOW

Reflect on what you have learned and predict how this information will be used in the future.

102^c.15 // HAIR CARE

ACHIEVE //

Following this lesson on *Hair Care*, you'll be able to:

>> Identify the steps involved in doing a hair evaluation prior to a salon service

>> Describe the common hair conditions a salon professional may encounter in the salon

>> Explain common scalp conditions a salon professional may encounter in the salon

>> Offer examples of various hair-loss conditions and available treatments

FOCUS //

HAIR CARE

Hair Evaluation

Common Hair Conditions

Common Scalp Conditions

Hair Loss

HAIR EVALUATION

1 DETERMINE HAIR TYPE AND DENSITY

Texture: _____

_____

Fine	Medium	Coarse
Feel of	Feel of	Feel of
_____	_____	_____

Visual examination: _____

_____

_____

Density: _____

_____

Identifiy the density of each hair fiber shown

2 DETERMINE CLIENT'S HAIR CONDITION:

Porosity: _____

_____

Average:	Resistant:	Extreme:	Uneven:
Cuticle is slightly	Cuticle is	Cuticle is	Porosities are
_____	_____	_____	_____
•	•	•	•
		•	
•	•	•	

Elasticity: _____
_____

Normal Dry Hair: Stretches _____%

Wet Hair: Stretches _____% to _____%

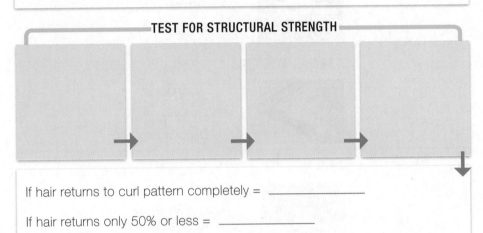

TEST FOR STRUCTURAL STRENGTH

If hair returns to curl pattern completely = _____

If hair returns only 50% or less = _____

3 **CONSIDER EFFECTS OF CLIMATE:**

The amount of moisture in air determines amount of moisture in hair.

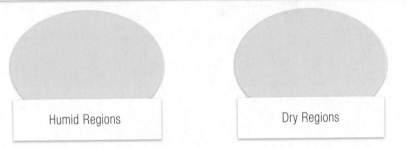

Humid Regions

Dry Regions

COMMON HAIR CONDITIONS

Number of cuticle scale layers: _____ to _____

Scales should lie flat along the _____

Acid mantle lubricates the outermost layer of the cuticle and reduces _____

Combing and brushing damages the _____

Condition:

Also Known As:

Description:

Condition:

Also Known As:

Description:

Condition:

Also Known As:

Description:

Condition:

Also Known As:

Description:

Condition:

Also Known As:

Description:

Condition: Matting

Also Known As:

Description:

Condition: Ringed Hair

Also Known As:

Description:

Condition: Hypertrichosis

Also Known As:

Description:

Condition: Hirsutism

Also Known As:

Description:

Mechanical Damage:

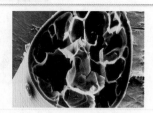

COMMON SCALP CONDITIONS

	DISORDER OR DISEASE	MEDICAL TERM	DESCRIPTION	TREATMENT
Scales				
Dandruff				
Dry Dandruff				
Greasy or Waxy Dandruff				

The leading cause of dandruff is a naturally occurring microscopic fungus called Malassezia.

EXTERNAL PARASITES

	DISORDER OR DISEASE	MEDICAL TERM	DESCRIPTION	TREATMENT
Ringworm				
Ringworm of the scalp				
Honeycomb Ringworm				
Itch Mite				
Head Lice				

HAIR LOSS

As a salon professional, you are often the first person asked to respond to questions about hair loss. So knowing how to address client concerns will greatly affect your client's well-being.

NORMAL HAIR LOSS

Lanugo Hair: _____

_____

Vellus Hair: _____

_____

Terminal Hair: _____

_____

Average daily hair loss of hairstrands = _____ to _____

ANDROGENETIC HAIR LOSS

Draw in the progressive miniaturization of the hair follicle.

Alopecia

-
-
-

Androgenetic Alopecia

-
-
-

RECOGNIZING ANDROGENETIC ALOPECIA

Men

-
-
-
-

Women

-
-
-
-

The degree of hair loss can be evaluated by rating the:

- Pattern: _____
- Density: _____

_____

Note: Because women experience a single pattern of hair loss, only density needs to be evaluated.

OTHER TYPES OF HAIR LOSS

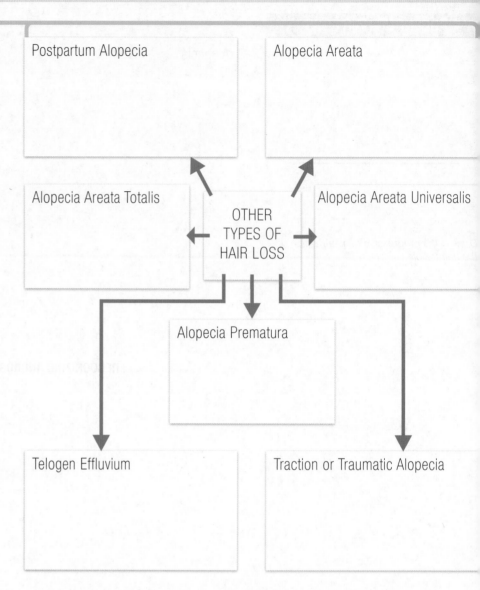

Postpartum Alopecia

Alopecia Areata

Alopecia Areata Totalis

OTHER TYPES OF HAIR LOSS

Alopecia Areata Universalis

Alopecia Prematura

Telogen Effluvium

Traction or Traumatic Alopecia

HAIR-LOSS TREATMENTS

TREATMENT OF ANDROGENETIC ALOPECIA

1.

2.

3.

4.

5.

SCRAMBLE

Unscramble these important terms from the lesson.

APOISISSR

YSENITD

LAAPECIO

ASFGIITIRL MCRIIUN

SPOOITYR

SAICNTEI

CELTIITYSA

LESSON CHALLENGE *Multiple choice. Indicate one correct answer for each question.*

1. The number of active hair follicles per square inch on the scalp refers to:
   a. color
   b. texture
   c. density
   d. porosity

2. The ability of the hair to absorb moisture, liquids or chemicals is known as:
   a. texture
   b. density
   c. capacity
   d. porosity

3. If the layers of the cuticle are very close together the hair has which type of porosity?
   a. uneven
   b. extreme
   c. average
   d. resistant

4. Which of the following refers to the ability of hair to stretch and return to its original shape without breaking?
   a. texture
   b. porosity
   c. elasticity
   d. breaking point

5. Small cracks starting in the cuticle and splitting the hair entirely are known as brittle hair, fragilitis crinium or:
   a. pityriasis
   b. trichoptilosis
   c. trichorrhexis nodosa
   d. pityriasis steatoides

6. Fragilitis crinium is the technical name for:
   a. matting
   b. alopecia
   c. split ends
   d. ringed hair

7. Lumps or swelling along the hair shaft is known as trichorrhexis nodosa or:
   a. alopecia
   b. gray hair
   c. matted hair
   d. knotted hair

8. The loss of pigment in the hair as a person ages is called:
   a. trichonodosis
   b. abraded hair
   c. plica polonica
   d. acquired canities

9. Excessive matting of the hair is referred to as:
   a. canities
   b. monilethrix
   c. plica polonica
   d. trichorrhexis nodosa

10. A condition in which beads or nodes form on the hair shaft is called:
    a. canities
    b. nodules
    c. monilethrix
    d. hypertrichosis

11. A disorder that refers to a chronic scalp condition with excessive flaking, which accumulates on the scalp or falls to the shoulders, is known as dandruff or:
    a. scabies
    b. pityriasis
    c. tinea capitis
    d. tinea favosa

12. A disorder that refers to thick, crusty patches of red irritated scalp is known as:
    a. psoriasis
    b. ringworm
    c. pityriasis capitis
    d. pediculosis capitis

13. The medical term for greasy or waxy dandruff is:
    a. tinea capitis
    b. tinea favosa
    c. pityriasis capitis
    d. pityriasis steatoides

14. An infestation of head lice on the scalp is called:
    a. scabies
    b. tinea favosa
    c. pediculosis capitis
    d. pityriasis steatoides

15. How should a salon professional handle a situation when areas of enlarged open follicles surrounded by clusters of red spots, indicating tinea capitis are observed?
  a. continue with the service
  b. refer the client to a physician
  c. cleanse with a medicated shampoo
  d. cleanse and massage the scalp with an antiseptic lotion

16. What scalp disease might be present if prior to a service several dry, yellow, encrusted areas on the scalp are noticed along with a peculiar odor?
  a. scabies
  b. pityriasis
  c. tinea favosa
  d. pediculosis capitis

17. Short, fine, non-pigmented hair found more abundantly on women is known as:
  a. cilia
  b. vellus
  c. lanugo
  d. terminal

18. What is the average amount of daily hair loss?
  a. 10 to 20 strands
  b. 40 to 100 strands
  c. 250 to 500 strands
  d. 1,000 strands

19. In men, male pattern baldness takes the shape of:
  a. irregular patches
  b. spots of baldness
  c. generalized thinning
  d. horseshoe-shaped fringe

20. Traction alopecia can be caused by:
  a. stress
  b. loose chignons
  c. protein conditioners
  d. tight cornrows

LESSON CHALLENGE REFERENCES

Check your answers. Place a check mark next to the page number for any incorrect answer. On the lines, jot down topics that you still need to review.

1. PAGE 190 _____
2. PAGE 190 _____
3. PAGE 190 _____
4. PAGE 191 _____
5. PAGE 192 _____

6. PAGE 192 _____
7. PAGE 192 _____
8. PAGE 192 _____
9. PAGE 193 _____
10. PAGE 193 _____

11. PAGE 194 _____
12. PAGE 194 _____
13. PAGE 194 _____
14. PAGE 195 _____
15. PAGE 195 _____

16. PAGE 195 _____
17. PAGE 196 _____
18. PAGE 196 _____
19. PAGE 197 _____
20. PAGE 198 _____

▶ GROW WHAT YOU KNOW

Reflect on what you have learned and predict how this information will be used in the future.

102ᶜ.16 //
SHAMPOO AND SCALP MASSAGE THEORY

ACHIEVE //

Following this lesson on *Shampoo and Scalp Massage Theory*, you'll be able to:

» List considerations for draping during a shampoo and scalp massage service

» Explain the purpose of shampooing and conditioning

» Compare the five types of massage movements used during a scalp massage

FOCUS //

SHAMPOO AND SCALP MASSAGE THEORY

Draping

Shampoo and Condition

Scalp Massage

Shampoo and Scalp Massage Service Considerations

DRAPING

DRAPING: Performed prior to hair care services, such as shampooing and scalp massage, to protect client's skin and _____

DRAPING CONSIDERATIONS

Towel

-
-

Plastic/Waterproof Cape

-
-

Neck Strip

-
-
-

Cloth Cape

-
-
-

SHAMPOO AND CONDITION

The purpose of shampooing is to cleanse the scalp and hair by removing dirt, oils and product _____

The purpose of conditioning is to fortify the damaged areas of the hair and protect it against further damage from _____

-
-
-
-

SHAMPOO SERVICE

-
-

WATER

SOFT WATER

-
-

HARD WATER

-
-

Always Remember

Monitor water temperature before applying water to your client's _____

Wipe up water spills to prevent _____

BRUSHING AND COMBING

- Removes _____
- Increases blood circulation to the _____
- Removes dust, dirt and product _____

Brushing prior to chemical service, or if any cuts or abrasions are evident, is

_____ _____.

REMOVING TANGLES FROM WET HAIR

- Start _____
- Release _____
- Begin _____
- Comb _____
- Part off _____
- Remove _____
- Continue throughout _____

SCALP MASSAGE

Massage: _____

_____

_____

Scalp Massage: Movements performed to relax muscles and increase blood circulation

-
-
-

SMARTNOTES

When massaging the scalp:

-
-
-
-

THE 5 BASIC MOVEMENTS OF MASSAGE

MOVEMENT	DESCRIPTION	EFFECT
1. Effleurage		
2. Petrissage		
3. Tapotement *Also known as percussion or hacking*		
4. Friction		
5. Vibration		

SHAMPOO AND SCALP MASSAGE CONSIDERATIONS

Draping, shampooing and conditioning preparation and procedures vary based on timing allowed for each service and each client's needs.

Examples:

-
-
-

QUICK DRAW

Draw your interpretation of the actions used for each of the five basic massage movements.

EFFLEURAGE	PETRISSAGE	TAPOTEMENT	FRICTION	VIBRATION

LESSON CHALLENGE *Multiple choice. Indicate one correct answer for each question.*

1. Which of the following statements is NOT true about draping?
   a. performed prior to hair care service
   b. protects client's skin and clothing
   c. performed after client removes jewelry
   d. performed after shampooing is complete

2. The capes used for shampooing, wet hair sculpting, designing and chemical services are made of plastic or:
   a. cloth
   b. rubber
   c. leather
   d. waterproof material

3. Which type of water is generally preferred for shampooing?
   a. hot
   b. cold
   c. hard
   d. soft

4. Before applying the water stream to a client's scalp when shampooing, always:
   a. add shampoo
   b. monitor the water temperature
   c. have the client put on protective eyewear
   d. ask the client to test the water temperature

5. When brushing the client's hair, you should begin:
   a. by brushing vigorously
   b. by first massaging the scalp
   c. from the scalp first, then toward the ends
   d. from the ends first, then toward the scalp

6. Which of the following types of hair tends to tangle easier than normal or natural hair?
   a. freshly sculpted hair
   b. newly layered hair
   c. newly conditioned hair
   d. chemically treated hair

7. What massage movement involves light or heavy kneading and rolling of the muscles?
   a. friction
   b. effleurage
   c. petrissage
   d. tapotement

8. Which massage movement involves light, gliding strokes and is often used to begin and/or end a treatment?
   a. friction
   b. petrissage
   c. tapotement
   d. effleurage

9. Which massage movement consists of a light tapping or slapping and is used to promote muscle contraction?
   a. friction
   b. effleurage
   c. petrissage
   d. tapotement

10. A highly stimulating, shaking motion describes which massage movement?
    a. friction
    b. effleurage
    c. vibration
    d. tapotement

LESSON CHALLENGE REFERENCES

Check your answers. Place a check mark next to the page number for any incorrect answer. On the lines, jot down topics that you still need to review.

1. PAGE 205 _____
2. PAGE 205 _____
3. PAGE 207 _____
4. PAGE 207 _____
5. PAGE 208 _____
6. PAGE 209 _____
7. PAGE 211 _____
8. PAGE 211 _____
9. PAGE 211 _____
10. PAGE 211 _____

▶ GROW WHAT YOU KNOW

Reflect on what you have learned and predict how this information will be used in the future.

102ᶜ.17 // SHAMPOO AND CONDITION GUEST EXPERIENCE

ACHIEVE //

Following this lesson on *Shampoo and Condition Guest Experience*, you'll be able to:

>> Identify the information found in the client record related to shampooing and scalp massage

>> Summarize the service essentials related to the shampoo and condition client visit

>> Explain how knowing the products, tools, supplies and equipment related to shampoo and condition services benefit your client and the salon

>> Provide examples of infection control and safety guidelines for shampoo, condition and scalp massage services

FOCUS //

SHAMPOO AND CONDITION GUEST EXPERIENCE

Guest Relations

Shampoo and Condition Products1Shampoo and Condition Tools and Supplies

Shampoo and Condition Equipment

Shampoo and Condition Infection Control and Safety

GUEST RELATIONS

The purpose for maintaining a client record is to be able to better meet the

_____

A TYPICAL CLIENT RECORD SHOULD INCLUDE:

MAKE SURE CLIENT RECORD INFORMATION IS:

Contraindications include:

-
-
-
-
-

During the consultation, be aware and take note of:

-
-
-
-
-

SHAMPOO AND CONDITION SERVICE ESSENTIALS (4 Cs)

CONNECT
-
-

CONSULT
-
-
-
-
-
-

CREATE
-
-
-

COMPLETE
-
-
-
-
-
-

Watch for signs of discomfort:
-
-
-
-

After-care advice should include:
-
-

SHAMPOO AND CONDITION PRODUCTS

SHAMPOO AND CONDITION TOOLS AND SUPPLIES

SHAMPOO AND CONDITION EQUIPMENT

SHAMPOO AND CONDITION INFECTION CONTROL AND SAFETY

Review information.

Always wear disposable non-latex gloves when using chemicals.

Contact dermatitis is an inflammation of the skin due to:

•

•

•

Symptoms are:

•

•

•

•

MATCHING

Place A, B, C or D on the line in front of the statement that matches the corresponding area.

A. PERSONAL CARE

B. CLIENT CARE PRIOR TO SERVICE

C. CLIENT CARE DURING SERVICE

D. SALON CARE

_____ Ensure shampoo area is clean and tidy

_____ Wash hands

_____ Test water temperature

_____ Drape client for specific service

_____ Use product and supplies economically

_____ Keep back of cape on outside of chair

_____ Maintain good posture

_____ Check and question client for contraindications

LESSON CHALLENGE
Multiple choice. Indicate one correct answer for each question.

1. All of the following information could be found in client records EXCEPT:
   a. date of last service
   b. price of the service
   c. client's social security number
   d. technique and application method

2. Which of the following locations might be sensitive during a scalp massage?
   a. at the crown
   b. along the hairline
   c. behind the earlobes
   d. at the sides of the head

3. This statement would occur during the Consult service essential:
   a. "Hello, welcome to the xxx salon."
   b. "Would you like to schedule your next appointment today?"
   c. "How frequently do you shampoo your hair?"
   d. "Is this water temperature okay for you?"

4. Which shampoo is recommended for removing residue such as product buildup?
   a. color
   b. clarifying
   c. conditioning
   d. pH-balanced

5. Which type of conditioner displaces excess moisture, providing the hair with more body?
   a. customized
   b. normalizing
   c. moisturizing
   d. body building

6. What is considered the appropriate water pressure for rinsing during a shampoo service?
   a. weak
   b. strong
   c. forceful and strong
   d. moderate to strong

7. How should you monitor the temperature of the water during rinsing?
   a. by keeping one finger in the water stream
   b. by running the water on the back of your hand
   c. by running the water on the inside of your wrist
   d. by running the water on the palm of your hand

8. Which of the following statements describes a technique for scalp massage movements?
   a. break contact often
   b. use fast, non-rhythmic motions
   c. do not break contact and use slow rhythmic motions
   d. use staccato-type movements followed by heavy vibration

9. Wipe up water-spills:
   a. immediately
   b. after the client leaves
   c. after checking with the manager
   d. after the client pays for the service

10. Which of the following items would be discarded following the shampoo service?
    a. client cape
    b. neck strip
    c. hair brush
    d. all-purpose comb

LESSON CHALLENGE REFERENCES

Check your answers. Place a check mark next to the page number for any incorrect answer. On the lines, jot down topics that you still need to review.

1. PAGE 217 _____
2. PAGE 218 _____
3. PAGE 220 _____
4. PAGE 222 _____
5. PAGE 223 _____
6. PAGE 226 _____
7. PAGE 226 _____
8. PAGE 226 _____
9. PAGE 226 _____
10. PAGE 227 _____

▶ GROW WHAT YOU KNOW

Reflect on what you have learned and predict how this information will be used in the future.

103ᶜ.1 // GOAL SETTING

ACHIEVE //

Following this lesson on *Goal Setting*, you'll be able to:

>> List actions that will help start a successful career

>> Describe the five aspects of S.M.A.R.T. goals

>> Explain the benefits of applying the 80/20 rule to your career

>> Compare and contrast guidelines for establishing short- and long-range goals

FOCUS //

GOAL SETTING

Goals: Getting Started

S.M.A.R.T. Goals

The 80/20 Rule

Professional Goals

GOALS: GETTING STARTED

Success happens with planning, focusing, taking advantage of opportunities and overcoming obstacles.

HIGH ACHIEVERS:

S.M.A.R.T. GOALS

Goal:

S_____ •

M_____ •

A_____ •

R_____ •

T_____ •

THE 80/20 RULE

Pareto's 80/20 pattern of distribution: _____

_____

80/20 rule: _____

_____

Make the 80/20 rule work for you by:

-
-
-
-
-

PROFESSIONAL GOALS

1. ESTABLISH A LONG-RANGE GOAL

Where you want your career to be in _____ _____

-
-
-

2. DETERMINE YOUR SHORT-RANGE GOALS

What you would like to achieve in the next _____

Examples:

-
-

3. CREATE A PLAN TO ACHIEVE YOUR GOALS

Be specific as you create a set of objectives and tasks

Examples:

-
-

4. REVIEW YOUR GOALS PERIODICALLY

Change your goals if they no longer reflect your chosen direction

Example:

-

SCRAMBLE

Unscramble these important terms from the lesson.

C F C I S P E I

E T I Y L M

B L M A S E E A U R

E L A R S I C I T

E L A C I E A V B H

MATCHING

S.M.A.R.T. GOAL MATCH: *Place "Yes" before the quote if you feel it correctly states the intent of the S.M.A.R.T. goal aspect. Place "No" before the quote if it doesn't correctly state the intent of the S.M.A.R.T. goal aspect.*

SPECIFIC

_____"I will get an entry-level position in a reputable salon after graduation."

_____ "I will get a job."

MEASURABLE

_____ "I will make several retail suggestions to clients this coming week."

_____"I will make at least five retail suggestions to my clients over the next week."

ACHIEVABLE

_____"This is something I can commit to."

_____ "Only Superman could complete this goal, but I will try anyway."

REALISTIC

_____ "I would like to earn enough money to open my own salon in six months."

_____ "I will own my own salon in five years."

TIMELY

_____ "I will get a job soon."

_____ "I will get a job in the next 60 days."

LESSON CHALLENGE *Multiple choice. Indicate one correct answer for each question.*

1. **Which of the statements below represents a specific goal?**
    a. I will get a job.

    b. I will very easily get a job.

    c. I will most likely get a job somewhere close to where I might live.

    d. I will get an entry-level position in a reputable salon after graduation.

2. **Measurable goals will help you get organized and:**
    a. track your progress
    b. force you to stretch

    c. stick with the status quo
    d. believe in what you can do

3. **Pareto's principle is called the:**
    a. 50/50 rule
    b. 60/40 rule

    c. 80/20 rule
    d. 90/10 rule

4. **Which of the following time periods identifies the consideration for a long-range goal?**
    a. 3 months
    b. 6 months

    c. 1 year
    d. 5 years

5. **All of the following actions describe how to create a plan to achieve your goals EXCEPT:**
    a. be specific
    b. consider your budget

    c. avoid alternate plans
    d. include alternate plans

LESSON CHALLENGE REFERENCES

Check your answers. Place a check mark next to the page number for any incorrect answer. On the lines, jot down topics that you still need to review.

1. PAGE 8 _____

2. PAGE 8 _____

3. PAGE 10 _____

4. PAGE 11 _____

5. PAGE 11 _____

▶ GROW WHAT YOU KNOW

Reflect on what you have learned and predict how this information will be used in the future.

103ᶜ.2 |
JOB SEARCH

ACHIEVE //

Following this lesson on *Job Search*, you'll be able to:

» List the elements of a resumé, cover letter and portfolio

» Identify the strategies that will help you gain a professional position in the salon industry

FOCUS //

JOB SEARCH

Resumé, Cover Letter and Portfolio

Job Interview

JOB SEARCH OPTIONS:

-
-
-
-
-
-
-

RESUMÉ, COVER LETTER AND PORTFOLIO

RESUMÉ:

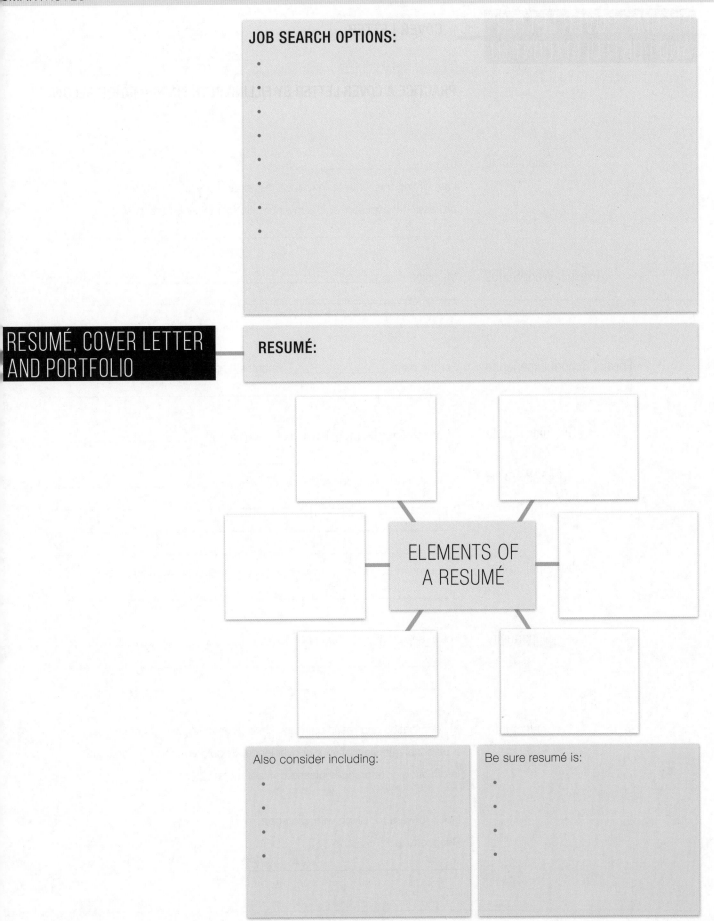

ELEMENTS OF A RESUMÉ

Also consider including:

-
-
-
-

Be sure resumé is:

-
-
-
-

RESUMÉ, COVER LETTER AND PORTFOLIO (CONT'D)

COVER LETTER:

PRACTICE A COVER LETTER BY FILLING IN THE INFORMATION BELOW:

Salon Name

Dear _____,

I am writing this letter to introduce myself and describe my personal and professional aspirations. It is my intention to interview for a position at

_____

Present Work Status

My name is _____ and I am

presently _____

_____

Formal School Experience

For the past _____ (months) I have studied cosmetology at

_____

Graduation Date

I plan to complete my schooling and licensure by _____

_____

Specialty Skills

In addition to my salon preparation, I have also _____

_____

_____

_____

Position Applied For

At this point in my career I am especially interested in working as a

_____

Opportunity

I have selected your salon because _____

_____

_____

Contact Info

My application and resumé are attached. Please know that I am available for a personal interview at your convenience. Should you require additional information or references please contact me at _____

I look forward to talking with you soon.

Respectfully,

_____

RESUMÉ, COVER LETTER AND PORTFOLIO (CONT'D)

PORTFOLIO:

Elements of a portfolio include special events, technical skills, accomplishments, references and continuing education overviews.

JOB INTERVIEW

- Stay _____

- Be yourself and be _____

PERSONAL APPEARANCE

- Neat
- Fashionably _____
- Flattering hair _____

- Healthy skin
- Properly applied _____

APPLICATION

Additional information beyond name/address/phone:

-
-
-
-

PUNCTUALITY

- Arrive _____
- Confirm exact _____
- Confirm parking availability and _____
- Determine travel _____

TECHNICAL AND COMMUNICATION SKILLS

THE INTERVIEWER MAY...

-
-
-

INTERVIEW QUESTIONS

Interview question types:

1. Questions to get to know the applicant:

   _____

2. Focus on the past so employers can predict your reaction in the future:

   _____

3. Concentrate on future performance rather than past performance:

   _____

If you are asked questions that seem to be discriminatory, politely decline answering them.

PERSONAL QUALITIES

- Sincerity and _____
- Motivation and _____
- Obvious desire to _____
- Integrity
- Compatibility and cooperative nature

ABILITIES AND ASPIRATIONS:

- Ability to:
  - Promote new service or retail _____
  - Organize and manage your _____
  - Accept constructive _____
- Understanding of the salon's goals
- Realistic career _____
- Educational and professional goals

INTERVIEW DO'S AND DON'TS

DO

Be prepared

Exhibit a positive _____

Maintain eye _____

Send thank-you _____

Tell interviewer you are interested (if you are)

DON'T

Falsify application or embellish

_____

Allow mobile device to

_____

Badmouth anyone

Bring anyone to _____

Give impression you are interested solely due to location or _____

MATCHING

Place the letter:
A before the question if it is an example of a standard interview question
B if it is a behavioral interview question
C if it is an example of a situational interview question

_____ Describe a time when you didn't get along with a colleague.

_____ Why do you want to work here?

_____ A client brings in a picture of a hairstyle she wants. At the end of the service, she lets you know that this is not what she wanted. How would you handle this?

_____ Tell me about yourself.

LESSON CHALLENGE *Multiple choice. Indicate one correct answer for each question.*

1. Which of these descriptions is NOT a guideline to be used when creating a resumé?
   a. list awards and special recognition
   b. show prior employment information
   c. provide at least eight pages of information
   d. write the resumé in a brief and concise manner

2. The item that offers an employer a brief summary of why you would like to be employed at the salon and what qualities you would bring to the salon is called a(n):
   a. profile
   b. resumé
   c. application
   d. cover letter

3. During a job interview it is very important to:
   a. tell a lot of stories
   b. stay calm and be yourself
   c. stretch the truth if necessary
   d. tell the interviewer whatever you think he or she wants to hear

4. Before an interview begins, you might be asked to fill out a(n):
   a. resumé
   b. cover letter
   c. portfolio
   d. application

5. Which of the following statements describes what you should do if you are asked a question that seems discriminatory?
   a. give a false answer
   b. remain defiantly silent
   c. politely decline to answer
   d. answer the question truthfully

LESSON CHALLENGE REFERENCES

Check your answers. Place a check mark next to the page number for any incorrect answer. On the lines, jot down topics that you still need to review.

1. PAGE 15 _____
2. PAGE 16 _____
3. PAGE 18 _____
4. PAGE 18 _____
5. PAGE 21 _____

▶ GROW WHAT YOU KNOW

Reflect on what you have learned and predict how this information will be used in the future.

103^c.3 |
FINDING A SALON THAT FITS

ACHIEVE //

Following this lesson on *Finding a Salon That Fits*, you'll be able to:

>> Identify criteria to keep in mind when considering a job offer

>> List the various types of salon businesses where you could apply for employment

>> Compare the types of job benefits salons might offer

>> Discuss key aspects of work ethic that are universally recognized in the salon profession

FOCUS //

FINDING A SALON THAT FITS

Salon Considerations

Selecting a Salon

Job Benefits

Your New Job

SALON CONSIDERATIONS

Write a question you could ask during an interview for each of the following salon considerations:

1. Owner/Manager –

2. Services –

3. Staff and Clientele –

4. Policies and Procedures –

5. Pay and Benefits –

SELECTING A SALON

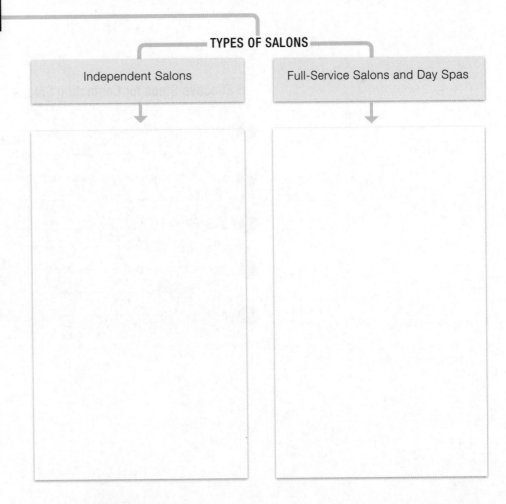

TYPES OF SALONS

Independent Salons	Full-Service Salons and Day Spas

SELECTING A SALON (CONT'D)

TYPES OF SALONS

Chain Salons and Franchises	Independent Contractor (Salon Suites or Booth Rentals)

5 Effective Steps for Contacting Salons

1 Make a list of salons or spas in your _____

2 Check salon's social media for hiring notices and/or updates

3 Watch for local _____

4 Contact salons by phone and/or through social _____

5 Stop by salon for a face-to-face introduction and drop off a _____

JOB BENEFITS

Rate the job benefits in the order of importance to you from 1-10.

_____ Paid holidays, bonuses

_____ Paid vacations

_____ Number of sick days allowed

_____ Insurance benefits (health, accident, life)

_____ Retirement plan

_____ Opportunities for travel

_____ Opportunity for advancement

_____ Educational seminars and events

_____ Ongoing salon educational programs

_____ Length and number of breaks

YOUR NEW JOB

TWO COMMON APPROACHES TO INSTRUCT NEW EMPLOYEES

Orientation Program:

Assistant or Apprentice:

WORK ETHIC

Showing up on time, ready to work shows _____.

Not wasting time or salon resources demonstrates _____.

Not always waiting to be told what to do is a sign of _____.

Working harmoniously within a group is called _____.

Making a conscious effort to get along with co-workers shows a positive

_____.

Loving what you do and bringing that to work with you every day shows your

_____.

EVALUATION AND FEEDBACK

When you start a new job, it's important you're clear on what your employer wants from you.

Keep tabs on your progress moving forward by:

Asking the manager or senior stylist to observe your interaction with

_____

Listening to suggestions on improving your

_____

WORK ETHIC
From the Jump Start Box match each statement to the key aspect of work ethic it describes.

DEPENDABILITY

EFFICIENCY

INITIATIVE

TEAMWORK

POSITIVE ATTITUDE

PASSION

JUMP START BOX

I love my job and coming to work every day.

I am always careful to use the correct amount of product for each service.

I look forward to working together with my colleagues to make this salon great.

If I see work that needs to be done I don't wait to be told, I do it.

I always try to be upbeat with my clients and co-workers.

I feel it is very important to show up on time for work each morning and be ready to go.

LESSON CHALLENGE *Multiple choice. Indicate one correct answer for each question.*

1. All of the following descriptions apply to an independent salon EXCEPT:
   a. may offer from 5-40 workstations
   b. owner makes all the decisions in terms of décor
   c. uses a set business plan provided by a parent company
   d. owner makes all the decisions in terms of pricing and services

2. Of the items listed below, which one is NOT considered a benefit?
   a. salary
   b. sick days
   c. paid vacation
   d. paid holidays

3. Insurance benefits might include all of the following EXCEPT:
   a. car insurance
   b. life insurance
   c. health insurance
   d. accident insurance

4. Dependability as a work principle can be described as:
   a. getting along with co-workers
   b. not waiting to be told what to do
   c. showing that you love what you do
   d. showing up on time and ready to work

5. Passion as a work principle can be described as:
   a. getting along with co-workers
   b. not waiting to be told what to do
   c. showing that you love what you do
   d. showing up on time and ready to work

LESSON CHALLENGE REFERENCES

Check your answers. Place a check mark next to the page number for any incorrect answer. On the lines, jot down topics that you still need to review.

1. PAGE 28 _____

2. PAGE 29 _____

3. PAGE 29 _____

4. PAGE 32 _____

5. PAGE 32 _____

▶ GROW WHAT YOU KNOW

Reflect on what you have learned and predict how this information will be used in the future.

103ᶜ.4 |
PROFESSIONAL RELATIONSHIPS

ACHIEVE //

Following this lesson on *Professional Relationships*, you'll be able to:

» Identify ways that networking is valuable to future career success

» List the keys to successful client relationships

» Give examples of how to establish a positive rapport with a salon owner or manager

FOCUS //

PROFESSIONAL RELATIONSHIPS

Networking

The Client Approach

The Team Approach

NETWORKING

NETWORKING

Process that gives you access to people and resources within the industry that can provide you with opportunities for career advancement and continuing education.

Benefits:

*

*

*

Valuable concepts used by successful business people in any industry:

1. Plan _____

2. Create a professional _____

3. Define your _____

4. Develop good professional _____

EDUCATION + ⬚ + ⬚ = ⬚

THE CLIENT APPROACH

KEYS TO SUCCESSFUL CLIENT RELATIONSHIPS

Serve	Organize	Explain	Suggest	Teach
◯	◯	◯	◯	◯

Recommend	Adjust	Share	Notify
◯	◯	◯	◯

THE TEAM APPROACH

The team concept revolves around several factors:

COMMON GOALS

Teamwork flourishes when a blending of personal and business goals occurs.

SHARING KNOWLEDGE

Sharing leads to loyal, satisfied _____.

HELPING OTHERS

Help your co-workers by managing your downtime _____.

REACHING OUT TO OTHER PROFESSIONALS

Make connections with fellow professionals who offer services you currently don't provide.

SALON MANAGER/OWNER RELATIONSHIP

Establish and maintain a positive rapport with your manager:

• Showing a desire to learn is all about:

_____

• Taking initiative is all about:

_____

• Being a trust builder is all about:

_____

• Shaking it off is all about:

_____

MATCHING

Place A, B, C, or D in front of the scenario that gives an example of how to gain a rapport with the salon owner/manager.

A. SHOW A DESIRE TO LEARN

C. BE A TRUST BUILDER

B. TAKE INITIATIVE

D. SHAKE IT OFF

_____
Your employer talked to you about sagging retail sales. They noticed that you were not recommending product. You listened respectfully and listened to suggestions on where and how you can improve your skills.

_____
The salon owner held a staff meeting on providing exceptional guest relations. After the meeting you volunteered to do additional research on the topic because you want to know more and have a desire to share the information.

_____
I am unsure of performing the service that Mrs. Jones requested. It will be my first time performing this complicated hair color service. Would it be appropriate to have Jennifer assist me since she completed the service many times?

_____
I spoke to the receptionist about the disorganization of the magazines and books in the reception area and offered to help come up with a better system of keeping them more inviting and available.

LESSON CHALLENGE *Multiple choice. Indicate one correct answer for each question.*

1. Networking provides all of the following benefits EXCEPT:
   a. leads to lifelong friendships
   b. gives access to people and resources within the industry
   c. provides a good way to learn about trends in the industry
   d. contacts create difficult situations that turn into real problems

2. Which of the following descriptions would be considered a key to successful client relationships?
   a. teach the client how to maintain their look at home
   b. ensure clients know you are busy by making them wait at least 15 minutes
   c. declare that you can make the client look like any photograph they bring in
   d. don't explain what you have in mind until you can show the client the finished look

3. When handling a client complaint you can turn a negative experience into a positive one by:
   a. restating back to the client what you heard
   b. avoiding any feedback the client might have
   c. not asking any additional questions to clarify concerns
   d. ignoring any signs that the client might be disappointed

4. Which of the following actions would represent taking the team approach?
   a. greet only your clients
   b. avoid referring your clients to other designers
   c. do only your work, helping others leads to problems
   d. offer guests something to drink while they are waiting

5. Which of the following characteristics will contribute to career success?
   a. avoiding criticism
   b. living in the past
   c. respecting knowledge of others
   d. avoiding change and acceptance

LESSON CHALLENGE REFERENCES

Check your answers. Place a check mark next to the page number for any incorrect answer. On the lines, jot down topics that you still need to review.

1. PAGE 36 _____   4. PAGE 39 _____

2. PAGE 37 _____   5. PAGE 41 _____

3. PAGE 38 _____

▶ GROW WHAT YOU KNOW

Reflect on what you have learned and predict how this information will be used in the future.

103ᶜ.5 |
KNOW YOUR CLIENT MARKET

ACHIEVE //

Following this lesson on *Know Your Client Market*, you'll be able to:

» Identify the components that make up the client factor

» Discuss the types of things that should be included in a client profile

» Explain how to calculate the financial value of one client

FOCUS //

KNOW YOUR CLIENT MARKET

The Client Factor

The Client Profile

The Financial Value of One Client

THE CLIENT FACTOR

Study your client market to know:

-
-
-
-

THE CLIENT PROFILE

Easiest way to get data is to ask:

-
-
-
-

Top customer demographic categories to note:

-
-
-
-
-

-
-
-
-
-

Possible Market Segment

- Age 38
- Female
- College-educated
- Full-time professional
- Married; 1.8 children
- Household income: $40,000+ per year

What are some assumptions you could make from this information?

-
-
-

CLIENT MARKET TRENDS

Current trends that could have an effect on a salon's marketing plan:

-
-
-
-

THE FINANCIAL VALUE OF ONE CLIENT

Salon industry experts tell us:

- Average loyal clients visit salon every _____ _____

- First-time clients rarely get more than a _____

- Only 1 in 10 first-time clients purchases _____

- Returning clients are more likely to purchase additional services

  or _____

- Exceptional service solidifies client/professional _____

- Regular clients ask for more advice and _____

- Average client spends $40 on services and $10 on product after

  approximately _____ _____

Average ticket:

CALCULATING THE FINANCIAL VALUE OF ONE CLIENT

What is the financial impact of losing just ONE client?

SATISFIED CLIENT:

UNHAPPY CLIENT:

The First 6 Months

- *Client visits every 6 weeks.* How many visits is this per year? _____

- *Client generates $25 in revenue per visit.* How much revenue is generated in the first 6 months? _____

From Then On (After the First 4 Visits in the First 6 Months)

- *Client generates a $50 average ticket.* How much revenue will this client generate each year (not including the first 6 months)? _____

- How much revenue will a client generate in the 2-year period following the initial 6 months? _____

Revenue in first 6 months (4 visits)		Revenue in next 2 years		Total client revenue over 2½ years
	+		=	

Explain how much revenue could be lost from one client who no longer visits the salon.

INCREASE YOUR AVERAGE TICKET

3 WAYS TO INCREASE YOUR AVERAGE TICKET WITHOUT RAISING PRICES

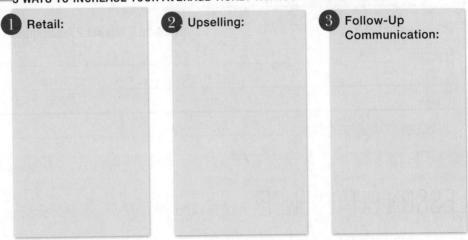

1 Retail:

2 Upselling:

3 Follow-Up Communication:

How Assessing the Client Market Can Improve Overall Business

The profitability of a salon can depend on a variety of things:

* Technical expertise and marketing _____
* Demographics and population _____
* Activeness of client base and client _____ _____

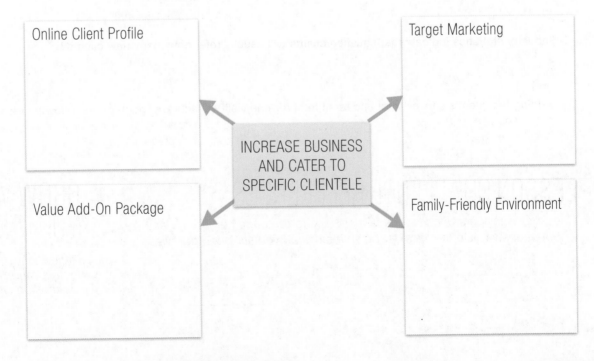

Online Client Profile

Target Marketing

INCREASE BUSINESS AND CATER TO SPECIFIC CLIENTELE

Value Add-On Package

Family-Friendly Environment

PROFILE OF A CLIENT

Column A identifies characteristics of a typical market segment. Column B provides a space for you to list assumptions you could make from the information in Column A.

Column A **Market 1**	Column B **Market 1 Assumptions**
Age 22	
Male	
Full-Time Student	

Column A **Market 2**	Column B **Market 2 Assumptions**
Age 65	
Female	
Retired	
$30K/Year Household Income	

LESSON CHALLENGE

Multiple choice. Indicate one correct answer for each question.

1. Important information about the client, combined with the financial value of a client, is referred to as the:
   a. client info
   b. client profile
   c. client factor
   d. target market

2. A client profile is a composite of market statistics that can be used to identify the general characteristics of individuals:
   a. within that market
   b. over the age of 65
   c. owning more than two vehicles
   d. who eat most meals in 5-star restaurants

3. According to statistics, how often does the average loyal client visit a salon?
   a. every 2 weeks
   b. every 6 weeks
   c. every 3 months
   d. twice per year

4. Industry statistics indicate that satisfied clients will usually refer how many new clients?
   a. 1
   b. 3
   c. 8
   d. 12

5. Adding the client's service total and retail total for one visit will achieve which of the following results?
   a. average visit
   b. average ticket
   c. average net profit
   d. average appointment

LESSON CHALLENGE REFERENCES

Check your answers. Place a check mark next to the page number for any incorrect answer. On the lines, jot down topics that you still need to review.

1. PAGE 44 _____

2. PAGE 45 _____

3. PAGE 50 _____

4. PAGE 50 _____

5. PAGE 50 _____

▶ GROW WHAT YOU KNOW

Reflect on what you have learned and predict how this information will be used in the future.

103ᶜ.6 |
BUILD YOUR CLIENTELE

ACHIEVE //

Following this lesson on *Build Your Clientele*, you'll be able to:

» Identify strategies for attracting and retaining clients

» Describe best practice techniques for building a clientele

FOCUS //

BUILD YOUR CLIENTELE

Attracting and Retaining Clients

Best Practices for Building a Clientele

ATTRACTING AND RETAINING CLIENTS

New clients generally come from 3 sources:

1.

2.   Your efforts

3.

Clientele:

Client Retention:

ATTRACTING AND RETAINING CLIENTS

Client Development:

Client Relations Management (CRM):

Full Book:

Four key elements of attracting and retaining clients

1 Practice target _____

2 Provide exceptional _____

3 Increase and meet market _____

4 Maintain a positive clientele-building _____

BEST PRACTICES FOR BUILDING A CLIENTELE

STRATEGIES FOR **ATTRACTING** CLIENTS

1.

2.

STRATEGIES FOR **RETAINING** CLIENTS

3.

4.

WORD-OF-MOUTH AND REFERRALS

Word-of-mouth advertising:

Referral:

Referral Source:

Referral Client:

Ensure that word-of-mouth about you is positive:

1. Deliver exceptional services

2. Make client _____

3. Correct situation if client expresses _____

Referrals are important

• Approximately 10% of all clients will be lost _____

Promoting Referrals:

• Ask satisfied clients to refer friends and _____

Referral Incentives:

• Place client's name on the back of your business card

• Friend of client brings in the card and receives _____

• Client receives _____

Why Clients Leave

Indifferent attitude of an employee	=	_____%
Product dissatisfaction	=	_____%
Competitive reasons	=	_____%
Other friends	=	_____%
Move away	=	_____%
Die	=	_____%

STRATEGIES FOR ATTRACTING CLIENTS	HOW IT WORKS	PROS	CONS
WORD-OF-MOUTH AND REFERRALS (CONT'D)	Satisfied clients recommend your services to others		Negative word-of-mouth spreads even faster than positive
	Ask existing clients to direct friends and colleagues to you and your salon		Incentives may be needed to motivate people to continue referring clients
DISTRIBUTING BUSINESS CARDS	Provides easy, effective and inexpensive way to attract new clients		Gives a negative impression if cards are not well-designed or stored carefully

STRATEGIES FOR RETAINING CLIENTS	HOW IT WORKS	PROS	CONS
UPSELLING	Sell specialized and/or additional salon services to clients during a current visit		Recommendations could seem overzealous to the client
PREBOOKING	Clients reserve a future appointment before leaving the salon during a current visit		Clients may forget their future appointment(s)

Using the Salon to Build a Clientele

Salon's promotional _____

Guest appearances

Correspondence

Your personal _____

BUILDING A CLIENTELE

Place **A** *in front of the statement if it falls under Client Development;*

place **B** *if it falls under Client Retention.*

_____
"The salon is getting so busy that I will need to increase my time in the salon to meet the client demand."

_____
"Here is my business card with my work schedule on the back. When one of your friends schedules a service and brings the card in at the time of service, your friend will get 50% off of the service that day, and you will get 50% off a future service."

_____
"Since you live in this neighborhood and we are open in the evenings, it would be very handy for you to stop in the salon on your way home from work."

_____
"I would love to give you a hand massage while we are waiting for your color to develop."

_____
"Would you like to prebook your next appointment? That way you can pick the time that works best for your schedule. I will call you a few days before as a reminder."

_____
"Would you like to have a beverage while you wait?"

_____
"I recently attended a class and learned a fabulous new color technique that I think will look great on you. Here is my business card, please give me a call if you are interested."

_____
"As a college student I know you are on a limited budget. This week my salon is running a ½-price special on haircuts for first-time clients."

LESSON CHALLENGE
Multiple choice. Indicate one correct answer for each question.

1. Which of the following descriptions identifies the meaning of clientele?
   a. persons who make habitual use of the services of another person
   b. persons who do not prebook appointments following the first visit
   c. persons who have never visited the salon and are not likely to vis
   d. persons who live out of the area and visit the salon only once in five years

2. A category title for tracking and overseeing clientele-building strategies is CRM which stands for:
   a. Client Referral Methods
   b. Client Retention Methods
   c. Client Retail Management
   d. Client Relations Management

3. Which of the following concepts involves converting existing clients to return clients?
   a. CRM
   b. client factor
   c. client profile
   d. client retention

4. If all of your appointment times have been scheduled with clients for a given day, the term to describe this is a:
   a. prebook
   b. full book
   c. client retention
   d. high market demand

5. An effective strategy to ensure a return visit from a client is to:
   a. limit your work hours
   b. provide exceptional service
   c. avoid using a business card
   d. promote negative word-of-mouth

6. Which of the following descriptions is NOT a best practice strategy for building a clientele?
   a. upselling
   b. prebooking
   c. referral
   d. client factor

7. The act of a highly satisfied client directing another person to see you for professional services is called a(n):
   a. upsell
   b. prebook
   c. referral
   d. client factor

8. For salon professionals just starting out, the most common and immediate source of referrals is:
   a. client profile
   b. target marketing
   c. promotional literature
   d. word-of-mouth recommendations

9. Offering an additional hair coloring service to the client who originally scheduled a haircut appointment is an example o
   a. full book
   b. balancing
   c. upselling
   d. target marketing

10. A client retention strategy that involves clients booking a future appointment before leaving the salon during a current visit is known as:
   a. upselling
   b. balancing
   c. prebooking
   d. word-of-mouth

LESSON CHALLENGE REFERENCES

Check your answers. Place a check mark next to the page number for any incorrect answer. On the lines, jot down topics that you still need to review.

▶ GROW WHAT YOU KNOW

Reflect on what you have learned and predict how this information will be used in the future.

THE SALON EXPERIENCE

ACHIEVE //

Following this lesson on *The Salon Experience*, you'll be able to:

» Identify elements of ambiance that create a comfortable and memorable atmosphere in the salon

» State why a personalized approach is the foundation of exceptional service

» Describe what it takes to create staff synergy

FOCUS //

THE SALON EXPERIENCE

Ambiance

Personalized Approach

Staff Synergy

Three critical components of the salon experience:

1.

2.

3.

AMBIANCE

Ambiance:

SALON AMBIANCE IN ACTION

MAIN COMPONENTS
OF AMBIANCE

PERSONALIZED APPROACH

Referred to as: _____ _____

- Treating the client like an important, valued _____

- Building trust and _____

THE SECRET OF THE PERSONALIZED APPROACH

Being truly interested in guest's well-being means you:

_____

_____

_____

_____

_____

_____

_____

_____

THE PERSONALIZED APPROACH IN ACTION

Little Things Are _____ _____

1 Showing sincere warmth and concern

2 Greeting guest by _____

3 Making sure the guest is _____

4 Smiling and staying _____

5 Showing enthusiasm

6 Remembering personal information

STAFF SYNERGY

STAFF SYNERGY

COOPERATION

Synergy is the action of two or more people working cooperatively together to achieve a total effect that is greater than could have been achieved _____.

> STAFF SYNERGY IS PEOPLE WORKING TOGETHER TO ACHIEVE MORE.

CONSISTENCY

Consistency:

SHARED ACCOUNTABILITY

The staff operates as part of a unit with a clear identity:

-
-

> SYNERGY CREATES A HARMONIOUS AND PREDICTABLE _____.

STAFF SYNERGY IN ACTION

Elements That Create Staff Synergy:

CLEAR, SHARED VISION

CLEAR PROCEDURES

OPEN AND CLEAR
COMMUNICATION

POSITIVE, COOPERATIVE
ATMOSPHERE

WITH-IT-NESS

PERSONALIZING YOUR APPROACH

*Study the three photos. Try to get a sense of who each person is from the photos and what might be important to each of the
Now, select one photo by putting a check mark in the box underneath and imagine this person will be your next guest. Make
list of all the ways you can think of to personalize your approach to show respect and make this guest feel important and value*

☐   ☐   ☐

I will personalize my approach with this guest by:

_____

_____

_____

LESSON CHALLENGE *Multiple choice. Indicate one correct answer for each question.*

1. The salon exterior, décor, music and sounds, and air and ventilation are all elements of:
   a. synergy
   b. ambiance
   c. with-it-ness
   d. personalized approach

2. A personalized approach is also referred to as:
   a. staff synergy
   b. salon experience
   c. chairside manner
   d. shared accountability

3. All of the following are the ways to demonstrate your personalized approach EXCEPT:
   a. securing your guest's valuables
   b. asking about important events in your guest's life
   c. responding to your guest's verbal and nonverbal expressions
   d. chatting with other designers during a salon service

4. What is meant by the term consistency?
   a. things happen in a haphazard way
   b. things happen in an uniform way
   c. things happen in a sloppy, messy way
   d. things happen in a pessimistic, doubtful way

5. Which of the following concepts creates a harmonious and predictable environment?
   a. synergy
   b. ambiance
   c. chairside manner
   d. personalized approach

6. Which of the following is NOT a necessary element for ensuring staff synergy?
   a. with-it-ness
   b. lack of procedures
   c. clear, shared vision
   d. open and clear communication

7. When staff members take individual initiative to stay on top of things and to pay attention to detail, they are practicing which of the following skills?
   a. cooperation
   b. with-it-ness
   c. problem-solving
   d. conflict management

8. Placing aromatic soaps and lotions in restrooms is an example of which of the following principles?
   a. follow the law
   b. poor client service
   c. big things make a little difference
   d. little things make a big difference

LESSON CHALLENGE REFERENCES

Check your answers. Place a check mark next to the page number for any incorrect answer. On the lines, jot down topics that you still need to review.

1. PAGE 68 _____
2. PAGE 71 _____
3. PAGE 71 _____
4. PAGE 72 _____
5. PAGE 72 _____
6. PAGE 73 _____
7. PAGE 73 _____
8. PAGE 73 _____

▶ GROW WHAT YOU KNOW

Reflect on what you have learned and predict how this information will be used in the future.

103ᶜ.8 |
SALON OWNERSHIP

ACHIEVE //

Following this lesson on *Salon Ownership*, you'll be able to:

» Identify common salon ownership types and their structures

» Describe requirements of salon ownership for the practice of good business

FOCUS //

SALON OWNERSHIP

Begin the Process of Owning a Salon

Requirements of Salon Ownership

BEGIN THE PROCESS OF OWNING A SALON

Understanding the inner workings of salons will create a foundation that will allow both the salon professional and the salon owner to meet goals together.

SELF-APPRAISAL

Review the self-appraisal ownership skills listed in this lesson. Decide on the 4 most important and list them in order here.

Most Important _____

Very Important _____

Somewhat Important _____

Also Imporant _____

PERSONAL FINANCIAL STATEMENT

Three basic elements of a financial statement:

1. All of the property you own:_____

2. All the money you owe: _____

3. Net worth: _____

TYPES OF SALON OWNERSHIP

Sole Proprietorship
•

Partnership
•

Corporation
•

Franchise
•

REQUIREMENTS OF SALON OWNERSHIP

To begin the process of salon planning, research:

1 Location
-

2 Market Need
-

3 Cost of Necessary Improvements
Examples include:
-
-

4 Compliance
-

GETTING THE RIGHT ADVICE

Accountant:

Insurance Agent:

Lawyer:

Distributor Sales Consultant:

The distributor might:
-
-
-

SPACE REQUIREMENTS AND FLOOR PLANS

General square footage per designer: _____

_____ x _____ = Square Ft.

Required areas for salon:

-
-
-
-

Develop a floor plan for a proposed location before trying to determine details

on _____

Sketch a basic floor plan that shows an efficient traffic pattern. The best design requires the fewest steps for the client and salon professional to travel.

BORROWING MONEY

Determine how much money is needed to:

Be willing to invest some of your own _____.

Make all loan payments on time to avoid _____.

RENTAL AGREEMENTS

Once you get a loan, you can enter into a rental agreement called a _____.

Leases normally should extend for _____ _____

As renter, or lessee, you promise to use the property according to the agreement and pay one of two types of _____.

FIXED RENT	VARIABLE RENT

TYPES OF INSURANCE

Malpractice:

Property or Premise:

Product Liability:

Unemployment:

Workers' Compensation:

TAXES

The salon owner pays the government:

- Taxes withheld from employees' _____
- Sales taxes collected on _____ and _____
- Income tax on business _____

EXPENSES AND INCOME

Revenue agencies like the IRS require you to keep a log of all your tips, which is income.

Did you know a salon owner is responsible for reporting employee tips?

INCOME	OPERATING EXPENSES

PROFIT	LOSS

Record keeping is required by law; keep records for 5 to _____ _____ .

Fill in the percentage for each cost of operating a business.

THE AVERAGE COST OF OPERATING A BUSINESS (BY % OF INCOME)		%
Compensation	Salaries or commissions for yourself and your employees, including payroll taxes	
Rent	Fixed or variable	
Supplies	Professional products used, retail products sold and miscellaneous equipment and tools	
Advertising	Promotion of salon	
Utilities	Water, electricity, gas, sanitation, phone	
Insurance	All types	
Employee Benefits	Education, vacation, pension or profit-sharing, health insurance	
Maintenance	Repairs, laundry, cleaning and replacement equipment	
Cost of Doing Business	Accounting, legal, licenses, subscriptions, professional dues, etc.	
Services of Debt	Capital improvements, equipment and original loan expense	
Depreciation	Account established to save for replacement of equipment; creates tax credit	
Miscellaneous	All other expenses	
Percentage of Income for Total Operating Expense =		

SALON PHILOSOPHY, POLICIES AND PROCEDURES

Philosophy, Policies and Procedures Handbook:

Provides a set of _____

Outlines the owner's expectations of _____

Informs employee about _____

List what you believe would be 5 of the most important items in a Salon Philosophy, Policies and Procedures Handbook.

1.

2.

3.

4.

5.

MATCHING

Match the term in the right column to its definition in the left column.

A. A list of all the property you own

B. A list of all the money you owe

C. Subtracting your liabilities from your assets

D. A business owned by two or more persons

E. A legal entity, separate from its shareholders, which is formed under legal guidelines

F. Protects the salon owner from financial loss resulting from employee negligence

G. Protects against financial loss arising because of injury or damage resulting from the use of a product.

H. A set dollar amount paid each month to the lessor

I. A set dollar amount paid per month to the lessor plus a percentage of the total monthly income

_____ net worth

_____ assets

_____ product liability insurance

_____ variable rent

_____ malpractice insurance

_____ partnership

_____ fixed rent

_____ corporation

_____ liabilities

LESSON CHALLENGE *Multiple choice. Indicate one correct answer for each question.*

1. Which of the following terms refers to all money owed?
   a. assets
   b. net worth
   c. liabilities
   d. financial status

2. Net worth is calculated by subtracting liabilities from which of the following?
   a. assets
   b. student loans
   c. loan balances
   d. charge accounts

3. The type of business ownership in which two or more persons share all costs of opening, operating and maintaining the business is a:
   a. franchise
   b. partnership
   c. corporation
   d. sole proprietorship

4. Which of the following business types is owned by the shareholders and formed under legal guidelines?
   a. franchise
   b. partnership
   c. corporation
   d. sole proprietorship

5. Location is the most important factor in:
   a. choosing a lawyer
   b. choosing a salon
   c. choosing a distributor
   d. opening a salon business

6. An efficient working space for each designer is:
   a. 50-75 square feet
   b. 120-150 square feet
   c. 200-300 square feet
   d. Over 300 square feet

7. To be granted future loans, it is important to pay loans on time and avoid:
   a. taxes
   b. default
   c. insurance
   d. compensation

8. Which type of insurance protects the salon owner from financial loss due to an employee's negligence?
   a. premise
   b. malpractice
   c. Social Security
   d. product liability

9. Workers' Compensation Insurance is needed to protect the:
   a. salon
   b. inventory
   c. employee
   d. advertiser

10. U.S. Social Security and Canadian Pension taxes are planned savings/retirement funds, and the money is collected by the:
   a. city council
   b. state government
   c. county government
   d. U.S. and Canadian governments

11. Who must apply for a state sales tax permit before collecting taxes on products or services sold?
   a. lawyer
   b. employee
   c. customer
   d. salon owner

12. Renting or leasing a workstation from a building owner would represent which of the following situations?
   a. partnership
   b. corporation
   c. sole proprietorship
   d. independent contractor

13. Which of the following items is reported to your revenue agency as employee income?
   a. tips received by an employee
   b. money paid to vendors for products
   c. operating expenses paid by the salon
   d. change given to a client following payment

14. What percentage of the total salon expenses generally represents compensation for the salon owner and employees?
   a. 10%
   b. 25%
   c. 50%
   d. 75%

15. Which one of the following items is usually the largest expense in operating a salon?
   a. rent
   b. supplies
   c. advertisement
   d. salaries or commissions

LESSON CHALLENGE REFERENCES

Check your answers. Place a check mark next to the page number for any incorrect answer. On the lines, jot down topics that you still need to review.

▶ GROW WHAT YOU KNOW

Reflect on what you have learned and predict how this information will be used in the future.

103ᶜ.9 |
SALON OPERATIONS

ACHIEVE //

Following this lesson on *Salon Operations*, you'll be able to:

>> List three common compensation structures for salon employees

>> Identify various advertising strategies for salons

>> Discuss why inventory control is important to salon operations

>> Explain the primary duties of a receptionist

FOCUS //

SALON OPERATIONS

Hiring

Pricing

Advertising

Inventory Control

Receptionist Duties

HIRING

Apply for a Federal Employer Identification Number before hiring employees.

Hire employees who meet your standards of honesty and _____.

Prior to hiring, employers must:

* Request proof of _____

* Complete I-9 form

* Place I-9 form and copy of supporting proof in employee's _____

List possible forms for proof of identity:

COMPENSATION

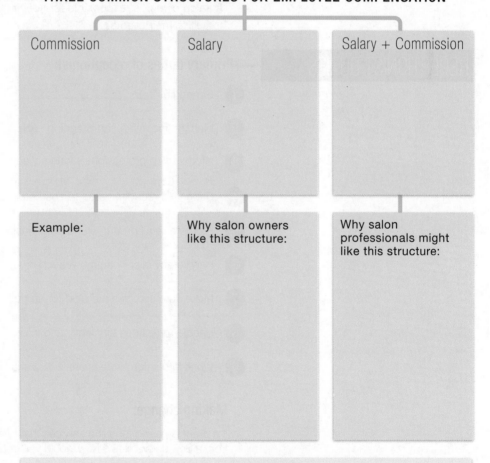

THREE COMMON STRUCTURES FOR EMPLOYEE COMPENSATION

Commission	Salary	Salary + Commission
Example:	Why salon owners like this structure:	Why salon professionals might like this structure:

PRICING

* If possible, determine prices by conducting a market _____

* Create a profile of potential clientele and target with _____

* Price services to fit income range of clientele you want to _____

*

*

*

ADVERTISING

Place a check mark in front of the 5 forms of advertising listed below that you believe will get the best results for a salon owner.

_____ Word-of-mouth

_____ Social media

_____ Direct mail

_____ Newspaper and magazine ads

_____ Television and radio ads

_____ Billboards

_____ Bus stop seats

_____ Public relation events

_____ Fundraising events for charities

_____ Community involvement

INVENTORY CONTROL

Inventory Control: Procedures used in the salon to ensure products are accounted for from receipt to sale.

•

•

A salon owner is responsible for keeping an inventory of products for employees to sell to their clients.

RECEPTIONIST DUTIES

Primary duties of receptionist:

1. Schedule _____ in a fair and efficient way.

2. Manage incoming and outgoing calls.

3. Inform salon professionals when clients _____.

4. Supervise reception area to ensure organization and efficiency.

5. Promote retail products and additional services.

6. Handle any client communication or _____.

7. Make sure services are paid for and documented.

8. Handle messages efficiently and in order of _____.

9. Work with salon professionals to make sure they remain on _____.

Making change:

If a client is paying for salon services that total $39.58, what would their change be from a $50 dollar bill and how would you count it back to them?

Change would be: _____

Change from $39.58:

Pennies = _____

Dimes = _____

Nickels = _____

Quarters = _____

Bills = _____

TELEPHONE TECHNIQUES

Telephone Answering Tips:

1. Answer the phone within:

2. Greet the client by saying:

3. Listen carefully for:

4. Book appointment and repeat back to client:

5. If you cannot help the client personally:

6. If a message is being left, include:

-
-
-
-
-

Repeat back the entire message to caller.
Deliver the message at an appropriate time.

Telephone communication is often the first impression a client will have of the salon.

SCHEDULING APPOINTMENTS

Important information noted in the appointment book or records includes:

-
-
-
-
-
-

Often additional information is added to the appointment book by using codes to describe various types of clients.

SCRAMBLE
Unscramble these important terms from the lesson.

S C O P N E A T I O N M

S O M I S C I O N M

R S A A Y L

N A D E T I S I G R V

O W D R F O T M U H O

O I E N T R Y V N

I M A O N P T E N T P

N R E E T I O I S T P C

LESSON CHALLENGE *Multiple choice. Indicate one correct answer for each question.*

1. Before a salon owner can hire employees, they need to apply for a:
   a. credit card
   b. Social Security card
   c. Social Insurance Number
   d. Federal Employer Identification Number

2. A set income given to an employee on a weekly or monthly basis is known as:
   a. stock
   b. salary
   c. booth rent
   d. commission

3. Earning additional payment based on the number of clients a salon professional brings into the salon is what type of compensation?
   a. salary
   b. pension
   c. insurance
   d. salary plus commission

4. What is the best form of advertising?
   a. television
   b. billboards
   c. pamphlets
   d. word-of-mouth

5. Which form of advertising involves sending postcards or flyers to prospective clients?
   a. direct mail advertising
   b. TV and radio advertising
   c. word-of-mouth advertising
   d. involvement in community affairs

6. Products purchased by the salon owner for use during client services and for retailing are known as stock in quantity or:
    a. turns
    b. overhead
    c. inventory
    d. commissions

7. Procedures in the salon that ensure all products are accounted for is known as:
    a. budgeting
    b. scheduling
    c. advertising
    d. inventory control

8. In many cases, the first person to greet a client is the:
    a. owner
    b. manager
    c. receptionist
    d. salon professional

9. When handling a phone call, always:
    a. maintain self-control
    b. match the client's anger
    c. promote salon discounts
    d. speak louder than normal

10. The salon professional's name, client's name, scheduled service, date and client's phone number should all be included in the:
    a. I-9 form
    b. appointment book
    c. state income tax form
    d. federal income tax form

LESSON CHALLENGE REFERENCES

Check your answers. Place a check mark next to the page number for any incorrect answer. On the lines, jot down topics that you still need to review.

1. PAGE 95 _____
2. PAGE 95 _____
3. PAGE 95 _____
4. PAGE 97 _____
5. PAGE 97 _____
6. PAGE 98 _____
7. PAGE 98 _____
8. PAGE 100 _____
9. PAGE 101 _____
10. PAGE 102 _____

▶ GROW WHAT YOU KNOW

Reflect on what you have learned and predict how this information will be used in the future.

103c.10 | RETAIL PRODUCTS

ACHIEVE //

Following this lesson on *Retail Products*, you'll be able to:

>> List the steps for effectively recommending products and services

>> Identify strategies for effective retailing in the salon

>> Compare and contrast different buyer types

>> Summarize retail display guidelines

FOCUS //

RETAIL PRODUCTS

Selling

Professional Products

Buyer Types

Effective Displays

SELLING

Retailing in the salon:

* Shows clients you are interested in their _____
* Ongoing process that takes effort and _____
* Requires you to look for new ways to interest your clients in the products you _____

Selling: Exchange of services, products, or expertise for _____

Art of professional _____

SALON PROFESSIONAL IS SELLING TWO IMPORTANT THINGS

1

2

RECOMMENDATIONS

Professional product recommendations will help establish a clientele loyal to you and products recommended

Successful salons have staff members who recommend their services and a quality line of retail products by:

*
*
*
*
*
*

PROFESSIONAL PRODUCTS

Becoming familiar with product _____ and

_____

* Practice recommending products
* Focus on how the client will _____
* Take advantage of _____
* Check with clients periodically
* Maintain a binder with information about products
* Try the products _____

FEATURES AND BENEFITS ——— Features + _____ = Incentive to _____

FEATURE	DESCRIPTION	BENEFIT
Size		Economical purchase
Ingredients	Product contains protein	
Concentrated formula		
Conversation should be _____ %		Conversation should be _____ %

STRATEGIES FOR SUCCESSFUL RETAILING IN THE SALON

Involve the _____
-
-
-
-

Suggest new _____
-
-
-

Close the _____
-
-
-
-
-

CONCLUSION OF THE RETAIL SALE

Reinforce that you expect the client to purchase the product using:

A positive _____

Explanation of benefits and _____

Knowledge of the _____

Customized _____

BUYER TYPES

BUYER TYPE	DESCRIPTION	STRATEGY
	• Open-minded • Takes a chance on new products	
Logical Buyer		• Explain what a product will do and how to use it • Supply client with available literature • Leave client alone to make decisions
	• Purchases more on personal reasons than facts • May react to color of packaging or aroma of product	
Bargain Buyer	• •	• Keep this buyer aware of any sale items or sale promotions offered • Do not push the client
	• Puts up a struggle • Has strong desire to debate	• • •

WHAT MOTIVATES BUYERS

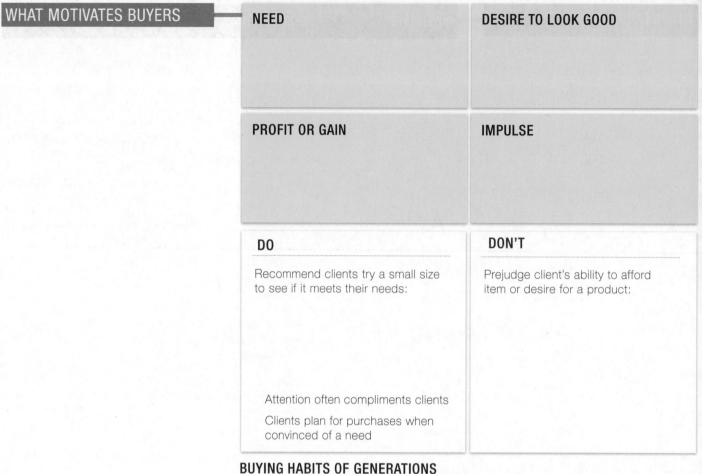

NEED

DESIRE TO LOOK GOOD

PROFIT OR GAIN

IMPULSE

DO

Recommend clients try a small size to see if it meets their needs:

Attention often compliments clients

Clients plan for purchases when convinced of a need

DON'T

Prejudge client's ability to afford item or desire for a product:

BUYING HABITS OF GENERATIONS

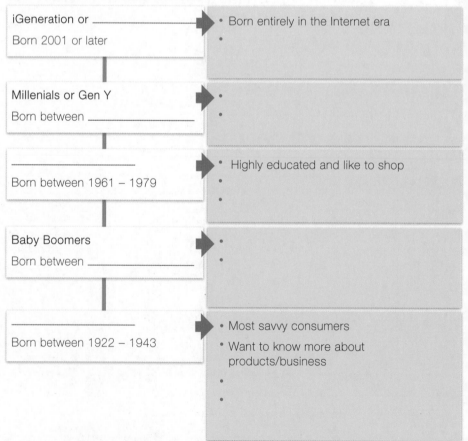

iGeneration or _____

Born 2001 or later

- Born entirely in the Internet era
-

Millenials or Gen Y

Born between _____

-
-

_____

Born between 1961 – 1979

- Highly educated and like to shop
-
-

Baby Boomers

Born between _____

-
-

_____

Born between 1922 – 1943

- Most savvy consumers
- Want to know more about products/business
-
-

FOLLOW-UP

BENEFITS OF WRITTEN INSTRUCTIONS

1. Reinforce professionalism of _____

2. Clarify product use for _____

3. Remind clients to do the treatments at _____

4. Help clients to remember suggested _____

5. Enable salon professional to select product from retail shelves

6. Help receptionist with retail _____

7. Offer referral opportunities

Examine the condition of the client's hair, skin or nails several weeks after you have sold them products

-

-

-

EFFECTIVE DISPLAYS

- Allocate adequate _____

- Display shelves for retail products—stocks or inventory—should:

  - Blend attractively with the _____

  - Be in interesting _____

RETAIL DISPLAY GUIDELINES

-
-
-

-
-
-

EXCEPTIONAL GUEST EXPERIENCE

FOUR REALMS AND HOW THEY CAN BE USED WITH PRODUCT DISPLAYS

Give an example of each type of realm in relation to the salon.

1 _____
Example:

2 _____
Example:

3 _____
Example:

4 _____
Example:

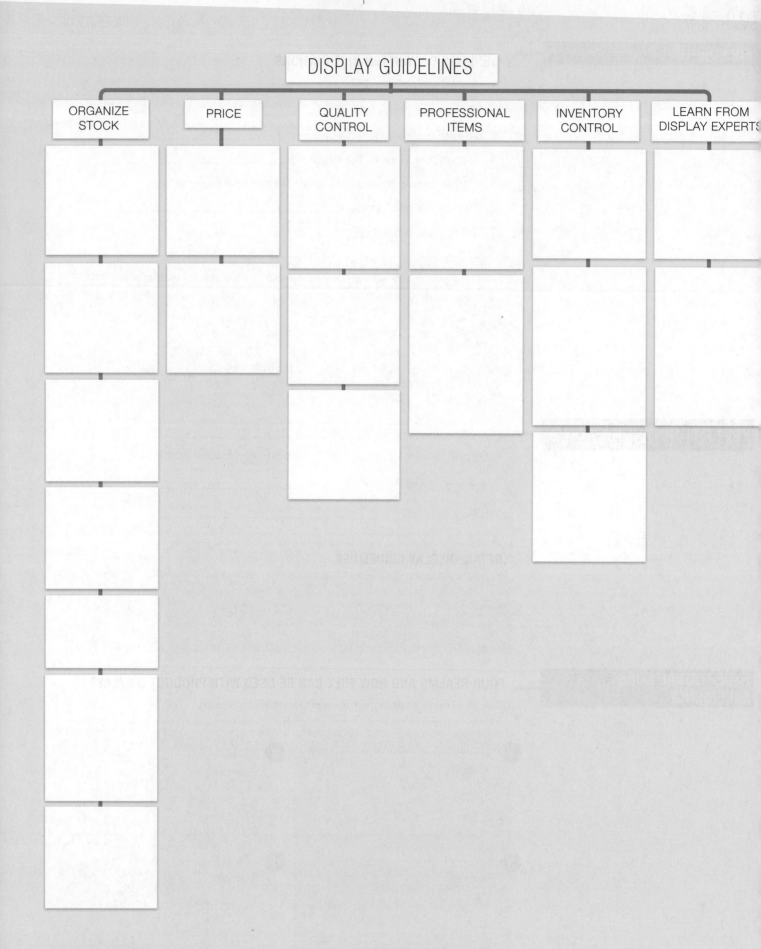

DISPLAY GUIDELINES

ORGANIZE STOCK

PRICE

QUALITY CONTROL

PROFESSIONAL ITEMS

INVENTORY CONTROL

LEARN FROM DISPLAY EXPERTS

LESSON CHALLENGE
Multiple choice. Indicate one correct answer for each question.

1. The term given for selling products for client home care is:
   a. retailing
   b. networking
   c. scheduling
   d. warehousing

2. Successful salons are those whose staff members are effectively recommending their services and a quality line of retail products by doing all of the following EXCEPT:
   a. listening to clients
   b. offering sound advice
   c. making negative comments
   d. communicating professionally

3. Features of a product are its characteristics, which might include:
   a. added shine
   b. size of container
   c. economical purchase
   d. re-conditioning effects

4. The following are all benefits of a product EXCEPT:
   a. adds shine
   b. aromatic ingredients
   c. reconditioning effect
   d. economical purchase

5. Which buyer type is open-minded and willing to take a chance on new products without hesitation?
   a. ready
   b. bargain
   c. logical
   d. stubborn

6. Which buyer wants to know all of the facts about the product and thinks carefully about buying, without much regard for who else likes or uses the product?
   a. ready
   b. bargain
   c. logical
   d. stubborn

7. The emotional buyer bases his or her purchases on:
   a. facts
   b. price
   c. personal reasons
   d. being a new product

8. Which buyer type wants to save money at all costs and is not as interested in quality of product as price?
   a. ready
   b. bargain
   c. logical
   d. stubborn

9. Which type of buyer puts up a struggle and has a strong desire to debate with you?
   a. ready
   b. bargain
   c. logical
   d. stubborn

10. Which of the following is perhaps the easier buyer motivation to recognize in the salon?
    a. want
    b. need
    c. like
    d. dislike

LESSON CHALLENGE REFERENCES

Check your answers. Place a check mark next to the page number for any incorrect answer. On the lines, jot down topics that you still need to review.

1. PAGE 105 _____
2. PAGE 106 _____
3. PAGE 108 _____
4. PAGE 108 _____
5. PAGE 110 _____

6. PAGE 110 _____
7. PAGE 110 _____
8. PAGE 110 _____
9. PAGE 110 _____
10. PAGE 111 _____

▶ GROW WHAT YOU KNOW

Reflect on what you have learned and predict how this information will be used in the future.

104ᶜ.1 //
DESIGN CONNECTION

ACHIEVE //

Following this lesson on *Design Connection*, you'll be able to:

>> Provide examples of how to see and think as a designer

>> Identify the three design elements that comprise every object in the world

>> Identify the four design principles related to the design elements

>> Provide examples of ways to create as a designer

>> Provide examples of ways to adapt as a designer

FOCUS //

DESIGN CONNECTION

See and Think As a Designer

Design Elements

Design Principles

Create As a Designer

Adapt As a Designer

DESIGN CONNECTION

Design is the arrangement of shapes, lines and ornamental effects to create an artistic whole.

The design connection process, also referred to as the Four Cornerstones of Design, is all about:

- Seeing as a designer
- Creating as a designer
- _____ as a designer
- _____ as a designer

SEE AND THINK AS A DESIGNER

SEE
-
-

THINK
-
-
-

QUALITATIVE ANALYSIS
-
-

QUANTITATIVE ANALYSIS

Determine the amount of each part relative to:
-
-
-

Proportion:

THREE LEVELS OF OBSERVATION

Selective seeing through the 3 levels of observation provides a system for studying, categorizing and communicating what you see.

What to look for:

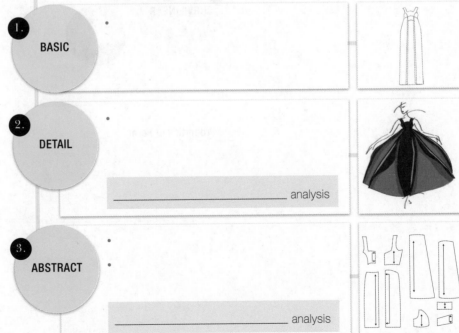

1. BASIC
-

2. DETAIL
-

_____ analysis

3. ABSTRACT
-
-

_____ analysis

DESIGN ELEMENTS

Three design elements, or major components of an art form are:

1.　　　　　　　　　　2.　　　　　　　　　　3.

FORM

Form is the 3-dimensional representation

of _____

Form consists of:

-
-
-

Shape is a 2-dimensional representation

of _____

Shape consists of:

-
-

HELPFUL HINT
In hair design, the terms "form" and "shape" are used interchangeably when describing the outer boundary, outline or silhouette of a design.

The 3 Major Categories of Forms and Shapes

	FORM	SHAPE	LINE
1. RECTILINEAR		• •	• •
2. TRIANGULAR		• • •	•
3. CURVILINEAR		• • • • • •	•

Properties of Form

-
-
-

LINE

- A point set in motion becomes a _____
- A line is a series of connected _____

Lines direct your eyes from one point to another

Draw an example of each below.

STRAIGHT LINES

HORIZONTAL
- _____ to horizon
- Weight and calmness

VERTICAL
- _____ to horizon
- Strength and weightlessness

DIAGONAL
- Between horizontal and vertical
- _____ _____

CURVED LINES

- Can be represented by any 3 _____ lines
- CONCAVE = _____ _____
- CONVEX = _____ _____

SHAPE

- A 2-dimensional representation of form consisting of length and width but not _____
- Consists of angles and, when extended into space, a shape becomes a _____

The celestial axis is a symbol that will support you in identifying straight and curved _____, _____ and _____

Horizontal

Vertical

Diagonal

Concave

Convex

2-dimensional

3-dimensional

Celestial axis

OBSERVING FORMS: NATURE, MANMADE AND HAIR

Studying forms and shapes will help you create inspirational new _____-_____ forms in hair.

1 2 3 4 5 6 7

SMART NOTES

TEXTURE

Texture is the _____ appearance or _____ of a surface, and it's the design element that creates interest within a design.

2 types of texture:

- Unactivated = _____

- Activated = _____

Line quality

OBSERVING TEXTURES: NATURE, MANMADE AND HAIR

Observing and feeling texture enables you to strengthen your observational skills and sense of _____.

Determine 3 examples that make you think of smooth or unactivated texture.

NATURE	MANMADE	HAIR

Determine 3 examples that make you think of rough or activated texture.

NATURE	MANMADE	HAIR

COLOR

Color is the visual perception of the reflection of light.

Color can add _____, _____ and the illusion of _____ to a form.

All colors are created by a combination of 3 primary colors, which are:

PRIMARY COLORS

_____

_____

SECONDARY COLORS

_____

_____

1 2 3 4 5 6 7

THREE CATEGORIES OF COLORS

WARM	COOL	NEUTRAL
yellow	blue	brown

OBSERVING COLORS: NATURE, MANMADE AND HAIR

Color and color patterns in _____ are limitless; can provide inspirational ideas for hair designs.

DESIGN PRINCIPLES

Artistic arrangement patterns for the _____ _____ to follow

The 4 design principles are:

1.	3.
2.	4.

REPETITION

Description: _____

_____

Show examples of repetition for each design element.

FORM	TEXTURE	COLOR

ALTERNATION

Description: _____

_____

Show examples of alternation for each design element.

FORM	TEXTURE	COLOR

PROGRESSION

Description: _____

_____

Show examples of progression for each design element.

FORM	TEXTURE	COLOR

CONTRAST

Description: _____

_____

Show examples of contrast for each design element.

FORM	TEXTURE	COLOR

BALANCE

Balance is the state of _____ existing between contrasting, opposite or interacting elements.

Types of Balance

1. Symmetrical
   - Weight is positioned _____ on both sides of a center axis
   - Focus remains on _____
2. Asymmetrical
   - Weight is positioned _____ from a center axis
   - Creates a sense of _____ and _____

CREATE AS A DESIGNER

- Practicing all aspects of hair design to build your expertise
- Perform with focus and precision to produce _____
  _____

CREATING FORM

Forms created through:

- _____
- _____
- _____

CREATING TEXTURE

Textures are created by:

* _____
* _____
* _____

Texture variables can be created through _____ _____

CREATING COLOR

Color can be added to hair with:

* _____ • _____

HELPFUL HINT
Color can:
* Lead your eye through a design or create a focal point
* Break up the surface appearance to create the illusion of texture

ADAPT AS A DESIGNER

Adapting is the highest level of design _____

Two components for adapting hair designs are:

1.	2.

Look at the images below. How does the new design reflect design adaptations of form, texture and color?

ADAPT: _____

_____

_____

_____

_____

ADAPT: _____

_____

_____

_____

_____

ADAPT: _____

_____

_____

_____

_____

HELPFUL HINT
Mastering the process of seeing, thinking, creating and adapting as a designer will set you apart from the average stylist in the salon.

THINKING MAP

Create a Thinking Map to help you make sense of how your notes fit together. Use words in the Jump Start Box as well as your own words and pictures to make a visual that will help you connect the important ideas in this chapter to each other. **Be creative!**

JUMP START BOX

Design Connection	Connect	Compose	Design Principles
See	Analyze	Personalize	Repetition
Think	Visualize	Design Elements	Alternation
Create	Organize	Form	Progression
Adapt	Practice	Texture	Contrast
Observe	Perform	Color	

LESSON CHALLENGE *Multiple choice. Indicate the correct answer for each question.*

1. Which of the following are you observing in the basic level of observation?
   a. color
   b. texture
   c. silhouette
   d. proportion

2. The 3 major design elements are form, texture and:
   a. basic
   b. color
   c. detail
   d. abstract

3. A 3-dimensional representation of shape is known as:
   a. line
   b. form
   c. point
   d. detail

4. Which of the following lines is parallel to the horizon?
   a. convex
   b. vertical
   c. diagonal
   d. horizontal

5. Which of the following lines is perpendicular to the horizon?
   a. convex
   b. vertical
   c. diagonal
   d. horizontal

6. The visual appearance or feel of a surface is known as:
   a. form
   b. color
   c. shape
   d. texture

7. The 4 design principles are repetition, alternation, progression and:
   a. line
   b. detail
   c. contrast
   d. proportion

8. Seeing as a designer is all about:
   a. observing and connecting
   b. analyzing and visualizing
   c. practicing and performing
   d. composing and personalizing

9. Creating as a designer is all about:
   a. observing and connecting
   b. analyzing and visualizing
   c. practicing and performing
   d. composing and personalizing

10. Adapting as a designer is all about:
    a. observing and connecting
    b. analyzing and visualizing
    c. practicing and performing
    d. composing and personalizing

LESSON CHALLENGE REFERENCES

Check your answers. Place a check mark next to the page number for any incorrect answer. On the lines, jot down topics that you still need to review.

1. PAGE 9 _____
2. PAGE 10 _____
3. PAGE 10 _____
4. PAGE 13 _____
5. PAGE 13 _____
6. PAGE 16 _____
7. PAGE 20 _____
8. PAGE 23 _____
9. PAGE 24 _____
10. PAGE 28 _____

GROW WHAT YOU KNOW

Reflect on what you have learned and predict how this information will be used in the future.

104.c2 //
CLIENT CONSIDERATIONS

ACHIEVE //

Following this lesson on *Client Considerations*, you'll be able to:

» Describe how hair designs can be adapted to complement different body types

» Identify various body shapes

» Provide examples of hair designs to complement various face shapes

» Identify clothing and lifestyles to consider when making design decisions for your clients

FOCUS //

CLIENT CONSIDERATIONS

Body Types and Shapes

Face Shapes

Hair Color and Natural Coloring

Clothing and Lifestyles

CLIENT CONSIDERATIONS

As a designer, you have the ability to help clients look and feel their best.

• _____

• _____

This requires careful analysis and an understanding of the client's _____

and _____ _____ .

BODY TYPES AND SHAPES

According to the standard proportion most artists use:

The head of a woman is:	The head of a man is:

BODY TYPES

	ECTOMORPH	MESOMORPH	ENDOMORPH
DESCRIPTION	• •	• •	• •
SHOULDERS/ HIPS		Dominant shoulders; Average hips	
LEGS/ARMS/ NECK	Long		Short
HEIGHTS	Women: Men:	Women: Men:	Women: Men:

BODY SHAPES

When considering the body shape:

• Identify the area that is the _____

• Visualize client's overall body _____

• Imagine amount of volume needed to bring widest area into _____

_____

On the illustrations below, sketch the shape that represents the body type listed.

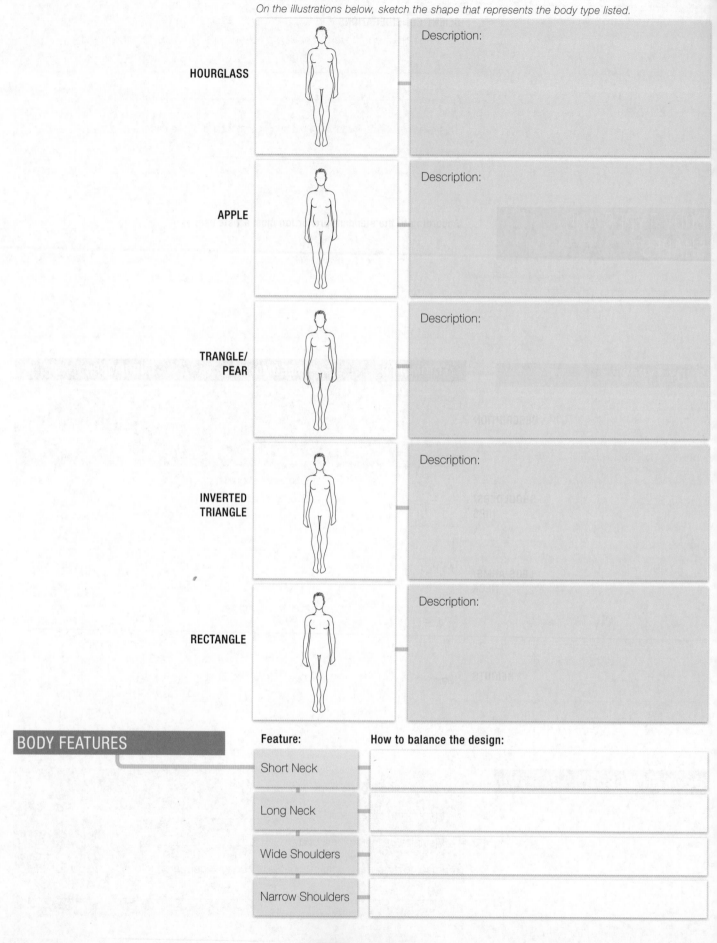

HOURGLASS

Description:

APPLE

Description:

TRANGLE/ PEAR

Description:

INVERTED TRIANGLE

Description:

RECTANGLE

Description:

BODY FEATURES

Feature:	How to balance the design:
Short Neck	
Long Neck	
Wide Shoulders	
Narrow Shoulders	

1 2 3 4 5 6 7

FACE SHAPES

To determine the most appropriate design, analyze the face using criteria such as:

-
-

-
-

3-SECTIONING

Section 1
Front hairline to middle of _____

Section 2
Middle of eyebrows to tip of _____

Section 3
Tip of nose to tip of _____

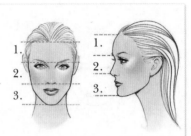

1.
2.
3.

HELPFUL HINT
Having the client observe in a mirror while 3-sectioning is a good way to lay the foundation so the client will understand the reasons behind the design decision you will be recommending.

Sections are considered harmonious if length of the sections are

_____

Hair designs and makeup can be used to create the illusion of

_____

COMMON FACE SHAPES

Being familiar with the different characteristics of each face shape will help you adapt hair designs to best suit your client.

Label the face shapes.

_____

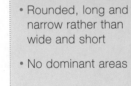

_____

_____

DESCRIPTION	DO	DON'T
• Rounded, long and narrow rather than wide and short • No dominant areas	• •	• Add too much height
• Looks circular • Appears short and wide rather than long and narrow	• • •	• Add a full fringe • Add width on the sides • Add equal fullness around entire face
• Short and wide • Looks angular with lots of straight lines	• • •	• Add solid lines at jawline • Add horizontal fringes or straight lines • Add height without width

Label the face shapes.

_____

_____

_____

_____

DESCRIPTION	DO	DON'T
• Long, narrow and angular • Jawline is wide and almost horizontal	• • •	• Add height without width • Style hair completely away from face
• Most often elongated • Forehead is narrow • Jaw is widest area	• •	• Accentuate the pear shape with narrowness at the temples and width at the jawline
• Elongated and angular • Widest areas are at cheekbones	• •	• Add width at cheekbones • Add height on top • Add short, cropped nape
• Long and angular • Chin is sometimes elongated and pointed; wide forehead	• •	• Add width at forehead or cheekbones

PROFILE

Profile: _____

_____

STRAIGHT

Slight outward curvature from front hairline to tip of nose to chin

CONVEX

Strong outward curvature; protruding nose or sloping forehead or chin

CONCAVE

Inward curve; often a protruding forehead and chin or small nose

Design Recommendation:

1 2 3 4 5 6 7

FACIAL FEATURES

Other features that may need special consideration:

RECEDING HAIRLINE

- _____
- _____
- _____

PROTRUDING EARS

- _____
- _____

_____

Selection of the eyeglass frames should also take into account:

EYEGLASSES

- _____
- _____
- _____
- _____

HAIR COLOR AND NATURAL COLORING

The right hair color can:

- _____
- _____
- _____

Analyze the pigmentation of their hair, skin, eyes and lips:

1. Determine whether the client's color scheme tends to be warm, cool

   or _____

2. Determine intensity of those colors (mild or _____)

CLOTHING AND LIFESTYLES

CLOTHING STYLES

Clothing and lifestyle complement each other and need to be considered when designing the hair.

Hair Design Preference:

CASUAL

Comfortable and low-maintenance

NATURAL

Wears colors and materials found in nature

CLASSIC

Wardrobe is coordinated

Color selections often include navy, black, white, cream, beige, brown and gray

ROMANTIC

Loves silk, flower prints, lace, beads and pastel shades

Often tone-on-tone

GAMINE

Fashion-oriented; enjoys wearing latest looks; small jewelry

DRAMATIC

Likes things out of the ordinary

Colorful clothing and accessories

LIFESTYLE FACTORS

Some lifestyle factors to consider in order to determine a hair design's practicality:

- _____
- _____
- _____

- _____
- _____
- _____

DRAWING BOARD

Practice your observation skills by tracing over the dominant characteristics of each face shape. This will reinforce your ability to recognize the different types of face shapes.

OVAL

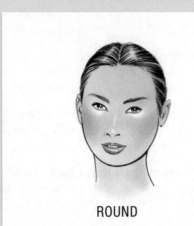

ROUND

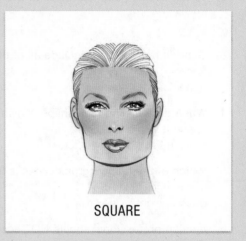

SQUARE

OBLONG

PEAR

DIAMOND

HEART

LESSON CHALLENGE *Multiple choice. Indicate the correct answer for each question.*

1. Tall and lanky clients generally need volume and/or:
   a. longer hair
   b. shorter hair
   c. flat styles
   d. braids

2. Which clients need hair designs with height and volume on the top?
   a. average
   b. very tall
   c. tall and lanky
   d. short and sturdy

3. General body shapes include all of the following names EXCEPT:
   a. pear
   b. apple
   c. triangle
   d. grapefruit

4. When determining face shape, which of the following is NOT a consideration?
   a. analysis of the hairline
   b. analysis of bone structure
   c. analysis of the least dominant area
   d. analysis of the widest and most dominant areas

5. Which of the following guidelines is true if the client has a round face shape?
   a. add a full fringe
   b. add height to the crown
   c. add width to the sides
   d. add equal fullness around the entire face

6. A salon professional should NOT accentuate the narrowness at the temples and width at the jawline in what type of face shape?
   a. pear
   b. heart
   c. square
   d. diamond

7. Which of the following should NOT be considered if the client has a diamond face shape?
   a. adding width at the jawline
   b. adding width at the forehead
   c. adding width at the cheekbones
   d. using a side part and diagonal fringe

8. Which of the following describes the term "profile"?
   a. a view of the face from the front
   b. an outline of the face from the side
   c. an outline of the face from the back
   d. a view from the top of the head looking down

9. A dominant, protruding forehead and chin or a small nose are characteristics of a:
   a. short profile
   b. convex profile
   c. straight profile
   d. concave profile

10. All of the following are true when choosing the right hair color, EXCEPT:
    a. emphasizes eye color
    b. emphasizes natural skin tone
    c. makes client look more radiant
    d. makes hair color last one-week longer

LESSON CHALLENGE REFERENCES

Check your answers. Place a check mark next to the page number for any incorrect answer. On the lines, jot down topics that you still need to review.

1. PAGE 37 _____
2. PAGE 37 _____
3. PAGE 38 _____
4. PAGE 42 _____
5. PAGE 44 _____
6. PAGE 45 _____
7. PAGE 46 _____
8. PAGE 47 _____
9. PAGE 47 _____
10. PAGE 50 _____

▶ GROW WHAT YOU KNOW

Reflect on what you have learned and predict how this information will be used in the future.

104ᶜ.3 //
CONNECT SERVICE ESSENTIAL

ACHIEVE //

Following this lesson on the *Connect Service Essential*, you'll be able to:

>> List the four Service Essentials

>> Demonstrate specific strategies for connecting with clients

>> Discuss additional elements that affect how well you connect with clients

>> Apply all five senses when using techniques to connect with clients

FOCUS //

CONNECT SERVICE ESSENTIAL

Connect Strategies

Connecting with the Five Senses

SERVICE ESSENTIALS: THE 4 Cs

1. **CONNECT**

   _____

   _____

2. **CONSULT**

   Analyzes client wants and needs, visualizes the end result, organizes the plan for follow-through and obtains client consent

3. **CREATE**

   Produces functional, predictable and pleasing results

4. **COMPLETE**

   Reviews the service experience and client satisfaction, offers product recommendations, expresses appreciation and provides follow-up

CONNECT STRATEGIES

Guidelines to help you connect with your clients and gain credibility:

1.

2.

3.

4.

In addition to communication skills, factors that affect ability to connect with clients include:

·

·

·

·

CONNECTING WITH THE FIVE SENSES

HOW WOULD YOU USE THE FIVE SENSES TO CONNECT WITH YOUR CLIENTS?

1. SIGHT
What colors would you plan for salon décor?

_____
_____
_____

2. SOUND
What type of music would your salon play in the background?

_____
_____
_____

3. TOUCH
How would you make your shampoo service standout as unique?

_____
_____
_____

4. SMELL
How would you take advantage of the sense of smell?

_____
_____
_____

5. TASTE
What refreshments would you offer in the salon?

_____
_____
_____

POSITIVE CHANGES

Christina has owned her salon for 5 years. The décor reflects her interest in nature, and quite often the image of the salon has been photographed and written about regarding its unique ambiance. In reality, Christina only has one major concern: her staff lacks consistency and synergy. No matter how much she tries to motivate the group, it seems that week after week, the same problems keep occurring. One of those problems is maintaining the image of the design area. Towels are draped over the cleansing area, hair is lying around the waste bins and there are too many products on the counter space. Christina met with her staff of 11 hair designers, 2 estheticians, 2 nail technicians and 1 receptionist and asked them to cooperate to make positive changes happen.

If you were a member of Christina's staff, what are some steps you could take to make positive changes happen within the salon?

_____
_____
_____
_____

LESSON CHALLENGE
Multiple choice. Indicate the correct answer for each question.

1. The four Service Essentials are Connect, Consult, Create and:
   a. Confirm
   b. Comfort
   c. Complete
   d. Communicate

2. Greeting the guest is an element of which of the following service essentials?
   a. Create
   b. Consult
   c. Connect
   d. Complete

3. The Connect service essential involves putting clients at ease and building:
   a. rapport
   b. finances
   c. disloyalty
   d. disagreement

4. Which of the following strategies is NOT a suggested Connect strategy?
   a. use the guest's name
   b. prebook an appointment
   c. introduce yourself to the guest
   d. give the client helpful direction

5. A client should be greeted within the first:
   a. 10 seconds
   b. 90 seconds
   c. 5 minutes
   d. 10 minutes

6. Why is it important to use a client's name?
   a. creates a barrier
   b. helps every client feel important
   c. develops a recognizable distance
   d. lets everyone around them know who they are

7. When introducing yourself to a client, use poised, calm movements to project confidence and:
   a. inability
   b. hesitation
   c. competence
   d. incompetence

8. All of the following statements describe positive environmental elements, EXCEPT:
   a. omit connecting time with the next client
   b. keep personal conflicts off the salon floor
   c. make sure music and reading material in waiting area are appropriate
   d. minimize distractions and make sure you always have your client's full attention

9. Which of the following words describes how clients should see your routine each time they visit?
   a. varied
   b. erratic
   c. irregular
   d. consistent

10. The five senses that will ensure your client's salon visit is exceptionally memorable are sight, sound, smell, touch and:
    a. walk
    b. humor
    c. taste
    d. balance

LESSON CHALLENGE REFERENCES

Check your answers. Place a check mark next to the page number for any incorrect answer. On the lines, jot down topics that you still need to review.

1. PAGE 62 _____
2. PAGE 63 _____
3. PAGE 63 _____
4. PAGE 63 _____
5. PAGE 63 _____

6. PAGE 63 _____
7. PAGE 63 _____
8. PAGE 64 _____
9. PAGE 66 _____
10. PAGE 66 _____

▶ GROW WHAT YOU KNOW

Reflect on what you have learned and predict how this information will be used in the future.

104^c.4 //
CONSULT
SERVICE
ESSENTIAL

ACHIEVE //

Following this lesson on the *Consult Service Essential*, you'll be able to:

» Discuss the four strategies that make up the Consult Service Essential

» Give examples of how you can connect with clients during the consultation

» Summarize the importance of keeping updated client records

FOCUS //

CONSULT SERVICE ESSENTIAL

Consult Strategies

Consultations Help You Connect

Consultation Records

SERVICE ESSENTIALS: THE 4 Cs

1. **CONNECT**

   Establishes rapport and builds credibility with each client

2. **CONSULT**

   _____

   _____

3. **CREATE**

   Produces functional, predictable and pleasing results

4. **COMPLETE**

   Reviews the service experience and client satisfaction, offers product recommendations, expresses appreciation and provides follow-up

CONSULT STRATEGIES

Consulting with your client is a 4-step process that includes:

1.

2.

3.

4.

CONSULTATIONS HELP YOU CONNECT

The Consult essential is extremely important for new clients:

• If clients feel you are listening to them, they are more likely to return and
   _____

• Be honest; maintain a kind smile and a reassuring _____

• Schedule enough time to consult before the service; schedule extra time for
   _____   _____

• Make sure consultation area offers privacy: noise level is minimal; lighting is good

• Use visual aids to help the client explain what they want

CONSULTATION RECORDS

A client record ensures that any staff member will be able to meet this client's service needs safely and effectively. It also serves as a record of how any long-term treatments or services are progressing.

Keep in mind:

- Do not leave records in view where anyone can _____ _____

- Keep all records safely secured and/or _____ _____

- Refer to client records before each consultation/visit

- Update client records at the end of consultation and/or _____

Tips for a Successful Consultation

1. Listen to your client and maintain _____ _____.

2. Sit next to your client during the consultation so they don't have to _____ _____.

3. Ask the client what he or she likes about their hair/skin/nails and find out how they care for it.

4. Establish what your client's hair concerns are, then tailor the conversation throughout the service around how/what products will _____ _____.

5. Add any relevant notes to the client consultation cards or records, and update your client records _____.

SCRAMBLE

Unscramble these important terms from the lesson.

UTCNOSL

IULEVSAZI

YZNEAAL

ZIOGNRAE

GENREAMET

OFFERING ALTERNATIVES

Work with a partner and determine ways you might offer positive alternative plans for a design that can't be performed for a client. Consider how you would inform the client without just saying "no." Practice back-and-forth conversation as partners, and then share with the class your best attempt at offering the alternative plan.

CLIENT RECORD

Practice filling out the client record by working with a partner and role playing completing the record by reversing the roles of professional and client.

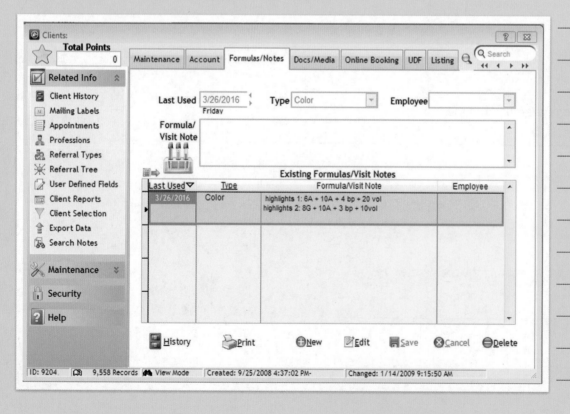

1 2 **3** 4 5 6 7

LESSON CHALLENGE
Multiple choice. Indicate the correct answer for each question.

1. All of the following strategies are part of the Consult service essential, EXCEPT:
   a. organizing a plan
   b. obtaining consent
   c. performing the service
   d. visualizing the end result

2. Analyzing the guest's wants and needs occurs during which service essential?
   a. Create
   b. Consult
   c. Connect
   d. Complete

3. Which of the following is an open-ended question?
   a. Is your skin dry?
   b. Do you like your current hair color?
   c. What final results do you want to see in your hair?
   d. You haven't had a facial for a while, right?

4. Select the term that could be used by a client to help uncover what they "want" in a hair service.
   a. flat
   b. drab
   c. shine
   d. lifeless

5. Select the term that could be used to help uncover problems or challenges that clients currently "have."
   a. dull
   b. soft
   c. shine
   d. smooth

6. Identifying the cost of the service is discussed during which of the following service essentials?
   a. Create
   b. Consult
   c. Connect
   d. Complete

7. If the guest feels hesitant about your suggestion made during the Consult service essential, you should:
   a. proceed with the service anyway
   b. offer to prebook the guest's next appointment
   c. convince the guest to change his or her mind
   d. ask additional questions to clarify what the guest really wants

8. At what point would you gain consent to move forward during the Consult service essential?
   a. after all questions have been clarified
   b. after analyzing the client's wants and needs
   c. right after viewing a photo the client brought
   d. before analyzing the client's physical attributes

9. Identify the environment used for the consultation.
   a. private area
   b. darkest area
   c. dispensary area
   d. noisiest spot in the salon

10. All of the following are true about the consultation record EXCEPT:
    a. keep safely secured
    b. refer to before consultation
    c. leave in view where anybody can read them
    d. update at end of consultation or service

LESSON CHALLENGE REFERENCES

Check your answers. Place a check mark next to the page number for any incorrect answer. On the lines, jot down topics that you still need to review.

1. PAGE 70 _____

2. PAGE 70 _____

3. PAGE 70 _____

4. PAGE 70 _____

5. PAGE 70 _____

6. PAGE 71 _____

7. PAGE 71 _____

8. PAGE 71 _____

9. PAGE 72 _____

10. PAGE 73 _____

▶ GROW WHAT YOU KNOW

Reflect on what you have learned and predict how this information will be used in the future.

104ᶜ.5 //
CREATE SERVICE ESSENTIAL

ACHIEVE //

Following this lesson on the *Create Service Essential*, you'll be able to:

» List the three most important steps in the Create essential

» Explain the difference between features and benefits of products

» Give examples of how to make each client's service exceptional

» Identify ways you can help customize a service for every client

FOCUS //

CREATE SERVICE ESSENTIAL

Create Strategies

Make the Client Experience Count

SERVICE ESSENTIALS: THE 4 Cs

1. **CONNECT**

   Establishes rapport and builds credibility with each client

2. **CONSULT**

   Analyzes client wants and needs, visualizes the end result, organizes the plan for follow-through and obtains client consent

3. **CREATE**

   _____

   _____

4. **COMPLETE**

   Reviews the service experience and client satisfaction, offers product recommendations, expresses appreciation and provides follow-up

CREATE STRATEGIES

SHOW—TELL—TEACH

1. SHOW _____

2. TELL _____

3. TEACH _____

FEATURES AND BENEFITS

As you teach clients about the products, share information about each product. Focus on the benefits, and briefly explain their features.

Feature of a product = its characteristics and _____

Examples: _____

Benefit of a product = _____

Examples: _____

MAKE THE CLIENT EXPERIENCE COUNT

Make your clients feel they've had an exceptional visit:

1.

2.

3.

4.

CUSTOMIZING EACH SERVICE EXPERIENCE

List examples of ways to focus on your client, and look for opportunities to exceed their expectations.

-
-
-
-

MAKE MEMORABLE VISITS

- Listen

- Keep the conversation _____

- Work with intent and _____

- Keep your work simple and make it _____

- Know your _____

- Remember that you are limited by the client's desires

MEMORABLE SALON VISITS

Identify ways you will plan to make clients remember their salon visits with you. Use the chart below to list strategies you would use to have a variety of clients feeling like they want to return.

CLIENT TYPE	STRATEGY TO CREATE A MEMORABLE EXPERIENCE
Female, age 35-45, Stay-at-home mom	
Female, age 55-70, Nurse	
Male, age 35-45, Lawyer	
Male, age 55-70, Welder	
Female, age 13-19, Athlete	
Male, age 13-19, Athlete	

FEATURES AND BENEFITS

Review the list below and determine whether the description is a word used to identify a feature or a benefit. Place an "F" on the line to the left if it is a feature, or place a "B" on the line to the left if it describes a benefit.

_____ Natural bristles

_____ Shine

_____ Almond oil

_____ Reduces frizz

_____ Soft to the touch

_____ Protects

_____ Relaxes

_____ Easy to pour

_____ Convenient

_____ Added volume

_____ Vitamin E

_____ Fragrance

_____ Affordable

_____ Added strength

_____ Coconut oil

LESSON CHALLENGE   *Multiple choice. Indicate the correct answer for each question.*

1. **Ensuring the client's comfort during the service describes which service essential?**
   a. Create
   b. Consult
   c. Connect
   d. Complete

2. **All of the following are things to keep in mind during the Create service essential, EXCEPT:**
   a. make the education process fun
   b. prebook your next appointment
   c. introduce each technique as quick and easy
   d. document products and services discussed with the client

3. **A strategy practiced during the Create service essential is called Show, Tell and:**
   a. Go
   b. Sell
   c. Teach
   d. Complete

4. **Which of the following statements could be used when making a recommendation to describe a benefit of a product?**
   a. This product will increase shine.
   b. This product contains almond oil.
   c. This brush is made of natural bristles.
   d. This product is developed with vitamin E.

5. **Select the description that could identify a feature when recommending a product?**
   a. reduces frizz
   b. added volume
   c. natural bristles
   d. protects and relaxes

6. **The following strategies all help the client feel they've had an exceptional experience, EXCEPT:**
   a. providing knowledge
   b. not suggesting add-on services
   c. offering additional food and drinks
   d. using various relaxation techniques

7. **Examples of topics to avoid when talking with the client include all of the following, EXCEPT:**
   a. money
   b. religion
   c. politics
   d. lifestyle

8. **How much time should be spent talking about yourself during the client's salon visit?**
   a. not at all
   b. not too much
   c. only when asked
   d. every chance possible

LESSON CHALLENGE REFERENCES

Check your answers. Place a check mark next to the page number for any incorrect answer. On the lines, jot down topics that you still need to review.

1. PAGE 77 _____

2. PAGE 77 _____

3. PAGE 78 _____

4. PAGE 78 _____

5. PAGE 78 _____

6. PAGE 79 _____

7. PAGE 81 _____

8. PAGE 81 _____

GROW WHAT YOU KNOW

Reflect on what you have learned and predict how this information will be used in the future.

104.6 //
COMPLETE SERVICE ESSENTIAL

ACHIEVE //

Following this lesson on the *Complete Service Essential*, you'll be able to:

>> Discuss strategies for solidifying your client relationship during the Complete service essential

>> Explain the best approach to recommending products and after-care advice

FOCUS //

COMPLETE SERVICE ESSENTIAL

Complete Strategies

After-Care Advice

1 2 3 4 5 6 7

SERVICE ESSENTIALS: THE 4 Cs

1. **CONNECT**

   Establishes rapport and builds credibility with each client

2. **CONSULT**

   Analyzes client wants and needs, visualizes the end result, organizes the plan for follow-through and obtains client consent

3. **CREATE**

   Produces functional, predictable and pleasing results

4. **COMPLETE**

   _____

   _____

   _____

COMPLETE STRATEGIES

1. Reinforce client _____

2. Make professional product recommendations

3. Prebook client's next appointment

4. End with a warm _____

5. Complete client _____

6. Provide follow-up after the salon visit

AFTER-CARE ADVICE

Be careful not to make negative comments about other _____.

Staying in the positive vibe will help keep the service exceptional and

_____.

Spell out the benefits of using products at home.

Explain to clients:

• Which product you have used on their hair/skin/nails

• _____

• _____

SCRAMBLE

Complete the statement by unscrambling the word(s).

Reinforce client **NASOTIITCSFA**

Make professional product **DRECOMENATINSMO**

Prebook client's **XNET NAOITMENTPP**

End with a **RWAM OOYDBEG**

Complete **NLIECT CREODR**

Provide follow-up **EAFTR TEH SALNO SVITI**

ATTENTION TO DETAIL

Creating an exceptional experience can be accomplished with special attention to the details of the Service Essentials. Match the action of each Service Essential listed in column B by placing the appropriate number on the line to the left in Column A.

COLUMN A

_____ CONNECT

_____ CONSULT

_____ CREATE

_____ COMPLETE

COLUMN B

1. Analyzes, visualizes and organizes the framework to move ahead

2. Establishes the client's satisfaction and future follow-up

3. Builds rapport

4. Produces functionally and aesthetically pleasing results

LESSON CHALLENGE *Multiple choice. Indicate the correct answer for each question.*

1. Of the following strategies, which one is used during the Complete service essential?
   a. analyze client wants and needs
   b. introduce yourself to the guest
   c. make product recommendations
   d. organize a plan for follow-through

2. All of the following strategies are used during the Complete service essential, EXCEPT:
   a. visualize the end result
   b. end with a warm goodbye
   c. complete client record card
   d. provide follow-up after the salon visit

3. Actions that can help reinforce client satisfaction during the Complete service essential include all of the following, EXCEPT:
   a. prompting clients to tell you how they feel
   b. summarizing the salon services performed
   c. asking questions to determine what the client wants
   d. reminding clients how great their total appearance looks

4. The technique that defines turning first-time clients into return clients is:
   a. prebooking
   b. follow-up care
   c. making product recommendations
   d. summarizing the salon services performed

5. Newsletters, birthday cards and thank-you cards are all ways to provide:
   a. follow-up
   b. upselling
   c. prebooking
   d. recommending

6. After-care advice includes explaining the benefits of using a product at home with all the following information, EXCEPT:
   a. which product to use
   b. how to use the product
   c. why you used the product
   d. why other products don't work

LESSON CHALLENGE REFERENCES

Check your answers. Place a check mark next to the page number for any incorrect answer. On the lines, jot down topics that you still need to review.

1. PAGE 85 _____

2. PAGE 85 _____

3. PAGE 86 _____

4. PAGE 86 _____

5. PAGE 87 _____

6. PAGE 88 _____

▶ GROW WHAT YOU KNOW

Reflect on what you have learned and predict how this information will be used in the future.

105ᶜ.1
SCULPTURE THEORY

ACHIEVE //

Following this lesson on *Sculpture Theory*, you'll be able to: ·

>> Describe the two ways to analyze the length arrangement of a hair sculpture

>> Illustrate the shape, texture and structure of the four basic forms

>> Classify combination forms within hair sculptures by the four basic forms

>> Evaluate the effects of different shapes and surface textures on the same client

FOCUS //

SCULPTURE THEORY

Sculpture Transformation

Hair Sculpture Analysis

Four Basic Forms

Combination Forms

Change the Sculpture, Change the Effect

HAIR SCULPTING: The artistic carving or removing of _____

_____ to create various forms and shapes.

SCULPTURE TRANSFORMATION

Sculpture transformation is all about changing the _____ (silhouette), the surface _____ and the

_____ of a hair design.

When creating a sculpture transformation for your client,

_____ is most important.

HAIR SCULPTURE ANALYSIS

3 levels of observation for hair sculpture analysis:

_____

_____

BASIC – FORM/SHAPE

Identify the basic form or shape by simply observing the outer boundary or

silhouette known as the _____ _____

Design is analyzed using only _____

DETAIL – TEXTURE

Identify the detail in the _____ or surface appearance

TWO TYPES OF TEXTURE

UNACTIVATED	ACTIVATED
•	•

ABSTRACT – STRUCTURE

Hair is viewed as if standing _____ _____

or projected at a 90° angle from the curves of the head

Arrangement of lengths across the curves of the head

A _____ graphic is a diagram that provides an abstract view of

_____ _____ to scale and proportion;

blueprint for final sculpture

TWO WAYS TO ANALYZE STRUCTURE

NATURAL FALL	NORMAL PROJECTION
•	•
•	•
•	•

Draw in the angles of normal projection.

FOUR BASIC FORMS

SOLID, GRADUATED, INCREASE-LAYERED, UNIFORMLY LAYERED

When used alone, or in combination, these forms make up all hair designs.

WEIGHT: Weight is created by the concentration of _____ within a given area.

CREST AREA: Widest area around the head, divides the _____, the area above the crest, from the _____, the area below the crest.

SOLID FORM

ALSO KNOWN AS:

SHAPE:

TEXTURE:

STRUCTURE:

WEIGHT:

Draw in the structure and texture of solid form.

GRADUATED FORM

ALSO KNOWN AS:

SHAPE:

TEXTURE:

STRUCTURE:

WEIGHT:

Draw in the structure and texture of graduated form.

INCREASE-LAYERED FORM

ALSO KNOWN AS:

SHAPE:

TEXTURE:

STRUCTURE:

WEIGHT:

Draw in the structure and texture of increase-layered form.

UNIFORMLY LAYERED FORM

ALSO KNOWN AS:

SHAPE:

TEXTURE:

STRUCTURE:

WEIGHT:

Draw in the structure and texture of uniformly layered form.

GRADATION: Also color-coded yellow; a very _____ version of the graduated form

COMBINATION FORMS

Two or more forms within a sculpture

INCREASE/SOLID — Illusion of _____ surface appearance with maximum perimeter _____

INCREASE/UNIFORM/GRADATION — Close-fitting _____; fringe creates height and _____

UNIFORM/GRADUATED — Lengths blend for a totally _____ surface texture

UNIFORM/INCREASE — Highly activated surface and elongation toward the _____

GRADUATION/UNIFORM/GRADATION — Close-fitting _____ blends to uniformly layered lengths; graduated interior lengths achieve _____ toward face

SQUARE (RECTILINEAR) FORM — Weight area is created where increase layering meets _____ form

CHANGE THE SCULPTURE, CHANGE THE EFFECT

Can transform a client's look in any number of ways—becoming more _____, more sophisticated, more professional or more _____-_____, just to name a few

MATCHING

Match the corresponding structure graphic and terms to their related fashion images.

○
_____
_____

○
_____
_____

○
_____
_____

○
_____
_____

JUMP START BOX

UNACTIVATED

UNACTIVATED/ACTIVATED

SHORTER INTERIOR/
LONGER EXTERIOR

EQUAL LENGTHS

RECTANGLE

OVAL

TRIANGLE

CIRCLE

A

B

C

D

LESSON CHALLENGE
Multiple choice. Indicate one correct answer for each question.

1. Sculpture transformation is all about changing the shape, surface texture and:
   a. detail
   b. structure
   c. color
   d. form line

2. At the basic level of observation, a hair sculpture can be identified by observing the outer boundary or silhouette known as the:
   a. detail
   b. structure
   c. texture
   d. form line

3. The surface appearance of hair is referred to as:
   a. texture
   b. density
   c. elasticity
   d. condition

4. When the hair is viewed abstractly as if it were projected at a 90° angle from the various curves of the head, it is referred to as:
   a. structure
   b. natural fall
   c. surface texture
   d. normal projection

5. The solid form is also known as a one-length cut, bob, Dutch boy, blunt cut or a:
   a. 90° haircut
   b. 45° haircut
   c. 0° haircut
   d. 60° haircut

6. In a graduated form, the line that divides the activated and unactivated textures is known as the:
   a. form line
   b. ridge line
   c. weight line
   d. perimeter line

7. The basic form that consists of shorter interior lengths that progress toward longer exterior lengths, is known as:
   a. solid
   b. graduated
   c. increase-layered
   d. uniformly layered

8. All of the following descriptions are true about the uniformly layered form EXCEPT:
   a. oval shape
   b. rounded shape
   c. activated texture
   d. same length throughout

9. The proportional relationship of each form within a combination produces the shape, texture and position of:
   a. color
   b. weight
   c. the interior
   d. the exterior

10. A change in hair sculpture can transform a client's look in any of the following ways EXCEPT:
    a. becoming more fit
    b. becoming more sporty
    c. becoming more professional
    d. becoming more sophisticated

LESSON CHALLENGE REFERENCES

Check your answers. Place a check mark next to the page number for any incorrect answer. On the lines, jot down topics that you still need to review.

1. PAGE 5 _____
2. PAGE 6 _____
3. PAGE 6 _____
4. PAGE 7 _____
5. PAGE 10 _____

6. PAGE 13 _____
7. PAGE 14 _____
8. PAGE 17 _____
9. PAGE 18 _____
10. PAGE 20 _____

▶ GROW WHAT YOU KNOW

Reflect on what you have learned and predict how this information will be used in the future.

105ᶜ.2 //
SCULPTURE TOOLS AND ESSENTIALS

ACHIEVE //

Following this lesson on *Sculpture Tools and Essentials*, you'll be able to:

» Describe the function of the five main sculpting tools

» Provide examples of supplies, products and equipment used to perform a hair sculpture

FOCUS //

SCULPTURE TOOLS AND ESSENTIALS

Shears

Taper Shears

Razors

Clippers

Combs

Sculpting Essentials

SCULPTING TOOLS: Sculpting tools are the hand-held tools used for cutting hair and require _____ after every use

SHEARS

Also known as: _____

Characteristics: _____

Primary Use: _____

PARTS OF THE SHEARS

Label the parts of shears

using this list:

Shank	Movable Blade
Tension Screw	Thumb Grip
Still Blade	Finger Grip
Finger Brace	

HOW TO HOLD THE SHEARS AND COMB

Insert ring finger to control _____ blade

Insert thumb to control _____ blade

Remove thumb and _____ shears to hold comb and shears in same hand

Alternative method of palming the shears is to rest shears on the _____ of the palm

Hold comb between _____ and _____

_____ of same hand; once hair is distributed, transfer comb to

_____ hand for sculpting

SCULPTING POSITIONS

	Palm Down	Palm Up	Palm-to-Palm	On Top of Fingers
POSITION				
COMMONLY USED FOR				

TAPER SHEARS

Also known as: _____

_____

Characteristics: 1 _____ blade, 1 _____ (serrated)
blade that holds the hair

_____

Primary Use: _____

_____

TYPES OF TAPER SHEARS

8 Teeth:	16 Teeth:	32 Teeth:	Channeling Shears: Wider notches produce dramatic _____ effects
_____	_____	_____	
_____	_____	_____	
_____	_____	_____	
_____	_____	_____	
_____	_____	_____	

RAZORS

May be used to sculpt entire form or to texturize within the form

Produces _____ or an angled effect on the end of each strand

When sculpting with a _____, it is essential that hair always be damp throughout.

PARTS OF THE RAZOR

Label the parts of razor

Blade	Handle
Guard	Tang
Shank	Shoulder

using this list:

HOW TO HOLD THE RAZOR

Foldable	Nonfoldable
_____	_____
_____	_____
_____	_____
_____	_____
_____	_____
_____	_____
_____	_____
_____	_____

CLIPPERS

Generally chosen to _____

Movable blade moves in a _____ -to- _____ motion as it sculpts the hair

PARTS OF THE CLIPPERS

ALERT!
Never use clipper blades that have broken teeth, and always align a new set of blades.

_____

_____

_____

HOW TO HOLD THE CLIPPERS

Position _____ over clippers and position

_____ on side of clippers

Alternative: Position _____ on top of clippers,

and position remaining fingers _____ clippers

COMBS

SHAMPOO	MASTER SKETCHER	CUTTING	TAPER/BARBER

MATCHING

Match the type of tool with its related function.

SCULPTING TOOL

1. SHEARS
2. TAPER SHEARS
3. RAZOR
4. CHANNELING SHEARS
6. CLIPPERS
7. MASTER SKETCHER COMB
8. TAPER COMB

FUNCTION

_____ Used for controlling larger amounts of hair with clipper-over-comb and shear-over-comb techniques

_____ Create a clean, blunt edge

_____ Allows you to sculpt as close to the scalp as possible while using shear-over-comb and clipper-over-comb techniques

_____ Produce clean, precise lines or a soft, broom-like effect

_____ Produces tapering or an angle effect on the end of each strand

_____ Produce dramatic chunky effects

_____ Produce alternation of short and long lengths; remove bulk

LESSON CHALLENGE   *Multiple choice. Indicate the correct answer for each question.*

1. Which finger should be placed in the finger grip to control the still blade when holding shears?
   a. ring
   b. pinky
   c. index
   d. thumb

2. To hold the comb and shears in the same hand without jeopardizing the client's safety, release the thumb grip and:
   a. close your palm over the shears
   b. close your fingers over the finger grip
   c. wrap your thumb around the finger grip
   d. wrap your fingers tightly around the blade

3. All of the following are sculpting positions EXCEPT:
   a. palm up
   b. palm down
   c. palm-to-palm
   d. hand-to-hand

4. When lifting the lengths on top of the head, you will need to sculpt the hair along which area of your fingers?
   a. the top
   b. the inside
   c. underneath
   d. the knuckle

5. Which of the following is true about the 32 teeth taper shears?
   a. create highly textured effects
   b. create lightly tapered effects
   c. produce dramatic chunky effects
   d. remove a minimal amount of hair within a parting

6. Channeling shears are primarily used for all of the following special effects EXCEPT:
   a. heavy fringes
   b. extreme length variations
   c. lightly tapered effects
   d. notched perimeter lengths

7. When sculpting with a razor, all of the following results are achieved EXCEPT:
   a. ends are tapered
   b. softer appearance to hair
   c. a diffused form line appears
   d. regular alternation of short and long lengths

8. When using clippers, the attachment that allows the hair to be sculpted at the same length is the:
   a. taper
   b. razor
   c. guard
   d. trimmer

9. As it sculpts the hair, the movable blade of the clippers moves:
   a. up and down
   b. to the left only
   c. to the right only
   d. from side to side

10. Which tool allows you to sculpt as close to the scalp as possible while using shear-over-comb and clipper-over-comb techniques?
    a. razor
    b. trimmer
    c. cutting comb
    d. taper/contour comb

LESSON CHALLENGE REFERENCES

Check your answers. Place a check mark next to the page number for any incorrect answer. On the lines, jot down topics that you still need to review.

1. PAGE 28_____
2. PAGE 28_____
3. PAGE 29_____
4. PAGE 29_____
5. PAGE 31_____

6. PAGE 31_____
7. PAGE 32_____
8. PAGE 34_____
9. PAGE 34_____
10. PAGE 36_____

▶ GROW WHAT YOU KNOW

Reflect on what you have learned and predict how this information will be used in the future.

105ᶜ.3 // SCULPTURE SKILLS

ACHIEVE //

Following this lesson on *Sculpture Skills*, you'll be able to:

» State the 7 Sculpting Procedures in the sequential order they are used to perform a hair sculpture

» Describe each of the 7 Sculpting Procedures

» List additional factors to consider when sculpting hair

FOCUS //

SCULPTURE SKILLS

The 7 Sculpting Procedures

Sculpting Considerations

THE 7 SCULPTING PROCEDURES

Unique system for producing predictable sculpture results

1.	5.
2.	6.
3.	7.
4.	

SECTION (1)

Many successful hair sculptures begin with _____.

Sectioning involves dividing the hair into _____ areas for the

purpose of _____.

The _____ of sections and types of sectioning _____

depend on the type of hair sculpture being created.

REFERENCE POINTS OF THE HEAD

Label the reference points of the head using this list:

CREST AREA
NAPE
INTERIOR
BACK
CROWN
EXTERIOR
SIDE
TOP
FRINGE AREA
APEX
OCCIPITAL

A. _____   G. _____

B. _____   H. _____

C. _____   I. _____

D. _____   J. _____

E. _____   K. _____

F. _____   L. _____

HEAD POSITION (2)

Actively positioning the client's head is an important part of the sculpting process.

The head position directly influences the _____ of the hair, which

affects the _____ and _____ of the sculpted line.

Upright	Forward	Tilted
•	•	•

PART (3)

Partings are lines that subdivide sections of hair in order to _____,

_____ and _____ the hair while sculpting.

List the 6 common parting lines:

1. _____   4. _____

2. _____   5. _____

3. _____   6. _____

Concave lines curve _____, like the inside of a sphere, while

convex lines curve _____, like the outside of a sphere.

The celestial axis is a symbol used to identify straight and curved lines, directions and projection angles.

DRAW IN THE PARTING LINES

Horizontal

Vertical

Diagonal Back

Diagonal Forward

DISTRIBUTE (4)

Distribution is the direction hair is combed in relation to its base parting.

4 TYPES OF DISTRIBUTION *(Draw in the distribution lines.)*

1. NATURAL

Draw natural distribution from horizontal and diagonal partings.

- Direction the hair assumes as it _____ _____ due to gravity
- Used from horizontal and _____ partings
- Primarily used to create _____ _____

2. PERPENDICULAR

Draw perpendicular distribution from horizontal, diagonal and vertical partings.

- Hair is combed at a _____ angle from its base parting
- Used from horizontal, _____ or _____ partings
- Primarily used to sculpt _____ and _____ forms

3. SHIFTED

Draw shifted distribution from horizontal, diagonal and vertical partings.

- Hair is combed out of _____ _____ in any direction except _____ to its base parting
- Used when sculpting most forms except _____
- Generally used for exaggerated _____ _____ and _____ within form

4. DIRECTIONAL

Draw directional distribution from curved partings.

- Hair is distributed _____ _____, _____ _____ or _____ _____ from the curve of the head
- Results in length _____ due to the curve of the head
- Used in **planar sculpting** technique

A technique in which the hair is sculpted along _____ and _____ planes

PROJECT (5)

Projection, also known as _____, is the angle at which the hair is held in relation to the _____ of the head prior to and while sculpting.

Identify the projection angles.

PROJECTION ANGLES

Most common projection angles in hair sculpting are _____, _____ and _____.

LOW PROJECTION: _____ – _____.

MEDIUM PROJECTION: _____ – _____.

HIGH PROJECTION: _____ – _____.

Projecting below 90° produces _____

Angles 90° and above begin to _____ hair and diminish _____.

PROJECTION ANGLE DIFFERENCES

SOLID FORM
- _____ projection or _____ _____; neither lifted away nor moved toward the scalp

GRADUATED FORM
- Most common projection angle is _____
- The _____ the projection angle, the _____ the amount of graduated texture

INCREASE-LAYERED FORM
- A _____, _____ or _____ projection angle is used
- Projection angle of the _____ design line is most important because it establishes where all lengths converge

UNIFORMLY LAYERED FORM
- Projection angle used is _____ from the curve of the head
- Also called _____ _____

FINGER/SHEAR POSITION (6)

Refers to the position of the fingers and the shears relative to the

_____ _____

 PARALLEL

 NONPARALLEL

* Fingers are positioned at an

_____ distance away

from the parting

* Results in _____

reflection of chosen line

* Also known as _____

_____

* Fingers are positioned

_____ away from

the parting

* Used to create exaggerated

_____ increases, to

blend between _____

lengths

DESIGN LINE (7)

A design line is the artistic _____ or _____ guide

used while sculpting

**2 TYPES OF
DESIGN LINES**

STATIONARY

* A _____ guide to which all lengths are directed

* Used for progression of lengths in _____ _____

* Used to sculpt _____ and _____-_____

forms and to achieve a _____ _____ in graduated

forms

MOBILE

* A _____ guide; sometimes called a traveling guide

* Small amount of previously sculpted hair used as a _____

_____ to sculpt subsequent partings

* Used to sculpt _____ and _____ forms and

_____ combination forms

*Indicate line
opposite original
parting pattern:*

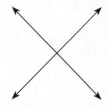

Cross-checking: _____

_____

_____

_____

SCULPTING CONSIDERATIONS

Important to check your work and enhance final results

GROWTH PATTERNS

- Adapt sculpting techniques to accommodate the natural growth patterns

- Natural growth patterns are determined by the angle and direction in which the hair grows out of the scalp

WIDOW'S PEAK	COWLICK	WHORL

FRINGE AND NAPE VARIATIONS

Fringe: _____

_____

_____

_____

Nape: _____

_____

_____

_____

CURLY HAIR CONSIDERATIONS

- Consider how hair will be worn naturally _____ or _____

  _____

- Consider using a comb versus fingers. Why? _____

  _____

  _____

List the advantages of sculpting hair dry:

-

-

-

THINKING MAP

Create a Thinking Map to help yourself make sense of how your notes fit together. Use words in the Jump Start Box as well as your own words and pictures to make a visual that will help you connect the important ideas of this lesson. Be creative!

LESSON CHALLENGE   *Multiple choice. Indicate the correct answer for each question.*

1. **The term used to describe dividing the hair into workable areas for control is:**
   a. designing
   b. texturizing
   c. sectioning
   d. positioning

2. **The apex refers to what part of the head?**
   a. occipital
   b. crest area
   c. crown area
   d. highest point

3. **When performing a hair sculpture, which of the following determines the size of the parting?**
   a. color
   b. length
   c. texture
   d. density

4. **What type of distribution results in a 90° angle from its base parting?**
   a. shifted
   b. parallel
   c. nonparallel
   d. perpendicular

5. What term, also known as elevation, is the angle at which the hair is held in relation to the curve of the head prior to sculpting?
   a. distribution
   b. projection
   c. texturizing
   d. cross-checking

6. Which of the following angles is considered to represent low projection (elevation)?
   a. 0° to 30°
   b. 30° to 60°
   c. 90° to 180°
   d. 60° to 90°

7. Projecting the hair below 90° would:
   a. build weight
   b. remove bulk
   c. remove weight
   d. shorten lengths

8. An angle of 45° would be considered what type of projection?
   a. low
   b. high
   c. medium
   d. very high

9. What type of form would result from using a 45° projection?
   a. solid
   b. graduated
   c. increase-layered
   d. uniformly layered

10. The projection angle used to create the arrangement of hair lengths that are the same throughout the head is:
    a. 0°
    b. 30°
    c. 45°
    d. 90°

11. With a parallel finger and shear position, the fingers are positioned:
    a. unequal distance away from the parting
    b. equal distance away from the parting
    c. one half the distance from the parting
    d. one fourth the distance from the parting

12. A design line that is used as a length guide for sculpting uniformly layered forms is referred to as:
    a. stable
    b. curved
    c. mobile
    d. stationary

13. Which of the following terms identifies the technique used to check the accuracy of a hair sculpture by using the opposite parting pattern?
    a. parting
    b. sectioning
    c. texturizing
    d. cross-checking

14. An uneven effect is created when sculpting curly hair that is:
    a. completely wet
    b. completely dry
    c. chemically treated
    d. partly wet and partly dry

LESSON CHALLENGE REFERENCES

Check your answers. Place a check mark next to the page number for any incorrect answer. On the lines, jot down topics that you still need to review.

1. PAGE 44 _____
2. PAGE 45 _____
3. PAGE 47 _____
4. PAGE 48 _____
5. PAGE 49 _____
6. PAGE 49 _____
7. PAGE 49 _____
8. PAGE 49 _____
9. PAGE 49 _____
10. PAGE 49 _____
11. PAGE 50 _____
12. PAGE 50 _____
13. PAGE 50 _____
14. PAGE 53 _____

▶ GROW WHAT YOU KNOW

Reflect on what you have learned and predict how this information will be used in the future.

105ᶜ.4 //
SCULPTURE GUEST EXPERIENCE

ACHIEVE //

Following this lesson on *Sculpture Guest Experience*, you'll be able to:

>> Summarize the service essentials related to hair sculpture

>> Provide examples of how to reassure or calm a child during a sculpting service

>> Provide examples of infection control and safety guidelines for sculpture services

FOCUS //

SCULPTURE GUEST EXPERIENCE

Sculpture Service Essentials

Children as Clients

Sculpture Infection Control and Safety

SCULPTURE SERVICE ESSENTIALS

CONNECT

Make a memorable impression on your client.

Two guidelines for welcoming a client:

-
-

CONSULT

Ask client about:

-
-
-

Analyze client's:

-
-
-

Assess:

-
-
- Visualize the end result

Explain:

-
-

Gain Feedback

-

CREATE

During Shampoo Service:

-
-

During Sculpture Service:

-
-

Explain and Teach:

-
-

COMPLETE

Request feedback and look for cues:

-
-

Escort client to the retail area:

-
-
-
-

CHILDREN AS CLIENTS

Some children need to be treated more carefully to help alleviate their fears and concerns.

A FEW SIMPLE STEPS FOR WORKING WITH CHILDREN

- Kneel down; make _____ _____

- Introduce yourself and explain what is about to take place

- Take child by hand if parent and child allow

- Maintain _____ and_____ contact while performing service

- Use visuals

- Offer a _____ for cooperation

- Know salon policy regarding unaccompanied minors requesting a service

SCULPTURE INFECTION CONTROL AND SAFETY

CLEANING

- _____ dirt and debris

- _____ growth of pathogens

DISINFECTION

- Does not kill _____

CLEANING AND DISINFECTION GUIDELINES

	SHEARS	RAZOR	CLIPPERS	COMBS
CLEAN	• Remove _____ and debris • Preclean with _____ and _____	• Discard blade after use in _____ _____ _____ • Preclean with soap and water	• •	• Remove _____ and debris • Preclean with _____ and _____
DISINFECT (with approved EPA-registered disinfectant)	•	• Solution, wipes or spray • Immerse _____ without _____	• Solution or _____ • Be guided by clipper manufacturer's directions for _____	•

PLASTIC/CLOTH CAPE

- Remove _____ from cape

- Wash in washing machine with _____ after each use

- Some regulatory agencies may require use of an approved EPA-registered disinfectant

NECK STRIP

- _____ after use

CARE AND SAFETY

PERSONAL CARE

- Minimize spread of _____ _____.

- Minimize fatigue during service by maintaining _____ _____.

CLIENT CARE PRIOR TO THE SERVICE

- Check scalp for _____ _____.

- Protect client's skin and clothing with a freshly laundered towel and _____ _____.

CLIENT CARE DURING THE SERVICE

- Be cautious and avoid nicking _____ _____.

- If you cut the client, stop service and apply _____ _____.

SALON CARE

- Ensure electrical cords are properly positioned to _____ _____.

- Sweep or vacuum and dispose of hair clippings at the _____ _____.

MATCHING

Match the service essential in the left column to its matching phrase in the right column.

1. CONNECT

2. CONSULT

3. CREATE

4. COMPLETE

_____ Ensure your client is protected by draping with a towel and plastic cape during the shampoo process.

_____ "What do you like, or dislike, about your previous haircut?"

_____ Analyze your client's face and body shape, physical features, hair and scalp.

_____ Escort client to the retail area and show the products you used.

_____ Build rapport and develop a relationship with the client.

_____ Perform a scalp massage to relax the client while shampooing their hair.

_____ Ask questions and look for verbal and nonverbal cues to determine your client's level of satisfaction.

_____ Meet and greet the client with a firm handshake.

_____ Personalize the hair sculpture after you air form the hair to add your signature touch!

_____ Explain to your client the products you are using throughout the service and why.

_____ Explain the cost and maintenance associated with all services.

_____ "Would you like layers in your hair?"

LESSON CHALLENGE *Multiple choice. Indicate the correct answer for each question.*

1. Communicating with your client prior to and during the service will help you avoid misunderstandings and ensure:
   a. predictable results
   b. a proper shampoo treatment
   c. their friends will give them compliments
   d. the sculpture is completed in a timely manner

2. All of the following are guidelines to follow during the Connect sculpture service essential EXCEPT:
   a. build rapport
   b. greet client with a firm handshake
   c. ask questions to discover client needs
   d. greet client with a pleasant tone of voice

3. Which of the following guidelines is used during the Consult sculpture service essential?
   a. complete a client record
   b. perform a scalp massage to relax the client
   c. communicate to develop a connection with the client
   d. ask specific questions such as "would you like your ears exposed?"

4. Teaching the client how to perform at-home hair care maintenance is important during which sculpture service essential?
   a. Create
   b. Consult
   c. Connect
   d. Complete

5. In order to determine your client's level of satisfaction, request feedback and look for:
   a. your tip
   b. your next client
   c. verbal and nonverbal cues
   d. approval from staff members

6. All of the following are ways to reassure or calm a child during a sculpting service EXCEPT:
   a. offering a reward
   b. using fun language
   c. asking them to keep quiet
   d. kneeling down to make eye contact

7. To keep a child from squirming, remind them that squirming may cause you to:
   a. cut yourself
   b. cut him or her
   c. never do their hair again
   d. tell their parents they were misbehaving

8. If an older child comes into the salon without a parent, consider:
   a. calling the parent first
   b. offering them the latest trends
   c. reducing the cost of the service
   d. having them sign a release form

9. All of the following are methods used to disinfect tools and equipment EXCEPT:
   a. rinse
   b. spray
   c. immersion
   d. disinfectant wipes

10. What is the first step in cleaning combs and brushes?
    a. remove hair and debris
    b. scrub with soap and water
    c. immerse in soap and water
    d. immerse in a disinfectant solution

LESSON CHALLENGE REFERENCES

Check your answers. Place a check mark next to the page number for any incorrect answer. On the lines, jot down topics that you still need to review.

1. PAGE 57 _____
2. PAGE 58 _____
3. PAGE 58 _____
4. PAGE 59 _____
5. PAGE 59 _____

6. PAGE 60 _____
7. PAGE 60 _____
8. PAGE 60 _____
9. PAGE 65 _____
10. PAGE 65 _____

▶ GROW WHAT YOU KNOW

Reflect on what you have learned and predict how this information will be used in the future.

105ᶜ.6 // SOLID FORM OVERVIEW

ACHIEVE //

Following this lesson on *Solid Form Overview*, you'll be able to:

» Identify the characteristics of solid form

» Provide examples of the 7 Sculpting Procedures related to solid form

» Give examples of guidelines to follow when sculpting solid form

» Provide fringe design variations that can be incorporated into solid form sculptures

FOCUS //

SOLID FORM OVERVIEW

Solid Form Characteristics

Solid Form Sculpting Procedures

Solid Form Guidelines

SOLID FORM CHARACTERISTICS

Solid form is also known as a blunt cut, one-length cut or a bob.

SHAPE

RECTANGULAR

STRAIGHT	ADDED TEXTURE
•	•
•	

TEXTURE

Unactivated with smooth, unbroken lines on the _____

Added texture causes the solid form to appear _____ and is a result of the _____ _____, not the sculpted form

STRUCTURE

Lengths progress from shorter at the _____ to longer in the _____

Weight is created at the perimeter form line in _____ _____

Color coded _____

Draw in the structure of solid form.

SOLID FORM SCULPTING PROCEDURES

SECTION (1)

Section hair for _____
Section hair between _____ _____ _____

HEAD POSITION (2)

Generally upright

Can be tilted forward when _____ nape hairline

PART (3)

Parallel to the design line

Draw in the solid form partings.

HORIZONTAL   DIAGONAL FORWARD   DIAGONAL BACK   CONCAVE   CONVEX

DISTRIBUTE (4)

NATURAL DISTRIBUTION

- Pay particular attention to the area above the _____

- Minimal _____

- _____

PROJECT (5)

Draw in the projection of natural fall.

Draw in the projection of 0°.

NATURAL FALL

-

0°

-

-

Maintain natural fall or 0° and avoid lifting the hair, which creates graduation.

Draw in the result of projection.

FINGER/SHEAR POSITION (6)

-

Hair can be controlled with fingers, a comb or the hand.

1.

2.

3.

4.

DESIGN LINE (7)

A stationary design line is used to sculpt solid forms.

The design line establishes the _____ _____

_____.

Draw in the solid form design lines.

HORIZONTAL   DIAGONAL FORWARD   DIAGONAL BACK   CONCAVE   CONVEX

All partings are distributed to the stationary design line.

SOLID FORM GUIDELINES

TENSION

Whether sculpting on straight or curly hair, too much tension will result in a

_____ _____.

Variations in the hairline and the protrusion of the ears can cause

_____ _____.

COMB CONTROL

·

·

FREEFORM

Another way to avoid tension when sculpting solid forms is to use freeform sculpting techniques.

CURLY HAIR

Appears much longer when tension is used.

Overlapping technique:_____

_____

Dry sculpting:_____

_____

LONGER LENGTHS

Turn the client's head and sculpt the sides either in front or in back of the

_____.

To create a horizontal line with a slight increase toward the sides, shift the hair

toward the _____.

SOLID FORM FRINGE VARIATIONS

Draw in the solid form fringe variation techniques.

DRAWING

Draw a picture or a symbol representing the possibilities for each procedure when sculpting a solid form.

1. SECTION

2. HEAD POSITION

3. PART

4. DISTRIBUTE

5. PROJECT

6. FINGER/SHEAR POSITION

7. DESIGN LINE

LESSON CHALLENGE
Multiple choice. Indicate one correct answer for each question.

1. Which of the following is NOT a characteristic of the solid form?
   a. interior activation
   b. unactivated texture
   c. maximum perimeter weight
   d. lengths fall to the same level

2. Solid form sculptures can be created along the following lines EXCEPT:
   a. convex
   b. vertical
   c. diagonal
   d. horizontal

3. Where are the shortest lengths found in the solid form?
   a. apex
   b. crown
   c. interior
   d. exterior

4. In natural fall, all lengths in the solid form fall to the same:
   a. level
   b. angle
   c. space
   d. guide

5. Generally, the parting pattern for the solid form is parallel to the:
   a. comb
   b. shears
   c. design line
   d. sectioning line

6. The distribution used to sculpt solid form is:
   a. natural
   b. shifted
   c. directional
   d. perpendicular

7. Which of the following projection angles are used to sculpt solid form?
   a. 0° and 45°
   b. 45° and 90°
   c. natural fall and 0°
   d. natural fall and 45°

8. What type of design line is used to sculpt solid form?
   a. mobile
   b. natural
   c. multiple
   d. stationary

9. What can cause a graduated appearance to occur over the ear when sculpting solid forms?
   a. tension
   b. no projection
   c. comb control
   d. freeform sculpting

10. The technique of sculpting each parting slightly longer as you work up the head is known as:
    a. blunt
    b. overlapping
    c. comb control
    d. cross-checking

LESSON CHALLENGE REFERENCES

Check your answers. Place a check mark next to the page number for any incorrect answer. On the lines, jot down topics that you still need to review.

1. PAGE 86 _____
2. PAGE 87 _____
3. PAGE 88 _____
4. PAGE 88 _____
5. PAGE 89 _____

6. PAGE 90 _____
7. PAGE 91 _____
8. PAGE 93 _____
9. PAGE 93 _____
10. PAGE 94 _____

▶ GROW WHAT YOU KNOW

Reflect on what you have learned and predict how this information will be used in the future.

105ᶜ.9 //
GRADUATED
FORM OVERVIEW

ACHIEVE //

Following this lesson on *Graduated Form Overview*, you'll be able to:

» Identify the characteristics of graduated form

» Identify the 7 Sculpting Procedures related to graduated form

» Provide fringe design variations that can be incorporated into graduated form sculptures

FOCUS //

GRADUATED FORM OVERVIEW

Graduated Form Characteristics

Graduated Form Sculpting Procedures

Graduated Form Guidelines

GRADUATED FORM CHARACTERISTICS

Graduated form is also known as a wedge, stacked bob, modern bob.

SHAPE

Identify/draw the triangular shape of each illustration.

Overall shape of the graduated form is _____ .

Shape is influenced by degree of _____ .

Weight is created above the perimeter _____ _____ .

TEXTURE

Interior: _____

Ridge line

Exterior: _____

STRUCTURE

Exterior lengths are _____ .

Interior lengths are _____ .

Ends stack up along an angle in _____ _____ .

Progression varies in _____ , _____ and

_____ graduated forms.

Color coded _____

GRADUATED FORM SCULPTING PROCEDURES

SECTION (1)

Section hair for _____ . Section hair when the _____

_____ or _____ changes.

HEAD POSITION (2)

Generally upright. Can be tilted forward.

PART (3)

Parallel to the _____ _____ .

Draw in the graduated form partings and resulting form line.

HORIZONTAL   DIAGONAL FORWARD   DIAGONAL BACK

A diagonal finger position is used with _____ _____ .

DISTRIBUTE (4)

NATURAL	PERPENDICULAR	DIRECTIONAL
•	•	•
	•	•
	•	•

PROJECT (5)

Projection for graduated form is measured from _____ .

Lower projection angles create _____ graduation and higher projection angles produce _____ graduation.

Identify the angle for low, medium and high projection.

90°

45°

0°

_____

_____

_____

_____

_____

_____

LINE OF INCLINATION
Identify the line of inclination.

LOW PROJECTION	MEDIUM PROJECTION	HIGH PROJECTION
•	•	•
•	•	•
•	•	•

FINGER/SHEAR POSITION (6)

PARALLEL	NONPARALLEL
•	•
•	•
•	•
	•
	•

DESIGN LINE (7)

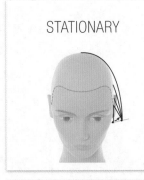

STATIONARY

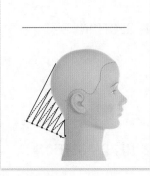

_____

_____

Any line from the celestial axis may be used to sculpt graduation.

GRADUATED FORM GUIDELINES

CROSS-CHECKING

SOFTENING THE WEIGHT AREA

PRESSURE GRADUATION

GRADUATED FORM FRINGE VARIATIONS

Identify and draw the types of fringes.

- _____
- _____
- _____

- _____
- _____
- _____

- _____
- _____
- _____

DRAWING

Draw a picture or a symbol representing the possibilities for each procedure when sculpting a graduated form.

1. SECTION

2. HEAD POSITION

3. PART

4. DISTRIBUTE

5. PROJECT

6. FINGER/SHEAR POSITION

7. DESIGN LINE

LESSON CHALLENGE *Multiple choice. Indicate one correct answer for each question.*

1. The shape of a graduated form is:
   a. oval
   b. round
   c. triangular
   d. rectangular

2. The weight in a graduated form is positioned:
   a. low
   b. high
   c. at the perimeter form line
   d. above the perimeter form line

3. The line that visually separates activated and unactivated textures in a graduated form is called the:
   a. form line
   b. ridge line
   c. inclination
   d. perimeter line

4. The visual contrast between textures in graduated form is reduced when sculpted on what type of hair?
   a. fine
   b. wavy
   c. thick
   d. straight

5. When sculpting graduated texture from horizontal and diagonal partings, natural distribution must be combined with:
   a. projection
   b. natural fall
   c. parallel finger position
   d. perpendicular distribution

6. When sculpting graduated forms, projection angles are measured from:
   a. a comb
   b. natural fall
   c. body position
   d. finger position

7. Which of the following projection angles is used to create medium graduation?
   a. above 0°, below 30°
   b. above 30°, below 60°
   c. above 60°, below 90°
   d. above 90°, below 120°

8. In most instances, which of the following finger/shear positions is used to sculpt graduation from horizontal or diagonal partings?
   a. parallel
   b. vertical
   c. curved
   d. nonparallel

9. Graduation can be created by using a vertical parting pattern and positioning your fingers along the intended:
   a. weight line
   b. perimeter form line
   c. line of inclination
   d. interior design line

10. Which of the following design lines is used to build a weight area in a graduated form?
    a. mobile
    b. vertical
    c. diagonal
    d. stationary

LESSON CHALLENGE REFERENCES

Check your answers. Place a check mark next to the page number for any incorrect answer. On the lines, jot down topics that you still need to review.

1. PAGE 117 _____
2. PAGE 118 _____
3. PAGE 118 _____
4. PAGE 118 _____
5. PAGE 121 _____
6. PAGE 122 _____
7. PAGE 122 _____
8. PAGE 124 _____
9. PAGE 124 _____
10. PAGE 125 _____

▶ GROW WHAT YOU KNOW

Reflect on what you have learned and predict how this information will be used in the future.

105°.12 //
INCREASE-LAYERED FORM OVERVIEW

ACHIEVE //

Following this lesson on *Increase-Layered Form Overview*, you'll be able to:

>> Identify the characteristics of increase-layered form

>> Identify the 7 Sculpting Procedures related to increase-layered form

>> Give examples of multiple design lines used to sculpt increase-layered forms

>> Provide perimeter design options used to customize increase-layered forms

FOCUS //

INCREASE-LAYERED FORM OVERVIEW

Increase-Layered Form Characteristics

Increase-Layered Form Sculpting Procedures

Increase-Layered Form Guidelines

INCREASE-LAYERED FORM CHARACTERISTICS

Increased-layered form may comprise the entire form or a component of a design.

SHAPE

Identify the oval shape in the image.

- Elongated/oval

- No buildup of _____

- No area of accentuated

   _____

TEXTURE

- Activated with visible hair ends that do not stack on each other

- Longer interior lengths result in a combination of textures

- Accentuated in _____ or _____ hair

STRUCTURE

Shorter _____ progresses to longer _____

Shorter interior lengths create _____

INCREASE-LAYERED FORM SCULPTING PROCEDURES

SECTION (1)

Subdivided into two sections from a _____ or

_____ part

HEAD POSITION (2)

Generally upright; can be tilted forward

PART/DISTRIBUTE (3/4)

Draw in the parting pattern and distribution. Identify the resulting texture.

| vertical | horizontal | diagonal forward | diagonal back |

Most common type of distribution is _____

PROJECT (5)

Stationary design line is usually projected at _____

- Stationary design line establishes the location to which all other lengths are

  _____.

- Projection angle can vary to either increase or decrease the distance that

  lengths _____.

FINGER/SHEAR POSITION (6)

PARALLEL	NONPARALLEL
Horizontal: • Vertical: •	•

Another technique used to sculpt increase-layered texture is

_____ _____

DESIGN LINE (7)

Any line from celestial axis; _____

The most common technique used to sculpt increase layering is

_____ _____

INCREASE-LAYERED FORM GUIDELINES

CUSTOMIZING THE PERIMETER DESIGN LINES

Draw examples of customizing the perimeter design lines and identify the achieved effect.

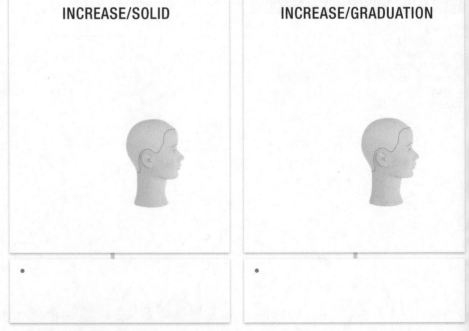

INCREASE/SOLID	INCREASE/GRADUATION
•	•

DRAWING

Draw a picture or a symbol representing the possibilities for each procedure when sculpting an increase-layered form.

1. SECTION

2. HEAD POSITION

3. PART

4. DISTRIBUTE

5. PROJECT

6. FINGER/SHEAR POSITION

7. DESIGN LINE

LESSON CHALLENGE *Multiple choice. Indicate one correct answer for each question.*

1. The shape or silhouette of the increase-layered form resembles which of the following shapes?
   a. oval
   b. round
   c. triangular
   d. rectangular

2. When interior increase layers are sculpted at longer lengths, the resulting texture of the hair sculpture will be:
   a. totally activated
   b. totally unactivated
   c. activated in the interior only
   d. a combination of unactivated and activated

3. The shortest lengths in an increase-layered form are found in the:
   a. nape
   b. interior
   c. directional
   d. perpendicular

4. The most common type of distribution used to sculpt increase-layered forms is:
   a. shifted
   b. natural
   c. directional
   d. perpendicular

5. When sculpting an increase-layered form, which parting pattern positions layered texture equally around the head?
   a. convex
   b. vertical
   c. concave
   d. horizontal

6. When a diagonal-forward perimeter is desired when sculpting increase-layered form, which parting pattern should be used?
   a. vertical
   b. horizontal
   c. diagonal back
   d. diagonal forward

7. The projection angle of the stationary design line is most important because it establishes the location to which all other lengths are:
   a. etched
   b. notched
   c. converged
   d. manipulated

8. The finger position used to conserve the most length when sculpting increase layers is:
   a. parallel
   b. nonparallel
   c. stationary
   d. perpendicular

9. The most common technique used to sculpt increase-layered forms is:
   a. notching
   b. razor etching
   c. conversion layering
   d. a mobile design line

10. If weight is desired at the perimeter of an increase-layered form, sculpt the perimeter design line in:
    a. natural fall
    b. normal projection
    c. increasing lengths
    d. decreasing lengths

LESSON CHALLENGE REFERENCES

Check your answers. Place a check mark next to the page number for any incorrect answer. On the lines, jot down topics that you still need to review.

1. PAGE 146 _____
2. PAGE 146 _____
3. PAGE 146 _____
4. PAGE 147 _____
5. PAGE 147 _____

6. PAGE 147 _____
7. PAGE 148 _____
8. PAGE 148 _____
9. PAGE 149 _____
10. PAGE 150 _____

▶ GROW WHAT YOU KNOW

Reflect on what you have learned and predict how this information will be used in the future.

105ᶜ.15 //
UNIFORMLY LAYERED FORM OVERVIEW

ACHIEVE //

Following this lesson on *Uniformly Layered Form Overview*, you'll be able to:

>> Identify the characteristics of uniformly layered form

>> Explain the 7 Sculpting Procedures related to uniformly layered form

>> Give examples of sculpting guidelines for uniformly layered form

FOCUS //

UNIFORMLY LAYERED FORM OVERVIEW

Uniformly Layered Form Characteristics

Uniformly Layered Form Sculpting Procedures

Uniformly Layered Form Guidelines

UNIFORMLY LAYERED FORM CHARACTERISTICS

Layered cut, or 90° angle cut

SHAPE

Identify/draw the round shape in this picture.

- Round
- No _____
- Parallels the curve of the _____

TEXTURE

- Totally _____
- Curl patterns, whether natural or chemically altered, will accentuate the surface texture adding _____ and _____.

STRUCTURE

All lengths are _____.

Draw in the structure graphic.

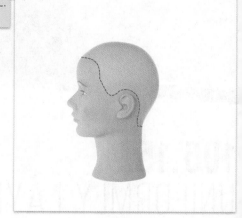

UNIFORMLY LAYERED FORM SCULPTING PROCEDURES

SECTION (1)

Section hair for _____.

HEAD POSITION (2)

Generally upright; can be tilted forward when _____ nape

PART (3)

Draw in and identify the uniformly layered form partings.

HORIZONTAL

VERTICAL AND/OR PIVOTAL

TOP

SIDES/BACK

FRONT

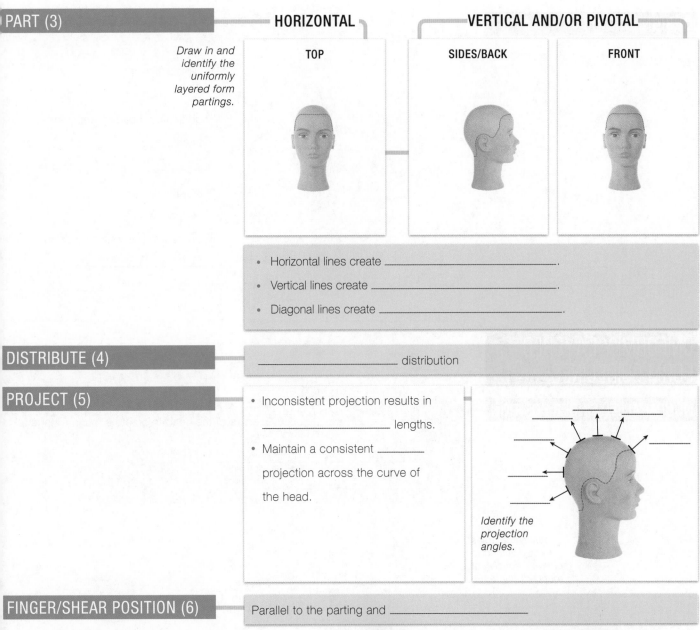

- Horizontal lines create _____.
- Vertical lines create _____.
- Diagonal lines create _____.

DISTRIBUTE (4)

_____ distribution

PROJECT (5)

- Inconsistent projection results in _____ lengths.
- Maintain a consistent _____ projection across the curve of the head.

Identify the projection angles.

FINGER/SHEAR POSITION (6)

Parallel to the parting and _____

Identify the palm position.

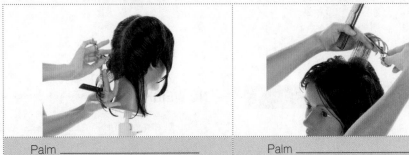

Palm _____

Palm _____

DESIGN LINE (7)

A _____ design line is used to sculpt uniformly layered forms.

Draw in the design line.

1. Sculpt design line.

2. Each sculpted parting becomes a new _____ _____ for the next parting.

3. Keep design line visible by using _____ _____

UNIFORMLY LAYERED FORM GUIDELINES

NONPARALLEL FINGER POSITION

Adapt for _____ areas of the head to create a round silhouette.

- _____ _____

   _____

Identify the areas to be adjusted to achieve a consistent rounded silhouette.

FORM VARIATIONS

NO WEIGHT

- Sculpt design line in _____ _____
- Design line is guide

NO WEIGHT (CONT'D)

Draw in the structure graphic based on the related technique.

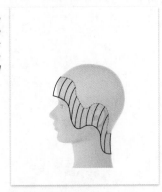 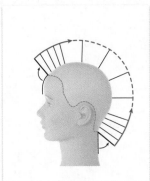 

MORE WEIGHT

- Larger _____ section
- Weight _____ is guide

Draw in the structure graphic based on the related technique.

 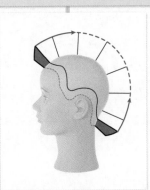 

ADD WEIGHT AND DEFINE FORM LINE

- Sculpt all lengths at _____
- Sculpt _____ last

Draw in the structure graphic based on the related technique.

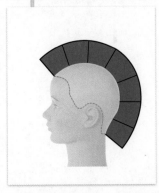 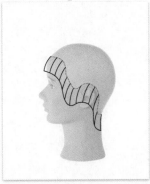 

TIGHTLY CURLED HAIR

Advanced technique, referred to as _____

_____

DRAWING

Draw a picture or a symbol representing the possibilities for each procedure when sculpting a uniformly layered form.

1. SECTION

2. HEAD POSITION

3. PART

4. DISTRIBUTE

5. PROJECT

6. FINGER/SHEAR POSITION

7. DESIGN LINE

LESSON CHALLENGE *Multiple choice. Indicate the correct answer for each question.*

1. **Which of the following describes the lengths of the uniformly layered form?**
   a. progress from shorter to longer
   b. progress from longer to shorter
   c. lengths are uneven
   d. lengths are all equal

2. **Which parting pattern creates the appearance of weight in a uniformly layered form?**
   a. pivotal
   b. diagonal
   c. vertical
   d. horizontal

3. **What type of distribution is used to sculpt uniform lengths?**
   a. natural
   b. shifted
   c. directional
   d. perpendicular

4. **Which projection angle is used to sculpt the uniformly layered form?**
   a. natural fall
   b. 0°
   c. 45°
   d. 90°

5. **What can be done while sculpting shorter uniform lengths to maintain equal distance from the head?**
   a. change palm position
   b. project lengths at the opposite angle
   c. visually assess lengths in natural fall
   d. extend little finger and rest it on the scalp

6. **What type of design line is used to sculpt uniform lengths?**
   a. mobile
   b. stationary
   c. combination
   d. multiple stationary

7. **When sculpting uniformly layered lengths, the design line should remain:**
   a. visible
   b. vertical
   c. horizontal
   d. stationary

8. **Which of the following can be done to establish more weight along the perimeter hairline when sculpting a uniformly layered form?**
   a. sculpt perimeter at a 45° projection angle
   b. sculpt perimeter at a 90° projection angle
   c. sculpt perimeter using shifted distribution
   d. sculpt larger perimeter section in natural fall first

9. **Which of the following statements is true when sculpting uniformly layered forms with tighter curl patterns?**
   a. the curl pattern will appear looser
   b. the curl pattern will appear more straight
   c. the hair will appear longer after sculpting
   d. the hair will appear shorter after sculpting

10. **An advanced technique used when sculpting uniform layers on tightly curled hair is called:**
    a. refine
    b. freeform
    c. stretching
    d. customizing

LESSON CHALLENGE REFERENCES

Check your answers. Place a check mark next to the page number for any incorrect answer. On the lines, jot down topics that you still need to review.

1. PAGE 169 _____
2. PAGE 170 _____
3. PAGE 171 _____
4. PAGE 171 _____
5. PAGE 172 _____

6. PAGE 172 _____
7. PAGE 172 _____
8. PAGE 173 _____
9. PAGE 174 _____
10. PAGE 174 _____

▶ GROW WHAT YOU KNOW

Reflect on what you have learned and predict how this information will be used in the future.

105^c.19 //
TEXTURIZING TECHNIQUES

ACHIEVE //

Following this lesson on *Texturizing Techniques*, you'll be able to:

>> Identify where texturizing can occur along the strand

>> List three categories of texturizing techniques

>> Provide examples of client-centered guidelines for texturizing

FOCUS //

TEXTURIZING TECHNIQUES

Texturizing Areas of the Strand

Texturizing Categories

Client-Centered Guidelines for Texturizing

Texturizing is also known as _____ or _____

SCULPTING SHORTER LENGTHS WITHIN THE FORM TO:

-
-
-
-
-

VARIETY OF TOOLS:

-
-
-
-

TEXTURIZING AREAS OF THE STRAND

TEXTURIZING MAY BE PERFORMED AT ANY OF THE 3 AREAS OF THE HAIRSTRAND:

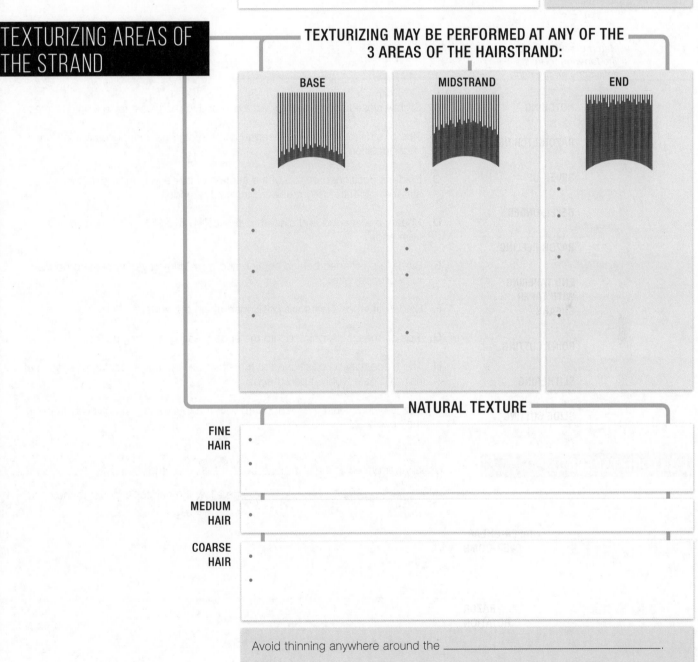

BASE

-
-
-
-

MIDSTRAND

-
-
-
-

END

-
-
-

NATURAL TEXTURE

FINE HAIR
-
-

MEDIUM HAIR
-

COARSE HAIR
-
-

Avoid thinning anywhere around the _____.

TEXTURIZING CATEGORIES

Three main categories of texturizing:

1.

2.

3.

FORM LINE TAPERING

Also known as: _____

Texturizing the ends of the hair along the form line:

•

•

Match the types of form line tapering to their definitions on the right.

NOTCHING	
RAZOR ETCHING	
BEVEL-UP	
BEVEL-UNDER	
RAZOR PEELING	
END TAPERING WITH TAPER SHEARS	
POINT CUTTING	
SLITHERING	
SLIDE CUTTING	

A. Slightly closed shears slide down the strand to produce a rapid length increase.

B. Tips of straight shears are inserted into the strands and movement is from finger position toward ends.

C. Blade is positioned on top of the section of hair and is moved in curved strokes; produces slight upward turn of the ends.

D. Shears are opened and closed rhythmically while sliding blades upward from ends.

E. Blade is positioned behind section and moved in curved strokes; produces turned-under effect.

F. Blades of taper shears are positioned along the ends.

G. Tips of shears are pointed into the ends creating a zigzag pattern.

H. The blade may be positioned at the side or at the top of parting or section of hair to create highly tapered ends.

I. Hair is held against the razor guard with the thumb as you pull away from the head.

CONTOUR TAPERING

Usually performed at the _____ and _____

to reduce _____ and allow the hair to lie closer to the head

TAPER-SHEAR-OVER-COMB

•

•

RAZOR ROTATION

•

•

EXPANSION TAPERING

Performed near the base or midstrand to create _____ and

_____

STRAND TAPERING WITH THE TAPER SHEARS

-
- Creates expansion and volume within the form
-

SLICING

-
-
- Amount of texture activation is controlled by how wide the shears are opened and the length of the stroke

CLIENT-CENTERED GUIDELINES FOR TEXTURIZING

Enhance client _____ and _____

TEXTURIZING TECHNIQUE TIPS

Keep the hair evenly damp when:

1.

2.

3.

Match a texturizing technique to the image and definitions on the right.

	NOTCHING
	RAZOR PEELING
	RAZOR ETCHING
	POINT CUTTING

A.

Shallow = _____

Deep = _____

B.

Use a sharp _____ and change the blade frequently. Blade of razor touches the hair at a slight angle.

Longer strokes = _____

C.

Use a razor with a _____.

Less end texture = _____

More end texture = _____

D.

Do not open the shears all the way. Avoid using dull shears, which could cause _____.

THINKING MAP

Create a Thinking Map to help yourself make sense of how your notes fit together. Use some or all of the words in the Jump Start Box, as well as your own words and pictures to make a visual that will help you connect the important ideas of this lesson. Be creative!

JUMP START BOX

FORM LINE	END TAPERING WITH THE TAPER SHEARS	CONTOUR	EXPANSION
NOTCHING	RAZOR ETCHING	TAPER-SHEAR-OVER-COMB	STRAND TAPERING WITH TAPER
POINT CUTTING	RAZOR PEELING	RAZOR ROTATION	SLICING
SLIDE CUTTING	BEVEL-UP		
SLITHERING	BEVEL-UNDER		

LESSON CHALLENGE
Multiple choice. Indicate the correct answer for each question.

1. Texturizing reduces bulk without:
   a. lengthening the hair
   b. adding volume to the hair
   c. adding additional movement to the hair
   d. shortening the overall length appearance of the hair

2. Base texturizing is performed up to:
   a. 1/2" (1.25 cm) from the scalp
   b. 1" (2.5 cm) from the scalp
   c. 1 1/2" (3.75 cm) from the scalp
   d. 2" (5.0 cm) from the scalp

3. Which type of texturizing technique is used to create expansion and fullness while removing weight at the base area?
   a. end texturizing
   b. base texturizing
   c. shear-over-comb
   d. midstrand texturizing

4. A technique performed on the ends of the hair to allow for mobility, soften the ends and blend weight lines is called:
   a. slithering
   b. razor rotation
   c. end texturizing
   d. base texturizing

5. Which of the following hair types should be texturized 1" (2.5 cm) away from the scalp?
   a. fine hair
   b. coarse hair
   c. blond hair
   d. medium hair

6. Which texturizing technique can be performed with shears or clippers?
   a. slicing
   b. etching
   c. pointing
   d. notching

7. Slithering, a technique in which the shears are opened and closed rhythmically while moving upward from the ends, is also called:
   a. etching
   b. effilating
   c. point cutting
   d. slide cutting

8. To perform a bevel-under effect, the blade is positioned behind the section of the hair and moved in:
   a. long strokes
   b. curved strokes
   c. zigzag strokes
   d. a back-and-forth motion

9. Which of the following techniques is performed by rotating the razor and the comb in a light circular motion?
   a. slide cutting
   b. razor etching
   c. razor peeling
   d. razor rotation

10. Which of the following is performed by gliding the open shears along the surface of the hair?
    a. slicing
    b. slithering
    c. point cutting
    d. taper-shear-over-comb

LESSON CHALLENGE REFERENCES

Check your answers. Place a check mark next to the page number for any incorrect answer. On the lines, jot down topics that you still need to review.

1. PAGE 206 _____
2. PAGE 207 _____
3. PAGE 207 _____
4. PAGE 207 _____
5. PAGE 207 _____

6. PAGE 208 _____
7. PAGE 209 _____
8. PAGE 210 _____
9. PAGE 211 _____
10. PAGE 211 _____

▶ GROW WHAT YOU KNOW

Reflect on what you have learned and predict how this information will be used in the future.

105ᶜ.20 //
COMBINATION FORM OVERVIEW

ACHIEVE //

Following this lesson on *Combination Form Overview*, you'll be able to:

» Describe the characteristics that each basic form adds to a combination form

» List factors to consider when determining the proportional relationship within a combination form

FOCUS //

COMBINATION FORM OVERVIEW

Combination Form Characteristics

Proportional Relationships

Combination form: Displays the characteristic of each form

COMBINATION FORM CHARACTERISTICS

Sculpting one form in one area and another form in another area of the design

SHAPE/TEXTURE/STRUCTURE

SHAPE

•

| Solid |
| Graduated |
| Increase |
| Uniform |

TEXTURE

•

STRUCTURE

•

KEEP IN MIND THE FOLLOWING:

• Section according to changes in desired line, shape and structure

Solid Form
•

Graduated Form
•

Increase Layering
•

Uniform Layering
•

Identify the characteristics for each combination form given below.

Square (Rectilinear) Form – Hair: Andrzej Matracki; Photography: Sylwia Sokolowska, Model: Marcin Wydych

		INTERIOR	EXTERIOR
INCREASE/ SOLID		• •	
INCREASE/ GRADUATED		• •	•
GRADUATED/ INCREASE		•	•
UNIFORM/ GRADUATED		•	•
UNIFORM/ INCREASE		•	• •

SQUARE (RECTILINEAR) FORM	INTERIOR: INCREASE/UNIFORM EXTERIOR: GRADUATED/UNIFORM/INCREASE
	• Created using the _____ _____ technique • Weight occurs where _____ / _____ meet

PROPORTIONAL RELATIONSHIPS

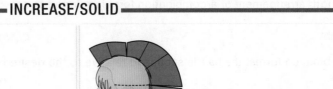

Determine the _____ and _____ techniques to be used

Consider the following when deciding the proportional relationship:

• Proportion of desired _____

• Placement of desired weight relative to _____

• Placement of desired weight relative to _____

Identify the proportions of each combination form.

— **INCREASE/SOLID** —

_____ INCREASE

_____ SOLID

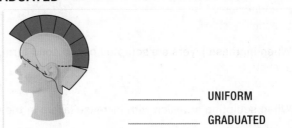

_____ INCREASE

_____ SOLID

— **UNIFORM/GRADUATED** —

_____ UNIFORM

_____ GRADUATED

_____ UNIFORM

_____ GRADUATED

— **UNIFORM/INCREASE** —

_____ UNIFORM

_____ INCREASE

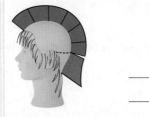

_____ UNIFORM

_____ INCREASE

MATCHING

Draw a line from the combination form to its related shape.

INCREASE/SOLID	Circle/Triangle
INCREASE/GRADUATED	Oval/Triangle
UNIFORM/INCREASE	Oval/Rectangle
UNIFORM/GRADUATED	Triangle/Oval
GRADUATED/INCREASE	Circle/Oval

LESSON CHALLENGE
Multiple choice. Indicate the correct answer for each question.

1. Sculpting one form in one area and another form elsewhere in the design refers to sculpting a:
   a. basic form
   b. long sculpture
   c. combination form
   d. similar structure throughout

2. The shape, texture and structure of a combination form depends on the proportions used and the:
   a. tool chosen
   b. position of activation
   c. position of volume
   d. length each form is sculpted

3. The length arrangement of a combination form is referred to as:
   a. shape
   b. weight
   c. texture
   d. structure

4. In combination forms, the hair is sectioned relative to the desired changes in line, shape and:
   a. angle
   b. structure
   c. length guides
   d. finishing direction

5. Which of the following forms adds volume and creates a rounded shape?
   a. solid
   b. graduated
   c. increase
   d. uniform

6. When sculpting an increase/solid combination form, a solid exterior will:
   a. add texture
   b. soften texture
   c. reduce perimeter weight
   d. add perimeter weight

7. When increase layers are sculpted over a solid form, the interior surface texture becomes:
   a. short
   b. rounded
   c. activated
   d. unactivated

8. When sculpting a design with increase layers in the exterior, the resulting form is generally:
   a. shorter
   b. angular
   c. rectilinear
   d. elongated

9. When sculpting graduated forms in the exterior, consider the:
   a. type of tool
   b. line of inclination
   c. parting pattern
   d. texturizing technique

10. Consider all of the following when deciding upon the proportional relationship of one form to another EXCEPT:
    a. desired texture
    b. desired texturizing techniques
    c. desired weight relative to head shape
    d. desired weight relative to facial features

LESSON CHALLENGE REFERENCES

Check your answers. Place a check mark next to the page number for any incorrect answer. On the lines, jot down topics that you still need to review.

1. PAGE 217 _____
2. PAGE 217 _____
3. PAGE 217 _____
4. PAGE 217 _____
5. PAGE 217 _____
6. PAGE 217 _____
7. PAGE 218 _____
8. PAGE 219 _____
9. PAGE 219 _____
10. PAGE 221 _____

▶ GROW WHAT YOU KNOW

Reflect on what you have learned and predict how this information will be used in the future.

106ᶜ.1 //
MEN'S SCULPTURE OVERVIEW

ACHIEVE //

Following this *Men's Sculpture Overview*, you'll be able to:

>> Define planar sculpting

>> Describe overcomb techniques

>> Explain the importance of outlining

>> Identify three facial hair designs

FOCUS //

MEN'S SCULPTURE OVERVIEW

Planar Sculpting

Overcomb Techniques

Outlining

Facial Hair Designs

Square form is a combination form, which is created using the planar sculpting technique.

PLANAR SCULPTING

- Technique in which the hair is sculpted along imaginary
  _____ and _____ planes
- The planar sculpting technique is used to create _____
  forms

SQUARE FORMS

STRAIGHT UP AND STRAIGHT OUT	STRAIGHT BACK	STRAIGHT OUT

Draw in directional distribution for square forms.

REDUCING WEIGHT CORNERS

Weight can be reduced or totally removed by rounding off the weight _____, which changes the interior from square to _____.

PLANAR SCULPTING GUIDELINES

Head position: _____

Use mirror to check:
- Directional distribution straight up, straight out, _____
- Finger position: _____ or _____.

OVERCOMB TECHNIQUES

Overcomb techniques rely on a comb to hold lengths when hair is so _____ it cannot be easily held between the fingers.

Larger Combs:

Cutting Combs:

Taper Combs:

SHEAR-OVER-COMB

- Shears positioned _____
- Thumb controls _____
- Comb and shears move upward in _____
- Repeat the technique many times to create a _____

CLIPPER-OVER-COMB

- Clippers positioned _____
- Clippers moved across comb _____
- Use _____ when working with taper combs to create extremely short hairlines

TAPER-SHEAR-OVER-COMB

Use taper-shear-over-comb to increase _____ and reduce density.

GRADATION

- Gradation is similar to graduation but gradation is very _____.
- The angle the comb is held controls the resulting length _____
- The higher the angle of the comb, the _____ the resulting length

3 TYPES OF GRADATION

Identify the projection angle used to sculpt gradation, and illustrate the line of inclination.

	LOW	MEDIUM	HIGH
TRANSPARENCY *Circle one.*	Least Medium Maximum	Least Medium Maximum	Least Medium Maximum
LOCATION			

FADE

- Ultra short version of gradation with a high degree of _____
- Some areas may be sculpted to the skin referred to as _____ fades
- Blend using a progression of attachments or _____

OUTLINING

Outlining: A technique used to _____ the

_____ _____

To work around the ear, _____ it slightly forward or backward

TOOLS USED FOR OUTLINING:

•

•

•

ALERT!
Cosmetologists may not be allowed to sculpt on the skin with a _____.
Be guided by your _____.

HAIR TATTOOS

Hair tattoos are creative outlines carved into the hair, and can be created with
_____ and/or a _____

FACIAL HAIR DESIGNS

Designing and trimming facial hair is a special service that may be offered in a salon.

Trimming unwanted hair as a grooming service includes removing excess hair from:

1.

2.

3.

Label the facial hair designs.

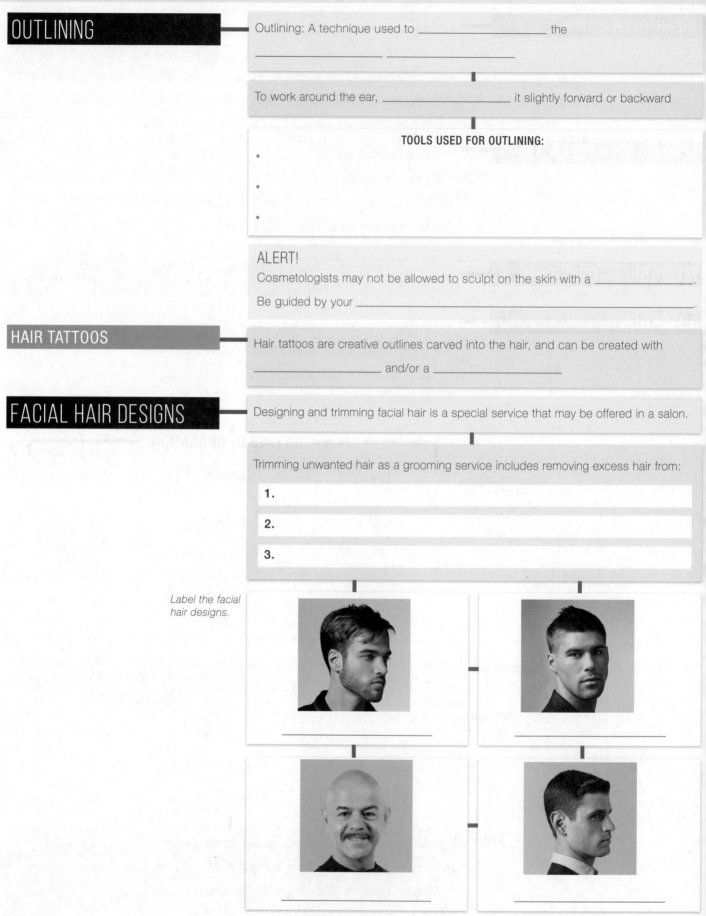

_____

_____

_____

_____

THINKING MAP

Create a Thinking Map to help yourself make sense of how your notes fit together. Use words in the Jump Start Box as well as your own words and pictures to make a visual that will help you connect the important ideas of this lesson. Be creative!

JUMP START BOX

MEDIUM	OUTLINING	FADES
GOATEE	CLIPPERS	GRADATION
CLIPPER-OVER-COMB	FACIAL HAIR	TRIMMERS
SQUARE FORM	PLANAR SCULPTING	LOW
TRANSPARENCY	COMB CONTROL	MUSTACHE
BEARD	HIGH	OVERCOMB
TIPS OF SHEARS	SIDEBURNS	SHEAR-OVER-COMB

LESSON CHALLENGE *Multiple choice. Indicate one correct answer for each question.*

1. The planar sculpting technique is used to create which of the following forms?
   a. solid
   b. uniform
   c. increase
   d. square

2. When planar sculpting you will automatically be creating:
   a. uniform lengths
   b. graduated lengths
   c. a combination form
   d. solid form lengths

3. All of the following are incorporated with directional distribution EXCEPT:
   a. straight up
   b. straight out
   c. straight back
   d. straight down

4. What technique is used when the lengths are too short to control between your fingers?
   a. notching
   b. overcomb
   c. planar
   d. pointing

5. To refine the perimeter in a shear-over-comb technique, designers use a:
   a. tail comb
   b. large comb
   c. taper comb
   d. wide-tooth comb

6. Which technique is used to create a flat top?
   a. notching
   b. parallel sculpting
   c. shear-over-comb
   d. clipper-over-comb

7. In gradation, the higher the angle of the comb, the greater the amount of:
   a. work
   b. space
   c. length
   d. transparency

8. Medium gradation generally extends into the:
   a. top
   b. crown
   c. interior
   d. occipital

9. When designing a fade, the placement of each zone should be predetermined so that the design is:
   a. transparent
   b. symmetrical
   c. asymmetrical
   d. well-balanced

10. Facial hair design includes beards, goatees, mustaches and:
    a. fades
    b. gradation
    c. sideburns
    d. planar form

LESSON CHALLENGE REFERENCES

Check your answers. Place a check mark next to the page number for any incorrect answer. On the lines, jot down topics that you still need to review.

1. PAGE 4 _____
2. PAGE 4 _____
3. PAGE 5 _____
4. PAGE 7 _____
5. PAGE 7 _____

6. PAGE 8 _____
7. PAGE 10 _____
8. PAGE 10 _____
9. PAGE 11 _____
10. PAGE 14 _____

▶ GROW WHAT YOU KNOW

Reflect on what you have learned and predict how this information will be used in the future.

107ᶜ.1 // HAIR DESIGN THEORY

ACHIEVE //

Following this lesson on *Hair Design Theory*, you'll be able to:

» List three reasons clients receive hair design services

» Identify two areas of hair design, and provide examples of each

» Explain the three levels of observation used in hair design analysis

» Summarize how sculpted forms are altered through hair design

» Provide examples of shapes used in hair design setting patterns

» Justify the value of creating different hair designs for the same client

FOCUS //

HAIR DESIGN THEORY

Hair Design Transformation

Hair Design Analysis

Hair Design's Influence on Sculpted Forms

Shapes in Hair Design

Change the Hair Design, Change the Effect

HAIR DESIGNING: _____

_____

HAIR DESIGN TRANSFORMATION

Reasons clients receive hair design services:

• The finish: _____

• A weekly or _____ _____

• _____ _____

HAIR DESIGN SERVICES

2 AREAS OF HAIR DESIGN

1. _____

• Structured, longer _____

• Dry under a _____

Examples include: _____

_____

_____

2. _____

• Softer, _____

• Dry by _____

Examples include: Air forming,

_____

_____

HAIR DESIGN ANALYSIS

3 LEVELS OF OBSERVATION

BASIC LEVEL (Form and Shape)

Look for: • _____

_____

• _____

Volume = | Indentation =

DETAIL LEVEL (Texture)

Look for: • _____

• _____

Surface Texture

Unactivated = | Activated =

Types of texture: _____

_____

ABSTRACT LEVEL (Direction)

Look for:

• _____

• _____

BASIC – FORM AND SHAPE

Form of a design can expand in any direction and includes:

Draw in and identify the areas of expansion.

_____

_____

_____

_____

_____

_____

DETAIL – TEXTURE

Natural texture can be temporarily changed through _____

_____ or _____ _____ .

The texture character achieved will be influenced by:

1. _____

2. Position of tool along the _____

1. UNACTIVATED

Draw in and identify the texture pattern.

_____

Tools used to achieve this pattern:

- _____
- _____

2. ACTIVATED

Draw in and identify the texture patterns.

_____ _____ _____ _____

Tools used to achieve these patterns:

- _____
- _____
- _____
- _____

Draw the speed of curls from slow to fast.

ABSTRACT – DIRECTION

Overall direction analyzed according to where the hair moves in relation to the face:

• Hair moving forward or _____

• Back or _____

• To one side

• Any combination

Directions within the design can be straight, curved or _____

HAIR DESIGN'S INFLUENCE ON SCULPTED FORMS

Hair design allows you to temporarily alter the shape of a sculpted form:

• Shift the position of _____

• Alter existing _____

• Change the _____

SOLID FORM

Addition of curls shifts weight area upward creating the illusion of a

_____ _____ .

GRADUATED FORM

Width and expansion of a graduated form can further be accentuated by adding

_____ and _____ texture patterns.

INCREASE-LAYERED FORM

The introduction of tighter curl patterns within a given area can drastically alter the overall:

1. _____

2. _____

UNIFORMLY LAYERED FORM

Wide array of styling options:

1. Break up rounded shape by adding _____

2. Elongate the shape by adding volume in one area while

_____ it in another

3. Enhance rounded shape by adding _____

COMBINATION FORMS

Can range from smooth to wavy to _____ finishes

SHAPES IN HAIR DESIGN

STRAIGHT SHAPES

Straight shapes create directional movement away from or toward the _____.

RECTANGLES

Draw in the shape and identify the directional movement.

_____

TRIANGLES

Draw in the shape and identify the directional movement.

_____
_____
_____

CURVATURE SHAPES

Curvature shapes create curved movement in the hair that are either

_____ or _____.

HALF-CIRCLE

Draw in the shape and identify the directional movement.

_____
_____
_____

OBLONGS

Draw in the shape and identify the directional movement.

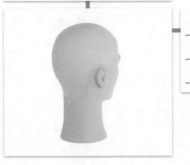

_____
_____
_____

CHANGE THE HAIR DESIGN, CHANGE THE EFFECT

Provide clients with:

• Freedom to change their _____

• More options for _____

• Flexibility to try new _____

MATCHING

Write the term number in the blank next to the corresponding description.

Term	Description
1. Wet design	_____ Slow speed
2. Oblongs	_____ Texture
3. Basic level	_____ Direction
4. Rectanglular shape	_____ Structured, longer lasting
5. Abstract level	_____ Smooth
6. Unactivated	_____ Softer, casual feeling
7. Tight curls	_____ Move half away and half towards the face
8. Triangle shapes	_____ Rough
9. Detail level	_____ Fast speed
10. Half-circle shapes	_____ Moves hair in one direction
11. Large waves	_____ Form/shape
12. Activated	_____ Wide to narrow, narrow to wide
13. Thermal design	_____ Two or more create a wave pattern

LESSON CHALLENGE

Multiple choice. Indicate one correct answer for each question.

1. Hair design is a temporary change in:
   a. volume
   b. indentation
   c. form, texture and color
   d. form, texture and direction

2. Which of the following is generally not a reason to receive a hair design service?
   a. weekly service
   b. special occasions
   c. hide color mistakes
   d. completion of another service

3. The two areas of hair design services are:
   a. roller setting and air forming
   b. wet design and thermal design
   c. straight and curly hair designing
   d. weekly service and special occasion

4. Hair design analysis includes which of the following levels of observation?
   a. form, color, texture
   b. basic, detail, texture
   c. basic, detail, abstract
   d. form, volume, indentation

5. The two categories of surface texture are known as:
   a. straight and wavy
   b. straight and curly
   c. unactivated and smooth
   d. unactivated and activated

6. Tighter curl patterns added to increase-layered forms create the illusion of:
   a. weight
   b. longer lengths
   c. shorter lengths
   d. geometric shapes

7. Rectangle shapes are usually used to move hair:
   a. asymmetrically
   b. in one direction
   c. in multiple directions
   d. in alternating directions

8. Curvature shapes used in hair design include:
   a. oblongs
   b. triangles
   c. rectangles
   d. trapezoids

9. The half-circle is most often used to move the hair:
   a. in one direction
   b. toward the face
   c. in alternating directions
   d. half toward, half away from the face

10. The temporary nature of hair design services provides clients with all of the following EXCEPT:
    a. styling options
    b. flexibility to try new designs for fun
    c. freedom to change without chemical commitment
    d. ongoing commitment to the same style

LESSON CHALLENGE REFERENCES

Check your answers. Place a check mark next to the page number for any incorrect answer. On the lines, jot down topics that you still need to review.

1. PAGE 5 _____
2. PAGE 6 _____
3. PAGE 7 _____
4. PAGE 8 _____
5. PAGE 8 _____
6. PAGE 14 _____
7. PAGE 16 _____
8. PAGE 16 _____
9. PAGE 16 _____
10. PAGE 17 _____

▶ GROW WHAT YOU KNOW

Reflect on what you have learned and predict how this information will be used in the future.

107ᶜ.2 //
HAIR DESIGN TOOLS AND ESSENTIALS

ACHIEVE //

Following this lesson on *Hair Design Tools and Essentials*, you'll be able to:

>> Describe the function of a variety of combs and brushes used in hair design

>> Describe the function of a variety of wet design tools

>> Describe the function of a variety of thermal design tools

>> Provide examples of supplies, products and equipment used to perform a hair design

FOCUS //

HAIR DESIGN TOOLS AND ESSENTIALS

Combs and Brushes

Wet Design Tools

Thermal Design Tools

Hair Design Essentials

Tools include combs, brushes, and wet and thermal design tools. Essentials include supplies, products and equipment.

COMBS AND BRUSHES

COMBS — **MAIN FEATURES OF A COMB**
-
-

BRUSHES — **MAIN FEATURES OF A BRUSH**
-
-
-

Select a tool from the list that is most commonly used to achieve the function below.

- Molding Comb
- Master Sketcher
- Fine-Tooth Tail Comb
- Wide-Tooth Tail Comb
- Vent Brush
- 7- or 9-Row Brush
- Round Brush
- Cushion Brush

	Backcomb and finishing techniques, separate curls and define texture
	Relax a set, dry mold, backbrush or smooth a surface
	Smooth wavy or curly textures; create curved end texture
	Distribute, mold, scale and part
	Allow greatest airflow; dry hair quickly
	Distribute and mold the hair
	Backcomb and smooth the hair
	Create volume, curved end texture or curls

WET DESIGN TOOLS

ROLLERS

Used to manipulate wet hair into desired shapes and movements and allowed to dry with tools in place

Identify the type of roller and complete the rest of the chart.

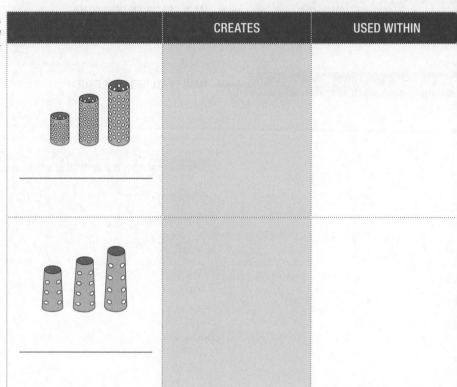

	CREATES	USED WITHIN
_____		
_____		

THERMAL DESIGN TOOLS

Used to dry or design hair into desired shapes and texture with heat

BLOW DRYER

Used to air form wet hair while using brushes, combs and fingers to

create _____ _____ and

_____ _____

MATCHING

Match the function to the image of the related thermal design tool.

FUNCTION

1. Create temporary curvilinear texture patterns

2. Press tightly curled hair

3. Straighten and silk hair

4. Create "S" pattern or wave formation

5. Create crimped texture pattern

6. Spread a gentle airflow over larger areas

7. Focus airflow to small area

_____ _____ _____ _____

_____ _____ _____

HAIR DESIGN ESSENTIALS

Include the supplies, products and equipment used to perform hair design services:

SUPPLIES

SINGLE-USE	MULTI-USE
•	•
•	•
	•
	•

PRODUCTS

Hair design products are used to add a range of _____ and _____

Characteristics:

	– Liquids to solids
	– Matte to high shine
	– Light to super firm

EQUIPMENT

Hair design equipment includes permanent furnishings and fixtures:

•

•

•

LESSON CHALLENGE
Multiple choice. Indicate the correct answer for each question.

1. The type of comb that is used for distribution, molding, scaling and parting the hair is called:
   a. teaser comb
   b. Master Sketcher
   c. fine-tooth tail comb
   d. wide-tooth tail comb

2. The type of comb that is used to backcomb the hair, separate curls and define texture is called:
   a. molding comb
   b. shampoo comb
   c. fine-tooth tail comb
   d. wide-tooth tail comb

3. The brush that allows the greatest airflow to the hair so lengths can be dried quickly while directing them into the lines of the design is called a:
   a. vent brush
   b. round brush
   c. cushion brush
   d. 9-row air-forming brush

4. Round brushes may have a core that is made of any of the following EXCEPT:
   a. wood
   b. metal
   c. plastic
   d. leather

5. The tool used to relax a set, backbrush or smooth the surface of the hair is referred to as a:
   a. vent brush
   b. 9-row brush
   c. round brush
   d. cushion brush

6. Conical rollers are used within curvature shapes and create a(n):
   a. repetition of curl diameters
   b. progression of curl diameters
   c. angular curl formation
   d. uniform curl formation

7. All of the following are examples of thermal design tools EXCEPT:
   a. flat iron
   b. blow dryer
   c. curling iron
   d. cylinder rollers

8. The blow dryer attachment that spreads airflow gently over a larger area is called a:
   a. diffuser
   b. hot comb
   c. lifter comb
   d. concentrator

9. Flat irons consist of two flat plates that include ceramic or:
   a. wood
   b. nylon
   c. metal
   d. plastic

10. The characteristics of styling products include all of the following EXCEPT:
    a. viscosity
    b. level of shine
    c. ingredients used
    d. level of hold/control

LESSON CHALLENGE REFERENCES

Check your answers. Place a check mark next to the page number for any incorrect answer. On the lines, jot down topics that you still need to review.

1. PAGE 24 _____
2. PAGE 24 _____
3. PAGE 25 _____
4. PAGE 25 _____
5. PAGE 25 _____

6. PAGE 26 _____
7. PAGE 27 _____
8. PAGE 27 _____
9. PAGE 27 _____
10. PAGE 29 _____

▶ GROW WHAT YOU KNOW

Reflect on what you have learned and predict how this information will be used in the future.

1 2 3 4 5 6 7

107ᶜ.3 // HAIR DESIGN SKILLS

ACHIEVE //

Following this lesson on *Hair Design Skills*, you'll be able to:

>> Describe the setting procedures used in hair design

>> Describe the finishing procedures used in hair design

FOCUS //

HAIR DESIGN SKILLS

Setting Procedures

Finishing Procedures

Hair design procedures fall into 2 main categories:

- Setting procedures

- Finishing procedures

SETTING PROCEDURES

TWO MAIN CATEGORIES OF SETTING:

_____

_____

5 wet-setting procedures:

Thermal setting procedures can be combined:

DISTRIBUTE

- Distribution is the direction the hair is combed or dispersed over the curve of the head

- Point of origin: _____

_____

PARALLEL DISTRIBUTION	RADIAL DISTRIBUTION
•	•
•	•

Draw in the distribution and identify major characteristics.

MOLD

Molding, also known as shaping, is designing wet hair in straight or curved lines to create a pattern or map out the direction hair will move.

SCALE

Carving out shapes in the proper size and proportion to establish the direction and lines of the design; also known as _____

Straight shapes or sections include:

RECTANGLE	TRIANGLE

Draw the distribution patterns for these straight shapes.

TRAPEZOID	DIAMOND/KITE

Curved shapes or sections include:

CIRCLE	HALF-CIRCLE	EXPANDED CIRCLE

Draw the curvature shapes and molding patterns within.

OVAL	EXPANDED OVAL	OBLONGS

PART

- Partings are lines that subdivide shapes or sections to help distribute and control the hair after _____ and _____

- Subsections are often called _____

Draw the parting pattern for the following shapes.

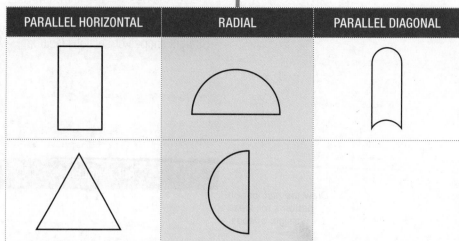

PARALLEL HORIZONTAL	RADIAL	PARALLEL DIAGONAL

APPLY

Hair is set by applying a tool such as a roller, round brush or curling iron to produce the desired amount of volume, indentation and degree of _____ and _____

- Size of the curl is determined by the tool or pincurl _____
- Tools with smaller diameter = Tighter or _____
- Tools with larger diameters = _____

3 COMPONENTS OF A CURL:

BASE	STEM (ARC)	CIRCLE
•	•	•
	•	•
•	•	•

HELPFUL HINT
There are 3 components of every curl, which are basically the same regardless of the tool or technique used to create it.

How will these 5 procedural steps for setting help you become a better hair designer?

_____

_____

FINISHING PROCEDURES

Also referred to as _____; steps are similar for rollers, pincurls or thermal designing

Finishing Checklist:

- Blend bases

- Retrace and reinforce lines

- Add height and control form

- Smooth surface and redefine lines

- Add finishing touches

5 Procedural Steps for Finishing:

Briefly describe the purpose of each step of the finishing phase of hair design.

RELAX
-
-

DRY MOLD
-

BACKCOMB/ BACKBRUSH
-
-
-

DEFINE THE FORM
-
-
-

DETAIL
-
-

MATCHING

Match the term in the Jump Start Box to the corresponding procedural image.

_____

_____

_____

_____

_____

_____

_____

_____

_____

_____

JUMP START BOX

APPLY	DEFINE THE FORM	DISTRIBUTE	MOLD	RELAX
BACKBRUSH	DETAIL	DRY MOLD	PART	SCALE

LESSON CHALLENGE *Multiple choice. Indicate one correct answer for each question.*

1. The place where motion begins is known as:
   a. radial
   b. parallel
   c. molding
   d. point of origin

2. Which of the following types of distribution refers to straight or curved lines that originate from a single point of origin and radiate outward in any direction, like the spokes of a wheel?
   a. radial
   b. parallel
   c. straight
   d. curved parallel

3. Which of the following shapes is used to move the hair in equal proportions from a center point of origin?
   a. oblong
   b. triangle
   c. half-oval
   d. half-circle

4. The 2nd direction, or bottom half of the oblong shape moves toward the:
   a. back end
   b. closed end
   c. convex end
   d. concave end

5. Two or more alternating oblongs create a(n)?
   a. "O-shape"
   b. "C-shape"
   c. "S-shape"
   d. figure eight

6. Which of the following base shapes is used within a circle?
   a. kite
   b. triangle
   c. rectangle
   d. rhomboid

7. The size of the curl will be determined by the:
   a. size of the base
   b. length of the stem
   c. direction of the curl
   d. diameter of the tool

8. Which component of a curl determines the amount of movement?
   a. arc
   b. base
   c. circle
   d. diameter

9. The finishing procedure that reinforces the established lines of the design is known as:
   a. relaxing
   b. dry molding
   c. backcombing
   d. backbrushing

10. A technique used to increase height and control form by creating a cushion or mesh at the base is called:
    a. comb-out
    b. dry molding
    c. backcombing
    d. relaxing the set

LESSON CHALLENGE REFERENCES

Check your answers. Place a check mark next to the page number for any incorrect answer. On the lines, jot down topics that you still need to review.

1. PAGE 36 _____
2. PAGE 36 _____
3. PAGE 39 _____
4. PAGE 40 _____
5. PAGE 40 _____
6. PAGE 41 _____
7. PAGE 42 _____
8. PAGE 43 _____
9. PAGE 45 _____
10. PAGE 46 _____

▶ GROW WHAT YOU KNOW

Reflect on what you have learned and predict how this information will be used in the future.

107^c.4 // HAIR DESIGN GUEST EXPERIENCE

ACHIEVE //

Following this lesson on *Hair Design Guest Experience*, you'll be able to:

» Summarize the service essentials related to hair design

» Provide examples of infection control and safety guidelines for hair design services

FOCUS //

HAIR DESIGN GUEST EXPERIENCE

Hair Design Service Essentials

Hair Design Infection Control and Safety

HAIR DESIGN SERVICE ESSENTIALS

Offer an exceptional hair design guest experience—from the greeting to completion.

CONNECT

2 guidelines for welcoming a client:

-
-

CONSULT

Ask client questions to determine:

-
-

Analyze client's:

-
-
-

Assess:

-
-

Summarize:

-
-
-

Gain Feedback

-

CREATE

- Replace plastic cape with cloth cape during the _____
- Explain how and why you are using products throughout _____
- Allow client to hold and _____ _____

COMPLETE

- Ask questions and look for _____ and _____ cues
- Recommend products to maintain the appearance and condition of _____

HAIR DESIGN INFECTION CONTROL AND SAFETY

CLEANING

-
- Slows growth of _____

DISINFECTION

- Does not kill _____

CLEANING AND DISINFECTION GUIDELINES

	COMBS/BRUSHES	ROLLERS
CLEANING GUIDELINES	• Remove hair and _____ • Preclean with _____ and _____	• Remove hair and _____ • Preclean with _____ and _____
DISINFECTION GUIDELINES	• Immerse in an approved _____ _____ _____	• Immerse in an approved EPA-registered disinfectant solution

	HAND-HELD DRYER	THERMAL IRONS/COMBS
CLEANING GUIDELINES	• Remove buildup from vent with _____ or _____ • Preclean filter with _____ and _____; allow to _____	• Allow iron to _____ • Remove buildup with _____ • Clean heavily soilded irons with _____ _____

DISINFECTION GUIDELINES	• Use an approved EPA-registered disinfectant .
	
	   ■ _____
	   ■ _____
		• Use an approved EPA-registered disinfectant
		
		   ■ Wipe
		   ■ Spray

CARE AND SAFETY

PERSONAL CARE

• Check that your personal standard of health and hygiene minimizes the

_____ of _____.

• Minimize fatigue by maintaining good _____.

CLIENT CARE PRIOR TO THE SERVICE

• Check the _____ for any _____

or _____.

• Ensure client does not have sensitivities to any _____.

CLIENT CARE DURING THE SERVICE

• Avoid using excess tension on the _____ and

_____.

• Perform thermal iron procedures only on _____.

• Periodically, ask your client if the heat from the blow dryer is too _____.

• Test the temperature of thermal irons or pressing combs before applying to

_____.

SALON CARE

• Disinfect all tools after _____.

• Ensure electrical equipment is in good condition and remember to

_____.

MATCHING

Match the description in the right column to its corresponding phase of care in the left column.

1. **PERSONAL CARE**

2. **CLIENT CARE PRIOR TO SERVICE**

3. **CLIENT CARE DURING THE SERVICE**

4. **SALON CARE**

_____ Clean/mop water spillage from floor to avoid accidental falls

_____ Check that your personal standards of health and hygiene minimize the spread of infection

_____ Check the temperature of stove-heated pressing combs and thermal irons by testing on a piece of white paper towel

_____ Ensure that the client does not have sensitivities to any styling products

_____ Protect the client's skin from thermal irons by positioning a hard-rubber or nonflammable comb underneath the iron

_____ Wear single-use gloves as required

_____ Refer to your regulatory agency for proper mixing/handling of disinfectant solutions

_____ Report malfunctioning furniture/equipment to manager's attention

_____ Check the scalp for any diseases or disorders

LESSON CHALLENGE
Multiple choice. Indicate the correct answer for each question.

1. During which of the following service essentials should you assess the facts and thoroughly think through your recommendations?
   a. Connect
   b. Consult
   c. Create
   d. Complete

2. During which of the following service essentials do you personalize the design to add your personal touch?
   a. Connect
   b. Consult
   c. Create
   d. Complete

3. During which of the following service essentials should you produce a functional, predictable and pleasing result?
   a. Connect
   b. Consult
   c. Create
   d. Complete

4. Which of the following guidelines relates to the Complete hair design service essential?
   a. produce a functional, predictable and pleasing result
   b. personalize the hair design to add your signature touch
   c. stay focused on delivering the hair design service to the best of your ability
   d. recommend products to maintain the appearance and condition of your client's hair

5. All of the following cleaning and disinfection guidelines are true about combs and brushes EXCEPT:
   a. remove hair and debris
   b. disinfect with fine steel wool
   c. preclean with soap and water
   d. immerse in an approved EPA-registered disinfectant

6. What is recommended to remove buildup from a cool iron barrel?
   a. a toothbrush
   b. a damp cloth
   c. spray cleaner
   d. soap and water

7. All single-use items must be:
   a. discarded after use
   b. cleaned after each use
   c. disinfected after each use
   d. washed in washing machine

8. Which guideline is performed prior to the hair design service?
   a. complete client record
   b. check scalp for any diseases or disorders
   c. ask client to purchase products
   d. schedule client's next appointment

9. All of the following guidelines are to be completed during the hair design service EXCEPT:
   a. perform thermal procedures on dry hair
   b. avoid excessive tension on hair when styling
   c. postpone treatment of burn until after the service
   d. test temperature of thermal irons before applying to hair

10. Which of the following is a guideline to follow to ensure salon care?
    a. only clean salon chair
    b. only clean workstation
    c. disinfect all porous items
    d. ensure equipment is clean and disinfected

LESSON CHALLENGE REFERENCES

Check your answers. Place a check mark next to the page number for any incorrect answer. On the lines, jot down topics that you still need to review.

1. PAGE 52 _____
2. PAGE 53 _____
3. PAGE 53 _____
4. PAGE 53 _____
5. PAGE 57 _____

6. PAGE 57 _____
7. PAGE 57 _____
8. PAGE 58 _____
9. PAGE 59 _____
10. PAGE 59 _____

▶ GROW WHAT YOU KNOW

Reflect on what you have learned and predict how this information will be used in the future.

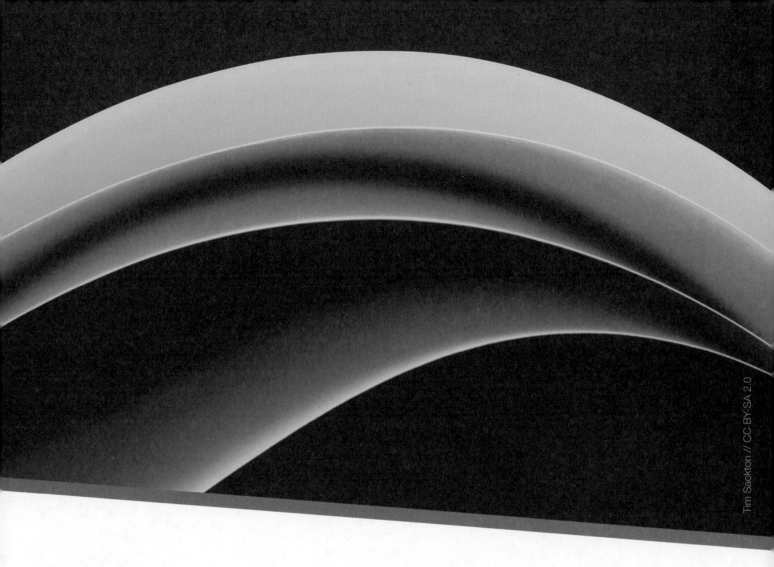

107ᶜ.6 //
STRAIGHT VOLUME AND INDENTATION

ACHIEVE //

Following this lesson on *Straight Volume and Indentation*, you'll be able to:

» List the effects of the five straight volume tool positions

» List the effects of the four straight indentation tool positions

» Give examples of how rollers are set within straight shapes

» Identify the base controls used in straight volume pincurls

FOCUS //

STRAIGHT VOLUME AND INDENTATION

Straight Base Control

Rollers in Straight Shapes

Pincurls in Straight Shapes

Straight Volume

• Creates _____ and

_____

• Base and strand are lifted and the

ends _____

Straight Indentation

• Creates _____

• Base and strand are flat and the

ends _____

STRAIGHT BASE CONTROL

Base Control

1._____

2._____

BASE SIZE

Includes both the width and the length of the base

• Base width is measured by _____ of the _____

• Base length is measured by _____ of the _____

Identify the base size.

_____

_____

_____

_____

TOOL POSITION

The position of the tool in relation to the base will affect the lift or volume achieved,

as well as the amount of _____ _____.

STRAIGHT VOLUME TOOL POSITION

TOOL POSITION	BASE SIZE	PROJECTION ANGLE	DESCRIPTION	EFFECT
ON BASE (FULL BASE)	1x		Tool sits completely within base	
HALF-OFF BASE (HALF-BASE)	1x Optional: 1½x, 2x		Tool sits half-off and half-on bottom parting	
OFF BASE	1x Optional: 1½x, 2x		Tool sits completely off bottom parting	
UNDERDIRECTED	1½x Optional: 2x		Tool sits in lower portion of base but not on or below parting	
OVERDIRECTED (VOLUME BASE)	1½x Optional: 2x		Tool sits in upper portion of base but not on or above parting	

STRAIGHT INDENTATION TOOL POSITION

Position of the tool and the size of the base influence the amount of
_____ space or _____ achieved.

TOOL POSITION	BASE SIZE	PROJECTION ANGLE	DESCRIPTION	EFFECT
ON BASE	1x		Tool sits completely on its base; rolled in an upward direction	
HALF-OFF BASE	1x Optional: 1½x, 2x		Tool sits half-off and half-on its base; rolled in an upward direction	
OFF BASE	1x Optional: 1½x, 2x		Tool sits completely off its base; rolled in an upward direction	
UNDERDIRECTED	1½x Optional: 2x		Tool sits within the base close to the bottom parting; rolled in an upward direction	

COMPONENTS OF A CURL

Identify the curl components.

There are 3 components of every curl:

1._____

2._____

3._____

BASE
-
-

STEM (ARC)
-
-
-

CIRCLE
-
-
-
-
-
  -
  -

ROLLERS IN STRAIGHT SHAPES

- Cylindrical rollers are usually used within _____ _____
- Hair is wrapped smoothly and evenly around the roller to avoid

  _____ _____ and _____

  _____.

- Roller chosen according to the desired curl patterns, repetition, alternation, progression or contrast
- Smaller rollers produce _____ _____
- Results vary according to _____ _____

ROLLERS WITHIN RECTANGLE SHAPES

- Used as a _____ or _____ shape
- Set from multiple _____ of _____
- Base controls chosen according to desired effects
- Partings used to create base shapes are _____

Draw rollers within a rectangle shape.

Rectangle
*
*
*

Draw rollers within a rectangle shape using a bricklay pattern.

Rectangle – Bricklay Pattern
*
*

ROLLERS WITHIN TRIANGLE SHAPES

* A progression of tool lengths is used to accommodate the narrow to wide shape
* Partings used to create base shapes are horizontal

Draw rollers within a triangle shape using a progression of roller lengths.

Triangle
*
*

Draw rollers within a diamond shape using a progression of roller lengths and a bricklay pattern.

Diamond/Kite
*
*

Draw rollers within a trapezoid shape using a progression of roller lengths and a bricklay pattern.

Trapezoid
* Created with _____ _____
* Often used as a fill-in shape
* Portion of a triangle

SETTING SHAPES WITH THERMAL TOOLS

The same base controls used for rollers also apply to thermal tools, such as the curling iron and round brush.

Curling Iron

Size of base is determined by

_____

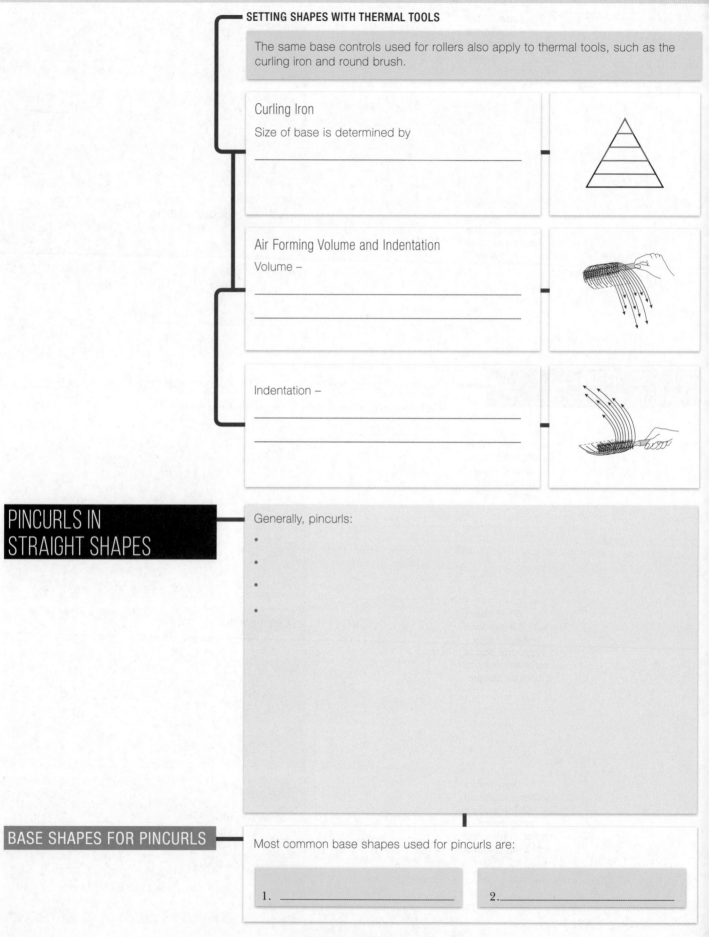

Air Forming Volume and Indentation

Volume –

_____

_____

Indentation –

_____

_____

PINCURLS IN STRAIGHT SHAPES

Generally, pincurls:

-
-
-
-

BASE SHAPES FOR PINCURLS

Most common base shapes used for pincurls are:

1. _____   2. _____

**BASE CONTROL
FOR PINCURLS**

Pincurl base control refers to:

•

•

STRAIGHT VOLUME PINCURL BASE CONTROLS

Identify and describe the base controls in the following illustrations.

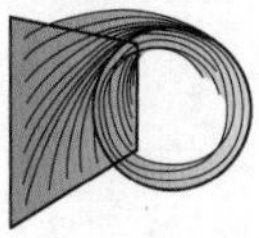

_____   _____   _____

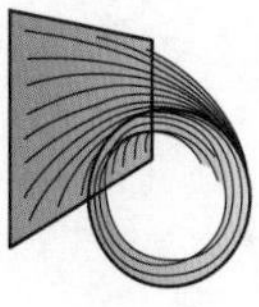

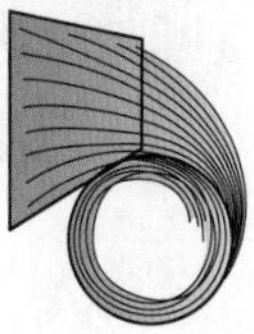

**FORMING STRAIGHT
VOLUME PINCURLS**

Straight volume pincurls:

• Large, stand-up pincurls that achieve a similar effect to hair wound around a roller, but result in _____

• Used within straight shapes to create _____ and

_____

• Also referred to as stand-up, _____ _____ and

_____ _____

Identify the steps used to create straight volume pincurls in the images below.

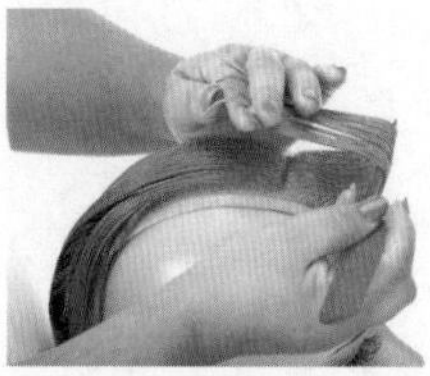

_____   _____   _____   _____

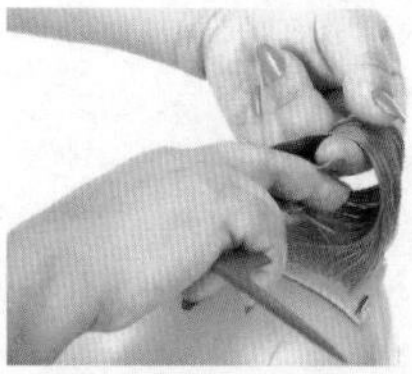

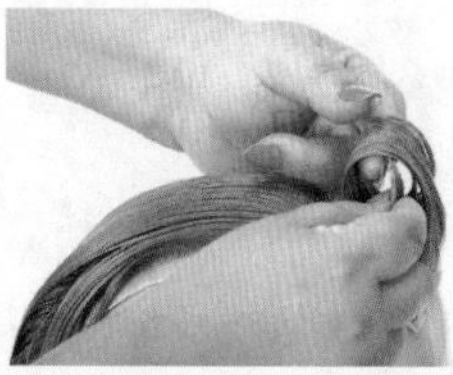

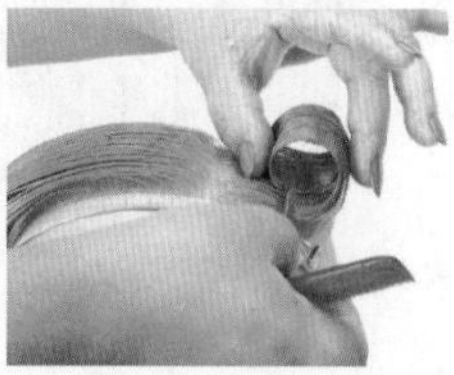

MATCHING

Match the image in the left column to the appropriate projection angle and base control in the right column.

1.

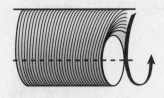

2.

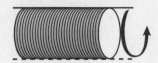

3.

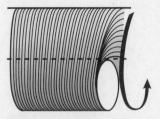

4.

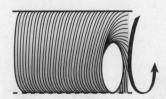

5.

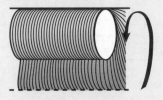

Projection Angle – Base Control

_____ 45˚ below center – 1x Off Base

_____ 90˚ from center – 1x Half-Off Base

_____ 45˚ above center – 1½x Overdirected

_____ 90˚ from center – 1½x Underdirected

_____ 45˚ above center – 1x On Base

LESSON CHALLENGE *Multiple choice. Indicate one correct answer for each question.*

1. The combination of the size of the base in relation to the diameter of the tool and the position of the tool in relation to the base is called:
   a. curl control
   b. base control
   c. diameter control
   d. combination control

2. Which base size means the same as the diameter of the tool?
   a. 1x
   b. 1½x
   c. 2x
   d. 2½x

3. An on-base tool position will result in the strongest base strength and:
   a. least volume
   b. least strength
   c. smallest diameter
   d. maximum volume

4. Which of the following tool positions will result in the least volume and the least base strength?
   a. on base
   b. off base
   c. half-off base
   d. underdirected

5. The tool sits in the lower portion of the base but not on or below the parting in which of the following tool positions?
   a. on base
   b. half-off base
   c. overdirected
   d. underdirected

6. What is the area between straight and curved partings within a shape, or the section of hair where the roller, thermal iron or round brush is placed called?
   a. arc
   b. base
   c. stem
   d. circle

7. What part of the curl determines the amount of movement of the curl?
   a. base
   b. stem
   c. circle
   d. shape

8. What determines the size of the circle of a curl?
   a. tool length
   b. tool diameter
   c. stem diameter
   d. base diameter

9. Stand-up, cascade and barrel curls are another name for which of the following pincurls?
   a. flat
   b. transitional
   c. straight volume
   d. straight indentation

10. When forming pincurls, the hair is smoothed to create:
    a. height
    b. closeness
    c. crimped ends
    d. a ribbon-like effect

LESSON CHALLENGE REFERENCES

Check your answers. Place a check mark next to the page number for any incorrect answer. On the lines, jot down topics that you still need to review.

1. PAGE 83 _____
2. PAGE 83 _____
3. PAGE 84 _____
4. PAGE 84 _____
5. PAGE 84 _____
6. PAGE 86 _____
7. PAGE 86 _____
8. PAGE 86 _____
9. PAGE 90 _____
10. PAGE 91 _____

▶ GROW WHAT YOU KNOW

Reflect on what you have learned and predict how this information will be used in the future.

107^c.8 //
CURVATURE VOLUME AND INDENTATION

ACHIEVE //

Following this lesson on *Curvature Volume and Indentation*, you'll be able to:

» Identify curvature volume and curvature indentation base controls

» Identify base shapes used to set various curvature shapes

» Describe the position of rollers within various curvature shapes

» Explain the effects of the three types of curvature pincurls

FOCUS //

CURVATURE VOLUME AND INDENTATION

Curvature Base Control

Rollers in Curvature Shapes

Pincurls in Curvature Shapes

Curvature Volume

Curvature Indentation

- Creates _____

- Creates _____

- Base and strand are lifted and the

- Strand is flat and the ends

ends _____

_____

Draw in the shapes that are used to set curvature volume and indentation to include direction within the shape.

Curvature volume and indentation are set within curvature shapes, such as:

CIRCLE

OVAL

OBLONGS

CURVATURE BASE CONTROL

Base Control

1. _____

2. _____

The base shapes used for curvature volume and indentation:

BASE SIZE AND TOOL POSITION

Base Size: _____

_____

- Base width is measured by _____ of the _____

- Base length is measured by _____ of the _____

CURVATURE VOLUME TOOL POSITION

Identify the illustration and the effect.

	BASE SIZE	PROJECTION ANGLE		
ON BASE	1x	45° above center		Effect:_____
UNDERDIRECTED	1½x, 2x	90° from center		Effect:_____
HALF-OFF BASE	1x, 1½x, 2x	90° from center		Effect:_____
OFF BASE	1x, 1½x, 2x	45° below center		Effect:_____

CURVATURE INDENTATION TOOL POSITION

- Tool position changes when setting curvature indentation
- _____
  _____

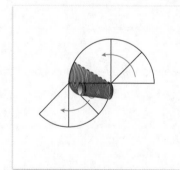

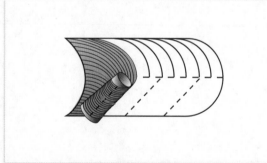

ROLLERS IN CURVATURE SHAPES

- Cone-shaped rollers are usually used within _____
  _____
- Cone rollers consist of a progression of _____
- Consist of a _____ and _____ end

CURVATURE SHAPES	POSITION	TO ACHIEVE	APPLIED USING
————————	Fringe area and/or sides	Curvature volume that directs equal amounts of hair off the face and on the face, with equal radial lines	• Equal-length rollers positioned one diameter away from a single center point of origin
———————— ————————	Fringe area and/or sides	Extends curvature movement toward the back	• Inner-and-outer technique • Inner circle set as a normal half-circle • Outer circle set using the inner circle point of origin • Rollers are positioned within their base, versus one diameter away from the point of origin for the inner circle
————————	Fringe area and/or sides	Curvature volume that directs hair with unequal radial lines	• Unequal-length rollers positioned one diameter away from a single point of origin
———————— ————————	Top-front or sides of the head	Curvature movement that travels toward the back	• Indirect technique • Each roller set from its own point of origin that is established at the front bottom corner of the previously set roller • Rollers positioned one diameter away from their point of origin
————————	Anywhere on the head in any direction	A strong wave pattern	• Rollers positioned diagonally and set from multiple points of origin • Volume oblongs begin at the convex end • Indentation oblongs begin at the concave end

PINCURLS IN CURVATURE SHAPES

Generally pincurls allow for a wide range of movement:

• _____

_____

• The size of the base and position of the circle in relation to the base affect the

amount of _____ and _____ achieved

Draw examples of pincurls within their related parting pattern.

Curvature volume and indentation pincurls are set within curvature shapes, such as the:

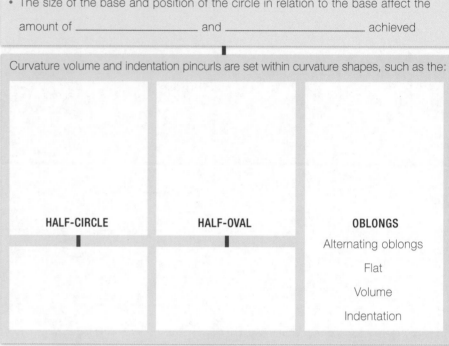

HALF-CIRCLE	HALF-OVAL	OBLONGS
		Alternating oblongs
		Flat
		Volume
		Indentation

Identify the base controls for curvature pincurls.

_____   _____   _____

_____   _____   _____

CURVATURE PINCURLS

The three common types of curvature pincurls are:

FLAT	VOLUME	INDENTATION
• Used for _____	• Create fullness and _____	• Create hollow space and_____
• Base, stem and circle are _____	• Base and stem are _____	• Base is _____
• Also known as carved or _____ curls	• Circle turns _____	• Stem (arc) and circle are _____

1 2 3 4 5 6 7

THINKING MAP

Create a Thinking Map to help yourself make sense of how your notes fit together. Use words in the Jump Start Box as well as your own words and pictures to make a visual that will help you connect the important ideas of this lesson. Be creative!

JUMP START BOX

CURVATURE	INNER/OUTER TECHNIQUE	PINCURLS
ALTERNATING OBLONGS	HALF-OVAL	FLAT
HALF-CIRCLE	EXPANDED OVAL	VOLUME
EXPANDED CIRCLE	INDIRECT TECHNIQUE	INDENTATION

LESSON CHALLENGE
Multiple choice. Indicate the correct answer for each question.

1. Which of the following tool positions is not used in curvature volume?
   a. on base
   b. off base
   c. overdirected
   d. underdirected

2. Which of the following results are created with cone-shaped rollers?
   a. straight shapes
   b. directional movement
   c. consistent rate of speed
   d. strong curvature movement

3. Which of the following shapes is used to direct the hair equally away and then toward the face?
   a. oblong
   b. triangle
   c. half-oval
   d. half-circle

4. Which of the following techniques is used to set an expanded circle?
   a. direct
   b. indirect
   c. narrow-to-wide
   d. inner-and-outer

5. Which of the following techniques is used to set an expanded oval?
   a. direct
   b. indirect
   c. narrow-to-wide
   d. inner-and-outer

6. The shape that is set with rhomboid-shaped bases is known as a(n):
   a. oblong
   b. half-oval
   c. half-circle
   d. expanded circle

7. Another name for an on-base curvature pincurl is:
   a. no stem
   b. full stem
   c. half stem
   d. undirected stem

8. Three common curvature pincurls are flat, volume and:
   a. barrel
   b. cascade
   c. stand-up
   d. indentation

9. Flat pincurls begin at which end of an oblong or shaping?
   a. first
   b. second
   c. convex
   d. concave

10. Which type of pincurl is used to create hollow space or flare?
    a. flat
    b. volume
    c. skip waves
    d. indentation

LESSON CHALLENGE REFERENCES

Check your answers. Place a check mark next to the page number for any incorrect answer. On the lines, jot down topics that you still need to review.

1. PAGE 102 _____
2. PAGE 104 _____
3. PAGE 104 _____
4. PAGE 106 _____
5. PAGE 109 _____
6. PAGE 110 _____
7. PAGE 113 _____
8. PAGE 114 _____
9. PAGE 114 _____
10. PAGE 116 _____

▶ GROW WHAT YOU KNOW

Reflect on what you have learned and predict how this information will be used in the future.

107:12 //
FINGERWAVING AND MOLDING

ACHIEVE //

Following this lesson on *Fingerwaving and Molding*, you'll be able to:

» Describe the process of creating fingerwaves

» Explain how to create a skip wave

» Identify the benefits of hair wrapping

FOCUS //

FINGERWAVING AND MOLDING

Fingerwaves

Skip Waves

Hair Wrapping

FINGERWAVES

The art of shaping and defining the hair in graceful waves is called:

Learning to fingerwave will help you develop:

1._____

2._____

3._____

A fingerwave is created by molding 2 alternating oblongs (shapings) that are connected by a _____.

Plan the direction of the wave pattern

Draw in specified wave pattern.

Horizontal	Diagonal	Vertical

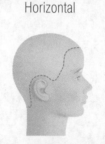 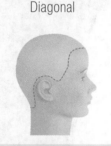 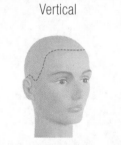

FINGERWAVING TECHNIQUE

Label the directions of an oblong, and identify the closed and open end.

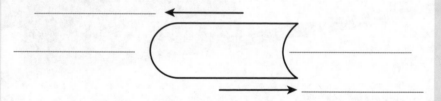

Mold 1st direction toward _____

Mold 2nd direction toward _____

Establish ridge beginning at the _____

Pinching or pushing the ridge will create over direction of the wave and is not recommended.

Each wave movement includes:

1. _____ (recess)   2. _____ (high ledge)

SHADOW WAVES: fingerwaves with _____ _____

2-COMB TECHNIQUE

Two combs can be used in place of your fingers to create small narrow waves with strong ridges:

• Effective on hair that is _____ _____

PAGES 148-149

SKIP WAVES

_____
_____
_____

RIDGE CURL: _____
_____

HAIR WRAPPING

_____
_____

• Creates smooth, straighter hair with a slight bend

CIRCLE WRAP

• Distribute hair from a _____

• Hair is molded around curves of the head section by section

THINKING MAP

Create a Thinking Map to help yourself make sense of how your notes fit together. Use words in the Jump Start Box as well as your own words and pictures to make a visual that will help you connect the important ideas of this lesson. Be creative!

JUMP START BOX

Fingerwaving

Skip Waves

2-Comb

Concave

Convex

1st Direction

2nd Direction

Open

Closed

LESSON CHALLENGE *Multiple choice. Indicate one correct answer for each question.*

1. **The first step in designing fingerwaves is to:**
   a. mold an oblong
   b. establish the ridge
   c. apply setting lotion
   d. plan direction of wave pattern

2. **The open end of an oblong is referred to as:**
   a. convex end
   b. concave end
   c. 1st direction
   d. 2nd direction

3. **The upper half of an oblong shape is the:**
   a. convex end
   b. concave end
   c. 1st direction
   d. 2nd direction

4. **At which area of the oblong does molding begin?**
   a. bottom of the shape
   b. open end of the shape
   c. convex end of the shape
   d. concave end of the shape

5. **Overdirection of the wave in fingerwaving may be caused by:**
   a. pinching or pushing the ridge
   b. use of styling lotion
   c. rolling your fingers off the ridge
   d. forming the ridge at the concave end

6. **Which of the following is NOT true about the 2-comb technique?**
   a. creates flat ridges
   b. creates strong ridges
   c. creates narrow waves
   d. effective on tightly curled hair textures

7. **Two alternating oblongs connected by a ridge where one oblong is molded and one oblong is set is called a(n):**
   a. skip wave
   b. fingerwave
   c. shadow wave
   d. alternating oblong

8. **Begin setting flat pincurls at the:**
   a. perimeter
   b. closed end
   c. convex end
   d. concave end

9. **Hair wrapping is a molding technique that is based on wrapping hair over the:**
   a. head
   b. iron
   c. brush
   d. roller

10. **The circle wrap is distributed from:**
    a. a side part
    b. a center part
    c. a single point of origin
    d. multiple points of origin

LESSON CHALLENGE REFERENCES

Check your answers. Place a check mark next to the page number for any incorrect answer. On the lines, jot down topics that you still need to review.

1. PAGE 144 _____
2. PAGE 145 _____
3. PAGE 145 _____
4. PAGE 146 _____
5. PAGE 147 _____

6. PAGE 147 _____
7. PAGE 148 _____
8. PAGE 148 _____
9. PAGE 149 _____
10. PAGE 149 _____

▶ GROW WHAT YOU KNOW

Reflect on what you have learned and predict how this information will be used in the future.

107ᶜ.15 //
THERMAL DESIGN

ACHIEVE //

Following this lesson on *Thermal Design*, you'll be able to:

>> Describe the three common ways to air form the hair

>> Contrast the various curling iron techniques

>> Summarize hair pressing

FOCUS //

THERMAL DESIGN

Air Forming

Thermal Ironing

Hair Pressing

THERMAL DESIGNING: The technique of drying and/or designing hair by using a hand-held dryer while simultaneously using your fingers, a variety of brushes, pressing comb and/or thermal irons.

How thermal design works:

1. Hydrogen bonds are _____ or broken down by water

   or _____

2. Protein chains shift and accept new _____

3. Heat is removed and hair cools

4. Bonds are _____

Helpful tip

Hair needs to cool completely prior to brushing or combing.

AIR FORMING

Air forming is also called

Blow dryers

- Available in different sizes and shapes
- Wattages vary from 1,000 to 1,800

Concentrators

- Focus airflow to a

   _____

- Used for a

   _____

Diffusers

- Spread airflow over a

   _____

- Used for freeform drying techniques

   such as _____

FINGERSTYLING

_____

_____

_____

SCRUNCHING

_____

_____

_____

- Best on wavy or _____ hair

- A diffuser is attached to the blow dryer to soften the airflow

- Hair is scrunched with the fingers to create _____

   _____

AIR FORMING WITH BRUSHES

Air forming with a blow dryer and a brush allows you to change the _____,

_____ and _____.

CHOICE OF BRUSH

Vent

Quickly dry the hair or to create specific directional movement, such as

_____

7- or 9-Row

_____

_____

Round

Change texture patterns by adding _____ or

_____ or by _____ - _____

_____

POSITION OF BRUSH

Volume

Brush is positioned

_____

_____

Indentation

Brush is positioned

_____

_____

AIR FORMING TIPS

• Use _____-_____ product

• Remove approximately 90% of moisture

• Dry hair on high setting; design on medium setting; set on _____

_____

• Air form in direction of the _____ _____

• Always keep dryer 3" to 5" (7.5 cm to 12.5 cm) from hair

• Use additional caution and lower heat settings when drying _____

_____

_____

THERMAL IRONING

Thermal ironing involves a variety of tools that are used to impart various texture patterns on dry hair—from straight to curly to crimped.

Name the 4 types of thermal irons:

1. _____

2. _____

3. _____

4. _____

CURLING IRONS

Thermal curling is the process of temporarily adding curl texture to dry hair through the use of heated irons (electric or stove-heated).

Thermal irons were first introduced in 1875; now are often called

_____ _____.

Label the parts of the curling iron.

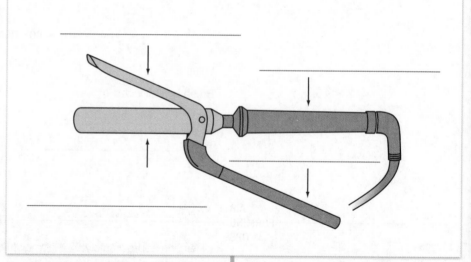

Electric Curling Iron

• The electric curling iron contains a heating element controlled by a thermostat

  that maintains a _____ _____.

• Never touch a curling iron with your fingers or by placing it near your

  _____ to _____ if it is hot.

• Lower temperatures are recommended for fine, _____

  _____ or lightened hair.

• Close a hot iron lightly on a damp towel before curling porous, white or

  _____ _____.

CLEANING THERMAL IRON

To remove residue, _____

_____

CURLING IRON TECHNIQUES

Various texture patterns can be achieved by varying the position of the iron along

the _____.

	POSITION OF IRON	ROTATION	EFFECT
BASE-TO-ENDS	•	•	•
			•
ENDS-TO-BASE	•	•	•
			•
ENDS TECHNIQUE	• Ends of hair • Volume: Indentation:	Volume: • Indentation: •	• •
MARCEL WAVES	• Barrel: • Shell:	• Direction of hair strand is encouraged beneath the barrel of the iron using the _____	•
SPIRAL	•	• Ends-to-base: • Base-to-ends:	• •

FLAT (STRAIGHTENING) IRONS

Parts:

_____

_____

Function:

_____

_____

CRIMPING IRONS

Parts:

_____

_____

Function:

_____

_____

UNDULATING IRONS

Parts:

_____

_____

Function:

_____

_____

MATCHING

Match the resulting effect on the left to the technique on the right.

Effect

_____ Stronger end curl progressing to a weaker base

_____ Elongated curls or a corkscrew effect

_____ Volume and support at the base and a consistent curl pattern throughout

_____ Alternating wave pattern along the hairstrand

_____ Curved under or bevel-up effect

Technique

1. Marcel Waves
2. Ends-to-Base
3. Ends
4. Spiral
5. Base-to-Ends

HAIR PRESSING

Hair pressing is a technique of temporarily straightening curly and tightly curled hair; also known as _____

- **First,** shampoo and _____
- **Next,** air form hair with a brush using _____
- **Then,** apply protective _____ or _____
- **Finally,** use a hot pressing comb on small _____

PRESSING COMBS

_____

_____

• Used on dry hair

• Pressing action is achieved with _____

Two types of pressing combs:

1. _____

2. _____

HAIR PRESSING TECHNIQUES

Two pressing techniques:

1. Soft Press:

2. Hard Press:

HAIR TEXTURE

Fine Texture

• Must be treated gently

• Less _____ and pressure to avoid breakage

Medium Texture

• Least difficult to press

• Requires no particular precautions

Coarse Texture

• Can be resistant

• Can tolerate _____ heat and pressure

PRESS AND CURL SERVICE

A press and curl service involves pressing the hair and then curling or waving the hair with a _____ _____.

TESTING TEMPERATURE

• Check the temperature by testing the pressing comb or thermal iron on a piece of

_____ _____ _____

• If the iron is too hot:

• _____

_____

• _____

_____

LESSON CHALLENGE
Multiple choice. Indicate one correct answer for each question.

1. The technique of drying and/or designing hair by using a hand-held dryer while simultaneously using your fingers and a variety of tools is known as:
   a. wet designing
   b. form designing
   c. thermal designing
   d. directional designing

2. Which bonds in the hair are weakened or broken by water or thermal heat?
   a. sulfur bonds
   b. oxygen bonds
   c. disulfide bonds
   d. hydrogen bonds

3. Before brushing or combing the hair after a thermal procedure, make sure the hair is:
   a. cool
   b. warm
   c. moist
   d. shampooed

4. The blow dryer attachment that fits on the nozzle and allows control of airflow to a small area is called:
   a. a diffuser
   b. a concentrator
   c. airflow control
   d. temperature control

5. Where is a hard-rubber or nonflammable comb positioned when curling the hair for a thermal design?
   a. between the barrel and groove
   b. in the palm of your opposite hand
   c. on top of the barrel away from the scalp
   d. between the curling iron and the scalp

6. Which of the following tools consists of 2 flat plates that are heated and used to straighten and silk the hair?
   a. flat iron
   b. crimping iron
   c. molding comb
   d. pressing comb

7. Pressing the hair twice with more pressure and heat during a hair pressing service is referred to as a:
   a. soft press
   b. curl press
   c. hard press
   d. stove press

8. Which product is used to prepare and protect the hair during pressing to prevent scorching and breakage?
   a. gel
   b. mousse
   c. pressing cream
   d. aerosol hairspray

9. Hair breakage may result from which of the following actions?
   a. pressing hair too often
   b. less pressure on the hair
   c. short contact time on the hair
   d. lower pressing comb temperature

10. Checking the temperature by testing the tool on a piece of white paper towel is performed for:
    a. blow dryers
    b. crimping irons
    c. electric thermal irons
    d. stove-heated thermal irons and combs

LESSON CHALLENGE REFERENCES

Check your answers. Place a check mark next to the page number for any incorrect answer. On the lines, jot down topics that you still need to review.

1. PAGE 170 _____
2. PAGE 170 _____
3. PAGE 170 _____
4. PAGE 171 _____
5. PAGE 180 _____

6. PAGE 182 _____
7. PAGE 183 _____
8. PAGE 184 _____
9. PAGE 184 _____
10. PAGE 185 _____

GROW WHAT YOU KNOW

Reflect on what you have learned and predict how this information will be used in the future.

ACHIEVE //

Following this lesson on *Long Hair Theory*, you'll be able to:

>> Explain the levels of observation used to analyze a long hair design

>> Restate in your own words how changing the long hair design can dramatically affect a client's appearance

FOCUS //

LONG HAIR THEORY

Long Hair Design Analysis

Change the Long Hair Design, Change the Effect

108ᶜ.1 //
LONG HAIR THEORY

LONG HAIR DESIGN ANALYSIS

Long hair designs are _____-dimensional and composed with attention to the elements of _____, _____ and _____.

LEVELS OF OBSERVATION

BASIC = _____ and _____

DETAIL = _____ and _____

ABSTRACT = _____

FORM AND SHAPE

Placement of mass, or _____, within the design

Focal Point: Position of _____ _____ _____ to which the eye is drawn

MATCHING

Match these illustrations to the correct description of the shape.

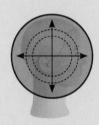
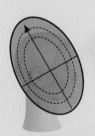
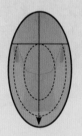
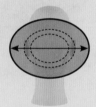

| More Width Than Height or Length | More Length Than Height | More Height Than Length | Volume Positioned Equally Throughout Design |

TEXTURE

Unactivated (smooth) and Activated (patterned)

Loops = _____ Texture

Tightly Formed Twists = _____ Texture

COLOR

Can lead eye through design

Can create focal point

DIRECTION

Determined by position of _____ or

_____ within design

Identify direction within a design as:

-
-
-
-
-

PROPORTION AND BALANCE:

Consider proportional relationship between:

_____, _____,

_____ and _____

Balance is either _____ or _____.

CHANGE THE LONG HAIR DESIGN, CHANGE THE EFFECT

Long hair design requires awareness of _____.

Gain agreement on mood or _____ to be expressed.

Remember to:

» Ask _____ questions.

» Listen carefully to your client's answers.

» Confirm _____

» Make effective design decisions for your clients.

IN YOUR OWN WORDS

In your own words, describe each of the designs in these pairs as you would to a client.

LESSON CHALLENGE *Multiple choice. Indicate one correct answer for each question.*

1. Which of the following is not considered one of the levels of observation?
   a. basic
   b. general
   c. detail
   d. abstract

2. Overall direction and directions within the form are determined through which level of observation?
   a. basic
   b. detail
   c. abstract
   d. none of the above

3. If a long hair design has equal height and width, where will volume be emphasized?
   a. front
   b. crown
   c. nape
   d. no particular area

4. What determines the direction of the form in long hair design?
   a. added color
   b. products used
   c. unactivated texture
   d. position of shapes

5. Which of the following is not critical to gain understanding of the mood or impression your long hair client wants to express?
   a. confirming understanding
   b. asking open-ended questions
   c. client's astrological sign
   d. listening carefully to client's answers

LESSON CHALLENGE REFERENCES

Check your answers. Place a check mark next to the page number for any incorrect answer. On the lines, jot down topics that you still need to review.

1. PAGE 5 _____
2. PAGE 5 _____
3. PAGE 8 _____
4. PAGE 12 _____
5. PAGE 14 _____

▶ GROW WHAT YOU KNOW

Reflect on what you have learned and predict how this information will be used in the future.

Mainstream // CC BY 2.0

Sarah-Rose // CC BY-ND 2.0

Hilary Dotson // CC BY-ND 2.0

108ᶜ.2 //
LONG HAIR TOOLS AND ESSENTIALS

ACHIEVE //

Following this lesson on *Long Hair Tools and Essentials*, you'll be able to:

>> Identify a variety of tools used in long hair design and describe their functions

>> Give examples of supplies commonly used in long hair design and their uses

>> Provide examples of products and equipment used in long hair design and describe their uses

FOCUS //

LONG HAIR TOOLS AND ESSENTIALS

Thermal Tools

Brushes

Combs

Long Hair Essentials

THERMAL TOOLS

- Use heat to set _____ _____ into hair
- Generally same as used in _____
- Mostly for hair preparation _____ putting it up

BLOW DRYERS/ATTACHMENTS

Blow Dryer – With attachments, used to air form wet hair using brushes, combs and fingers to create temporary _____ and _____ changes

Concentrators/nozzles _____ _____ to a _____ _____

Diffusers _____ a _____ _____ over _____ _____

_____

THERMAL IRONS

CURLING IRONS

- Temporary _____ _____
- _____, _____, _____
- Variety of _____
- Professional curling irons also called _____ _____

FLAT IRONS

- Temporarily _____ and _____ hair
- Consist of 2 _____

_____

_____

THERMAL ROLLERS

Also called _____ _____

Used on _____ _____ to quickly add _____ and _____ _____

BRUSHES

AIR FORMING BRUSHES

Allow greatest _____ to hair

Lengths can be _____ _____ while directing

them into the _____ of the _____

MATCHING

Match these images to the correct description.

| 7- or 9-Row | Vent | Paddle |

ROUND BRUSHES

Create _____ and _____

end texture

Vary in:

- _____
- Type of _____
- _____ of bristles

CUSHION BRUSHES

Dense bristles can be made of:

- _____ fiber
- _____ fiber
- _____

Use on _____ hair to increase

_____ and to _____ hair

COMBS

Main features are:

- _____
- _____ _____ _____
- Pointed end/tail, used to _____, _____ or _____

Hair reflects _____ and _____ of teeth

MATCHING

Match these images to the correct name.

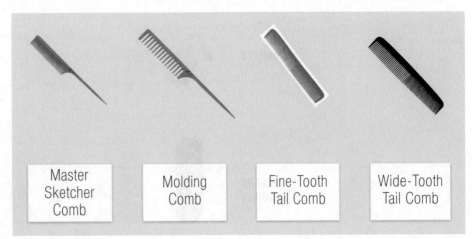

| Master Sketcher Comb | Molding Comb | Fine-Tooth Tail Comb | Wide-Tooth Tail Comb |

LONG HAIR ESSENTIALS

SUPPLIES

- Support and secure
- Available in a variety of _____ and _____ to conceal hair

BOBBY PINS

- Secure _____ or _____ sections to other areas
- Usually _____ slightly and then slid into hair to secure
- Closed pin can also be used, depending on _____

LOCKING:

Creates extra _____

Bobby pins are _____ _____

_____ _____

Create _____ of bobby pins

ELASTIC BANDS

Hold _____ in position

Secure the ends of _____ or

_____ strands

Covered hair bands = _____ on _____

HAIRPINS

Secure _____, _____ areas

Easier to _____

Often placed closer to _____ of design

Longer Hairpins = _____ hold hair in place;

_____ when the design is complete

HAIRNETS

Extra _____ and _____ in areas that are especially heavy or long

Also used to create _____

FILLERS (PADDING)

Provide _____ and _____

_____ hair fibers, backcombed and placed in

_____

Allows for _____ shape and volume

Also called _____

ALERT! Always follow _____ directions

for the proper use, _____ and

_____ of long hair essentials

PRODUCTS

Long hair is exposed to more stress than _____

_____

Natural Stress

• _____

• _____

Physical Stress

• _____ _____

• Ponytails or braids worn too _____ or

too _____

Use the right products to:

• _____ unruly hair

• Make hair look _____

• Add _____ and _____ to design

Carefully choose which products to use:

• Prior to _____ _____ or _____

• _____ air forming or setting

• While _____ or putting hair up

• While finishing and _____

LESSON CHALLENGE *Multiple choice. Indicate one correct answer for each question.*

1. The blow dryer attachment that focuses the airflow to a small area is called the nozzle or:
   a. switch
   b. handle
   c. diffuser
   d. concentrator

2. To create temporary texture changes, thermal rollers are used on:
   a. dry hair
   b. wet hair
   c. damp hair
   d. damaged hair

3. Of the following, the tool that allows the greatest airflow to the hair while directing it into the lines of the design is called a:
   a. long hairpin
   b. cushion brush
   c. fine-tooth comb
   d. 9-row air forming brush

4. The type of comb that is used for backcombing and smoothing the surface of the hair is called a:
   a. molding comb
   b. Master Sketcher comb
   c. fine-tooth tail comb
   d. wide-tooth tail comb

5. During which of the following is it important to carefully choose which product(s) you use?
   a. while designing
   b. during air forming or setting
   c. prior to air forming or setting
   d. all of the above

LESSON CHALLENGE REFERENCES

Check your answers. Place a check mark next to the page number for any incorrect answer. On the lines jot down topics that you still need to review.

1. PAGE 20 _____

2. PAGE 20 _____

3. PAGE 21 _____

4. PAGE 22 _____

5. PAGE 24 _____

▶ GROW WHAT YOU KNOW

Reflect on what you have learned and predict how this information will be used in the future.

108^c.3 //
LONG HAIR
SKILLS

ACHIEVE //

Following this lesson on *Long Hair Skills*, you'll be able to:

» State the importance of preparing the hair before creating a long hair design

» Provide examples of the five long hair procedures used to ensure predictable results

» Provide examples of the six common long hair techniques

FOCUS //

LONG HAIR SKILLS

Long Hair Preparation

Long Hair Procedures

Long Hair Techniques

LONG HAIR SKILLS:

Mastering long hair _____ and using organized, efficient
_____ = matching client's expectations every time

LONG HAIR PREPARATION

Long hair design preparation steps are followed by long hair design
_____ resulting in _____ _____
_____ _____.

Carefully choose proper:

- _____
- _____
- _____
- _____

The direction of the set should reflect _____ direction and
direction within _____ _____.

Techniques and tools commonly used:

_____   _____   _____

                                               _____

Describe the preparation steps used in these examples:

_____   _____   _____

_____   _____   _____

_____   _____   _____

_____   _____   _____

_____   _____   _____

LONG HAIR PROCEDURES

Following step-by-step procedures ensures _____ of the
_____ as a long hair design is created.
Not every design requires every _____ _____.
Working in a _____ _____ is just as critical.

DISTRIBUTE

Distribution is used throughout a long hair design service and:

• Defines the _____ _____ of the design.

• Determines the _____ in which the eye will travel

   _____ _____ _____.

• Can lead the eye to a _____ _____.

Overall, distribution is performed to prepare for the position of

_____ or _____.

Options include:

• _____   • _____

• _____   • _____

• _____

Distribution of individual strands or partings creates _____ and

_____ that _____ the eye through the design

and create _____.

SECTION

In long hair design, sectioning is used for _____, separates

areas with different _____, and helps designer stay

_____ and follow the _____.

Sectioning options for long hair design include:

• _____   • _____   • _____

• _____   • _____

• _____   • _____

Proper sectioning ensures accuracy of:

• _____ positioned in most favorable spot

• Overall _____

• _____ of focal point

Ponytail position results in: Concentration of _____

Increased number of ponytails or sections: Varies position of _____

and influences _____.

If no ponytails are used, you may need to section as you work to

_____ the hair and the position of _____.

PART

PARTINGS

• Used to _____ larger sections for _____.

• Specific techniques applied to individual partings; when combined create

   _____ _____ of design.

PART (CONT'D)

Direction of partings may be:

- _____
- _____

- _____
- _____

MORE PARTINGS = MORE:

- _____
- _____

- _____

APPLY

FOUNDATIONAL TECHNIQUES

- _____ - _____ - _____
- _____ - _____ - _____

_____

_____

BACKCOMBING/BACKBRUSHING:

Usually performed with loop or roll designs; increases

_____ or _____

Securing the Design:

Usually with _____ or _____ intended to be

_____ or _____

SECURING PONYTAILS

1-Bobby-Pin Technique:

- Slide a _____ _____ through elastic hair band.
- Hook _____ _____ around thumb.
- Hold _____ _____, wrap band around hair.
- Insert the end of band from around thumb into bobby pin.
- Pull pin up slightly, turn it downward and push under base of ponytail.

2-Bobby-Pin Technique:

- Slide 2 bobby pins onto _____ _____ .
- Insert 1 bobby pin at base of intended _____ .
- Push hand firmly against head to hold bobby pin in place.
- Wrap _____ around hair.
- Push second pin into hair, crisscrossing first pin and making an " _____ ."

DETAIL

Refers to finishing touches performed during a long hair design, or as final phase to personalize.

- _____
  _____
  _____

- _____
  _____
  _____

- _____

- _____

MATCHING

Match to identify the procedural steps used for long hair design.

Distribute	Section	Part	Apply	Detail

LONG HAIR TECHNIQUES

Off-the-Scalp Designs _____

On-the-Scalp Designs _____

TWISTS

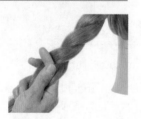

- _____
  _____
  _____

- _____

- Single-strand twists: _____

- 2-Strand Twists: _____

- 2-Strand Double Twists: _____
  _____
  _____

- 3-Strand Twists: _____

KNOTS

Interlacing or tying together of 1 or 2 strands to create a knot

- _____
- _____
- _____

Small individual partings = _____

Single-Strand Knots: _____
_____

2-Strand Knots: _____

OVERLAPS

Crossing of 2 strands over one another, creating a _____ effect

- _____
- _____
- _____
_____
- _____

BRAIDS

_____ or _____ of 3 or more strands
of hair
Other terms associated with braiding are: _____,
_____, _____,
_____, _____ and
_____

Most common methods: classified by number of strands

- _____
_____
- _____
- _____

3-strand overbraid:

- _____
- _____

3-strand underbraid:

- _____
- _____

Cornrows

- _____

- _____

- _____

Multiple _____ create a wider pattern of _____

_____

LOOPS

_____, _____ or _____

of hairstrands, which are then secured in a _____.

Can be varied in:

- _____   • _____

- _____   • _____

Single-Loop Technique: _____

_____

Double-Loop Technique: _____

_____

ROLLS

Consist of hair that is _____ or _____ within

_____.

- Shape of roll can be _____ or _____

- Size and shape of roll determined by:

  ▪ _____ _____

  ▪ _____ _____

  ▪ _____ of _____ _____

MATCHING

Match the technique name to the design.

| Twists | Knots | Overlaps | Braids | Loops | Rolls |

LESSON CHALLENGE *Multiple choice. Indicate one correct answer for each question.*

1. The long hair design procedures are distribute, section, part, apply and:
   a. mold
   b. relax
   c. detail
   d. backcomb

2. One, 2 or 3 strands of hair intertwined and/or rotated to form a rope-like appearance is called a:
   a. knot
   b. loop
   c. twist
   d. braid

3. The interlacing or tying together of a single strand or 2 strands of hair is called a:
   a. knot
   b. loop
   c. twist
   d. braid

4. Two strands crossed to opposite sides, in a downward or upward direction to create a crisscross effect is known as:
   a. knots
   b. loops
   c. braids
   d. overlaps

5. Twine, plait and interlock are some terms used to describe the long hair design method of crossing or weaving 3 or more strands of hair, also known as a(n):
   a. knot
   b. loop
   c. braid
   d. overlap

6. The two most common braiding methods are the 3-strand underbraid and the:
   a. 7-strand braid
   b. 5-strand braid
   c. 9-strand braid
   d. 3-strand overbraid

7. The 3-strand overbraid is also known as what type of braid?
   a. Italian
   b. French
   c. visible
   d. cornrow

8. Which braid is created when the outside strands are crossed under the center strand?
   a. weaving
   b. overlapping
   c. 3-strand overbraid
   d. 3-strand underbraid

9. The long hair design technique that consists of the folding, bending or encircling of strands that are then secured in a curvature shape is:
   a. rolls
   b. loops
   c. knots
   d. overlaps

10. In which long hair design technique is the hair wrapped or wound around itself?
    a. rolls
    b. loops
    c. knots
    d. overlaps

LESSON CHALLENGE REFERENCES

Check your answers. Place a check mark next to the page number for any incorrect answer. On the lines, jot down topics that you still need to review.

1. PAGE 34 _____
2. PAGE 44 _____
3. PAGE 45 _____
4. PAGE 46 _____
5. PAGE 47 _____

6. PAGE 47 _____
7. PAGE 47 _____
8. PAGE 47 _____
9. PAGE 48 _____
10. PAGE 49 _____

▶ GROW WHAT YOU KNOW

Reflect on what you have learned and predict how this information will be used in the future.

108ᶜ.4 //
LONG HAIR GUEST EXPERIENCE

ACHIEVE //

Following this lesson on *Long Hair Guest Experience*, you'll be able to:

>> Summarize the service essentials related to long hair designing

>> Restate in your own words the client considerations and communication guidelines used to ensure a successful long hair design

>> Provide examples of infection control and safety guidelines for long hair design services

FOCUS //

LONG HAIR GUEST EXPERIENCE

Long Hair Service Essentials

Long Hair Client Considerations

Long Hair Infection Control and Safety

LONG HAIR SERVICE ESSENTIALS

CONNECT

Guidelines for welcoming a client:

• Meet and greet with a firm _____ and pleasant tone of voice

• Communicate to build rapport and develop connection with client

CONSULT

Ask client about:

• _____

• _____ in event

Ask what client will be wearing; listen for details relating to:

• _____   • _____

• _____   • _____

Analyze client's:

• _____ and _____

• _____

• _____

• _____

Assess:

• _____

• _____

• Explain _____ including _____ or _____

Assess:

• Consider where _____ should be placed from all angles

Gain feedback:

• _____

CREATE

Protect client:

• _____ _____

• _____ _____

• Begin with _____ if already shampooed

• Ensure client _____ during the service

LONG HAIR SERVICE ESSENTIALS (CONT'D)

CREATE

Teach client:

* _____
* _____

COMPLETE

Request feedback and look for cues:

* _____   • _____

Escort client to retail area

* _____

* _____

* Suggest future appointment for next special occasion

* _____

* Complete client record

LONG HAIR CLIENT CONSIDERATIONS

FACIAL FEATURES

* Volume placement affects _____ _____.
* Delicate features usually better with _____ detailing around face.
* Bolder facial features can carry off _____ detail around the face.

BODY STRUCTURE

* Identify client's body shape.
* Short and sturdy clients benefit from _____ height and volume.
* Tall and lanky clients require _____ height and volume.

Refer to the *Client Considerations* lesson for additional information.

HAIR LENGTH, DENSITY AND TEXTURE

* _____
  _____

* Shorter hair will present more limitations than longer lengths; _____ may be an option.

* Determine if density and texture are sufficient to support desired style.

* Use _____ to build up the hair.

* _____ or _____ can also be used to support shapes.

OCCASION

Consider:

- Nature and _____ of occasion

- _____

- _____

  _____

  _____

WARDROBE

Consider:

- Lines garments create on body, especially at _____

- Amount of volume (full sleeves, full skirt)

- _____ gown offers different options than a high or

  closed neckline

IMPRESSION

How does client want to be perceived at event? Options might include:

- Elegant and _____

- Soft and _____

- Cutting-edge and _____

- _____

LONG HAIR INFECTION CONTROL AND SAFETY

CLEANING AND DISINFECTION GUIDELINES

Cleaning

-

-

-

Disinfection

- Kills certain _____

- Does not kill _____

-

-

-

-

Porous items must be _____ after each use.

LONG HAIR INFECTION CONTROL AND SAFETY (CONT'D)

TOOLS, SUPPLIES AND EQUIPMENT	CLEAN	DISINFECT
Combs and Brushes		
Thermal Tools		
Bobby Pins, Hairpins*		
Elastic Bands*		
Hairnets*		
Filler/ Padding*		

*Client will usually take these supplies home as part of the style.

Cape (plastic/cloth)

- _____

- _____

Neck Strip

- _____

CARE AND SAFETY

PERSONAL CARE

Personal standards of health and hygiene minimize the spread of infection.

·

·

Clean and _____ tools appropriately.

·

·

Refer to your area's regulatory agency for proper mixing/handling of disinfection solutions.

CLIENT CARE PRIOR TO THE SERVICE

Protect client's skin and clothing from water with freshly laundered towel and

_____ _____. If shampoo service is performed,

replace towel with _____ _____.

• Protect client's skin and clothing with a neck strip and

_____ _____.

CLIENT CARE DURING THE SERVICE

• Be aware of _____ _____ while combing,
  brushing or styling client's hair.

• Be aware of any sensitivity to tightness of _____ or positioning

  of _____ _____ or _____.

Work carefully around _____-_____ jewelry/piercings.

• Be aware of _____ _____ the client may be conveying.

SALON CARE

Promote professional image by ensuring your workstation is clean and tidy throughout service.

Ensure electrical cords are properly positioned to avoid accidental _____.

Clean/mop _____ _____ from floor to avoid accidental falls.

MATCHING

Match the service essential to the appropriate descriptor.

| Connect | Consult | Create | Complete |

Teach the client how to use a light holding spray if necessary as the day and the event progress.

Stay focused on delivering the long hair design service to the best of your ability.

Analyze your client's face and body shape, physical features, hair and scalp.

Offer sincere appreciation to your client for visiting the school or salon.

Assess the facts and thoroughly think through your recommendations.

Ask questions and look for verbal and nonverbal cues to determine your client's level of satisfaction.

Meet and greet the client with a firm handshake and a pleasant tone of voice.

Ask questions to discover client needs.

Communicate to build rapport and develop a connection with the client.

Ask your client to describe what she will be wearing; listen for details.

Escort client to the retail area and show the products you used.

Ensure client comfort during the service.

LESSON CHALLENGE *Multiple choice. Indicate one correct answer for each question.*

1. Communicating with your client prior to and during the long hair design service will help you avoid misunderstandings and ensure:
   a. predictable results
   b. a proper shampoo treatment
   c. their friends will give them compliments
   d. the service is completed in a timely manner

2. Each of the following guidelines is used during the Connect long hair service essential, EXCEPT:
   a. build rapport
   b. meet client with a firm handshake
   c. explain recommended solutions
   d. greet client with a pleasant tone of voice

3. Which of the following is a guideline to be followed during the Complete long hair service essential?
   a. meet and greet the client with a smile and a firm handshake
   b. teach the client how to use a light holding spray if necessary
   c. ask specific questions such as "What type of impression would you like to convey?"
   d. ask questions and look for verbal and nonverbal cues to determine your client's level of satisfaction

4. Ensuring your client's comfort during the service is important during which long hair service essential?
   a. Create
   b. Consult
   c. Connect
   d. Complete

5. In order to determine your client's level of satisfaction look for verbal and nonverbal cues and:
   a. ask for referrals
   b. request feedback
   c. recommend products for purchase
   d. seek approval from staff members

6. When hair density and texture are not sufficient to support the desired long hair design, which of the following is NOT a suggested solution?
   a. use a filler
   b. use padding
   c. shampoo the hair twice
   d. use specific products to build up the hair

7. Which is NOT a method used to disinfect tools and equipment?
   a. heat
   b. spray
   c. immersion
   d. disinfectant wipes

8. To clean combs and brushes, begin by:
   a. rinsing with hot water
   b. removing hair and debris
   c. immersing in soap and water
   d. immersing in a disinfectant solution

9. Which of the following is recommended to be disposed of after use on a long hair design client?
   a. cape
   b. comb
   c. brush
   d. hairnet

10. When completing the client record after a long hair service, which of the following is NOT necessary to note?
    a. hair condition
    b. scalp condition
    c. weather conditions
    d. long hair techniques used

LESSON CHALLENGE REFERENCES

Check your answers. Place a check mark next to the page number for any incorrect answer. On the lines, jot down topics that you still need to review.

1. PAGE 56 _____
2. PAGE 57 _____
3. PAGE 57 _____
4. PAGE 57 _____
5. PAGE 57 _____

6. PAGE 59 _____
7. PAGE 62 _____
8. PAGE 62 _____
9. PAGE 62 _____
10. PAGE 64 _____

▶ GROW WHAT YOU KNOW

Reflect on what you have learned and predict how this information will be used in the future.

109ᶜ.1 // WIG THEORY

ACHIEVE //

Following this lesson on *Wig Theory*, you'll be able to:

>> List the reasons clients wear wigs

>> State the different materials used in the composition of wigs

>> Explain the J and L Color Ring used for wigs

>> Describe the two general categories used to classify the construction of wigs and hairpieces

>> Compare the three methods used to attach hair or fiber to the wig cap or base

FOCUS //

WIG THEORY

History of Wigs

Composition, Colors and Construction

HISTORY OF WIGS

WIGS: Artificial hair items designed to cover the entire head.

-

-

DRAW IN AND COMMENT ON THE WIGS THAT WERE WORN THROUGHOUT HISTORY

EGYPTIANS:

ROMANS AND GREEKS:

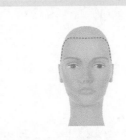

ELIZABETHAN ERA:

FRENCH REVOLUTION:

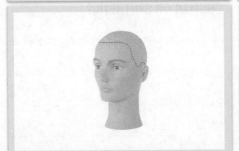

1950s AND 1960s:

Actors and actresses have worn wigs throughout the ages.

Advances in technology and design have made it so much easier to take advantage of the wide range of wigs available.

COMPOSITION, COLORS AND CONSTRUCTION

WIG COMPOSITION

3 TYPES OF WIGS

1.	2.	3.
•	•	•
•	•	•
	•	•
•		
	•	
•		
	•	
•		

The highest grade of human hair:	Examples of synthetic fibers include:	
_____	_____,	
	_____,	
	_____	

HUMAN OR SYNTHETIC?

• Hold several strands of each over a _____.

• Human hair will _____.

• Synthetic fiber will _____

_____

WIG COLORS

J AND L COLOR RING

• Standard hair color ring used by wig and hairpiece manufacturers

• Standardized colors = _____

• Contains numbered samples from _____

• Allows manufacturers to select from a variety of colors

WIG CONSTRUCTION

TWO GENERAL CATEGORIES:

CAP WIGS

-
-
-

CAPLESS WIGS

-
-
-

Hair and/or synthetic fibers may be attached to the wig cap or base in one of three methods:

Hand-Tied (hand-knotted)	Machine-Made	Semi-Hand-Tied

When Helping a Client Select a Wig...

-
-
-

WEB

From the Jump Start Box, select the term(s) or phrase(s) that belong in each box of the web.

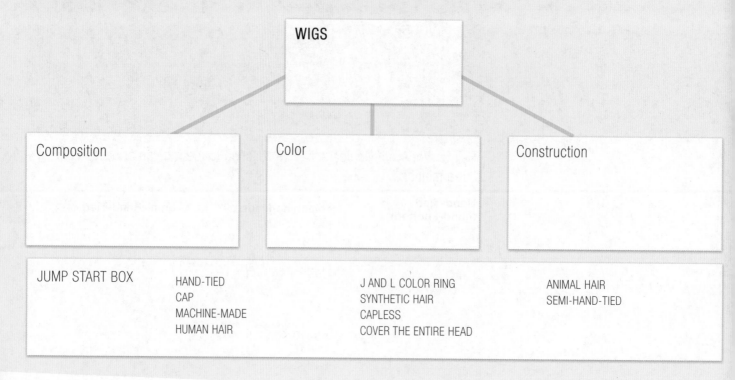

WIGS

Composition	Color	Construction

JUMP START BOX

HAND-TIED
CAP
MACHINE-MADE
HUMAN HAIR

J AND L COLOR RING
SYNTHETIC HAIR
CAPLESS
COVER THE ENTIRE HEAD

ANIMAL HAIR
SEMI-HAND-TIED

LESSON CHALLENGE *Multiple choice. Indicate one correct answer for each question.*

1. The type of human-hair wig that is the most costly is:
   a. Asian
   b. Indian
   c. European
   d. South American

2. Generally, hair from India is wavy, while hair from Asia is:
   a. long
   b. curly
   c. short
   d. straight

3. What type of hair is formulated with petroleum products?
   a. yak hair
   b. animal hair
   c. human hair
   d. synthetic hair

4. Human hairstrands will produce which of the following results when held over a match flame?
   a. burn slowly
   b. burn rapidly
   c. melt on the ends
   d. produce no odor

5. How many standardized colors are on the J and L Color Ring?
   a. 50
   b. 60
   c. 70
   d. 80

6. Which type of wig is available in several sizes and most often hand-tied?
   a. cap wig
   b. capless wig
   c. synthetic wig
   d. machine-made wig

7. Which of the following is NOT a characteristic of a capless wig?
   a. weighs only a few ounces
   b. most popular form of wigs
   c. consists of an elasticized mesh-fiber base
   d. consists of rows of hair wefts sewn to strips of elastic

8. Which of the following wig types simulates natural hair growth patterns and creates a natural look?
   a. cap
   b. hand-tied (hand-knotted)
   c. machine-made
   d. semi-hand-tied

9. It is difficult to perform a design service on which of the following wig types, since the direction of the hair is determined by the position the weft is sewn to the cap?
   a. cap
   b. hand-tied (hand-knotted)
   c. machine-made
   d. semi-hand-tied

10. Combinations of hand-tied and machine-made wigs and hairpieces are called:
    a. cap
    b. synthetic
    c. hand-knotted
    d. semi-hand-tied

LESSON CHALLENGE REFERENCES

Check your answers. Place a check mark next to the page number for any incorrect answer. On the lines, jot down topics that you still need to review.

1. PAGE 7 _____
2. PAGE 7 _____
3. PAGE 7 _____
4. PAGE 7 _____
5. PAGE 8 _____

6. PAGE 9 _____
7. PAGE 9 _____
8. PAGE 10 _____
9. PAGE 10 _____
10. PAGE 10 _____

▶ GROW WHAT YOU KNOW

Reflect on what you have learned and predict how this information will be used in the future.

109ᶜ.2 // WIG SERVICES

ACHIEVE //

Following this lesson on *Wig Services*, you'll be able to:

>> List some points to keep in mind when communicating with a client for a wig service

>> State different wig services you can offer a client

>> Summarize the differences between cleaning and conditioning a human-hair wig versus a synthetic wig

>> Explain different techniques and tips for cutting and shaping a wig

FOCUS //

WIG SERVICES

Wig Measurements and Fitting

Wig Cleaning and Styling

WIG SERVICES

Regardless of the reason(s) that the client desires the service, discretion is of great importance.

WIG SERVICE CONSIDERATIONS

-
-
-
-
-

WIG MEASUREMENT AND FITTING

WIG MEASUREMENT

WIG MEASUREMENT GUIDELINES

Brush the client's hair smooth.
For ready-to-wear wigs, measure the:

-

For custom-made wigs, also measure the:

-
-

PUTTING ON A WIG

PUTTING ON A WIG GUIDELINES

- Brush hair back from face and up from back _____.
- Cover hair with a _____ _____.
- Place front hairline over/slightly lower than client's front hairline.
- Adjust wig _____.

WIG BLOCKING

BLOCKING:

WIG BLOCKS:

WIG BLOCKING GUIDELINES

- Select the correct size canvas _____.
- Cover with clear plastic and secure plastic with _____ _____.
- Place wig on block and secure at:
  - ▪
  - ▪
  - ▪
  - ▪

CUSTOMIZING OR FITTING A WIG

TWO TYPES OF ALTERATIONS WHEN A GREATER CHANGE IS NEEDED:

Draw in the two types of alterations and label the parts of the wig.

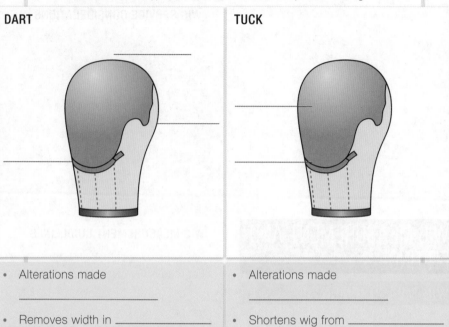

DART

TUCK

- Alterations made

  _____

- Removes width in _____

- Alterations made

  _____

- Shortens wig from _____

  to _____

STRETCHING OR SHRINKING CAP WIGS

STRETCHING CAP WIG: GUIDELINES

-
-
-
-
-

SHRINKING CAP WIG: GUIDELINES

-
-
-
-
-

Dry the wig under a warm dryer only if the wig is human hair; heat can distort curl patterns of _____ _____ .

WIG CLEANING AND STYLING

CLEANING AND CONDITIONING

HUMAN-HAIR WIGS	SYNTHETIC-HAIR WIGS
Cleaning and Conditioning Guidelines	*Cleaning Guidelines*
	Repeat same procedure as human hair except:
•	
•	•
•	
	•
•	
•	
•	
•	
•	

COLORING SERVICES

- Color should not be applied to wigs that are _____.
- Before coloring, perform a _____ _____.
- Keep color off the wig cap.

CUTTING AND SHAPING

- _____
- You may use thinning shears or a razor on _____ _____.
- Razors are not recommended for _____ _____.
-
-

SETTING AND FINISHING

-
-

ALERT!

Don't put synthetic wigs under dryer, since excessive heat can melt the fiber.

MATCHING
Match the wig service to the correct image.

1. Cutting   **2. Wig Measurement**   **3. Customizing a Wig**   **4. Wig Blocking**   **5. Putting on a Wig**

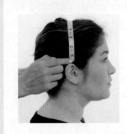   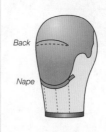 

_____   _____   _____   _____   _____

LESSON CHALLENGE
Multiple choice. Indicate one correct answer for each question.

1. When fitting a client with a wig, measure the circumference of the head, running the tape measure just:
   - a. on the ears
   - b. over the eyes
   - c. under the ears
   - d. above the ears

2. When putting the wig on the client, start at the:
   - a. nape
   - b. crown
   - c. sideburn area
   - d. front hairline

3. Which of the following terms identifies the procedure for sizing a wig?
   - a. pinning
   - b. blocking
   - c. matching
   - d. synthesizing

4. Dart alterations for a wig are made vertically to:
   - a. add width in the nape area
   - b. remove width in the nape area
   - c. shorten a wig from the front to the nape
   - d. avoid excess bulk close to the perimeter

5. How often should human-hair wigs be cleaned?
   - a. daily
   - b. once a week
   - c. every 2-4 weeks
   - d. every 2 months

6. What is the purpose of thinning a wig?
   - a. add weight
   - b. remove bulk
   - c. prevent frizzing
   - d. provide volume

LESSON CHALLENGE REFERENCES

Check your answers. Place a check mark next to the page number for any incorrect answer. On the lines, jot down topics that you still need to review.

1. PAGE 18 _____

2. PAGE 19 _____

3. PAGE 20 _____

4. PAGE 22 _____

5. PAGE 23 _____

6. PAGE 26 _____

GROW WHAT YOU KNOW

Reflect on what you have learned and predict how this information will be used in the future.

109ᶜ.3 //
HAIRPIECES AND HAIR ADDITIONS

ACHIEVE //

Following this lesson on *Hairpieces and Hair Additions*, you'll be able to:

>> Identify three types of fiber used in hairpieces and hair additions

>> List the different types of hairpieces and where they are most likely positioned

>> Compare strand-by-strand to weft hair additions

>> Explain why additional care is required during a hairpiece or hair addition consultation

FOCUS //

HAIRPIECES AND HAIR ADDITIONS

Hairpiece and Hair Addition Fibers

Hairpieces

Hair Addition Methods

Hairpiece and Hair Addition Service Essentials

- Hairpieces consist of: _____

  _____

- Hair additions consist of: _____

  _____

HAIRPIECE AND HAIR ADDITION FIBERS

HUMAN HAIR	SYNTHETIC FIBER	ANIMAL HAIR
•	•	•
•	•	•
•	•	•
•	•	
	•	
	•	

HAIRPIECES

Hairpieces are categorized or named according to their purpose and where they are designed to be worn.

TYPES OF HAIRPIECES

Classic Hairpieces	
Bang	
Cascade	
Chignon	
Fall	
Pony	
Toupée	
Wiglet	

HAIRPIECE ATTACHMENTS

COMBS:

CLIPS:

INTEGRATION:

ADHESIVES:

TOUPÉES

Hairpieces designed to cover _____

_____

HAIR ADDITION METHODS

TWO MAIN CLASSIFICATIONS

Strand-by-Strand/Points	Wefts/Lines
Loose or prepared strands of hair or fiber that are added to natural hair along _____ _____	Strands of hair or fiber sewn or bonded along one edge and added to natural hair along _____ _____
Draw a representation of strand-by-strand/points.	*Draw a representation of weft/lines.*

STRAND-BY-STRAND METHODS

CLIP-IN:

THERMAL FUSION:

COLD FUSION:

BEADING/TUBING:

BRAIDING:

WEFT ATTACHMENT METHODS

TAPING/CLIPPING

TRACK-AND-SEW

BONDING

TAPING

LIQUID ADHESIVE

TRACK-AND-SEW	
Tracks	**Sewing Methods**
• Strips of hair parted off to be _____	Needles may be straight and/or curved with _____ _____
•	Overcast Stitch:
•	
•	Lock Stitch:
•	Double-Lock Stitch:

HAIRPIECE AND HAIR ADDITION SERVICE ESSENTIALS

Keep in mind when communicating with a client:

•

•

•

•

•

•

•

SCRAMBLE

Unscramble these important words from the lesson.

TETISNYHC BERIF

GNIONCH

SADEACC

GNIONCH

ALFL

EPOUET

GLIWTE

REMLAHT ISUOFN

LESSON CHALLENGE   *Multiple choice. Indicate one correct answer for each question.*

1. Hair additions are an appropriate choice for clients who want to add length, density, texture and/or:
    a. color
    b. wiglet
    c. cascade
    d. short hair

2. Long hair fiber attached to an oblong-shaped dome base is referred to as a:
    a. fall
    b. toupée
    c. wiglet
    d. cascade

3. Which hairpiece is made up of hair fibers 6" or less in length attached to a round-shaped, flat base?
    a. switch
    b. wiglet
    c. chignon
    d. curl segment

4. A hairpiece worn by men to cover bald or thinning hair spots, particularly on top of the head, is called a:
    a. fall
    b. braid
    c. toupée
    d. chignon

5. Which type of hairpiece allows the client's hair to be pulled through for blending purposes?
    a. switch
    b. cascade
    c. integration
    d. curl segment

6. What is the hair addition method that uses a bonding agent activated by a heating element to affix loose hair fiber to small sections of the client's own hair?
    a. thermal fusion
    b. gluing
    c. track-and-sew
    d. on-the-scalp braiding

7. Which of the following methods describes attaching hair wefts to the client's hair by using a special adhesive?
    a. liquid bonding
    b. track-and-sew
    c. on-the-scalp braiding
    d. off-the-scalp braiding

8. Which method of applying hair additions requires a patch test?
   a. sewing
   b. bonding
   c. stitching
   d. braiding

9. Which braid is used as a support structure when performing the track-and-sew hair addition method?
   a. any off-the-scalp braid
   b. 5-strand, off-the-scalp braid
   c. 3-strand, on-the-scalp braid
   d. 3-strand, off-the-scalp braid

10. Which of the following stitches is used to secure a weft at either end or across the length of the weft/track?
    a. lock stitch
    b. overcast stitch
    c. cross-over stitch
    d. double-lock stitch

LESSON CHALLENGE REFERENCES

Check your answers. Place a check mark next to the page number for any incorrect answer. On the lines, jot down topics that you still need to review.

1. PAGE 32 _____
2. PAGE 35 _____
3. PAGE 35 _____
4. PAGE 35 _____
5. PAGE 36 _____

6. PAGE 40 _____
7. PAGE 43 _____
8. PAGE 43 _____
9. PAGE 44 _____
10. PAGE 45 _____

▶ GROW WHAT YOU KNOW

Reflect on what you have learned and predict how this information will be used in the future.

109ᶜ.4 // WIG, HAIRPIECE AND HAIR ADDITION ESSENTIALS

ACHIEVE //

Following this lesson on *Wig, Hairpiece and Hair Addition Essentials*, you'll be able to:

» Identify the products, tools and supplies needed to perform wig, hairpiece and hair addition services

» Recognize equipment used in wig, hairpiece and hair addition services

» Summarize infection control and safety concerns before, during and after a wig, hairpiece or hair addition service

FOCUS //

WIG, HAIRPIECE AND HAIR ADDITION ESSENTIALS

Overview: Wig, Hairpiece and Hair Addition Essentials

Wig, Hairpiece and Hair Addition Infection Control and Safety

OVERVIEW: WIG, HAIRPIECE AND HAIR ADDITION ESSENTIALS

Be familiar with the essentials needed to meet the needs of your clients when dealing with wigs, hairpieces and hair additions.

WIG, HAIRPIECE AND HAIR ADDITION PRODUCTS

PRODUCTS	FUNCTION
Nonflammable Liquid Shampoo	
Mild Shampoo	Cleans synthetic wigs, hairpieces and hair additions
Synthetic Wig Shampoo	
Conditioner	Keeps the wigs, hairpieces and hair additions in good condition
Synthetic Wig Conditioner	
Holding Spray	Holds finished human-hair wig, hairpiece and hair addition designs in place

WIG, HAIRPIECE AND HAIR ADDITION TOOLS

TOOLS	FUNCTION
Comb	
Brush	
Shears	Shape and customize wigs, hairpieces and hair additions
Thinning Shears	
Razor	Tapers and blends; removes bulk and excess fiber
Rollers	Allow temporary curl placement for human-hair wigs and hairpieces
Clips	
J and L Color Ring	

WIG, HAIRPIECE AND HAIR ADDITION SUPPLIES

SUPPLIES	FUNCTION
Wig Cap	
Bobby Pins	Secure client's hair under wig; sometimes used to hold wig in place
Hairpins	
Needle and Thread	Create darts and tucks in wigs; secure wefts in track-and-sew technique; used to sew wefts for fantasy hairpieces
Wig Pins	
Styrofoam Heads	Store and display wigs
Chin Strap	
Measuring Tape	Measures client's head to determine correct wig size
Plastic Bag	Covers and protects canvas blocks
Cloth Cape	
Hair Addition Fiber/Hair	

WIG, HAIRPIECE AND HAIR ADDITION EQUIPMENT

EQUIPMENT	FUNCTION
Canvas Block (various sizes)	
Wig Dryer	Dries human-hair wigs that have been wet set (on canvas blocks)
Fusion Machine	Attaches hair additions to client's hair
Hackle	
Drawing Board	

WIG, HAIRPIECE AND HAIR ADDITION INFECTION CONTROL AND SAFETY

It is essential to keep your client's safety in mind at all times.

INFECTION CONTROL AND SAFETY – BEFORE THE SERVICE

-
-
-
-

INFECTION CONTROL AND SAFETY – DURING THE SERVICE

-
-
-
-

INFECTION CONTROL AND SAFETY – AFTER THE SERVICE

-
-
-

WEB

From the Jump Start Box select the phrases that describe the terms found in the outer boxes.

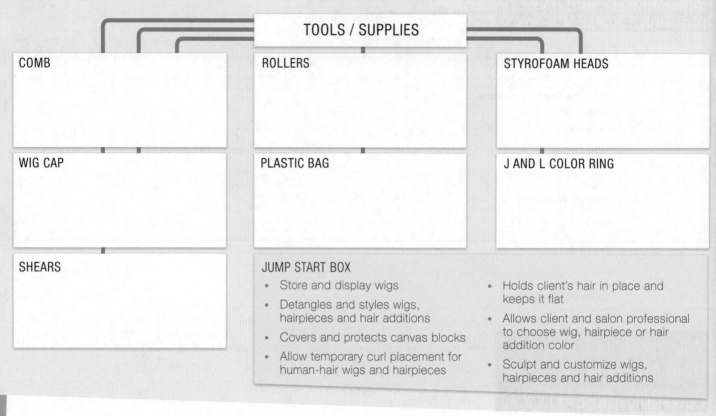

TOOLS / SUPPLIES

COMB

ROLLERS

STYROFOAM HEADS

WIG CAP

PLASTIC BAG

J AND L COLOR RING

SHEARS

JUMP START BOX

- Store and display wigs
- Detangles and styles wigs, hairpieces and hair additions
- Covers and protects canvas blocks
- Allow temporary curl placement for human-hair wigs and hairpieces

- Holds client's hair in place and keeps it flat
- Allows client and salon professional to choose wig, hairpiece or hair addition color
- Sculpt and customize wigs, hairpieces and hair additions

LESSON CHALLENGE

Multiple choice. Indicate one correct answer for each question.

1. What holds a finished wig and hairpiece design in place?
   a. holding spray
   b. wig conditioner
   c. synthetic wig shampoo
   d. nonflammable liquid shampoo

2. The following tool detangles and styles wigs, hairpieces and hair additions:
   a. comb
   b. razor
   c. shears
   d. rollers

3. All of the following implements are used to shape, taper and remove bulk, EXCEPT:
   a. shears
   b. razor
   c. rollers
   d. thinning shears

4. What is used to hold a wig or hairpiece in place on a canvas block during designing, cleaning and maintenance services?
   a. wig cap
   b. wig pins
   c. hairpins
   d. bobby pins

5. A flat mat used to hold hair extension fibers during a hair addition service is known as a:
   a. hackle
   b. wig cap
   c. canvas block
   d. drawing board

6. A metal plate with rows of pointed needles used to blend or straighten fiber/hair during a hair addition service is called a:
    a. dryer
    b. block
    c. hackle
    d. drawing board

7. For a wig service, when should you wash your hands?
    a. before the service
    b. during the service
    c. only when visibly dirty
    d. only when the client requests it

8. Work in a well-ventilated area when working with:
    a. gel
    b. conditioner
    c. anti-druff shampoos
    d. liquid dry shampoos

9. All of the following statements are true about wig, hairpiece and hair addition services EXCEPT:
    a. use a fresh drape on every client
    b. disinfect all tools properly
    c. it is not necessary to drape the client
    d. work with liquid dry shampoo in a well-ventilated area

10. Which of the following steps is required prior to disinfection?
    a. allow appropriate contact time
    b. store tools in a dry, covered container
    c. store tools in a hot, uncovered container
    d. clean and remove debris from all tools and multi-use supplies

LESSON CHALLENGE REFERENCES

Check your answers. Place a check mark next to the page number for any incorrect answer. On the lines, jot down topics that you still need to review.

1. PAGE 52 _____

2. PAGE 53 _____

3. PAGE 53 _____

4. PAGE 53 _____

5. PAGE 54 _____

6. PAGE 54 _____

7. PAGE 55 _____

8. PAGE 55 _____

9. PAGE 55 _____

10. PAGE 55 _____

▶ GROW WHAT YOU KNOW

Reflect on what you have learned and predict how this information will be used in the future.

110ᶜ.1 //
COLOR THEORY

ACHIEVE //

Following this lesson on *Color Theory*, you'll be able to:

>> Restate in your own words the law of color

>> Identify the three primary colors and explain how they are used to create secondary and tertiary colors

>> Distinguish the characteristics of color, including hue, value and intensity

FOCUS //

COLOR THEORY

The Law of Color

Color Wheel

Warm and Cool Colors

Complementary Colors

Characteristics of Color

COLOR THEORY

Color is the visual perception of the _____ of _____; without light there would be no color.

Each color is a group of electromagnetic waves, also called _____.

Wavelengths that can be seen create color and are known as _____ _____.

THE LAW OF COLOR

The three "pure" colors are _____, _____ and _____. When mixed together, these three primary colors create _____.

3 COLOR CATEGORIES

PRIMARY COLORS

Cannot be created by mixing any other colors:

-
-
-

SECONDARY COLORS

2 of the 3 primary colors mixed in varying proportions:

-
-
-

TERTIARY COLORS

A primary and a secondary color mixed in varying proportions:

-
-
-
-
-
-

COLOR WHEEL

Label the color hues in the color wheel.

A 12-hue wheel that can be used as a tool in which _____ primary, _____ secondary and _____ tertiary colors are positioned in a circle

Any mixed color can be described in relation to the _____ colors.

WARM AND COOL COLORS

Also known as warm and cool _____

WARM COLOR TONES

Generally, _____, _____ and
_____ fall into the warm half of the color wheel

COOL COLOR TONES

Generally, _____, _____ and
_____ fall into the cool half of the color wheel

HELPFUL HINT

In addition to knowing a client's hair type and color, it is important to know whether
a client's _____ _____ is warm or cool when
designing hair color to complement their natural coloring.

COMPLEMENTARY COLORS

Colors found _____ one another on the color wheel
Two complementary colors combined = a mix of all three _____
_____ /

When complementary colors are mixed together in varying proportions, they
neutralize or cancel out one another, producing a _____ color.

Neutral colors do not exhibit _____ or _____
tones, including certain shades of gray, brown and black.

HELPFUL HINT

In hair coloring, complementary colors are often used to neutralize
_____ _____.

Example: Client's hair is lightened to a brassy orange tone
Check color wheel: Complementary color to orange is _____
Correction: _____
Result: _____

COMPLEMENTARY MATCH:

A client's hair color is too drab (greenish). Correct it with slightly _____ toner or color rinse.

After lightening a client's hair to a light blond, it is very yellow. Correct it with a(n) _____ toner.

A desired medium blond resulted too brassy (orange). Correct it with a(n) _____ toner or color.

CHARACTERISTICS OF COLOR

Color has 3 main characteristics:

-
-
-

HUE

Hues are named and abbreviated based on color wheel position.

Colors are abbreviated by first initial and are used by manufacturers and salons to identify specific hues of hair coloring products:

Yellow = _____ Red-orange = _____

LEVEL/VALUE

Degree of _____ or _____ of a color relative to itself and to other colors

FIELDS OF COLOR

All hair colors can be broadly categorized into _____ major fields of color:

-
-
-

LEVEL SYSTEM

Level System = Numbering system that identifies the _____ or _____ of hair colors

Divides natural and _____ hair colors in _____ categories numbered 1-12; some manufacturers use 1-10

_____ = 1

_____ = 10 or 12

INTENSITY

Intensity refers to the vividness, brightness or saturation of a color within its own _____.

Hair color intensity can range from _____ to _____.

WORD SCRAMBLE:

Unscramble the words.

1. OLORC _____

2. HEU _____

3. NSINTTYIE _____

4. IRPRMYA ORCLO _____

5. COLRO ELWEH _____

6. CDRYAONES OLCRO _____

7. ALUVE _____

8. TTRRIEAY OCOLR _____

9. MPLYRAMCNETOE ROLOC _____

10. OOLC LOOCR _____

11. ARWM RCOOL _____

LESSON CHALLENGE *Multiple choice. Indicate one correct answer for each question.*

1. All of the following statements are true about color, EXCEPT:
   a. it is a phenomenon of light
   b. it is a group of electromagnetic waves
   c. it can be seen if wavelengths are reflected off an object
   d. it does not depend on the presence of light

2. What are the 3 primary colors?
   a. red, blue and yellow
   b. green, black and purple
   c. green, orange and purple
   d. red, white and blue

3. What colors are produced by mixing 2 primary colors in varying proportions?
   a. secondary
   b. tertiary
   c. infrared
   d. ultraviolet

4. A mixture of red and yellow creates what color?
   a. blue
   b. green
   c. violet
   d. orange

5. Varying proportions of blue and yellow create what color?
   a. black
   b. green
   c. violet
   d. blue

6. An example of a tertiary color would be:
   a. yellow-orange
   b. blue-yellow
   c. violet
   d. blue

7. Mixing varying proportions of a primary color with its neighboring secondary color will produce:
   a. white
   b. black
   c. gray
   d. a tertiary color

8. Which of the following combinations is NOT a tertiary color?
   a. red-violet
   b. blue-green
   c. red-orange
   d. blue-yellow

9. Which of the following descriptions identifies warm colors?
   a. colors that contain blue hues
   b. colors that contain green hues
   c. colors that fall into the orange and red half of the wheel
   d. colors that are opposite each other on the color wheel

10. Cool colors include:
    a. blues
    b. yellows
    c. reds
    d. oranges

11. Mixing colors found opposite one another on the color wheel produces which color?
    a. green
    b. white
    c. gray, black or brown
    d. blue

12. Colors found opposite each other on the color wheel are called:
    a. complementary colors
    b. primary colors
    c. secondary colors
    d. tertiary colors

13. An application of which colors would help rid a client of unwanted orange tones?
    a. green-based
    b. brown-based
    c. blue-based
    d. black-based

14. A level 12 color is:
    a. the darkest level
    b. the lightest level
    c. a medium level
    d. a neutral level

15. The vividness, brightness or saturation of a color is referred to as:
    a. level
    b. texture
    c. intensity
    d. porosity

LESSON CHALLENGE REFERENCES

Check your answers. Place a check mark next to the page number for any incorrect answer.
On the lines, jot down topics that you still need to review.

1. PAGE 6 _____

2. PAGE 7 _____

3. PAGE 7 _____

4. PAGE 7 _____

5. PAGE 7 _____

6. PAGE 7 _____

7. PAGE 7 _____

8. PAGE 7 _____

9. PAGE 9 _____

10. PAGE 9 _____

11. PAGE 10 _____

12. PAGE 10 _____

13. PAGE 11 _____

14. PAGE 13 _____

15. PAGE 16 _____

▶ # GROW WHAT YOU KNOW

Reflect on what you have learned and predict how this information will be used in the future.

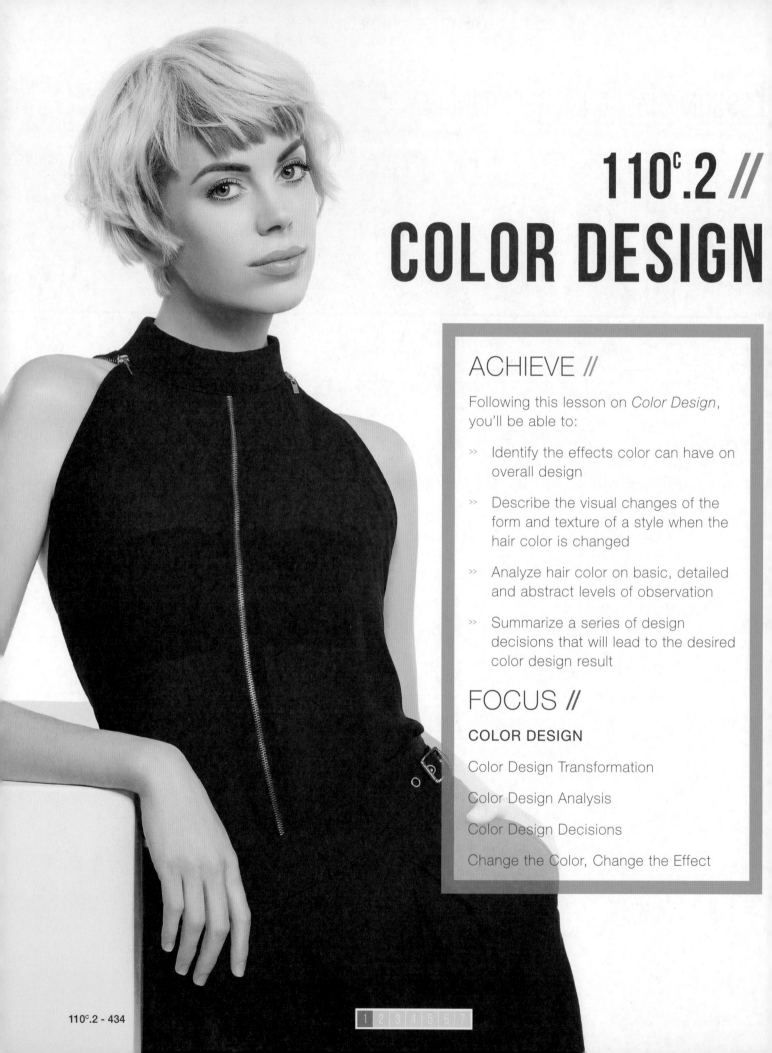

110ᶜ.2 //
COLOR DESIGN

ACHIEVE //

Following this lesson on *Color Design*, you'll be able to:

>> Identify the effects color can have on overall design

>> Describe the visual changes of the form and texture of a style when the hair color is changed

>> Analyze hair color on basic, detailed and abstract levels of observation

>> Summarize a series of design decisions that will lead to the desired color design result

FOCUS //

COLOR DESIGN

Color Design Transformation

Color Design Analysis

Color Design Decisions

Change the Color, Change the Effect

COLOR DESIGN TRANSFORMATION

EFFECTS OF COLOR ON FORM

A repetition of color throughout a design draws attention away from
_____ and focuses on _____.

EFFECTS OF COLOR ON TEXTURE

The texture of a design can be either emphasized or de-emphasized based on
the _____ and the _____ between the
colors chosen.

EFFECTS OF COLOR AS A FOCAL POINT

Color placed in specific area to lead the _____ or enhance
_____.

COLOR DESIGN ANALYSIS

Color designing is part of a _____ _____
and includes identifying:

•

•

Start by analyzing a color as a designer would, using the 3 levels of observation:

1. Basic:

2. Detail:

3. Abstract:

THINKING MAP:

LEVELS OF OBSERVATION

BASIC	DETAIL	ABSTRACT
_____	_____	_____
_____	_____	_____
_____	_____	_____

HAIR COLOR ANALYSIS

COLOR DESIGN DECISIONS

SCULPTED FORM

The sculpted form serves as the inspiration for _____ _____ and patterns.

Color designs can be used to _____ or _____ the _____ and _____ of a haircut.

EXISTING/DESIRED LEVEL

Dark colors visually _____ and emphasize _____ and _____.

Lighter colors create the _____ of more _____.

What are 3 questions you should ask yourself when planning color transformations?

1.

2.

3.

COLOR PLACEMENT

Draw in the areas and zones for color placement.

COLOR WITHIN ZONES

Patterns subdivide _____ into _____ create color design with a combination of colors.

Examples of areas or zones: _____ _____.

Draw in the areas and zones for color placement.

COLOR WITHIN SHAPES

Shapes are used to _____ _____ and create color _____.

Size and position of shapes are decided by _____ _____.

Shapes commonly used: _____ _____.

DESIGN PRINCIPLES

Artistic arrangement patterns for the design elements of:

-
-
-

REPETITION:

ALTERNATION:

PROGRESSION:

CONTRAST:

Label the design principles using the graphic organizer.

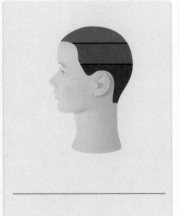

_____

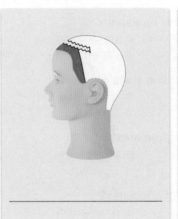

_____

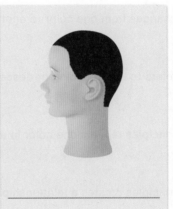

_____

_____

CHANGE THE COLOR, CHANGE THE EFFECT

Analyze the images and identify how the effect was changed. Compare your assessment results with your classmates' to discover how color perceptions differ and why it is important to use visual examples when consulting about hair color.

_____

_____

_____

LESSON CHALLENGE *Multiple choice. Indicate one correct answer for each question.*

1. Common reasons for a color change include:
   a. cover gray
   b. enhance existing hair color
   c. create a fashion statement
   d. all of the above

2. What color design principle can draw attention away from the texture of a design and focus on the silhouette?
   a. alternation
   b. progression
   c. repetition
   d. contrast

3. The texture of a hair design can be emphasized or de-emphasized based on:
   a. sectioning
   b. color patterns
   c. detail
   d. head position

4. Selective color placement in a specific area can create a:
   a. focal point
   b. color pattern
   c. secondary color
   d. all of the above

5. The three levels of observation are basic, detail and:
   a. formal
   b. structured
   c. abstract
   d. natural

6. Which design principle changes from one color to another repeatedly?
   a. repetition
   b. alternation
   c. progression
   d. contrast

7. Which design principle refers to an ascending or descending scale of colors?
   a. repetition
   b. alternation
   c. progression
   d. contrast

8. Which of these design principles repeats one color in a given area?
   a. repetition
   b. alternation
   c. progression
   d. contrast

9. Which of these design principles creates a relationship of opposites?
   a. repetition
   b. alternation
   c. progression
   d. contrast

LESSON CHALLENGE REFERENCES

Check your answers. Place a check mark next to the page number for any incorrect answer. On the lines, jot down topics that you still need to review.

1. PAGE 20 _____
2. PAGE 21 _____
3. PAGE 22 _____
4. PAGE 22 _____
5. PAGE 23 _____

6. PAGE 29 _____
7. PAGE 29 _____
8. PAGE 29 _____
9. PAGE 29 _____

▶ GROW WHAT YOU KNOW

Reflect on what you have learned and predict how this information will be used in the future.

110ᶜ.3 //
IDENTIFYING EXISTING HAIR COLOR

ACHIEVE //

Following this lesson on *Identifying Existing Hair Color*, you'll be able to:

» Describe the difference between eumelanin (brown/black pigment) and pheomelanin (red/yellow pigment)

» Identify the categories for gray hair mixtures of non-pigmented and pigmented hair

» Identify the natural hair color levels

» Explain how manufacturers identify and name artificial hair colors, including by level and tone, and by tone or name

» Review the hair analysis considerations prior to a color service, including texture and porosity

FOCUS //

IDENTIFYING EXISTING HAIR COLOR

Identifying Natural Hair Color

Identifying Artificial Hair Color

Additional Considerations

IDENTIFYING NATURAL HAIR COLOR

Contributing pigment + artificial pigment = _____

Contributing pigment = Client's naturally present _____ or

a combination of _____ and previously applied artificial

_____ remaining on hair

- _____

  _____

MELANIN

Pigment that gives hair its _____ and is

determined through _____

Brown/black natural pigment: _____

Red/yellow natural pigment: _____

Dense concentration of eumelanin = _____ hair

Small population of eumelanin = _____ hair

Predominant amount of pheomelanin = _____ hair

Two Types of Melanin

GRAY HAIR

Melanin production _____ and hair strand loses its

_____; results in white hair

Gray hair is a _____ of non-pigmented and _____ hair

Primary factor is _____

Percentages of Gray Hair

Prior to a color application, determine the _____ of gray

your client has; may need to use different color _____ to

accommodate different percentages of gray

25% GRAY	50% GRAY	75%-80% GRAY

If a client has:

* _____ %-30% gray hair, apply a color _____ level lighter than desired shade

* 75%-80% apply one level _____ than desired color

  When working with _____ hair, may need to pre-soften or prelighten hair first

IDENTIFYING NATURAL LEVEL AND TONE

For the best results, analyze a client's natural hair color to determine:

*
*
*

Steps to Analyze Color

1 FIRST:

2 THEN:

3 FINALLY:

IDENTIFYING ARTIFICIAL HAIR COLOR

If your client has already had a color service in the past, you will need to identify the:

*
*

TONES/BASE COLORS

Color Selection Considerations:

Predominant underlying tone of color formulation: _____

Intensity of color: Lessened by adding a _____ color; increased by adding a _____ color

HELPFUL HINT

Manufacturers identify and name artificial colors in several ways:

By level and _____, such as level 5RV (red-violet)

By _____ and tone, such as medium red-violet

By base color or _____, such as red-violet or mahogany

Name of base colors often indicate _____ or _____ of a color or its tone

ADDITIONAL CONSIDERATIONS

TEXTURE

Draw the three different textures and porosity diameter.

| Fine | Medium | Coarse |

POROSITY

Texture (diameter) and porosity of your client's hair influence _____

_____ and _____.

Texture = _____

_____

Coarse: _____

_____

Fine: _____

Medium: _____

Porosity = _____

Determined by number of _____ layers and how _____

they overlap.

Main factor for:

• _____ • _____

• _____ • _____

Resistant porosity (cuticle layers are smooth): _____

_____

Average porosity (cuticle is slightly raised): _____

_____

Extreme porosity (cuticle is lifted and/or missing): _____

_____

Reasons for Uneven Porosity:

•

•

•

•

HELPFUL HINT

Uneven or extreme porosity may require a _____ to ensure

even _____ absorption.

GIVE IT A TRY

Look at the picture and identify the Field, Level and Tone.

| FIELD | LEVEL | TONE |

LESSON CHALLENGE

Multiple choice. Indicate one correct answer for each question.

1. A small concentration of eumelanin will produce:
   a. black hair
   b. red hair
   c. light blond hair
   d. dark brown hair

2. Red hair color would be determined due to a:
   a. small concentration of eumelanin
   b. dense concentration of eumelanin
   c. small concentration of pheomelanin
   d. dense concentration of pheomelanin

3. Which hair texture may tend to process slightly lighter than the intended level?
   a. coarse
   b. medium
   c. fine
   d. thinning

4. Which type of porosity may take longer to absorb coloring?
   a. normal
   b. average
   c. extreme
   d. resistant

5. With resistant porosity, cuticles are:
   a. slightly raised
   b. smooth
   c. missing
   d. open

LESSON CHALLENGE REFERENCES

Check your answers. Place a check mark next to the page number for any incorrect answer.
On the lines, jot down topics that you still need to review.

1. PAGE 35 _____

2. PAGE 35 _____

3. PAGE 42 _____

4. PAGE 42 _____

5. PAGE 42 _____

▶ GROW WHAT YOU KNOW

Reflect on what you have learned and predict how this information will be used in the future.

110ᶜ.4 | NONOXIDATIVE COLOR PRODUCTS

ACHIEVE //

Following this lesson on *Nonoxidative Color Products,*
you'll be able to:

>> Identify the two main types of nonoxidative color products

>> Describe the characteristics of temporary color products

>> Describe the characteristics of semi-permanent color products

>> Describe the characteristics of vegetable, metallic
and compound dyes

FOCUS //

**NONOXIDATIVE
COLOR PRODUCTS**

Temporary Colors

Semi-Permanent Colors

Vegetable, Metallic and
Compound Dyes

NONOXIDATIVE COLOR PRODUCTS

Nonoxidative = _____ change; _____ effect

Add pigment but do not _____ existing hair color

Used to _____ color, impart _____

and add _____ tones as well as _____

unwanted tones

Not mixed with a _____; used directly out of bottle

Two Types of Nonoxidative Colors

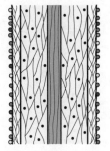

Temporary

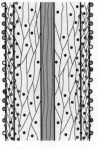

Semi-Permanent

TEMPORARY COLORS

- Last from shampoo to

  _____

- Not rinsed out once

  _____

- _____ color

  molecules only coat surface of cuticle

  creating _____

  change

- Does not require a patch or

  _____ test

  Examples:

SEMI-PERMANENT COLORS

- Fade _____ with

  each shampoo; no line of

  _____

- Large and small molecules—large

  molecules _____;

  small molecules penetrate

  _____ and

  enter _____

- Predisposition test required if

  containing an _____

  _____

  Examples:

VEGETABLE, METALLIC AND COMPOUND DYES

Least common types of hair coloring products used today

Use is discouraged since they are _____ and

sometimes _____

VEGETABLE DYES

Vegetable dyes utilize _____ products to color the hair

Henna – Most common, _____

_____

Chamomile – _____

METALLIC DYES

Also known as: progressive or _____ dyes; not recommended

because metals do not mix with other chemicals used in salon services

COMPOUND DYES

Combination of _____ and _____ dyes

MATCHING

Match the term with the correct description.

A. Temporary

B. Semi-Permanent

C. Henna

D. Chamomile

E. Metallic Dyes

F. Compound Dyes

_____ Combination of metallic and vegetable dyes

_____ Produces reddish highlights

_____ Last from shampoo to shampoo

_____ Also known as progressive or gradual dyes

_____ Gradually fades with each shampoo

_____ Produces golden highlight

LESSON CHALLENGE

Multiple choice. Indicate one correct answer for each question.

1. Which colors coat only the surface of the cuticle and do not enter the cortex?
   a. semi-permanent
   b. long-lasting permanent
   c. permanent
   d. temporary

2. A nonoxidative process that uses large and small color molecules and allows small color molecules to penetrate the cuticle and enter the cortex is called:
   a. temporary coloring
   b. semi-permanent coloring
   c. demi-permanent coloring
   d. permanent coloring

3. Which of the following characteristics does NOT describe semi-permanent colors?
   a. only deposits color
   b. retouch services are not required
   c. leaves a line of demarcation
   d. does not involve a chemical change to alter hair

4. A vegetable dye that produces reddish highlights is commonly known as:
   a. henna
   b. metallic dyes
   c. filler
   d. chamomile

5. Chemical services should not be performed on hair that has been colored with any of the following products, EXCEPT:
   a. henna
   b. metallic dyes
   c. compound dyes
   d. weekly rinses

LESSON CHALLENGE REFERENCES

Check your answers. Place a check mark next to the page number for any incorrect answer. On the lines, jot down topics that you still need to review.

1. PAGE 49 _____

2. PAGE 51 _____

3. PAGE 51 _____

4. PAGE 52 _____

5. PAGE 52 _____

► GROW WHAT YOU KNOW

Reflect on what you have learned and predict how this information will be used in the future.

110ᶜ.5 | OXIDATIVE COLOR PRODUCTS

ACHIEVE //

Following this lesson on *Oxidative Color Products*, you'll be able to:

» Identify the two types of oxidative color products

» Explain the relationship of developer strength and levels of the desired color

» Describe the characteristics of fillers, concentrates, intensifiers and drabbers

» State the difference between the on-the-scalp lighteners and off-the-scalp lighteners

» Identify the 10 stages of decolorization

» List four main steps in color formulation

FOCUS //

OXIDATIVE COLOR PRODUCTS

Long-Lasting Semi-Permanent (Demi-Permanent) Colors

Permanent Colors

Developers

Fillers, Concentrates, Intensifiers and Drabbers

Lighteners

Basic Color Formulation Guidelines

OXIDATIVE COLOR PRODUCTS

Deposit color only _____ (lighten) and _____ color in a _____ process; mixed with an _____ (developer) to create _____ change (_____ of _____) with longer lasting effect.

Not designed to lift _____ pigment.

Two major classifications of oxidative colors are:

1   Oxidative without ammonia = _____

2   Oxidative with ammonia = _____

Two Types of Oxidative Colors

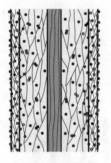

Long-Lasting Semi-Permanent

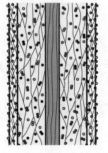

Permanent

Since permanent colors contain aniline derivatives, a predisposition test (patch test) is required.

LONG-LASTING SEMI-PERMANENT

- Also known as _____ _____ demi-permanent; or _____ without _____ colors
- Contain little or no _____
- Deposit color, add _____ to hair, does not lighten _____ color
- Required to have _____ test
- Generally last _____ to _____ weeks
- Mixed with low volume of hydrogen _____ creating a _____ change
- 3 types:
    - ▪
    - ▪
    - ▪
- Contain small color molecules that _____ the cortex
- Last _____ to _____ weeks

PERMANENT

- Sometimes called oxidative tints with ammonia or _____ _____ tints
- Mixed with varying strengths of _____ _____
- Capable of lightening _____ pigment and depositing _____ pigment in a _____ process
- Required to have _____ test
- Ammonia and hydrogen peroxide allow for _____ and _____
- 3 types:
    - ▪
    - ▪
    - ▪
- 2 types of dye intermediates that can be found in permanent tint are _____ and _____

DEVELOPERS

Oxidizing agents with pH of _____ to _____ used with semi-permanent and permanent colors, lighteners and toners

- Measured by volume: 10, 20, 30 and 40 volume in the _____
- Measured by the percentages: 3%, 6%, 9% and 12% in _____
  - Lower volume = _____ achieved
  - Higher volume = _____ achieved
  - Most commonly used developer in hair coloring products is _____

DEVELOPER STRENGTHS

As a general rule:

10 volume (3%) developer lifts up to _____ color level

20 volume (6%) developer lifts up to _____ color levels

30 volume (9%) developer lifts up to _____ color levels

Prelightening may be required if the desired amount of lift is not achieved using a single-process color.

FILLERS, CONCENTRATES, INTENSIFIERS AND DRABBERS

Products designed to increase vibrancy or to neutralize unwanted tones.

FILLERS

Equalize porosity of hair and deposit _____ color in one application

Two types of fillers:

- Conditioning: _____
  _____

- Color: _____
  _____

CONCENTRATES, INTENSIFIERS AND DRABBERS

Concentrates: _____ or _____ tones

Intensifiers: _____

Drabbers: _____ unwanted tones

Can be _____ with color applied _____ to prelightened hair

LIGHTENERS

Also known as bleaches; used to _____, remove or diffuse pigment

Utilize ingredients, such as _____ and _____, for oxidation

Penetrates the cortex, causing _____ to break into _____ pieces

2 types:

-

-

ON-THE-SCALP LIGHTENER

-

-

-

OFF-THE-SCALP LIGHTENER

-

-

-

-

DEGREES OF DECOLORIZATION

Approximately _____ stages or degrees of _____

Hair should _____ be lightened to white to avoid extreme _____

If hair is _____, a _____ may make hair appear ashy, gray or too cool

LABEL THE DEGREES

Write in the correct degree of decolorization:

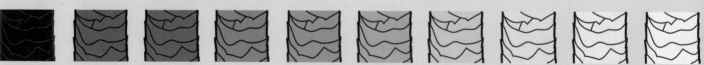

_____

TONERS

Light _____ colors used to add _____ or

_____ to prelightened hair

Deposit color and _____ unwanted pigment remaining after

prelightening: _____ golds or _____

Degree of _____ will help determine level of toner

A predisposition test is _____

All toners should be selected in relation to the _____

DOUBLE-PROCESS

Hair that is lightened (decolorized) first and then colored (recolorized) to
desired shade

2 common reasons for recolorizing:

1.

2.

Performed in two steps:

1.

2.

BASIC COLOR FORMULATION GUIDELINES

Requires an understanding of the laws of color, _____

and _____ pigment

Performed in four steps:

1

2

3

4

Always follow _____

for mixing ratios and procesing times

COLOR FORMULATION PRACTICE

Follow the color formulation steps and recommend the formula.

EXISTING LEVEL AND TONE:

Level 5, natural

25% gray

DESIRED LEVEL AND TONE:

Level 5, natural gold

COLOR FORMULA:

DEVELOPER:

EXISTING LEVEL AND TONE:

Level 9, natural golden blond

DESIRED LEVEL AND TONE:

Level 6, golden red

COLOR FORMULA:

DEVELOPER:

EXISTING LEVEL AND TONE:

80% gray

20% level 6 natural light brown

DESIRED LEVEL AND TONE:

Level 9, beige blond

COLOR FORMULA:

DEVELOPER:

COLOR FORMULA:

EXISTING LEVEL AND TONE:

DESIRED LEVEL AND TONE:

DEVELOPER:

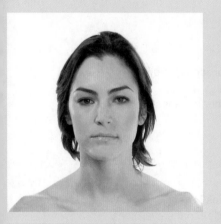

COLOR FORMULA:

EXISTING LEVEL AND TONE:

DESIRED LEVEL AND TONE:

DEVELOPER:

LESSON CHALLENGE   *Multiple choice. Indicate one correct answer for each question.*

1. Hair color products that are mixed with a developer to create a chemical change are called:
    a. oxidative color
    b. nonoxidative color
    c. temporary color
    d. semi-permanent color

2. A type of hair color that uses a low-volume hydrogen peroxide that can only deposit color or add tone to the hair would be:
    a. temporary
    b. semi-permanent
    c. permanent
    d. long-lasting semi-permanent

3. Long-lasting semi-permanent colors will generally last:
    a. 1 to 2 weeks
    b. 2 to 3 weeks
    c. 4 to 6 weeks
    d. at least 3 months

4. Demi-permanent colors are NOT designed to:
    a. add tone
    b. last 4 to 6 weeks
    c. deposit color
    d. lighten existing color

5. Permanent hair colors are sometimes called:
    a. oxidative tints with ammonia
    b. temporary colors
    c. semi-permanent colors
    d. oxidative tints without ammonia

6. The combination of hydrogen peroxide and which of the following items will allow for the lift and lightening of the hair's natural color?
    a. shampoo
    b. relaxer
    c. pigment
    d. ammonia

7. Which of the following products requires the use of a skin patch test?
    a. temporary color
    b. color mousse
    c. permanent color
    d. weekly rinse

8. What may be required if the desired amount of lift is not achieved using a single-process color?
    a. prelightening
    b. addition of a temporary color
    c. addition of a filler
    d. addition of a demi-permanent color

9. Which item is the most commonly used developer or oxidizing agent?
    a. aniline
    b. nitrogen
    c. oxygen
    d. hydrogen peroxide

10. Which of the following statements is true of products that contain aniline derivatives?
    a. they are always temporary
    b. a skin patch test is not required
    c. they may be applied to the eyelashes
    d. a skin patch test is required

11. A 20 volume hydrogen peroxide solution will generally lift the hair:
    a. two levels
    b. three levels
    c. four levels
    d. five levels

12. A 30 volume hydrogen peroxide solution will generally lift the hair how many more levels than a 20 volume solution?
    a. one level
    b. two levels
    c. three levels
    d. four levels

13. Which product is used before a color service to provide an even base?
    a. toner
    b. intensifier
    c. filler
    d. drabber

14. Which of the following statements is true of lighteners?
    a. used to add melanin to the hair
    b. used to add polymers and melanin
    c. generally applied to wet hair
    d. used to diffuse or remove pigment

15. On-the-scalp lighteners have a pH of:
    a. 2.5 to 3.5
    b. 4.0 to 5.5
    c. 6.5 to 7.5
    d. about 9.0

16. Off-the-scalp lighteners are generally used for:
    a. virgin coloring
    b. retouch coloring
    c. special effects such as highlighting
    d. soap capping

17. Which process involves lightening the hair and then recoloring to the desired color result?
    a. tint back
    b. cap method
    c. double-process
    d. weaving

LESSON CHALLENGE REFERENCES

Check your answers. Place a check mark next to the page number for any incorrect answer.
On the lines, jot down topics that you still need to review.

1. PAGE 58 _____
2. PAGE 59 _____
3. PAGE 59 _____
4. PAGE 59 _____
5. PAGE 60 _____
6. PAGE 60 _____

7. PAGE 61 _____
8. PAGE 61 _____
9. PAGE 61 _____
10. PAGE 61 _____
11. PAGE 62 _____
12. PAGE 62 _____

13. PAGE 64 _____
14. PAGE 65 _____
15. PAGE 65 _____
16. PAGE 65 _____
17. PAGE 67 _____

▶ GROW WHAT YOU KNOW

Reflect on what you have learned and predict how this information will be used in the future.

COLOR TOOLS
AND ESSENTIALS | 110ᶜ.6

ACHIEVE //

Following this lesson on *Color Tools and Essentials*, you'll be able to:

>> Describe the functions of the main coloring tools

>> Provide examples of supplies, products and equipment used to perform a color service

FOCUS //

COLOR TOOLS AND ESSENTIALS

Color Tools

Color Essentials

COLOR TOOLS

Color tools are the _____ tools you use.

Tools are selected based on desired _____ result and

_____ preference.

COLOR BOWL

- Holds the color formula
- Has the measurement guide for _____
- Used for products that have a _____ or creamy consistency

COLOR APPLICATOR BOTTLE

- Has a _____ applicator tip
- Bottle is marked with a _____ guide
- Used for products that have a _____ consistency

COLOR BRUSH

- Is made with _____ bristles
- One end applies color, pointy end _____ hair
- Chosen according to the _____ and _____ of area worked in

COLOR COMBS

TAIL COMB

A tail comb is used for combing and _____ the hair.
Many stylists prefer _____ tail combs.

PALETTE COMB

A palette comb is used for a faster, more _____ alternative to foiled highlights.
A palette comb has _____ at the end to hold the hair at the scalp and a _____ to hold surrounding hair while painting.

FOIL/THERMAL STRIPS

Foils and thermal strips are both used to _____ the colored hair from the _____ .

MATCHING

Match the term with the correct image.

Thermal Strip

Tail Comb

Palette Comb

COLOR ESSENTIALS

MATCHING

Match the type of tool with its related function.

1. Color Brush   _____ Isolates woven or sliced strands from untreated hair

2. Color Applicator Bottle   _____ Protects client's clothing

3. Foil   _____ Protects hands during chemical services

4. Tail Comb   _____ Protects skin from direct contract with cape

5. Protective cape   _____ Consists of nylon bristles and used to apply color

6. Neck Strip   _____ Has a pointed end; used for parting and combing hair

7. Protective Gloves   _____ Holds color formula and pointed tip is used to part and apply color

LESSON CHALLENGE

Multiple choice. Indicate one correct answer for each question.

1. Which color tool is used to apply a thick or creamy color consistency?
   a. applicator bottle
   b. tail comb
   c. color brush
   d. wide-tooth comb

2. What consists of nylon bristles on one end and a pointed tip on the other?
   a. 9-row brush
   b. tail comb
   c. wide-tooth comb
   d. color brush

3. Which color tool is commonly used to apply color products with a liquid consistency?
   a. applicator bottle
   b. tail comb
   c. color bowl
   d. wide-tooth comb

4. A(n) _____ is used to comb and part the hair.
   a. palette comb
   b. tail comb
   c. wide-tooth comb
   d. applicator bottle

5. What tool is commonly used when highlighting?
   a. foils
   b. sculpting comb
   c. water bottle
   d. applicator bottle

LESSON CHALLENGE REFERENCES

Check your answers. Place a check mark next to the page number for any incorrect answer. On the lines, jot down topics that you still need to review.

1. PAGE 75 _____

2. PAGE 75 _____

3. PAGE 75 _____

4. PAGE 76 _____

5. PAGE 76 _____

▶ GROW WHAT YOU KNOW

Reflect on what you have learned and predict how this information will be used in the future.

110^c.7 |

COLOR SKILLS

ACHIEVE //

Following this lesson on *Color Skills*, you'll be able to:

» State the color procedures in the sequential order they are
  used to perform a color service

» Describe each of the six color procedures

» Explain additional factors to consider when coloring hair

FOCUS //

COLOR SKILLS

Color Design Procedures

Color Considerations

COLOR DESIGN PROCEDURES

A system for producing _____ color results.

SECTION

_____ = Dividing the hair into _____ areas

for _____

RECTANGULAR

• Positioned for a _____ or _____ part
• May _____ through crown

CIRCULAR

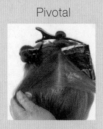

• Distinguishes color patterns between the _____ and

_____

TRIANGULAR

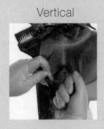

• _____ section of hair in fringe
• Adds interest to _____ _____

_____ = Determines how evident the color pattern

is in _____ _____ _____

PART

• Horizontal slices placed in the interior: Definite _____ of color
• Diagonal slices placed in the interior: _____ effect

Consider product _____, hair _____ and

desired _____ _____ when choosing

_____ of parting.

MATCHING PARTING DIRECTIONS

Match the technical image to the matching illustration and the parting direction.

Horizontal	Pivotal	Vertical	Diagonal	Zigzag

Dimensional
Coloring
Techniques

Positioning hightlights and/or _____ on the surface of _____ or to _____ strands throughout the design. Dimensional coloring involves theory that darker colors _____ and add _____, while lighter colors come _____ and add _____.

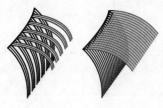

WEAVING AND SLICING

What: _____

_____

Why: _____

_____

FREEFORM PAINTING

What: _____

_____

Why: _____

_____

END LIGHTS

What: _____

_____

Why: _____

_____

CAP METHOD

What: _____

_____

Why: _____

_____

RETOUCH

What: _____

_____

Why: _____

_____

APPLY

Typically done with a _____ _____

_____ or _____ bottle

COLOR APPLICATION TECHNIQUES

A _____ and _____ are used to apply cream colors and lighteners.

An applicator bottle is used to apply _____ and

_____ hair colors.

COLOR ALONG THE STRAND

Techniques described according to placement of color along the strand:

Base to Ends (Darker Result):

Ensure the product thoroughly penetrates _____ _____.

Away From the Base (Lighter Result):

Holding the brush _____ or at an angle will result in softer

_____ _____.

Base:

Used for _____ color service on new growth only

Draw each technique in the boxes provided.

BASE TO ENDS (DARKER)	AWAY FROM THE BASE (LIGHTER)	BASE (RETOUCH)

PROCESS

_____ = Allow time for color to _____

and _____

_____ .

TEST

_____ color product from select strands to ensure proper

development.

REMOVE AND CONDITION

Follow _____ _____

to remove color products and condition hair.

COLOR CONSIDERATIONS

May serve as an inspiration for color _____ .

When more than one color is added to the surface, _____

_____ are acheived.

SOLID FORM

_____ reflects light more evenly.

GRADUATED FORM

_____ softens the form through the _____

and draws attention to the _____ .

INCREASE-LAYERED FORM

_____ from darker to lighter visually adds

_____ to the top and _____ to

the perimeter.

UNIFORMLY LAYERED FORM

_____ used to darken the exterior will make the form look

_____ in the shape.

LESSON CHALLENGE

Multiple choice. Indicate one correct answer for each question.

1. Which technique is performed on the surface of the hair to create a highlighted or lowlighted color effect?
   a. virgin lighter
   b. color glazing
   c. freeform painting
   d. lighter result touch-up

2. A highlighting technique in which a crochet hook is used to pull hairstrands through a perforated cap is called:
   a. reverse highlighting
   b. cap method
   c. double-process blond
   d. weaving

3. Which coloring technique is used to ensure the product thoroughly penetrates the entire strand?
   a. midstrand to ends
   b. ends to base
   c. base to ends
   d. ends to midstrand

4. Which of the following techniques is generally referred to as a retouch application?
   a. base to ends
   b. base
   c. ends to base
   d. base, then midstrand to ends

5. A technique popular with clients who request ombré is:
   a. stripping
   b. base to ends coloring
   c. lightening
   d. away from the base coloring

LESSON CHALLENGE REFERENCES

Check your answers. Place a check mark next to the page number for any incorrect answer.
On the lines, jot down topics that you still need to review.

1. PAGE 89 _____

2. PAGE 90 _____

3. PAGE 92 _____

4. PAGE 92 _____

5. PAGE 92 _____

▶ GROW WHAT YOU KNOW

Reflect on what you have learned and predict how this information will be used in the future.

110ᶜ.8 | COLOR GUEST EXPERIENCE

ACHIEVE //

Following this lesson on *Color Guest Experience*, you'll be able to:

>> Summarize the service essentials as they relate to color services

>> Discuss examples of infection control and safety guidelines for color services

FOCUS //

COLOR GUEST EXPERIENCE

Color Service Essentials

Color Infection Control and Safety

COLOR SERVICE ESSENTIALS

Proper lighting is essential for an accurate _____ _____ and _____ _____.

Incandescent lighting = _____

Fluorescent lighting = _____

To avoid any misunderstandings, practice reflective listening skills to include: Listening _____ and then _____ what your clients have said to you.

CONNECT

Meet and greet the client with a _____ _____ and pleasant tone of voice

_____ and build rapport to develop a _____ with client

CONSULT

Ask questions about past services to understand client's wants and _____

Gain feedback and _____

CREATE

_____ ensures client protection

Inform the client about at-home care _____

COMPLETE

_____ client satisfaction

_____ single-use supplies, _____ tools and arrange workstation

MATCHING

Match the service essential in the left column to its matching phrase in the right column.

1. Connect   _____ Analyze face, body shape, physical features, eyes and skin tone

2. Consult   _____ Communicate to build a relationship with client

3. Create   _____ Ensure client protection by draping the client with a cape and towels

4. Complete   _____ Reinforce guest's satisfaction with the overall experience

                                 _____ Ask questions to discover information about past color experiences

                                 _____ Meet and greet client with a firm handshake

                                 _____ Prebook guest's next appointment

                                 _____ Stay focused on delivering the color service to the best of your abilities

CLIENT CHEMICAL RECORD

The client record contains the following information:

- _____ information
- Color _____
- _____ methods and _____ time

CLIENT CHEMICAL COLOR RELEASE FORM

- Is not a _____ document
- Does not absolve colorist from _____

PROMOTING HAIR COLOR SERVICES

Listen to cues that offer an opportunity to recommend services

When communicating with clients, use professional terminology, which includes:

- _____ (versus bleach)
- _____ (versus dye)
- _____ (versus darker)

COLOR INFECTION CONTROL AND SAFETY

Protect your client by following _____ _____ and _____ guidelines.

Cleaning: _____

_____

Disinfecting: _____

_____

Available in varied forms, including:

- _____
- _____

- _____
- _____

The salon industry uses _____-_____ products.

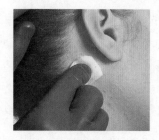

PREDISPOSITION (SKIN PATCH) TEST

All color products containing an aniline derivative ingredient _____

_____

_____

to the hair color service.

PREDISPOSITION (SKIN PATCH) TEST GUIDELINES

Cleanse area

- _____
- _____

APPLY INTENDED FORMULA

- _____
- _____

CHECK FOR RESULTS

- Analyze results; determine if reaction is negative (no signs) or positive
  - ›› Signs include: _____
    _____

- If reaction is _____, proceed with service; if reaction is
  _____, do not proceed with service
- Record _____ in client record
- Clean work area

COLOR DEVELOPMENT STRAND TEST

Allows to monitor the color _____

Allows you to assess stress on _____ and _____

CLEANING AND DISINFECTION GUIDELINES

Only nonporous tools, supplies and equipment can be _____.

Any single-use items must be _____ after each use.

CARE AND SAFETY

FOLLOW INFECTION CONTROL PROCEDURES FOR PERSONAL CARE AND CLIENT SAFETY

PERSONAL CARE

Wash _____ and dry thoroughly with single-use towel.

Wear protective _____.

CLIENT CARE PRIOR TO SERVICE

Check scalp for _____ or _____.

Perform skin test _____ _____ before color service.

Protect client's skin and clothing by draping with a _____ and
_____ for a color service.

CLIENT CARE DURING SERVICE

Protect client's skin by applying _____ _____ around
the hairline.

Do not permit _____ to come in contact with eyes.

Be sure the _____ stays in place, and the client's arms
are _____ the cape.

SALON CARE

Use only _____ or _____ bowls to mix color.

Use mixed products _____.

LESSON CHALLENGE

Multiple choice. Indicate one correct answer for each question.

1. The guest experience begins with:
   a. draping
   b. the consultation
   c. gaining feedback and approval
   d. building rapport and trust

2. Greeting your client with a firm handshake is part of the _____ service essential.
   a. Consult
   b. Connect
   c. Complete
   d. Create

3. Producing a functional, predictable and pleasing result is part of the _____ service essential.
   a. Consult
   b. Connect
   c. Complete
   d. Create

4. Asking questions and analyzing the client's anatomical features is part of the _____ service essential.
   a. Consult
   b. Connect
   c. Complete
   d. Create

5. Reinforcing the guest's satisfaction is part of the _____ service essential.
   a. Consult
   b. Connect
   c. Complete
   d. Create

6. The client record houses the following information, EXCEPT:
   a. contact information
   b. color formulation
   c. processing time
   d. legal information

7. Draping for a color service should include a cape and _____.
   a. neck strip
   b. towels
   c. plastic
   d. cotton oil

8. A predisposition test should be performed how many hours before a color service?
   a. 36-58
   b. 2-6
   c. 24-48
   d. 40-60

9. A skin patch test will help determine:
   a. the processing time for a lightener
   b. the correct formula
   c. the processing time for a coloring procedure
   d. if the client has a sensitivity or an allergic reaction

LESSON CHALLENGE REFERENCES

Check your answers. Place a check mark next to the page number for any incorrect answer. On the lines, jot down topics that you still need to review.

1. PAGE 103 _____
2. PAGE 103 _____
3. PAGE 103 _____
4. PAGE 103 _____
5. PAGE 103 _____

6. PAGE 105 _____
7. PAGE 109 _____
8. PAGE 109 _____
9. PAGE 109 _____

▶ GROW WHAT YOU KNOW

Reflect on what you have learned and predict how this information will be used in the future.

111ᶜ.1 //
PERM THEORY

ACHIEVE //

Following this lesson on *Perm Theory*, you'll be able to:

» State the breakthroughs that influenced the perm texture systems used today

» Explain the two phases involved when performing a perm texture service

FOCUS //

PERM THEORY

History of Perming

Phases of Perming

HISTORY OF PERMING

Perming is a chemical texture service that involves the process of

using _____ and _____ actions to

_____ change the texture of hair, giving your clients the

straight-to-wavy or curly looks they desire. Clients request a perm service texture:

- To add _____, _____ and _____
  _____ to flat, limp hair

- To add _____ _____ throughout or in selected
  areas of the head

- To have the option of wearing their hair straight or textured

MATCHING

Match the treatment descriptions below with the appropriate techniques in the chart.

A.   Thioglycolic acid or derivatives

B.   Possible sulfur derivatives in the mud

C.   Strong alkaline chemicals

D.   Neutral low-pH alkaline and low/no thio;
     Digital Perms

E.   Consists of strong alkaline solutions

F.   Thio derivatives; glyceryl monothioglycolate

G.   Used bisulfides

HISTORY OF PERMING	POPULAR TECHNIQUE	SPECIALIZED TREATMENT
Today	Constantly evolving	
1970	Acid/endothermic – add heat; Exothermic – generate their own heat	
1938	Cold waves; no heat	
1931	Overnight wave; no electricity; chemical reaction	
1926	Croquignole; preheat method; ends to scalp	
1905	Spiral method; heat machine; scalp to ends	
Ancient Egypt	Wrap hair on sticks, applied mud, baked in sun	

PEOPLE TO KNOW

Charles Nessler _____

_____

Evans & McDonough _____

Arnold F. Willatt _____

PHASES OF PERMING

Today's perms involve two major phases:

-
-

PHYSICAL PHASE

Desired _____ and _____ of the new wave or curl

pattern achieved by _____ hair around perm rods with

_____ sizes and shapes.

Hair needs to be wrapped _____ and _____

around each rod, using appropriate _____ without

_____; ensures hair takes on the desired shape.

CHEMICAL PHASE

The two chemicals used during the chemical phase are _____

_____ (reducing agent) and _____ (oxidizing agent).

Perm solution is also known as _____ lotion or

_____ lotion.

Perm solution is applied to break disulfide bonds and soften the

_____ structure.

After the perm solution is thoroughly rinsed, the neutralizer is applied to

_____ and _____ the hair into its new wavy or

curly shape, then thoroughly rinsed.

LESSON CHALLENGE

Multiple choice. Indicate one correct answer for each question.

1. What length of hair was Charles Nessler's heat permanent waving machine suitable for?
   a. medium
   b. short
   c. long
   d. very short

2. In 1926, the croquignole method of wrapping hair from the ends to the scalp was created. What is another name for this wrapping method?
   a. spiral method
   b. overlap method
   c. clamp method
   d. none of the above

3. In what year was the first cold wave created?
   a. 1938
   b. 1905
   c. 1931
   d. 1970

4. What was the active ingredient used in the first cold wave?
   a. glyceryl monothioglycolate
   b. bisulfides
   c. thioglycolic acid or a derivative
   d. none of the above

5. Which phase of perming is the most important?
   a. physical phase
   b. chemical phase
   c. both are equally important
   d. neither

LESSON CHALLENGE REFERENCES

Check your answers. Place a check mark next to the page number for any incorrect answer. On the lines, jot down topics that you still need to review.

1. PAGE 6 _____

2. PAGE 6 _____

3. PAGE 7 _____

4. PAGE 7 _____

5. PAGE 11 _____

▶ GROW WHAT YOU KNOW

Reflect on what you have learned and predict how this information will be used in the future.

111.2 // PERM DESIGN

ACHIEVE //

Following this lesson on *Perm Design*, you'll be able to:

-> Summarize a series of design decisions involved when adding texture that will lead to a desired texture result

-> Identify the most commonly used basic perm patterns

FOCUS //

PERM DESIGN

Perm Design Decisions

Perm Patterns

Change the Texture, Change the Effect

PERM DESIGN DECISIONS

Before reaching for a perm product or perm tools, the designer must first _____ the final texture outcome. With that picture in mind, the designer then makes specific _____ based on the following questions:

- What is the _____ and _____ texture?
- What _____ will I be working with?
- Where will I _____ the texture?
- Which _____ _____ will I use?

EXISTING AND DESIRED TEXTURE

In perming, the basic decision when moving from the client's existing texture to the desired texture includes the following:

- Type of texture desired which determines _____ and _____ (shape) of perm rods:

- Tight, _____ curls
- Large, _____ curls
- Waves or _____ curls
- Technique used to wrap _____ around _____

OVERLAP (CROQUIGNOLE) TECHNIQUE

- Produces _____ and _____ - _____
- Achieves _____ lift, strong _____ curl
- Best suited for _____ to _____ hair

SPIRAL TECHNIQUE

- Positions revolutions of hair next to one another
- Creates an _____ texture pattern
- Consistent along the _____ of the strand
- Most often used on _____ to _____ hair

FORM

As added texture _____ the form:

- Illusion of shorter length is created
- Form line and weight area shift upward

Describe in your own words how the addition of texture affects the following forms.

Solid Form:

_____

_____

_____

Increase-Layered Form:

_____

_____

_____

TEXTURE PLACEMENT

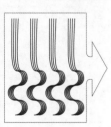

ZONES

Zonal or partial perms position added texture within specific areas of a design to:

• _____

• _____

• _____

Adding texture to the fringe can _____.

Add texture to the interior to _____ the form and

create _____.

TEXTURE ALONG THE STRAND

Base

Adding texture only at the base, called _____ _____,

is usually done for one of two reasons:

1 To create _____ and _____ for

added _____ and _____

of the overall hair design

2 More commonly, to add texture to _____ in

order to _____

_____ along the strand

Away From the Base

Adding texture _____ from the base creates

_____ textures that can result in progressive

designs or a natural-looking finish.

MATCHING

Identify the direction in which the hair is distributed:

Toward the face

Alternating clockwise and counterclockwise directions

Away from the face

From a side part

DESIGN PRINCIPLES AND ROD CHOICE

Identify the design principle for the following images:

_____

_____

_____

_____

PERM PATTERNS

PERM PATTERNS

• Also known as _____ _____

• Help _____ and _____ how perm service is performed

• Affect the final look of _____ _____ _____

RECTANGLE PATTERN

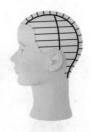

- Also known as _____
- Consists primarily of rectangular _____ subdivided into rectangular _____
- Center rectangle usually positioned _____ _____ to _____

CONTOUR PATTERN

- Versatile and adapts to contours or _____ of head
- Includes a central _____ and 2 sections at each side
- Indirect partings from multiple points of origin are used in sections adjacent to center rectangle; _____ partings gradually become _____ toward back/exterior

BRICKLAY PATTERN

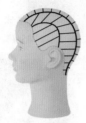

- Positions rods in a _____ configuration to avoid _____
- Bases within each row are _____ from previous row so _____ lines do not line up
- Pattern resembles the way a bricklayer deliberately arranges bricks in a building, _____ _____

SPIRAL BRICKLAY PATTERN

- Features _____ rows subdivided in a staggered bricklay pattern
- Rods are positioned _____ within _____ bases
- Used in conjunction with _____ bricklay pattern

ZONAL PATTERN

- Zonal perms also called _____ perms
- Involves adding texture in certain _____, or _____ of head
- Adds _____ and _____ _____ to otherwise straight hair in selected areas

CHANGE THE TEXTURE, CHANGE THE EFFECT

Explain how the addition of texture changes the effect of these looks.

_____

_____

_____

_____

LESSON CHALLENGE

Multiple choice. Indicate one correct answer for each question.

1. **What length of hair is the spiral technique most often used on?**
   a. long only
   b. short to long
   c. medium to long
   d. short to medium

2. **As added texture expands the form:**
   a. the form is no longer apparent
   b. the illusion of shorter length is created
   c. the illusion of longer length is created
   d. form line and weight area shift downward

3. **What are the 2 basic wrapping techniques for rotating strands around a perm tool?**
   a. twist and overlap
   b. wave and overlap
   c. spiral and overlap
   d. overlap and croquignole

4. **The overlap (croquignole) technique produces which result?**
   a. undulating waves and curls
   b. revolutions of hair next to one another
   c. both a and b
   d. neither a nor b

5. Positioning texture in one or more specific areas or zones of the head, or along only a certain portion of the hairstrand is called:
    a. zoning
    b. texture placement
    c. strand placement
    d. none of the above

6. You can apply the design principles of repetition, alternation, progression and contrast:
    a. along the strand
    b. to texture within zones
    c. throughout an entire composition
    d. all of the above

7. What term refers to the way perm tools are arranged around the client's head while wrapping?
    a. molding
    b. circle wrap
    c. distribution
    d. perm pattern

8. Zonal perms are also called:
    a. end perms
    b. base perms
    c. sub perms
    d. partial perms

LESSON CHALLENGE REFERENCES

Check your answers. Place a check mark next to the page number for any incorrect answer. On the lines, jot down topics that you still need to review.

1. PAGE 17 _____

2. PAGE 17 _____

3. PAGE 17 _____

4. PAGE 17 _____

5. PAGE 19 _____

6. PAGE 22 _____

7. PAGE 23 _____

8. PAGE 25 _____

▶ GROW WHAT YOU KNOW

Reflect on what you have learned and predict how this information will be used in the future.

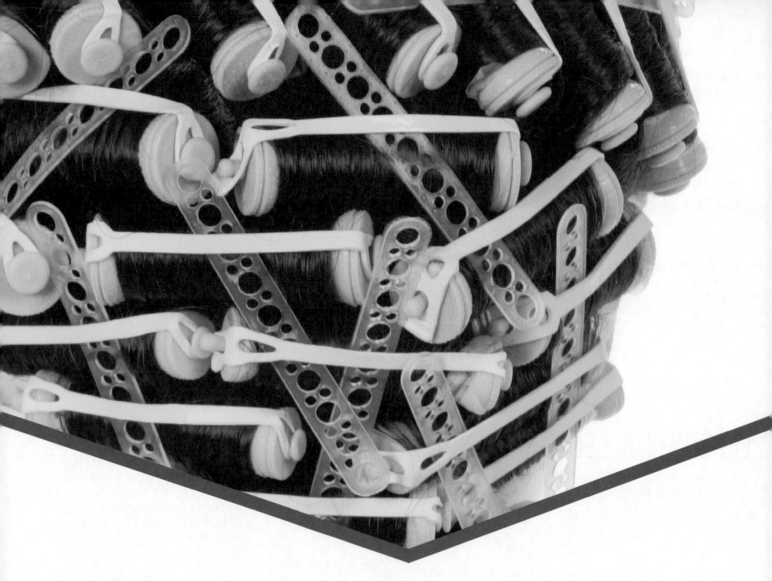

111^c.3 // PERM PRODUCTS AND ESSENTIALS

ACHIEVE //

Following this lesson on *Perm Products and Essentials*, you'll be able to:

» Explain the types of perm products and their usage

» Describe the functions of the main tools used for perming

» Provide examples of products, tools and equipment used to perform a perm service

FOCUS //

PERM PRODUCTS AND ESSENTIALS

Perm Products

Perm Essentials

PERM PRODUCTS

_____ (or permanent waving) allow you to chemically _____ hair from straight to wavy or curly formation.

- Hair is wrapped around perm rods chosen to reflect desired
_____

- Processing (waving) lotion is applied to break _____ bonds
  - _____ protein structure
  - Allows protein chains to shift and assume _____ of perm rod

- Rinsing _____ processing lotion

- Second chemical product, _____ (rebonding lotion), reforms disulfide bonds in a new _____

TYPES OF PERM SOLUTIONS (LOTIONS)

Select appropriate _____ based on your client's hair and the _____ of the curl desired.

ALKALINE (COLD) PERMS

- Processed without heat
- Perm solution chemically breaks or reduces disulfide bonds while hair is wrapped on perm rods
- Also known as
  "_____ _____,"
  are processed without heat
- pH of approximately
  _____ to _____
- Main ingredient is
  _____
  _____
  or its derivatives and
  _____
  _____, which
  _____ the
  processing time
- High alkalinity—use caution to
  prevent _____ to
  hair structure or chemical burns to
  the skin
- Should be wrapped without
  _____ (minimal
  stretching or straining of the hair)
- Hair starts to process as soon as the
  _____ is applied

ACID (HEAT) PERMS

- Generally processed
  _____ heat
- _____,
  _____ and
  _____ solution
  break disulfide bonds
- Acid perms, also known as
  "_____ _____,"
  are processed with heat
- pH range of
  _____ to _____
- Acid perms cause only minimal
  swelling; therefore it is essential
  that the hair be wrapped with
  _____, even
  _____
- Insufficient _____
  before neutralizing can trap odor in
  the hair

ADVANTAGES OF ALKALINE AND ACID PERMS

Alkaline Perms

- _____ curl pattern
- Faster _____ time
- Better for _____ hair
- No need for _____

Acid Perms

- _____, natural curl pattern
- Gentler to hair
- More control due to _____ processing time
- Better for _____ or chemically treated hair

OTHER PERM PRODUCT TYPES

Exothermic Perms

- Exothermic perms are _____-heating and _____-timing
- _____ is mixed with perm solution to create heat through a chemical reaction
- The _____ can vary, so they can be either alkaline or acidic

LOW/NO THIO

- Has a different reducing agent known as _____ _____
- Used on clients who may have _____ reaction to thioglycolic acid

The "Heat" Perm

- Is also referred to as a "hot perm," "ionic perm," "_____ _____" or "digital perm"
- Produces soft-looking waves and curls, which are more defined when _____ and looser when _____
- Thermally _____ the hair using the perm solution and heated rods
- Generally does not require _____ _____, _____ or _____ to achieve curl
- Last from _____–_____ months, depending on hair

NEUTRALIZER

- Neutralizing is the _____ chemical step in the perm process
- _____ and restores the disulfide bonds
- Main ingredient found in most neutralizers or (or bonding lotions) is

  _____ _____, _____

  _____, or _____ _____

- pH ranges from _____ to _____, depending on type
- Reduces the swelling caused by the _____ of the

  perm solution

- _____, or fixes, the disulfide bonds into the new

  _____ position, determined by size of perm rod, making

  the texture change "_____"

BARRIER/PROTECTIVE CREAMS

BARRIER CREAM

- Protects client's _____ when applied to hairline

  _____ using chemicals

- Applied to _____ and _____
- Helps hold _____ in place

PROTECTIVE CREAM

- Protects parts of _____ not being processed during a

  retouch service, prevents perm solution from being absorbed into hair

MATCHING

Match the perm products to their descriptions.

1. Neutralizer   _____ Self-heating and self-timing

2. Protective Cream   _____ Should not use tension when wrapping

3. Exothermic Perm   _____ Use heat to process

4. Alkaline Perm   _____ Protects the hair not being processed

5. Acid Perm   _____ pH range of 2.5-7

PERM ESSENTIALS

PERM TOOLS

APPLICATOR BOTTLE

Controls and _____ perm solution or neutralizer

Nozzle or tip used for better _____

PERM RODS

Determine the _____ and _____ of new

curl configuration

Different _____ produce different degrees of curl

_____

STYLING COMB

_____, distributes and parts hair to be wrapped within

a section

TAIL COMB

_____ off sections of hair and individual bases

when wrapping

LABELING ACTIVITY

Label the perm tools shown in the images.

_____

_____

_____

_____

_____

_____

PERM SUPPLIES

Identify the main function of the various supplies listed below.

Plastic Shampoo Cape

_____
_____
_____
_____

End Papers

_____
_____
_____
_____

Cloth Towels

_____
_____
_____
_____

Picks/Stabilizers

_____
_____
_____
_____

Cotton Strips

_____
_____
_____
_____

Spray Bottle

_____
_____
_____
_____

Plastic Sectioning
Clips

_____
_____
_____
_____

Protective Gloves

_____
_____
_____
_____

EQUIPMENT	FUNCTION
HEAT EQUIPMENT; INFRARED LAMPS, HOOD DRYER	Provide _____ for acid perms during processing as required by the manufacturer's directions
PLASTIC CAP	Prevents perm solution from _____ out during processing
TIMER	_____ designer to check for test curls, processing and neutralizing times as recommended by the manufacturer
SHAMPOO BOWL	Holds client's _____ and hair for shampooing prior to service and for rinsing perm solution and neutralizer from hair
STYLING CHAIR	Provides _____ seat for client; _____ for best working height

LESSON CHALLENGE

Multiple choice. Indicate one correct answer for each question.

1. What structure must be permanently broken to change the hair from straight to curly state?
   a. eumelanin
   b. carbon
   c. disulfide bonds
   d. melanocytes

2. Alkaline perms carry a pH of:
   a. 8.0-9.5
   b. 10-14
   c. 6.0-7.5
   d. 4.5-5.5

3. In addition to tension and perm solution, what do acid perms use to perform the processing action?
   a. alkalinity
   b. drying
   c. cold
   d. heat

4. Which of the following statements is true about alkaline perms?
   a. strong curl pattern
   b. slower processing time
   c. need heat
   d. better for fragile hair

5. Which perm tool determines the size and shape of the new curl texture?
   a. tail comb
   b. perm rod
   c. stabilizer
   d. applicator bottle

LESSON CHALLENGE REFERENCES

Check your answers. Place a check mark next to the page number for any incorrect answer. On the lines, jot down topics that you still need to review.

1. PAGE 29 _____

2. PAGE 30 _____

3. PAGE 32 _____

4. PAGE 32 _____

5. PAGE 35 _____

GROW WHAT YOU KNOW

Reflect on what you have learned and predict how this information will be used in the future.

111ᶜ.4 //

PERM SKILLS

ACHIEVE //

Following this lesson on *Perm Skills*, you'll be able to:

» Explain how the hair is analyzed prior to a perm service

» Identify and explain the procedural steps during the physical and chemical phases of a perm service

FOCUS //

PERM SKILLS

Pre-Perm Analysis

Perm Procedures

PRE-PERM ANALYSIS

Perform a pre-perm analysis to include assessing the hair's:

-
-

Pre-perm analysis helps choose the right _____ size, _____ size and the proper _____ _____, as well as manage _____ time.

POROSITY

Refers to hair's ability to _____ - _____, _____ or _____.

The more _____ , the more perm solution is _____.

POROUS/HIGHLY POROUS HAIR

Porous hair or excessively porous hair

- Mild _____ perm recommended
- _____ before any perm service
- Use _____ product to equalize porosity
- Select gentler, _____ perm

RESISTANT HAIR

- _____ _____
- Requires stronger alkaline _____ to _____ _____; allows perm chemicals be absorbed

POROSITY TEST

Run thumb and finger along a strand of hair from _____ to _____.

If rough it will be due to _____ and _____ cuticle scales, indicating that hair is more _____ and _____.

Record results in client's record.

ELASTICITY

Hair's ability to be _____ and _____ to its original shape without breaking.

Normal dry hair: _____ _____

Wet hair: _____

With _____ elasticity, hair will not return to its original state after stretched.

Hair that lacks _____ or resiliency and shows any signs of _____ is not safe to perm.

ELASTICITY TEST
(STRUCTURAL STRENGTH)

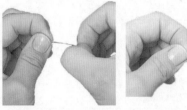

The purpose of an elasticity test is to check hair's ability to stretch and return to its _____ shape without _____.

Assesses the damage to the internal structure of the hair (cortex), prior to a chemical or styling service. Note that this test is intended for straight or wavy hair.

- Remove strand of hair from side of head, above ears
- Hold between thumb and forefinger
- With thumbnail and index finger of other hand, run distance of hair rapidly creating a series of small curls
- Gently pull hair taut for 10 seconds and release

If good condition: _____

_____

If structurally weak: _____

_____

TEXTURE

Degree of _____ or _____ of the hair fiber.

_____: May be more resistant due to finely packed cuticle

_____: Has average of 7-12 cuticle layers; accepts products well

_____: May be resistant due to the increased number of cuticle layers

DENSITY

Refers to the _____ of hair _____ per square inch; does not always correspond to hair _____.

Denser hair requires a _____ base size to avoid wrapping _____ hair around the perm rods.

MATCHING *Match terms to their definitions.*

Porosity	Elasticity	Texture	Density
Degree of coarseness or fineness of hair fiber	Amount of hair follicles per square inch; does not always correspond to hair texture	Hair's ability to absorb moisture, liquids or chemicals	Hair's ability to be stretched and return to its original shape

PERM PROCEDURES

A system for producing _____ perm results

First three steps are part of the _____ phase and last two

steps are part of the _____ phase of perming

PHYSICAL PHASE OF PERMING

Desired size and shape of the new wave or curl pattern are achieved by wrapping the hair around the perm tools with corresponding sizes and shapes. Important to wrap hair smoothly and evenly around perm tool; tool becomes the mold for new texture

DISTRIBUTE

Direct, or distribute, the hair in the _____ in which the client

will _____ their hair.

Label the direction of the distribution of hair.

_____   _____   _____

_____   _____   _____

SECTION

Helps _____ and create _____,

which are areas between two _____.

The _____ of a base is largely determined by the shape of

the _____ it is in.

RECTANGULAR	**CIRCULAR**	**OBLONG**
Rectangular sections — _____ bases	Circular sections — _____ and _____ bases	Oblong sections — _____ _____ bases

WRAP

Actual application and _____ of the perm rods.

Wrapping techniques and base control affect:

-
-
-

OVERLAP (CROQUIGNOLE) TECHNIQUE

Hair is rotated or

_____ around

rod from the ends of the strand up to

the _____

- Hair _____ itself
  with each revolution

- Strand should overlap around the
  perm rod at least _____
  for complete curl pattern

- Produces curls and

  _____ _____

- Used to achieve _____

  _____ and strong
  end curl

SPIRAL TECHNIQUE

Revolutions of hair are positioned

_____ to

_____

to create an

_____

texture pattern

- Texture pattern is _____

  _____

  and reflects shape and

  _____ of rods

- Best suited for

  _____

Can be wrapped in one of 2 ways:

- _____

- _____

PERM TOOLS

Come in various types, lengths, _____ and shapes.
Choose diameter and shape according to desired texture speed and character.
The _____ the diameter, the greater the visual length

_____.

Large-diameter tools:

- _____

Medium-diameter tools:

- _____

- _____

Small-diameter tools:

- _____

- _____

TOOL POSITION AND BASE CONTROL

Base control refers to the combination of:

1 The _____ of the base in relation to the _____ of
the rod

2 The _____ of the rod in relation to the _____

BASE

Refers to: _____

_____

Also called: _____

BASE SIZE

1x base

1½x base

2x base

- _____
- _____

- _____
_____

- _____
- _____

TOOL POSITION

Refers to: _____
_____

Determined by:

- _____
- _____

4 BASIC TOOL POSITIONS

1 On Base: _____
_____
_____

2 Half-Off Base: _____
_____
_____

3 Underdirected: _____
_____
_____

4 Off Base: _____
_____
_____

END-PAPER TECHNIQUES

Ensure _____, _____ curl; cover
ends of hair to manage _____; reduce
_____; eliminate crimping or _____
on hair ends.

END-PAPER TECHNIQUES (CONT'D)

Bookend

Double-Paper (Double-Flat)

_____

_____

_____

_____

_____

_____

_____

_____

_____

_____

Single Paper

Cushion

_____

_____

_____

_____

_____

_____

_____

_____

_____

_____

SECURING PERM TOOLS

Ensure all perm rods are securely in their proper positions; use

_____ or _____ .

ERGONOMIC TIPS FOR PHYSICAL PHASE OF PERMING

Stand directly behind the section to be wrapped, not to one side or the other.

Place perm tools, end papers and spray bottle within easy reach of your free hand.

Do not bend over, stoop or raise your shoulders uncomfortably while wrapping.

PROCESS

To permanently change the hair from _____ to curly,

strong disulfied bonds in the cortex are _____ and

_____ .

Fill in the basic steps for processing a perm:

1.   3.

2.   4.

APPLYING

_____
_____
_____

**TIMING AND
TESTING**

_____
_____
_____

Test curl: _____
_____
_____

RINSING

_____
_____

Use gentle _____ to avoid disturbing hair

on perm rods.

BLOTTING

Removes excess _____ before neutralizing, so neutralizer

is not _____.

NEUTRALIZE

Saturate hair on each perm tool applying to

_____.

Do not leave neutralizer on hair longer than recommended; could

_____

or, in severe cases, cause breakage.

**APPLY, RINSE,
AND REMOVE**

1st Rinsing Method: _____
_____

2nd Rinsing Method: _____
_____

ALERT!
Always read manufacturer's instructions to achieve the best reuslts from their perm products.

LESSON CHALLENGE

Multiple choice. Indicate one correct answer for each question.

1. The hair characteristics to assess in a pre-perm analysis are porosity, elasticity, texture and:
   a. natural pigment
   b. density
   c. styling
   d. length

2. The method of wrapping hair from the end to the scalp is known as:
   a. spiral
   b. bricklay
   c. contour
   d. croquignole

3. The size of the base and the angle at which the hair is held while wrapping determines the tool position or:
   a. base control
   b. base width
   c. roller size
   d. curl diameter

4. The four basic tool positions in perming are on base, half-off base, underdirected and:
   a. off base
   b. overdirected
   c. highly directed
   d. one-time directed

5. Which of the following descriptions identifies the bookend technique for end-paper placement?
   a. one end paper on top
   b. one end paper folded in half
   c. two end papers folded in half
   d. additional end papers along the strand

6. Water left in end papers after rinsing the perm solution will dilute the neutralizer and:
   a. crimp the curl ends
   b. weaken the curl formation
   c. create a crease at the base of the hair
   d. cause the curl to be tighter

7. The chemical phase of perming involves all the following EXCEPT:
   a. applying neutralizer
   b. applying perm solution
   c. wrapping hair around the perm rod
   d. rinsing the perm solution from the hair

LESSON CHALLENGE REFERENCES

Check your answers. Place a check mark next to the page number for any incorrect answer. On the lines, jot down topics that you still need to review.

1. PAGE 42 _____

2. PAGE 49 _____

3. PAGE 52 _____

4. PAGE 53 _____

5. PAGE 54 _____

6. PAGE 55 _____

7. PAGE 56 _____

▶ # GROW WHAT YOU KNOW

Reflect on what you have learned and predict how this information will be used in the future.

111:5 //

PERM GUEST EXPERIENCE

ACHIEVE //

Following this lesson on *Perm Guest Experience*, you'll be able to:

» Summarize the service essentials related to perm services

» Provide examples of infection control and safety guildlines for perm services

FOCUS //

PERM GUEST EXPERIENCE

Perm Service Essentials

Perm Infection Control and Safety

PERM SERVICE ESSENTIALS

Perm service factors include:

_____

CONNECT

Meet and greet the client with a _____ _____ and pleasant tone of voice.

_____ to build rapport and develop a

_____ with the client.

CONSULT

Ask questions about past services to understand client's _____

and _____.

Ask about your client's perming _____.

Assess the facts and thoroughly think through your _____.

Use _____ to ensure clear communication.

Gain feedback and _____.

CREATE

_____ ensures client protection.

Pay particular attention to preventing the perm chemicals from dripping onto your

client's _____ and neck and _____ the scalp.

Inform the client about home hair-care _____.

COMPLETE

_____ client satisfaction.

Recommend products to maintain the healthy condition of your client's hair.

Suggest a future appointment time for client's next visit.

Update client _____.

MATCHING

Match the example on the right column to its matching term in the left column.

1. Connect
2. Consult
3. Create
4. Complete

_____ Update client record

_____ Communicate to build a relationship with client

_____ Meet and greet client with firm handshake

_____ Recommend at-home care

_____ Pay attention to prevent perm chemicals from dripping onto your client's face and neck

_____ Ask questions to discover information about past perm experiences

_____ Ensure client protection by draping the client with a cape and towels

_____ Climate effects, hair and scalp type, condition, prior product usage

CLIENT RECORD/ RELEASE FORM

The client record contains the following information:

* _____ information
* Perm _____, pattern, product, _____ time
* _____ methods and _____ time

* Is not a _____ document
* Does not absolve hairstylist from _____

COMMUNICATION GUIDELINES

Respond to client cues in a way that encourages _____, loyalty and open communication.

PERM INFECTION CONTROL AND SAFTEY

Protect your client by following _____ and _____ guidelines.

Cleaning – _____
_____

Disinfection methods – _____

Disinfectants are available in varied forms, including:

*
*

*
*

The salon industry uses _____ products; follow manufacturer's guildines.

SAFETY PRECAUTIONS

PRIOR TO PERM SERVICE	DURING PERM SERVICE
•	•
•	
•	•
•	•
•	
•	•
•	
•	
•	

DRAPING FOR CHEMICAL SERVICES

Draping protects the client's _____ and helps prevent skin _____ or burns caused by the _____.

Write a number before each instruction to place in proper order.

_____ Have client remove jewelry and eyeglasses; store in a secure place

_____ Turn collar under

_____ Fold edge of towel down over cape and drape second towel over shampoo cape; fasten securely with clamp

_____ Wash hands

_____ Place towel around neck and fasten plastic shampoo cape over towel, covering back of chair; check that cape is not too tight, yet fits to prevent water or solution from dripping onto clothing

SCALP ANALYSIS

- Look for any abnormalities on the scalp, such as _____, _____, _____, _____.
- If needed, _____ the perm service until the scalp is healthy again.
- Never apply chemicals over any _____ scalp condition.
- Proceed with service when the scalp is _____ and hair is _____ competent.

PRELIMINARY TEST CURLS

Help determine how hair will react to _____

Critical if hair is _____, _____, damaged or has been colored with henna or possibly with _____ salts

1.

2.

3.

4.

5.

6.

7.

Hair is ready when _____ _____ automatically forms a strong, well-defined S-shape or pattern

SMARTNOTES

TEST FOR METALLIC SALTS

If metallic salts are suspected: Perform a _____ prior to perm service. Remove 20 strands of hair, immerse in _____ peroxide and 20 drops of 28% _____ in glass bowl for _____ minutes.

HAIR REACTION	TYPE OF METALLIC SALT	RESPONSE
Lightens slightly		
Lightens quickly		
No reaction in 30 minutes		
Solution boils/odor/hair pulls apart		

ALERT!

Do not perm until metallic product has been cut out of hair.

CLEANING AND DISINFECTION GUIDELINES

Only nonporous tools, supplies and equipment can be _____

All single-use items must be _____ after each use

TOOLS, SUPPLIES AND EQUIPMENT

Applicator Bottle: _____
_____
_____

Perm Tools/Rods: _____
_____
_____

Comb: _____
_____
_____

Plastic Sectioning Clips: _____
_____
_____

Spray Bottle: _____
_____

Plastic Shampoo Cape or Perm Bib/Neutralizing Cape: _____
_____
_____
_____

Towels: _____
_____
_____

Store disinfected tools and multi-use supplies in a clean, dry, _____

container or _____ .

ALERT!

If tools, multi-use supplies or equipment have come in contract with blood or body fluids, the following disinfection procedures must take place:

Use an EPA-registered hospital disinfectant according to manufacturer's directions and as required by your area's regulatory agency.

CARE AND SAFETY

Follow infection control procedures for personal care and client safety.

PERSONAL CARE

Wash _____ and dry thoroughly with single-use towel.

Wear protective _____.

CLIENT CARE PRIOR TO SERVICE

Check scalp for _____ or _____.

Perform a test _____ to see how hair reacts to perm.

Protect client's skin and clothing by draping with a _____ and _____ for a chemical service.

CLIENT CARE DURING SERVICE

Protect client's skin by applying _____ _____ around the hairline.

Do not permit _____ to come in contact with eyes.

Be sure the _____ stays in place and the client's arms are _____ the cape.

SALON CARE

Discard any _____ or _____ perm solution or neutralizer once the service is complete.

Update the client record noting the perm _____, perm _____, pattern, _____ time, any sensitivities experienced.

LESSON CHALLENGE

Multiple choice. Indicate one correct answer for each question.

1. The guest experience begins with:
   a. draping
   b. the consultation
   c. gaining feedback and consent
   d. building rapport and trust

2. Greeting your client with a firm handshake is part of the _____ service essential.
   a. Consult
   b. Connect
   c. Complete
   d. Create

3. Producing a functional, predictable and pleasing result is part of the _____ service essential.
   a. Consult
   b. Connect
   c. Complete
   d. Create

4. Asking questions and analyzing the client's perm history and hair is part of the _____ service essential.
   a. Consult
   b. Connect
   c. Complete
   d. Create

5. Reinforcing the client's satisfaction is part of the _____ service essential.
   a. Consult
   b. Connect
   c. Complete
   d. Create

6. The client record houses the following information EXCEPT:
   a. perm rods used
   b. perm product
   c. processing time
   d. legal information

7. Draping at the beginning of a perm service should include a plastic cape and _____.
   a. neck strip
   b. towels
   c. paper towels
   d. cotton coil

8. What is applied to a client's hairline prior to the chemical phase of the perm service?
   a. conditioner
   b. moisturizer
   c. protective cream
   d. neutralizer

LESSON CHALLENGE REFERENCES

Check your answers. Place a check mark next to the page number for any incorrect answer. On the lines, jot down topics that you still need to review.

1. PAGE 62 _____
2. PAGE 62 _____
3. PAGE 63 _____
4. PAGE 63 _____
5. PAGE 63 _____
6. PAGE 64 _____
7. PAGE 69 _____
8. PAGE 73 _____

▶ GROW WHAT YOU KNOW

Reflect on what you have learned and predict how this information will be used in the future.

111^c.12 //
RELAXER
THEORY

ACHIEVE //

Following this lesson on *Relaxer Theory*, you'll be able to:

>> State the early breakthroughs that influenced relaxer services as we know them today

>> Name the basic relaxer services offered in salons

>> Explain the two phases involved when performing a relaxer service

FOCUS //

RELAXER THEORY

History of Relaxing

Phases of Relaxing

Relaxing refers to the loosening or _____ of the hair's

_____ _____ as when straightening curly or tightly

curled hair.

It is not recommended that more than _____ of the

_____ _____ is removed, as it can damage most hair

types.

HISTORY OF RELAXING

Made of: _____ (or _____),

_____ _____ and _____.

pH of _____; very caustic

Later variation known as "_____" contained eggs

as well

PEOPLE TO KNOW

MADAM C.J. WALKER (Sarah Breedlove)

Invented: _____

_____

How it works: _____

_____

_____

_____

GARRETT A. MORGAN

Invented: _____

_____

BASIC RELAXER SERVICE

Four Basic Relaxer Services:

1. _____   3. _____

2. _____   4. _____

MATCHING

Match the example on the right column to its matching term in the left column.

1. Curl diffusion

2. Virgin relaxer

3. Retouch relaxer

4. Zonal relaxer

_____ Performed in selected areas of the head

_____ Used on natural, untreated or "virgin" hair

_____ Loosens or relaxes tightly curled hair patterns by approximately 50%

_____ Straighten up to 85%

_____ Performed only on new growth to match previously relaxed hair

_____ Also called chemical blowout

_____ Usually in the nape area or hairline

PHASES OF RELAXING

CHEMICAL PHASE

SECTION

As in perming, relaxing the hair involves both _____ and _____ steps.

For better organization and _____ during _____ of the relaxer product

APPLY

The 2 most commonly used relaxer products are:

• _____ _____

■ Used on _____ _____ or _____ hair

■ Can be more _____ due to its strength

■ Requires the use of a _____ _____ applied to entire scalp, hairline and ears

• _____ _____

■ Used on _____ to curly hair

■ Does not require _____ _____ to be applied to scalp

Applying the proper _____ relaxer product based on the client's _____ _____ is critical to the success of the relaxer service.

PHYSICAL PHASE

The second phase of a relaxer service, the physical phase, involves:

• _____ or combing

• Timing and _____

• Rinsing and _____

• _____

SMOOTH OR COMB

_____ relaxation of curl pattern and _____ of bonds to new straightener position

TIME AND TEST

Time according to _____ directions and/or standard salon _____.

Relaxation test - known as a comb test; determines whether hair is _____ to the desired degree or whether more _____ is required

RINSE AND BLOT

Rinsing removes chemicals and any chemical _____ and stops the chemical _____.

Blotting removes excess _____ and helps neutralizing product to be more _____.

NEUTRALIZE

_____ to _____ hair in its new straighter shape

For sodium hydroxide-based relaxers

Use a _____ _____

For ammonium thioglycolate-based relaxers:

Use a _____ _____

LESSON CHALLENGE

Multiple choice. Indicate one correct answer for each question.

1. It is not recommended to remove more than what percentage of the hair's natural texture?
   a. 85%
   b. 50%
   c. 15%
   d. 100%

2. What was the pH of early relaxer products?
   a. 7
   b. 1
   c. 14
   d. none of the above

3. In the early 1900s, the temporary method of hair relaxing was invented by:
   a. Garrett A. Morgan
   b. Madam C.J. Walker
   c. Charles Nessler
   d. none of the above

4. Which phase of relaxing is the most important?
   a. physical phase
   b. chemical phase
   c. neither
   d. both are equally important

5. Which relaxer ingredient requires the use of a base cream on the scalp to prevent irritation?
   a. ammonium thioglycolate
   b. neutralizer
   c. sodium hydroxide
   d. none of the above

LESSON CHALLENGE REFERENCES

Check your answers. Place a check mark next to the page number for any incorrect answer. On the lines, jot down topics that you still need to review.

1. PAGE 122 _____

2. PAGE 124 _____

3. PAGE 124 _____

4. PAGE 125 _____

5. PAGE 126 _____

GROW WHAT YOU KNOW

Reflect on what you have learned and predict how this information will be used in the future.

111ᶜ.13 // RELAXER PRODUCTS AND ESSENTIALS

ACHIEVE //

Following this lesson on *Relaxer Products and Essentials*, you'll be able to:

» Explain the types of relaxer products and their usage

» Describe the functions of the main tools used for relaxing

» Provide examples of products, supplies and equipment used to perform a relaxer service

FOCUS //

RELAXER PRODUCTS AND ESSENTIALS

Relaxer Products

Relaxer Essentials

RELAXER PRODUCTS

2 major categories of relaxer products:

Sodium hydroxide

*

*

*

* Use on:

  ▪

  ▪

  ▪

Ammonium thioglycolate

* Use on:

  ▪

  ▪

  ▪

TYPES OF RELAXER PRODUCTS

Select appropriate _____ based on your client's hair and chemical _____

SODIUM HYDROXIDE RELAXERS

* Formulated with 2% to 3% _____ _____ in a heavy cream base
* Strong _____ product
* Alkaline pH of _____ to _____
* Designed to straighten _____ curled hair

Also known as:

* _____ relaxers
* _____ relaxers

Prior to 1960s

* Known as _____ relaxers, required a base cream prior to relaxer to protect the scalp

Following 1960s

* _____ sodium relaxers
* Contain _____ and _____ agents to protect hair and scalp from irritation
* Gentler

No-lye relaxers:

* Contain a derivative of _____ _____
* Contain one of the following active ingredients:

  ▪

  ▪

  ▪

  ▪

Recommended for _____ resistant hair and require frequent _____ conditioning treatments

AMMONIUM THIOGLYCOLATE RELAXERS

- Formulated with 4% to 6% thioglycolic acid or its derivatives with 1% ammonium hydroxide

- _____ base is also usually added

- pH of _____

- Chemical reducing agent that causes hair to soften and swell

- Affect the hydrogen and _____ bonds during thio processing

- Disulfide bonds break between the two sulfur atoms in the _____ amino acids

- _____ process causes the split cysteine amino acids to rejoin

Relaxer strengths are categorized as:

- _____ – Used on healthy, color-treated hair, fine-textured or porous hair

- _____ – Used on curly to medium-textured hair

- _____ – Used on tightly curled, coarse-textured or resistant hair

ALERT!

Don't apply sodium hydroxide to extremely porous hair that has been colored with permanent hair color or lightened hair (decolorized, bleached).

Also, do not apply sodium hydroxide to hair that has been permed or relaxed previously with ammonium thioglycolate. Multiple services performed over the hair reduced the number of bonds in the hair, which can result in severe breakage.

NEUTRALIZER

Acid-balanced neutralizing _____ or stabilizer to _____ (lock) the hair into its new, _____ shape

- Shampoo or _____
- Reduces _____ caused by alkaline formulas
- Causes _____, which _____ broken down _____ bonds
- pH _____ to _____

For sodium hydroxide relaxer, use _____
For ammonium thioglycolate relaxer, use _____

_Follow manufacturer's directions regarding how _____ _____ to shampoo and how _____ the neutralizing product should be left on the hair._

PRODUCTS	FUNCTION Fill in the main function of the relaxer products listed below.
Shampoo	
Base Cream	
Protective Cream	
Chemical Relaxer Product	
Neutralizer or Neutralizing Shampoo	
Protein/Moisturizing Conditioner/ Sealer	
Styling Lotion	
Styling Products	

MATCHING

Draw a line matching the relaxer tool to its function.

RELAXER ESSENTIALS

RELAXER TOOLS

FUNCTION

APPLICATOR BRUSH

PLASTIC BOWL

TAIL COMB (NON-METAL)

SHAMPOO COMB

Parts out sections of hair; used for smoothing during processing

Holds relaxer product during application

Distributes neutralizer through the hair, eliminating tangles and minimizing damage to swollen hair using smooth, wide teeth of the comb

Applies relaxer and neutralizer to hair with less product waste, greater control and efficiency

RELAXER ESSENTIALS

RELAXER SUPPLIES

Identify the item based on its function.

Protects client from chemicals and water

_____
_____

Absorb and remove water, relaxer solution and neutralizer through blotting

_____
_____

Catches excess chemicals as they run off the scalp; protects client

_____
_____

Hold hair in place in controlled sections before and during wrapping procedure

_____
_____

RELAXER SUPPLIES (CONT'D)

Identify the item based on its function.

Holds relaxer product during application

_____

_____

Protects stylist's clothing from relaxer product

_____

_____

Removes relaxer and/or other products from containers for application, keeping supply of original product uncontaminated

_____

_____

Shield stylist's hands from chemicals during processing

_____

_____

RELAXER EQUIPMENT

FUNCTION

HEAT EQUIPMENT; PLASTIC CAP, INFRARED LAPS, HOOD DRYER

Provide and capture heat when _____ following relaxer service; help restore hair's structural integrity

TIMER

_____ to check for appropriate time allowed for relaxer to be on hair and scalp; also for monitoring neutralizing times as recommended by manufacturer

SHAMPOO BOWL

Needed for rinsing _____ chemicals and _____ from hair

STYLING CHAIR

Provides _____ seat for client; _____ for best working height

LESSON CHALLENGE

Multiple choice. Indicate one correct answer for each question.

1. Sodium hydroxide relaxers have a pH of:
   a. 5-6.5
   b. 11.5-14
   c. 6.5-8
   d. 8.5-10

2. Relaxer strengths for ammonium thioglycolate are categorized as all of the following EXCEPT:
   a. mild
   b. regular
   c. super
   d. heavy

3. Ammonium thioglycolate is a chemical reducing agent that causes the hair to:
   a. grow
   b. harden
   c. shrink
   d. soften

4. Sodium hydroxide relaxers are generally used on which type of hair?
   a. straight
   b. non-resistant
   c. tightly curled
   d. fragile hair

5. A salon professional should never use an ammonium thioglycolate product on a client's hair if it has been previously treated with:
   a. conditioner
   b. neutralizer
   c. sodium hydroxide
   d. shampoo

LESSON CHALLENGE REFERENCES

Check your answers as you did before. Place a check mark next to the page number for any incorrect answer. On the lines, jot down topics that you still need to review.

1. PAGE 133 _____

2. PAGE 133 _____

3. PAGE 133 _____

4. PAGE 133 _____

5. PAGE 135 _____

▶ # GROW WHAT YOU KNOW

Reflect on what you have learned and predict how this information will be used in the future.

111꜀.14 // RELAXER SKILLS

ACHIEVE //

Following this lesson on *Relaxer Skills*, you'll be able to:

>> Explain how the hair is analyzed prior to the relaxer service

>> Identify and explain the five procedural steps during the relaxer service

FOCUS //

RELAXER SKILLS

Pre-Relaxer Analysis

Relaxer Procedures

PRE-RELAXER ANALYSIS

An analysis of the porosity, elasticity, texture and density of the client's hair will help you determine:

The appropriate _____ of relaxer service

Type and _____ of relaxer product

Amount and time of _____ or _____ required

POROSITY

Refers to hair's ability to _____ moisture, liquids or chemicals

Match the appropriate guildeline for selecting relaxer product with the correct image.

_____   _____

A. When the hair is more **resistant**, you will need to select a stronger product, sometimes labeled as super strength.
B. With **porous** hair, choose a product labeled as mild.

ELASTICITY

Hair's ability to _____ and _____ without breaking, also known as the pull test

Write the type of elasticity, "Good" or "Poor," next to the appropriate statement.

Flexes back and forth as it is gently pulled   _____

In case of extreme breakage, you may need to cut off the damaged hair before a relaxer service   _____

If not extreme, you may chemically relax the hair and offer a course of treatment following the relaxer service   _____

Requires milder chemicals   _____

Can usually tolerate stronger chemicals   _____

SMARTNOTES

TEXTURE

Identify the texture diameter.

_____   _____   _____

**IDENTIFYING NATURAL
TEXTURE PATTERNS**

_____ _____ _____,
also called _____ _____, can be identified
by their visual characteristics.

Four major texture patterns determined by the _____ of the
hair follicle.

**STAGES OF RELAXING
TIGHTLY CURLED HAIR**

Identify the shape of each texture pattern below.

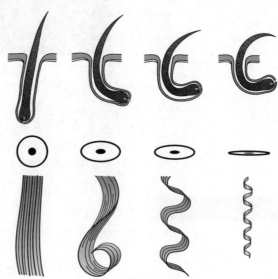

Straight   _____

Wavy   _____

Curly   _____

Tightly curled   _____

It is not advisable to relax tightly curled hair to the _____
relaxation level because this can overprocess the hair, leaving it limp and
susceptible to breakage.

DENSITY

Refers to the number of hair follicles per square inch and can be classified as
either light, medium or _____
In relaxing, density helps to determine the proper size _____
to use during the relaxer application.

RELAXER PROCEDURES

The _____ phase in relaxing includes sectioning the hair and applying the relaxer product.

The _____ phase includes smoothing or combing the hair, performing relaxation tests and neutralizing.

SECTION

- The first procedure step is to section the hair for _____ and _____, during the chemical application process
- Section a certain area or zone, such as the top, fringe, sides or nape
- Section only in the areas where texture will be _____ or _____

Before applying relaxer product, it is important to protect the skin around the hairline and ears with _____ _____.

_____ is the main ingredient in base creams.

APPLY

- Primary application method is with a _____
- Product is applied to _____ of the strand depending on the requirements of the service being performed
- Apply relaxer _____, without missing any areas to prevent an _____ pattern of straight or curly hair or ridges that could be hard to control

RELAXER APPLICATION METHODS

Write the appropriate application method for each.

VIRGIN	RETOUCH
- Relaxer first applied to most _____ area (usually crown or lower) - First applied ¼" (.6 cm) to ½" (1.25 cm) away from _____ _____, up to _____ ends - Next applied to area _____ _____	- Uses same procedures as virgin application, except product is applied only to _____ _____ - Overlapping product onto previously relaxed hair may result in - Apply _____ _____ to previously treated hair

ZONAL	CURL DIFFUSION
- Product is applied to _____ areas of head Depending on the desired result: - Use _____ application technique, or - Use _____ application technique	- Product generally applied to _____ _____ of hair - _____ _____ used to section and control hair - Brush used to apply product to _____ of hair

COMB OR SMOOTH

Match the statement to the appropriate image.

_____   _____   _____

A. Comb (instead of smoothing) the relaxer through the hair to reduce the curl pattern only by about 50%.

B. Smoothing is performed from base to ends in a downward direction for virgin applications.

C. For retouch applications, be careful not to overlap or smooth previously relaxed hair.

TIMING AND TESTING

The two primary ways to know when to stop smoothing and rinse the relaxer from the hair are:

1

2

TIMING FOR THIO RELAXERS

STRENGTH	CONDITION OF THE HAIR	TIMING
Mild		Up to _____ minutes
Regular		Up to _____ minutes
Super		Up to _____ minutes

TIMING FOR SODIUM HYDROXIDE RELAXERS

STRENGTH	CONDITION OF THE HAIR	TIMING
Mild		Up to _____ minutes
Regular		Up to _____ minutes
Super		Up to _____ minutes

RELAXATION TEST

Also known as the _____ _____, allows you to determine when the hair is relaxed to the desired degree or whether additional smoothing is required

1 Clear excess _____ from base or scalp area using back or tail of comb

2 Press the back or tail of the comb against the scalp area to determine the degree of relaxation by the amount of _____ that occurs

- Curl pattern reverts or "beads" = _____

  _____

- Strong amount of indentation = _____

  _____

RINSING AND BLOTTING

Points to remember:

- Hair must be rinsed for a long period of time to _____ the chemical action and completely rid the hair of any _____

  _____.

- Check closely in the _____ _____ and _____ the ears, which are more difficult to rinse.

- Chemicals left in the hair will remain _____ and could cause _____ _____ and/or _____

  _____.

Use an _____-_____ neutralizing _____ or _____ to _____ the hair into its new, straighter shape.

NEUTRALIZE

RELAXER TYPE	NEUTRALIZE USING
Sodium Hydroxide	_____
Ammonium Thioglycolate	_____

CREATING THE NEW RELAXED CURL PATTERN

Guiding steps to creat new, relaxed texture patterns for your clients:

1.

2.

3.

4.

5.

6.

MATCHING

Match the relaxer procedure step with its related image.

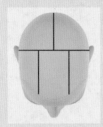

Apply   Neutralize   Test   Comb or Smooth   Section

LESSON CHALLENGE

Multiple choice. Indicate one correct answer for each question.

1. The hair's ability to absorb moisture, liquids or chemicals is known as:
   a. density
   b. porosity
   c. texture
   d. elasticity

2. Which of the following texture patterns is associated with an elliptical follicle?
   a. curly
   b. relaxed
   c. wavy
   d. straight

3. What protects the hairline, ears and scalp from chemical irritation?
   a. conditioner
   b. relaxer
   c. base cream
   d. neutralizer

4. Sodium hydroxide relaxers are generally used on what type of hair?
   a. tightly curled
   b. non-resistant
   c. wavy
   d. straight

5. Which chemical relaxer strength is safe to use on color-treated hair?
   a. extra-strength
   b. regular
   c. super
   d. mild

LESSON CHALLENGE REFERENCES

Check your answers. Place a check mark next to the page number for any incorrect answer. On the lines, jot down topics that you still need to review.

1. PAGE 142 _____

2. PAGE 144 _____

3. PAGE 147 _____

4. PAGE 150 _____

5. PAGE 150 _____

▶ GROW WHAT YOU KNOW

Reflect on what you have learned and predict how this information will be used in the future.

111^c.15 // RELAXER GUEST EXPERIENCE

ACHIEVE //

Following this lesson on *Relaxer Guest Experience*, you'll be able to:

» Summarize the service essentials related to relaxer services

» Provide examples of infection control and safety guidelines for relaxer services

FOCUS //

RELAXER GUEST EXPERIENCE

Relaxer Service Essentials

Relaxer Infection Control and Safety

Before applying any _____ _____ to the hair, have a thorough _____ to ensure an understanding regarding the desired new texture pattern.

RELAXER SERVICE ESSENTIALS

To determine the type and strength relaxer, ask the client about:

Preferred way of _____ and wearing hair on regular basis

"How much of the _____ texture would you like reduced?"

"What are the recent past _____ services you've had and has there been any _____ that resulted?"

Any fears, worries or _____ they may be concerned with

CONNECT

Meet and greet the client with a _____ _____ and pleasant tone of voice

_____ to build rapport and develop a

_____ with the client

CONSULT

Ask questions about past services to understand client's _____ and _____

Gain feedback and _____

CREATE

Ensure client protection through proper _____

_____ all steps of the relaxer service to the best of your ability

COMPLETE

_____ products to maintain the healthy condition of the hair

_____ single-use supplies, _____ tools and arrange workstation

IDENTIFY

Identify whether the information listed below belongs with a **client chemical release form**, or the **client chemical relaxer record:**

Client chemical release form

Client chemical relaxer record

Is not a legal document

Lists the products used and processing time

Does not absolve stylist from responsiblity

Contains contact information

Lists past services

COMMUNICATION GUIDELINES

Listen for cues that offer an opportunity to recommend services.

Communication guidelines help create an _____ of things clients might say during a relaxer service and how to respond in ways to encourage _____ _____.

Respond to each individual client with _____ and _____.

RELAXER INFECTION CONTROL AND SAFETY

Protect your client by following _____ _____ and _____ guidelines.

Cleaning – _____

_____

Disinfection methods – _____

_____

Disinfectants are available in varied forms, including:

-
-

-
-

The salon industry uses _____ products.

DRAPING FOR CHEMICAL SERVICES

Proper draping procedures for a relaxer service _____ the client's clothing and help prevent _____ _____ or _____.

SCALP ANALYSIS

When performing a scalp analysis look for any _____, such as:

-
-

-
-

Remember, _____ apply chemicals over any abnormal scalp conditions.

PRELIMINARY STRAND TEST

Allows you to evaluate the overall _____ of the hair to determine if it can withstand a _____ service

TEST FOR METALLIC SALTS

Color products that _____ color or _____ darken the hair (sometimes called hair _____) contain metallic salts.

_____ can form a residue on the hair that interferes with a chemical action.

TEST FOR METALLIC SALTS (CONT'D)

Performing a chemical service on hair with metallic salts can result in:

-
-
-
-

If metallic salts are suspected, perform a _____ test.

CLEANING AND DISINFECTION GUIDELINES

Only nonporous tools, supplies and equipment can be

_____.

All single-use items must be _____ after each use.

CARE AND SAFETY

Follow infection control procedures for personal care and client safety.

PERSONAL CARE

Wash _____ and dry thoroughly with single use towel.

Wear protective _____.

CLIENT CARE PRIOR TO SERVICE

Check scalp for _____ or _____.

_____ the client's hair to determine the correct

_____ use.

CLIENT CARE DURING SERVICE

Protects client's skin by applying _____ _____.

Do not permit _____ to come in contact with eyes.

Be sure the _____ stays in place and the client's arms are

_____ the cape.

SALON CARE

Use _____ applicator bottles, brushes and combs.

_____ any left over _____ _____

once the service is complete.

LESSON CHALLENGE

Multiple choice. Indicate one correct answer for each question.

1. The client record houses the following information EXCEPT:
   a. contact information
   b. name
   c. processing time
   d. legal information

2. The guest experience begins with:
   a. draping
   b. the consultation
   c. gaining feedback
   d. a firm handshake

3. Greeting your client is part of the _____ service essential.
   a. Consult
   b. Connect
   c. Complete
   d. Create

4. Ensuring client comfort is part of the _____ service essential.
   a. Consult
   b. Connect
   c. Complete
   d. Create

5. Checking into your client's relaxer history is part of the _____ service essential.
   a. Consult
   b. Connect
   c. Complete
   d. Create

6. Requesting feedback from the client is part of the _____ service essential.
   a. Consult
   b. Connect
   c. Complete
   d. Create

7. During the scalp analysis prior to a relaxer check for any cuts, bruises, sores and _____.
   a. dandruff
   b. abrasions
   c. oiliness
   d. wrinkles

8. Draping for a relaxer service should include a cape and _____.
   a. neck strip
   b. towels
   c. plastic
   d. cotton coil

LESSON CHALLENGE REFERENCES

Check your answers. Place a check mark next to the page number for any incorrect answer. On the lines, jot down topics that you still need to review.

1. PAGE 158 _____
2. PAGE 159 _____
3. PAGE 159 _____
4. PAGE 159 _____
5. PAGE 159 _____
6. PAGE 159 _____
7. PAGE 162 _____
8. PAGE 163 _____

▶ GROW WHAT YOU KNOW

Reflect on what you have learned and predict how this information will be used in the future.

111ᶜ.20 // CURL REFORMATION THEORY

ACHIEVE //

Following this lesson on *Curl Reformation Theory*, you'll be able to:

» State the milestones that influenced curl reformation services as we know them today

» Explain the two processes involved in performing a curl reformation service

» Provide examples of products, supplies and equipment used to perform a curl reformation service

» Identify and explain the six procedural steps during the curl reformation service

» Describe the three areas of a curl reformation service

FOCUS //

CURL REFORMATION THEORY

History of Curl Reforming

Curl Reforming Processes

Curl Reformation Products and Essentials

Curl Reformation Skills

Curl Reformation Guest Experience

Curl Reformation Service

Curl Reformation Rubric

Curl reformation is a chemical service designed to change _____ _____ hair to curly or wavy hair. Curl reformation is also known as _____ _____, reformation curls or double-process perm. The hair is first _____ to reduce the natural curl pattern and then _____ to create a new curl pattern.

Actions in the curl reformation process include:

- _____ the existing curl pattern
- _____ to produce a new curl pattern around perm tools
- _____ to fix (neutralize) the chemical bonds and lock in the new curl pattern

HISTORY OF CURL REFORMING

DR. WILLIE MORROW
- Started a company in the 1970s called _____
- Created a cold wave formulated to produce soft curls for

_____ _____ _____

JHERI REDDING
- Co-founder of Redken, Jhirmack and Nexxus®
- Credited with creation of pH-balanced shampoo
- Developed the _____, which was also a

_____ _____ _____ _____,

forumlated for tightly curled hair

COMER COTTRELL
- Founder of Pro-Line Products
- Created the first at home curl reformation called the _____

Today, the curl reformations products have been reformulated and are often known as _____ - _____ systems. These systems produce beautiful _____ _____ without the wet, oily look of earlier systems.

BASIC CURL REFORMATION SERVICES

There are two basic curl reformation services:

VIRGIN REFORMATION
A **virgin curl reformation service** is used on _____, _____ or _____ hair to reform tightly curled texture into a looser curl wave pattern.

RETOUCH REFORMATION
A **retouch curl reformation service** is performed on the _____ _____ only to _____ the previously curl reformed hair.

CURL REFORMING PROCESSES

The first process involves relaxing or _____ the natural curl pattern:

- Apply a _____ product known as a curl _____.

- _____ the hair to relax or reduce natural curl pattern.

The second process involves perming or _____ and _____ the hair into a new curl or wave pattern:

- Wrap and secure the hair using perm tools to _____ hair to new curl or wave pattern.

- Any _____ _____ _____ can be used to wrap the hair, once the desired direction is established.

- Apply a _____ _____ to the hair

- _____ _____.

- Rinse and apply neutralizer to _____ hair into new curl or wave pattern.

CURL REFORMATION PRODUCTS AND ESSENTIALS

CURL REFORMING PRODUCTS

In the **reducing** step, the _____ _____ is the product used to reduce or relax the natural curl pattern:

- _____ _____ is the main ingredient found in curl rearrangers.

In the **reforming** step, a _____ _____, or perm solution, is applied to the hair:

- Mild, creamy form of ammonium thioglycolate.

During the **rebonding** step, the neutralizer:

- _____

- Reduces _____ caused by alkaline formulas

- Causes oxidation, which _____

- Results in hair being held in new _____ _____

PRODUCTS	FUNCTION Explain the function of each curl reformation product.
Curl Rearranger	
Curl Booster	
Curl Activator	
Instant Moisturizer	

1 2 3 4 5 6 7

ESSENTIALS

CURL REFORMING TOOLS

- _____ – Determine the size and shape of new curl

CURL REFORMING SUPPLIES

- _____ – Hold perm rods in position

CURL REFORMATION SKILLS

PRE-CURL REFORMATION ANALYSIS

Before beginning a curl reformation service, you will perform a _____

_____ to properly assess the condition of your client's hair. The

porosity, _____, texture, density, type of curl pattern

and overall _____ of the hair will help you determine

the appropriate _____ and strength of curl

reformation products to use.

CURL REFORMATION STEPS

The steps that are performed within a curl reformation service are:

1.

2.

3.

4.

5.

6.

SECTION

Hair can be sectioned into _____ or _____

sections, just like in a relaxer service.

APPLY CURL REARRANGER

- In a virgin application, the rearranger is applied to the

_____ or cold shaft first, then to the

_____ and the _____.

- In the retouch application, the rearranger is only applied to the

_____ - _____ area without overlapping onto previously

treated hair.

SMOOTH

- The _____ of a comb is used to smooth hair, just as

in a relaxer service.

- A virgin application is smoothed from _____-_____-

_____.

- Only the new growth is smoothed in a _____

application, with a special care not to overlap product onto previously

treated hair.

CURL REFORMATION STEPS (CONT'D)

SECTION AND WRAP

Sectioning will be based on the _____ _____.

- Use _____ base control.
- Picks or stabilizers _____.
- Tool _____ and _____

  should be checked before proceeding to the next application step.

APPLY CURL BOOSTER

To ensure saturation, the curl booster is applied to the

_____ and _____ of each rod.

Well-experienced designers sometimes choose to apply the curl booster

section by section _____ to wrapping.

NEUTRALIZE

The process is very similar to _____ a perm.

Generally done while the hair is still _____ on the

perm rods.

Follow manufacturer's instructions for _____ and

_____ neutralizer.

MATCHING

Match the term with the correct image.

| Section | Apply Curl Rearranger | Smooth | Section and Wrap | Apply Curl Booster | Neutralize |

CURL REFORMATION GUEST EXPERIENCE

COMMUNICATION GUIDELINES

Before _____ any curl reforming chemicals to the hair:

- Have a thorough _____ with the client
- Listen carefully and _____ all the important

  information in the chemical record; be sure you _____

  the new texture pattern your client desires
- Ask questions to _____ past and current products

  used on the hair

SMARTNOTES

**CURL REFORMATION
INFECTION CONTROL
AND SAFETY**

The following are safety precautions that you should always adhere to
_____ to and _____ a curl
reformation service to _____ the client and yourself:

- Shampoo the client's hair only _____ prior
  to a curl reformation service to avoid _____
  the scalp. Use _____ finger pressure
  and _____ water pressure with a
  _____ temperature.

- Never perform a curl service on hair that has been relaxed with a
  _____ _____ _____. The
  results could be _____ _____ and
  _____ .

LESSON CHALLENGE
Multiple choice. Indicate one correct answer for each question.

1. How many processes are involved when performing a curl reformation?
   a. two
   b. three
   c. four
   d. five

2. During a curl reformation service, what causes hair to soften and swell in order to reform it into a new curl or wave pattern?
   a. oil
   b. booster
   c. rearranger
   d. neutralizer

3. What is the name of the product used to reduce the curl pattern?
   a. curl booster
   b. neutralizer
   c. curl rearranger
   d. none of the above

4. What is the main ingredient in curl boosters?
   a. bisulphides
   b. ammonium thioglycolate
   c. glycerol monothioglycolate
   d. none of the above

5. Which curl reformation service can be performed over hair relaxed with sodium hydroxide-based product?
   a. virgin curl reformation
   b. retouch curl reformation
   c. both services
   d. neither service

LESSON CHALLENGE REFERENCES

*Check your answers. Place a check mark next to the page number for
any incorrect answer. On the lines, jot down topics that you still need to
review.*

1. PAGE 206 _____

2. PAGE 208 _____

3. PAGE 208 _____

4. PAGE 208 _____

5. PAGE 210 _____

▶ GROW WHAT YOU KNOW

*Reflect on what you have
learned and predict how this
information will be used in
the future.*

112ᶜ.1 // SKIN THEORY

ACHIEVE //

Following this lesson on *Skin Theory*, you'll be able to:

>> Define the six basic functions of the skin

>> Describe the main composition of the skin

>> Offer examples of how to protect the skin by reducing the sun's harmful effects

>> Explain the basic type of skin surfaces

FOCUS //

SKIN THEORY

Functions of the Skin

Composition of the Skin

Skin Pigmentation and Sunscreen

Types of Skin

Skin is the largest organ of the body.

The study of the skin, its structure, functions, diseases and treatment is called

_____.

In the industry, the process of cleansing, toning, moisturizing, protecting and enhancing the skin is known as _____.

FUNCTIONS OF THE SKIN

6 BASIC FUNCTIONS

Reaction to a sensation is called a reflex.

① **S**

② **H**

③ **A**

④ **P**

⑤ **E**

Sebum is a complex mixture of fatty substances.

⑥ **S**

COMPOSITION OF THE SKIN

LABEL THE 3 MAIN LAYERS OF SKIN

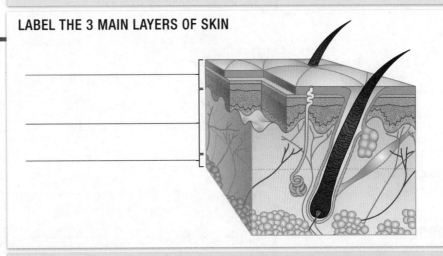

EPIDERMIS

Outermost protective layer

-
-
-
-

Label the 5 main layers of the epidermis.

Stratum _____
Hardened, "cornified," "horny" cells

Stratum _____
Transparent, clear (lucid) cells on soles and palms

Stratum _____
Grain-like cells

Stratum _____
"Spiny," irregularly shaped cells

Stratum _____
(Basal or Basement Layer): Cell growth

5 LAYERS OF THE EPIDERMIS

LOWEST

Stratum _____

Description: _____

_____

Function: _____

Special Cells: _____

Stratum _____

Description: _____

_____

Function: _____

Special Cells: _____

Stratum _____

Description: _____

_____

Function: _____

Special Cells: _____

Stratum _____

Description: _____

_____

Function: _____

Special Cells: _____

Stratum _____

Description: _____

_____

Function: _____

Special Cells: _____

Basic Melanin
(What you are born with)

Hyperpigmentation
(Result of external factors)

UPPERMOST

DERMAL

Composed mostly of keratinized cells

Also known as the: _____

Cells are alive or dead? *(Circle one)*

25 times thicker than the _____

Made up of connective tissues that give skin its _____

Two Layers of Dermal

PAPILLARY

* Directly beneath the

  _____

* Rich in blood vessels and

  _____

* Finger-like projections extend into epidermis and nourish the skin

* Tactile corpuscles are responsible for sensitivities to light

  _____

RETICULAR

* Lowest layer of dermal

* In direct contact with

  _____

* Contains:
  * Collagen and _____
  * Sudoriferous and sebaceous glands
  * Sensory nerve endings/receptors
  * Blood vessels
  * Arrector pili _____
  * Major portions of hair

  _____

Label the sudoriferous gland, sebaceous gland and the subcutaneous layer.

SUDORIFEROUS GLANDS

* Coiled base and tube-like duct opening on the surface of the skin that form a

  _____ _____

* Control and regulate _____ _____

* Excrete _____ _____

* Help maintain the acidic pH factor of skin

SEBACEOUS GLANDS

* Sac-like glands attached to the hair follicles that produce _____
* Keep skin _____
* Prevent dirt and grime from entering the _____
* Prevent skin from drying or _____

Sebum + sweat on the surface of the skin = _____ _____

SUBCUTANEOUS

Adipose (fatty) layer below the dermal layer

* Protective cushion for _____
* Shock absorber for _____
* Supports blood vessels/nerve endings
* Gives body contour and _____
* Provides reservoir of food and _____
* Composed of fatty and loose _____

Subcutaneous tissue contains blood vessels, sense organs, and

_____

SKIN PIGMENTATION AND SUNSCREEN

Melanin-producing cells called melanocytes are located in the basal layer of the
_____.

Melanin is distributed throughout all epidermal cells and forms an effective barrier from the penetration of _____ _____.

Two Types of Melanin

Brown/black =	Red/yellow =
_____	_____

Studies show 90% of wrinkles are caused by excessive exposure to the sun, and only 10% by the natural aging process.

The type of melanin produced is determined by amount and type of melanin present along with _____

Skin tanning is a result of accelerated melanin production to protect the skin from _____ _____.

Sunscreen helps keep skin from absorbing ultraviolet rays.
SPF rating system helps determine how long you can stay in the sun without _____.

American Academy of Dermatology recommends:

- Apply sunscreen with SPF of at least _____
- Reapply every _____
- Wear protective, tightly woven clothing
- Avoid surfaces, such as water, that can reflect up to _____ of damaging rays

SPF = _____

TYPES OF SKIN

From a salon professional's point of view, the surface of the skin falls into four basic types:

DRY SKIN

_____
_____

OILY SKIN

_____
_____
_____

NORMAL SKIN

_____
_____

COMBINATION SKIN

_____
_____

CROSSWORD

ACROSS

6. Chemical conversion of living cells into dead protein cells

7. Pigment that gives skin its color

8. One of the protein fibers that helps give skin its elastic quality

9. Outermost layer of the skin

10. Skin layer that is completely alive

DOWN

1. Skin layer that acts as a shock absorber to protect the bones

2. Another name for sudoriferous glands (Two words)

3. Most common skin type

4. Layer of epidermis that is being constantly shed (Two words)

5. Skin type characterized by signs such as peeling and flaking

LESSON CHALLENGE   *Multiple choice. Indicate one correct answer for each question.*

1. Functions of the skin include regulation of body temperature and:
   a. digestion
   b. protection
   c. circulation
   d. reproduction

2. Which of the following layers of skin does not contain any blood vessels?
   a. cutis
   b. dermal
   c. corneum
   d. epidermis

3. Where does mitosis (cell division) or replacement of the skin cells take place?
   a. stratum basale
   b. stratum lucidum
   c. stratum corneum
   d. stratum granulosum

4. Which of the following items determines the color of the skin?
   a. keratin
   b. melanin
   c. elastin fiber
   d. collagen protein

5. The stratum lucidum layer is found only on the:
   a. scalp
   b. elbows
   c. tops of hands
   d. soles of the feet and palms of hands

6. Which layer of the skin contains collagen protein and elastin fibers which lend support to the epidermis and give the skin its elastic quality?
   a. dermal
   b. epidermis
   c. stratum lucidum
   d. stratum granulosum

7. Sweat is excreted by what gland?
   a. adrenal
   b. endocrine
   c. sebaceous
   d. sudoriferous

8. The greatest concentration of sudoriferous glands is found on the:
   a. arms
   b. eyelids
   c. midsection of the body
   d. palms, soles, scalp and forehead, and underarms

9. What is the function of sebum?
   a. carry melanin
   b. produce sweat
   c. give skin elasticity
   d. mix with sweat to form the acid mantle

10. Most skin problems are caused by:
    a. the eccrine glands
    b. the sebaceous glands
    c. the sudoriferous glands
    d. the arrector pili muscles

11. Which layer of skin is located below the dermal layer and composed of adipose (fatty) and loose connective tissue?
    a. dermis
    b. epidermis
    c. subdermis
    d. subcutaneous

12. Nerve bundles in the subcutaneous tissue branch into the stratum granulosum layer and respond to:
    a. pain
    b. light
    c. taste
    d. sound

13. All of the following statements identify ways to protect the skin from the sun's harmful rays EXCEPT:

    a. apply oil every 2 hours
    b. apply sunscreen every 2 hours
    c. avoid surfaces, such as water, that can reflect up to 85% of the sun's damaging rays
    d. be aware that damaging UVA and UVB rays can penetrate windows, car windshields, clothing and clouds

14. Which skin type has a rough texture with blackheads and enlarged pores?
    a. dry
    b. oily
    c. normal
    d. combination

15. Which skin type is recognized by the shiny T-zone?
    a. dry
    b. oily
    c. normal
    d. combination

LESSON CHALLENGE REFERENCES

Check your answers. Place a check mark next to the page number for any incorrect answer.
On the lines, jot down topics that you still need to review.

▶ GROW WHAT YOU KNOW

Reflect on what you have learned and predict how this information will be used in the future.

112ᶜ.2 // SKIN DISEASES AND DISORDERS

ACHIEVE //

Following this lesson on *Skin Diseases and Disorders*, you'll be able to:

» Identify primary and secondary lesions

» Offer examples of pigmentation abnormalities

» Describe disorders of the sebaceous and sudoriferous glands

» Summarize common skin infections

FOCUS //

SKIN DISEASES AND DISORDERS

Lesions

Pigmentation Abnormalities

Disorders

Skin Infections

Only dermatologists or other medical doctors diagnose and treat skin diseases and disorders.

Symptoms of a disease are divided into two classifications.

1 _____

Those that can be

_____.

Examples:

_____,

_____,

_____

2 _____

Those that can be

_____.

Examples:

_____,

_____,

_____

In some cases, both objective and subjective symptoms may be present and can be indications of an _____.

SIX SIGNS OF INFECTION

- _____   - _____
- _____   - _____
- _____   - _____

Avoid performing services on skin where symptoms indicate an infection.

IMPORTANT VOCABULARY

Sensitivity that may develop from contact with normally harmless substances: _____

Objective symptom of redness, pain, swelling and/or increased temperature: _____

Term used to identify conditions that are frequent and habitual: _____

Term used to identify conditions that are brief and severe: _____

A disease communicable by contact: _____

Disease influenced by weather: _____

The study of causes of diseases: _____

The study of diseases: _____

EYES ON CANCERˢᴹ
GO BEAUTY, STOP CANCER.

Changes in skin that require physician evaluation:

A symmetry   **C** _____   **E** volution (take a picture)

B _____   **D** _____

CONTACT DERMATITIS
Two Types

1 IRRITANT
Caused by:

_____,

_____

Reaction:

_____

_____

_____

2 ALLERGIC
Caused by:

_____,

_____

Reaction:

_____

_____

_____

Infection control practices establish standards regarding protective items, such as gloves, to assist in avoiding occupational disorders.

Occupational disorders occur in certain types of employment

Dermatitis venenata (contact dermatitis): Skin becomes red, sore or inflamed after direct contact with a substance.

LESIONS

Lesions: _____

Three main categories:

-
-
-

As a salon professional, you need to recognize primary and secondary lesions.

PRIMARY SKIN LESIONS — CHANGES IN THE STRUCTURE OF THE SKIN AT THE ONSET OF A DISEASE

NAME	DESCRIPTION	EXAMPLE	SERVICE?
MACULES			
	Fluid-filled elevations; accumulation of fluids or blood just below epidermis		
	BULLA Like vesicles but larger		No service on affected areas
	HERPES SIMPLEX VIRUS Contagious, chronic condition characterized by a single or group of vesicles on a red, swollen base	Fever blister, cold sore	
PAPULES			
PUSTULES			
WHEALS		Mosquito bite	
		Hives	
TUMORS			

SECONDARY SKIN LESIONS — APPEAR AS DISEASE PROGRESSES TO LATER STAGES OF GROWTH

NAME	DESCRIPTION	EXAMPLE	SERVICE?
SCALES			Yes – Service
	PSORIASIS	Scales	
	Dried masses; remains of oozing sore		No service on affected areas
EXCORIATIONS		Scratch	
FISSURES	Cracks in the skin		
	Cicatrix; formations resulting from a lesion as part of healing process		
ULCERS		Loss of portion of the dermal layer	No service on affected areas

NAME	DESCRIPTION	EXAMPLE	SERVICE?
HYPERTROPHIES	*Overgrowth or excess skin (new growth)*		
CALLUS	Hyperkeratosis or keratoma; thickening of skin; occurs from pressure and friction		Yes – Service
VERRUCA	Variety of warts; caused by a virus; can be contagious	Warts	
SKIN TAGS		Small benign nodule	

PIGMENTATION ABNORMALITIES

CONDITIONS OF TOO MUCH COLOR OR TOO LITTLE COLOR IN PARTICULAR AREA OF THE SKIN

NAME	DESCRIPTION	EXAMPLE	SERVICE?
MELANODERMA	*Hyperpigmentation caused by overactivity of the melanocytes in the epidermis*		
CHLOASMA			
MOLES		Mole	
NEVUS		Birthmark, congenital mole	
LEUKODERMA	*Hypopigmentation of the skin caused by a decrease in activity of melanocytes*		
ALBINISM			
VITILIGO		Patches of hypopigmentation seen on the face, hands and neck	

DISORDERS

DISORDERS OF THE SEBACEOUS GLANDS

NAME	DESCRIPTION	SERVICE?
COMEDONES		
MILIA	Keratin-filled cysts; form a hard ball beneath the outer layer of skin	
ACNE		
ROSACEA		No service on affected areas Facial can be performed with physician's approval
ASTEATOSIS		
SEBORRHEIC DERMATITIS		Yes – Service

NAME	DESCRIPTION	SERVICE?
	Cyst or wen; subcutaneous tumor filled with sebum	
FURUNCLES		
	Cluster of furuncles; acute bacterial infection of adjoining hair follicles	No service on affected areas

DISORDERS OF THE SUDORIFEROUS GLANDS

NAME	DESCRIPTION	SERVICE?
BROMIDROSIS		Yes – Service
	Inability to sweat normally	
HYPERHIDROSIS		Yes – Service
MILIARIA RUBRA (prickly heat)		No service on affected areas

SKIN INFECTIONS

NAME	DESCRIPTION	SERVICE?
DERMATITIS		No service on affected areas
	Dry or moist lesions with inflammation; may be chronic or acute; should be referred to a physician for treatment	
IMPETIGO		No service on affected areas
	Infection in hair follicles; caused by bacteria, shaving or clothing irritation; red pimples with a hair in the center	
PSEUDOFOLLICULITIS BARBAE		
CONJUNCTIVITIS		No service on affected areas

Tinea = Medical term for ringworm

Contagious fungal disease characterized by a _____

_____

Caused by a fungal vegetable _____

1 2 3 4 5 6 7

▶ **WORD** FIND

In the Word Find, circle the words listed in the Jump Start Box. Words are listed forward, backward and diagonally. Listings that have punctuation or two words are found without spaces in the puzzle. How many of these words can you define?

JUMP START BOX

ACNE
DERMATITIS
ECZEMA
LESIONS
MELANODERMA
PSORIASIS
SEBACEOUS GLANDS
VESICLES
VITILIGO

```
U E N C A D N I X J D Q F A N T I L V N
U I L K T D I E F Q I U O H W K O T Z B
Y S G N C M R O F W F N J X T R X B N J
P N R V X S P A M R E D O N A L E M D Q
X L S K N N T S O B B I T N R M P L G J
Z N F E Y E L E U Q R P I O V S O K P X
K Q T A E Z T B Q M B B A O O G C E I G
V W R M N A B A D Z T M Q R I U I E J L
F E E E Q C D C S F B Y I L T D G G E X
V P J Z N L A E C X J A I H G G Z S V H
X G R C V C K O J A S T R J V P N L T I
J V S E X A S U W I I E I Y P W X T L F
S P T Y C N G S S V U T M S B Y S V Q P
B X W J O C T G J E S I T I T A M R E D
J W O I C D T L E Q L X J V R D R M C W
E C S F E C I A G X X V D S I M L K Z W
W E S X X I O N D H M A Z U X D J W H T
L E D Z L F N D V T U X X D M J P X A M
G D V P I B U S K F T S E L C I S E V P
E L Y U E M U G H R C D M Q O V C Z N A
```

LESSON CHALLENGE

Multiple choice. Indicate one correct answer for each question.

1. **An example of a subjective symptom would be:**
   a. itching
   b. swelling
   c. redness
   d. discharge

2. **Chronic is the term used to identify conditions that are:**
   a. visible
   b. brief and severe
   c. frequent and habitual
   d. influenced by weather

3. **A disease influenced by weather is referred to as:**
   a. serial
   b. rational
   c. seasonal
   d. inflammable

4. **A papule is an example of a:**
   a. tertiary lesion
   b. primary skin lesion
   c. subjective symptom
   d. secondary skin lesion

5. **Which of the following primary lesions are small elevations of skin similar to vesicles in size and shape but contain pus?**
   a. wheals
   b. tumors
   c. pustules
   d. macules

6. **A secondary lesion appearing as round, dry patches of skin covered with rough, silvery scales is called:**
   a. acne
   b. eczema
   c. psoriasis
   d. herpes simplex

7. Which of the following skin lesions usually appear as cracks or lines and often occurs when skin loses its flexibility due to exposure to wind, cold and water?
   a. stain
   b. tumor
   c. fissure
   d. papule

8. The lesion found following the normal healing process of an injury is called a(n):
   a. scar
   b. fissure
   c. vitiligo
   d. excoriation

9. Which of the following terms is another name for a keratoma?
   a. wart
   b. callus
   c. tumor
   d. birthmark

10. Verruca is a name given to a variety of:
    a. warts
    b. ulcers
    c. fissures
    d. skin tags

11. What is the technical term for a decrease in activity of melanocytes?
    a. acne
    b. verruca
    c. leukoderma
    d. melanoderma

12. An open comedone is the technical name for:
    a. nevus
    b. macule
    c. blackhead
    d. birthmark

13. Pearly white, enclosed keratin-filled cysts which form a hard ball beneath the outer layer of the skin are known as:
    a. acne
    b. milia
    c. rosacea
    d. comedones

14. Persons exposed to excessive heat may develop small red vesicles with burning and itching of the skin called prickly heat or:
    a. eczema
    b. anhidrosis
    c. bromidrosis
    d. miliaria rubra

15. Which of the following terms is an infection in the hair follicles caused by bacteria, shaving or clothing irritation?
    a. eczema
    b. impetigo
    c. folliculitis
    d. pseudofolliculitis barbae

LESSON CHALLENGE REFERENCES

Check your answers. Place a check mark next to the page number for any incorrect answer. On the lines, jot down topics that you still need to review.

▶ GROW WHAT YOU KNOW

Reflect on what you have learned and predict how this information will be used in the future.

112ᶜ.3 // SKIN CARE

ACHIEVE //

Following this lesson on *Skin Care*, you'll be able to:

>> Identify the skin care regimen recommended for healthy skin

>> State the benefits of each of the five types of massage movements used during facial massage

>> Describe the types of common facial masks used for skin

FOCUS //

SKIN CARE

Skin Care Regimen

Massage

Facial Masks

SKIN CARE REGIMEN

Proper skin care is a combination of concerted efforts toward a good home-maintenance program, a well-balanced diet, proper intake of water, limited exposure to the sun, exercise, rest and professional skin care treatments and products.

4 DAILY SKIN CARE STEPS

1 _____
   •

2 _____
   •

3 _____
   •

4 _____
   •

EXFOLIATION

Exfoliation: _____
_____

2 MAIN WAYS

1 **MECHANICAL (** _____ **)**
   Methods: _____

2 **CHEMICAL**
   Ingredients: _____

MASSAGE

Massage: Systematic, therapeutic method of manipulating the body by rubbing, pinching, tapping, kneading or stroking with the hands, fingers or an instrument.

BENEFITS OF MASSAGE
Applying pressure to motor points soothes and stimulates the nerves and muscles. Additional benefits of massage include:

1.

2.

3.

4.

5.

6.

CONTRAINDICATIONS FOR MASSAGE

Contraindications: _____

_____

CONTRAINDICATIONS	REASONS
MEDICAL CONDITIONS	
Pregnancy	
Heart conditions/pacemaker, high blood pressure	
Sensitive, redness-prone skin	
Metal bone pins or plates	
Known allergies	
Autoimmune diseases	
Diabetes	
Open sores, herpes simplex virus 1 and 2	
Facial surgery or laser treatment	
CERTAIN MEDICATIONS	
Accutane, exfoliating medications, certain antibiotics for acne treatment	
Blood thinners	
Oral steroids	

THE 5 BASIC MOVEMENTS OF MASSAGE

Keep in mind:

Never massage over an area exhibiting redness, swelling, pus, disease, bruises, and/or broken or scraped skin.

Massage movements should be directed toward the origin of the muscles.

When performing facial massage, an even tempo or rhythm is essential.

_____

Light, gliding, gentle stroking or circular movement
Relaxing and soothing

_____

Light or heaving kneading and rolling of muscles
Deep simulation of muscles, nerves and skin glands

_____

Light tapping or slapping with fingertips or flexed fingers
Stimulates nerves, muscle contraction and blood circulation

_____

Circular, or wringing movement; no gliding
Stimulates nerves and increases blood circulation

_____

Shaking movement in the arms
Highly stimulating

1 2 3 4 5 6 7

FACIAL MASKS

Facial masks (or packs) are used for many different reasons including:

-
-
-
-
-
-

TYPES OF FACIAL MASKS

MASKS	RECOMMENDED FOR WHICH SKIN TYPE(S)?
Clay/Mud	
Cream	
Gel	
Modeling	
Paraffin	

BENEFITS OF FACIAL MASKS

1.
2.
3.
4.
5.
6.
7.

MATCHING

Match the term from the left with its description on the right.

A. Petrissage

B. Friction

C. Vibration

D. Effleurage

E. Tapotement

_____ Shaking movement in the arms of the salon professional while the fingertips or palms are touching the client

_____ Circular, or wringing movement with no gliding; usually carried out with the fingertips or palms of hands

_____ Light or heavy kneading and rolling of the muscles

_____ Light, gliding, gentle stroking or circular massage movement

_____ Light tapping or slapping movement applied with the fingertips are partly flexed fingers

LESSON CHALLENGE *Multiple choice. Indicate one correct answer for each question.*

1. Products that help to cleanse, soothe and smooth the skin while bringing it to a normal pH are known as:
   a. oils
   b. toners
   c. massage creams
   d. manual exfoliants

2. A term that is used to describe moisturizing is:
   a. oiling
   b. toning
   c. hydrating
   d. cleansing

3. All of the following examples are possible mechanical exfoliation methods EXCEPT:
   a. brush
   b. scrubs
   c. enzymes
   d. facial cloths

4. Which of the following skin care products removes dead skin cells by using enzymes and hydroxy acids?
   a. massage cream
   b. cleansing lotion
   c. chemical exfoliant
   d. manual exfoliant

5. Applying pressure to motor points will have which of the following effects?
   a. increase body tension
   b. inflame and irritate muscles
   c. decrease production of keratin
   d. soothe and stimulate nerves and muscles

6. A massage can provide all of the following results EXCEPT:
   a. weaken muscle tissue
   b. stimulate glandular activity
   c. improve the texture of the skin
   d. increase blood circulation to the skin

7. If a client suffers from high blood pressure or has suffered a stroke, massage movements should:
   a. significantly reduce blood pressure
   b. reduce the chance of second stroke
   c. reduce the chance of heart attack
   d. be avoided since massage increases circulation

8. All of the following terms are basic massage movements EXCEPT:
   a. cleansing
   b. petrissage
   c. effleurage
   d. tapotement

9. The gentle massage movement that often begins and ends a massage treatment is called:
   a. friction
   b. petrissage
   c. effleurage
   d. tapotement

10. Effleurage is a massage movement that involves:
    a. circular movement with no gliding
    b. light tapping or slapping movement
    c. light, gentle stroking or circular movement
    d. light or heavy kneading and rolling of muscles

11. The massage movement that consists of light or heavy kneading and rolling of the muscles is called:
    a. friction
    b. vibration
    c. petrissage
    d. tapotement

12. The massage movement that involves a light tapping or slapping movement while increasing blood circulation and stimulating nerves is known as:
    a. friction
    b. vibration
    c. petrissage
    d. tapotement

13. Which of the following massage movements is a circular or wringing movement usually carried out with the fingertips or palms of the hands?
    a. friction
    b. vibration
    c. petrissage
    d. tapotement

14. A shaking movement in the arms of the salon professional while the fingertips or palms are touching the client is known
    a. friction
    b. vibration
    c. petrissage
    d. tapotement

15. Areas of the skin that are diseased, broken, bruised or scraped:
    a. require vibration
    b. should not be massaged
    c. require petrissage movements
    d. require tapotement movements

1 2 3 4 5 **6** 7

16. To avoid damage to muscle tissues, massage movements should be directed toward the:
    a. end of the muscle
    b. belly of the muscle
    c. center of the muscle
    d. origin of the muscle

17. Which of the following items is NOT a type of facial mask?
    a. clay
    b. cream
    c. modeling
    d. astringent

18. A facial mask that hardens to a rubber-like consistency and can be pulled from the face in one piece is a:
    a. gel mask
    b. cream mask
    c. paraffin mask
    d. modeling mask

19. All of the following statements are true about paraffin masks EXCEPT:
    a. heated then applied
    b. applied over a layer of gauze
    c. made from clay, sand, zinc, oxide or mud
    d. acts to draw oil and perspiration to the top layer of skin

20. All of the following statements identify a benefit of a facial mask EXCEPT:
    a. removes surface oil
    b. softens and smooths the skin
    c. decreases blood circulation in the areas treated
    d. increases skin's firmness temporarily

LESSON CHALLENGE REFERENCES

Check your answers. Place a check mark next to the page number for any incorrect answer.
On the lines, jot down topics that you still need to review.

▶ GROW WHAT YOU KNOW

Reflect on what you have learned and predict how this information will be used in the future.

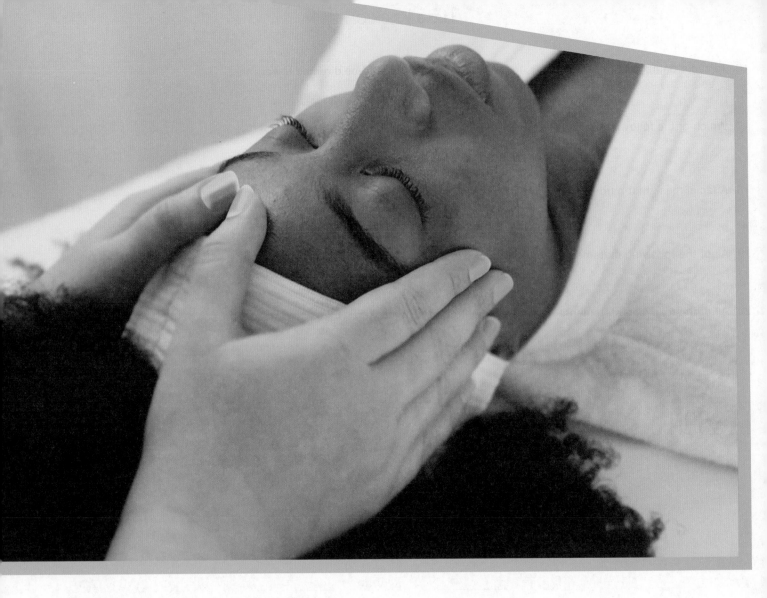

112ᶜ.4 // SKIN CARE GUEST EXPERIENCE

ACHIEVE //

Following this lesson on *Skin Care Guest Experience*, you'll be able to:

>> Identify the service essentials related to skin care

>> Provide examples of infection control and safety guidelines for skin care services

>> Define the products used for skin care services

>> Explain the three areas of a basic facial service

FOCUS //

SKIN CARE GUEST EXPERIENCE

Skin Care Service Essentials

Skin Care Infection Control and Safety

Basic Facial Service Overview

Basic Facial Rubric

SKIN CARE SERVICE ESSENTIALS

CONNECT

Form that is filled out with client:

_____ _____ _____ _____

Information recorded on this form:

*
*
*

CONSULT

Form that is used to record your treatment plan:

_____ _____ _____

Information recorded on this form:

*
*
*

*
*

CREATE

* Ensure client _____
*
*

COMPLETE

* Suggest future appointment time and offer to _____
* Discard single-use items and clean and disinfect _____
* Record recommended products on _____ _____

COMMUNICATION GUIDELINES

Respond to common client cues in a way that encourages client trust and open communication.

SKIN CARE INFECTION CONTROL AND SAFETY

CLEANING	DISINFECTING
•	•
•	
•	

SKIN CARE CLEANING AND DISINFECTION

TOOLS/SUPPLIES/EQUIPMENT	CLEANING	DISINFECTING
Spatula	If single-use item: • Must be _____ If multi-use item: • Preclean with _____ and _____; rinse well	If multi-use item: • Immerse in an approved EPA-registered _____ _____ • Rinse well
Gloves Cotton pads/Swabs Facial tissue	Single-use item: • Discard	Cannot be disinfected

SKIN CARE CLEANING AND DISINFECTION (CONT'D)

TOOLS/SUPPLIES/EQUIPMENT	CLEAN	DISINFECT
Fan brush Mixing bowls	• Preclean with soap and water • _____	• Immerse in an approved EPA-registered _____ _____ • Rinse well
Headband or head covering Sheets Blankets Client robe/gown Towels	• •	• •
Facial steamer Magnifying lamp Infrared lamp Wood's lamp Vacuum High-frequency electrodes Facial bed		•
	Store disinfected tools and multi-use supplies in covered container or cabinet that is clean and _____	

CARE AND SAFETY

PERSONAL CARE

• Check that your personal standard of hygiene minimizes the spread of _____

• Refer to your regulatory agency for proper mixing/handling of _____ _____

CLIENT CARE PRIOR TO SERVICE

• Drape client using the _____ _____

• Identify conditions or factors that serve as reasons to withhold certain treatments known as _____

CLIENT CARE DURING SERVICE

• When analyzing the skin or applying masks, protect and soothe the eyes by using _____ _____

• Remove all products from jars with a clean _____

• If any tools or multi-use supplies are dropped be sure to pick them up, then _____ and _____

SALON CARE

• Ensure equipment is cleaned and disinfected before and after _____ _____

• Keep labels on all containers and store products in a _____ _____

SKIN CARE PRODUCTS

PRODUCTS	FUNCTION
Cleanser	
	Brings skin to a normal pH
Exfoliant	
	Reduces friction and provides "slip" to skin during massage
	Cleanses, hydrates, tightens, exfoliates, reduces excess oil, offers nourishment to skin
Moisturizer	
Sunscreen	

BASIC FACIAL SERVICE OVERVIEW

PREPARATION

- Clean and disinfect workstation and facial bed
- Arrange appropriate facial tools and supplies
- Wash hands
- Ask client to remove jewelry; store in a secure place

PROCEDURE

1.   6.

2.   7.

3.   8.

4.   9.

5.   10.

COMPLETION

- Recommend products
- Prebook next appointment
- Follow proper infection control and safety procedures

MATCHING

List the tool, supply or equipment from the Jump Start Box in the appropriate column.

JUMP START BOX
Wood's lamp
Fan brush
Facial bed
Magnifying lamp
Multi-use spatula
Infrared lamp
Mixing bowls

IMMERSE IN AN EPA-REGISTERED DISINFECTANT AND RINSE WELL	WIPE DOWN WITH AN APPROVED EPA-REGISTERED DISINFECTANT AFTER EACH USE

LESSON CHALLENGE

Multiple choice. Indicate one correct answer for each question.

1. During which of the following service essentials should you complete a skin care record form with the client?
    a. Connect
    b. Consult
    c. Create
    d. Complete

2. During which the following service essentials should you teach the client how to perform their home skin-care regimen?
    a. Connect
    b. Consult
    c. Create
    d. Complete

3. During which the following service essentials should you discard single-use items and clean and disinfect multi-use supplies?
    a. Connect
    b. Consult
    c. Create
    d. Complete

4. Which of the following guidelines occurs during the Complete skin care service essential?
    a. ensure client comfort during service
    b. record recommended products on the client record for future visits
    c. stay focused on delivering the skin care service to the best of your ability
    d. explain recommended solutions, the products that will be used, and price of service

5. All of the following cleaning and disinfection guidelines are true about fan brushes EXCEPT:
    a. rinse well
    b. clean with acetone
    c. preclean with soap and water
    d. immerse in an approved EPA-registered disinfectant

6. All of the following statements are true about sheets and blankets EXCEPT:
    a. dry thoroughly
    b. remove hair and debris
    c. wash once at the end of each day
    d. use an approved laundry additive

7. All of the following are examples of possible contraindications for performing a facial service EXCEPT:
    a. dry skin
    b. diabetes
    c. pregnancy
    d. medication

8. Of the following steps, which comes first in a basic facial procedure?
    a. tone
    b. mask
    c. exfoliate
    d. massage

9. Of the following steps, which comes last in a basic facial procedure?
    a. mask
    b. massage
    c. exfoliate
    d. moisturize

LESSON CHALLENGE REFERENCES

Check your answers. Place a check mark next to the page number for any incorrect answer. On the lines, jot down topics that you still need to review.

▶ GROW WHAT YOU KNOW

Reflect on what you have learned and predict how this information will be used in the future.

112ᶜ.6 //

HAIR REMOVAL THEORY

ACHIEVE //

Following this lesson on *Hair Removal Theory*, you'll be able to:

>> Describe the six different methods of temporary hair removal

>> Compare laser hair reduction and photoepilation

FOCUS //

HAIR REMOVAL THEORY

Temporary Hair Removal

Permanent Hair Reduction

HAIR REMOVAL THEORY

Society and personal preferences have long dictated a person's need or desire for removing unwanted or superfulous hair.

The condition of unwanted or superfluous hair is referred to as

_____.

The condition where women grow dark hair in areas of the body that men typically grow more hair is known as _____.

There are two categories of hair removal:

-
-

TEMPORARY HAIR REMOVAL

Clients may choose to perform temporary hair removal services at home, such as:

-
-
-

Temporary hair removal services most often performed in the salon are:

-
-
-

SHAVING

The hair removal method most often used when unwanted hair covers large areas is _____.

Shaving can be performed using:

-
-
-

CHEMICAL DEPILATORIES

A **chemical depilatory** is a painless method of hair removal that dissolves the hair at _____ _____.

The bonds that are broken to allow the softened hair mass to be scraped away are the _____ _____.

The main ingredient of these products is a _____ _____ _____.

Chemical depilatories are usually found in one of the following forms:

-
-
-

TWEEZING

Tweezing is the hair removal method most commonly used to remove unwanted hairs from smaller areas, such as:

-
-
-

TWEEZING (CONT'D)

To tweeze, an individual hair is grasped with the tweezers and removed in the direction of hair growth, effectively extracting it from beneath the

_____ _____.

Eyebrow guidelines to achieve a well-arched eyebrow:

-
-
-

EYEBROW TWEEZING PROCEDURE

Draw an eye and eyebrow. Add dotted lines to show where the brow should begin, the peak and the point where the brow should end.

WAXING

Waxing is a procedure that is beneficial for temporarily removing hair from both _____ and _____ _____.

There are two types of wax: _____ and _____.

The majority of professional waxing services are performed with _____ _____.

Soft Wax Guidelines

Assess	Apply	Dust
Discard	Apply	Obtain
Apply	Hold	Apply

Waxing contraindications

- Do not _____
- Do not _____
- Avoid _____

Hard wax is ideal for small areas and _____.

- Great for clients that can't tolerate _____

Hard Wax Guidelines

Assess	Apply	Obtain
Hold	Discard	Apply
Apply		

THREADING

Threading is an ancient method of hair removal that utilizes 100% cotton thread that is twisted and rolled along the _____.
The results last approximately _____.
Threading requires additional _____.

SUGARING

Sugaring is a hair removal technique that utilizes a paste made primarily of sugar that is applied to the skin in a _____ _____.
Sugar paste adheres only to the hair, not the skin, and is easily removed with _____.

A benefit of sugaring is that _____
_____

PERMANENT HAIR REDUCTION

Methods of permanent hair reduction that are used by professionals trained in these particular areas are:

1.
2.

ELECTROLYSIS

Permanent hair reduction, known as electrolysis, uses electric current to damage the cells of the papilla and disrupt hair growth.

An electrologist has advanced training specifically in the study of electrolysis or is a _____ _____.

Three methods of permanent hair reduction:

1. _____

2. _____

3. _____

Galvanic

• Destroys hair by decomposing _____

• Galvanic electrolysis is also called _____

Thermolysis

• Involves inserting a single needle into the _____

• Thermolysis is also called _____

Blend

• Combination of galvanic and _____

LIGHT

• Light-based treatments are only effective when hair is in the _____ _____

• Two categories:

  ▪ _____

  ▪ _____

Laser Hair Reduction

• Use light to penetrate and diminish or destroy _____ _____

• Laser emits a beam of _____

Laser

L _____

A _____

S _____

E _____

R _____

Photoepilation

• This type of light is a _____ _____

• The benefit of this type of light is it can treat _____ _____

MATCHING

Rearrange the items below into the correct sequential order, and place the number on the lines provided.

BASIC SOFT WAX PROCEDURE

1. Apply removal strip; press and smooth strip _____

2. Apply pressure _____

3. Apply cleansing gel _____

4. Apply wax _____

5. Hold skin taut and remove strip _____

6. Assess direction of growth _____

7. Discard spatula _____

8. Wash hands _____

9. Lightly dust the area with powder _____

10. Obtain wax _____

LESSON CHALLENGE

Multiple choice. Indicate one correct answer for each question.

1. **All of the following are methods of treating hypertrichosis EXCEPT:**
    a. waxing
    b. shaving
    c. applying antiseptic lotion
    d. applying chemical depilatories

2. **Why is it not recommended to wax lanugo hair?**
    a. skin may lighten
    b. skin may darken
    c. hair won't grow back
    d. hair may lose softness

3. **Apply soft wax at a 45° angle:**
    a. in any direction
    b. in a circular direction
    c. in the direction of the hair growth
    d. in the opposite direction of hair growth

4. **What direction do you pull removal strips during a soft wax treatment?**
    a. toward the floor
    b. toward the ceiling
    c. away from client and yourself
    d. in opposite direction of hair growth

5. **What hair removal method is available for clients who cannot tolerate soft wax treatments?**
    a. shaving only
    b. electrolysis only
    c. hard wax treatment
    d. bleaching or lightening only

6. **Used hard wax should be disposed of after:**
    a. 12 hours
    b. 24 hours
    c. every client
    d. every 5 clients

7. Which of the following hair removal methods utilizes 100% cotton thread that is twisted and rolled along the surface of the skin?
   a. waxing
   b. tweezing
   c. sugaring
   d. threading

8. What hair removal method removes hair by decomposing the papilla?
   a. blend
   b. waxing
   c. shaving
   d. Galvanic

9. Inserting a single needle into a hair follicle for hair removal is called high frequency/short-wave electrolysis or:
   a. waxing
   b. shaving
   c. hydrolysis
   d. thermolysis

10. Which hair reduction treatment uses an intense, pulsed light beam that creates a burst of energy to destroy hair bulbs?
    a. thermolysis
    b. blend method
    c. photoepilation
    d. laser hair reduction

LESSON CHALLENGE REFERENCES

Check your answers. Place a check mark next to the page number for any incorrect answer.
On the lines, jot down topics that you still need to review.

1. PAGE 57 _____
2. PAGE 60 _____
3. PAGE 60 _____
4. PAGE 60 _____
5. PAGE 60 _____

6. PAGE 60 _____
7. PAGE 61 _____
8. PAGE 62 _____
9. PAGE 63 _____
10. PAGE 64 _____

▶ GROW WHAT YOU KNOW

Reflect on what you have learned and predict how this information will be used in the future.

112ᶜ.7 //

HAIR REMOVAL GUEST EXPERIENCE

ACHIEVE //

Following this lesson on *Hair Removal Guest Experience*, you'll be able to:

>> Identify the service essentials related to hair removal services

>> Summarize the tools and essentials related to hair removal

>> Provide examples of infection control and safety guidelines for hair removal services

>> Explain the three areas of a hair removal service

FOCUS //

HAIR REMOVAL GUEST EXPERIENCE

Hair Removal Service Essentials

Hair Removal Infection Control and Safety

Hair Removal Service Overview

Hair Removal Rubrics

HAIR REMOVAL SERVICE ESSENTIALS

CONNECT

Three guidelines for welcoming a client:

1.
2.
3.

CONSULT

Ask client questions to determine:

•

Assess:

•

•

Gain Feedback:

•

Analyze:

•

•

Summarize:

•

•

•

CREATE

• Ensure client _____

• Stay focused on delivering the service to the best of _____

   _____

COMPLETE

• Ask your client for _____

• Recommend _____

HAIR REMOVAL INFECTION CONTROL AND SAFETY

CLEANING AND DISINFECTING GUIDELINES

TOOLS, SUPPLIES AND EQUIPMENT	FUNCTION	CLEANING GUIDELINES	DISINFECTION GUIDELINES
SMALL SCISSORS	• Trim _____	• Remove hair and _____ • Open hinged area to allow for thorough _____ • Preclean with _____ and _____	• Use an approved EPA-registered _____ _____ or _____
BROW BRUSH	• Combs brow hair prior to _____	• Remove hair and _____ • Preclean with _____ and _____	• Immerse in an approved EPA-registered _____

TOOLS, SUPPLIES AND EQUIPMENT	FUNCTION	CLEANING GUIDELINES	DISINFECTION GUIDELINES
TWEEZERS	• Remove _____ _____	• Remove hair and _____ • Pre-clean with _____ and _____	• Immerse in an approved EPA-registered _____
WAX WARMER (POT)	• Melts and _____	• Remove any _____	
REMOVAL STRIPS	• Aid in removing hair; applied over _____	• Single-use item; must be _____	• Cannot be disinfected
SPATULA	• Removes wax from _____ • _____ _____	• Single-use item; must be _____	• If multi-use item, disinfect by immersing in an approved EPA-registered disinfectant
GLOVES	• Protect the _____	• Single-use item; must be _____	• Cannot be disinfected
SHEET	• Protects the _____	• Remove hair and _____ • Wash in washing machine after _____	• Use an approved laundry additive if required by your area's regulatory agency • _____ _____
HEADBAND	• Holds hair _____ _____ _____ _____	• Remove hair and _____ • Wash in washing machine after _____	• Use an approved laundry additive if required by your area's regulatory agency • _____ _____
PLASTIC BAG	• Holds _____	• Single-use item; must be _____	• Cannot be disinfected
SOFT SINGLE-USE TOWEL	• Aids in removal of _____	• Single-use item; must be _____	• Cannot be disinfected
FACIAL CHAIR	• Holds _____	• _____ _____	• Wipe down chair with a _____ _____
HANDHELD MIRROR	• Allows clients to view results		• Use an approved EPA-registered disinfectant _____

CARE AND SAFETY

Infection control and safety guidelines are essential while performing hair removal services in order to protect the health and well-being of you and your client. Good-to-remember points in this area are 1) Be guided by your area's regulatory agency, and 2) Read and follow manufacturer's directions.

PERSONAL CARE

- Check that your personal standard of hygiene minimizes the spread of _____

- Wash hands and dry thoroughly with a _____ _____

- Minimize fatigue by maintaining good _____

CLIENT CARE PRIOR TO SERVICE

- Analyze the skin and area in need of _____ _____

- Test temperature of the wax on the _____ _____ _____

- Perform an _____ _____

CLIENT CARE DURING SERVICE

- Beware of skin _____

- Do not wax over moles; warts; irritated, abraded or sunburned skin; _____ or _____ _____

- Keep product away from client's _____

SALON CARE

- Disinfect all tools after _____ _____

- Ensure equipment is _____ and _____

- Dispose of wax after _____ _____

HAIR REMOVAL PRODUCTS

Cleaning gel – _____

Antiseptic – _____

Wax – _____

Wax remover – _____

Soothing toner, gel, toner – _____

Powder – _____

Chemical depilatory – _____

MATCHING

Write the number of the service essential step from the left column on the line next to the appropriate guideline.

1. Connect

2. Consult

3. Create

4. Complete

_____ Stay focused on delivering the service to the best of your ability

_____ Gain feedback and consent from your client

_____ Have client fill out a client record form

_____ Suggest a future appointment time for your client's next visit

_____ Ask questions to discover client needs

_____ Request satisfaction feedback from your client

_____ Analyze client's skin where hair will be removed

_____ Ensure client comfort during the service

_____ Greet client with a firm handshake

LESSON CHALLENGE

Multiple choice. Indicate one correct answer for each question.

1. During which of the following service essentials should you ask questions to determine your client's needs?
   a. Connect
   b. Consult
   c. Create
   d. Complete

2. During which the following service essentials should you gain consent from your client?
   a. Connect
   b. Consult
   c. Create
   d. Complete

3. During which the following service essentials should you ensure client comfort?
   a. Connect
   b. Consult
   c. Create
   d. Complete

4. During which of the following service essentials should you recommend products?
   a. Connect
   b. Consult
   c. Create
   d. Complete

5. All of the following cleaning and disinfection guidelines are true about small scissors EXCEPT:
   a. remove hair and debris
   b. disinfect with fine steel wool
   c. preclean with soap and water
   d. use an approved EPA-registered disinfectant

6. All of the following supplies need to be discarded after each use EXCEPT:
   a. wax
   b. sheets
   c. removal strips
   d. single-use gloves

7. Which of the following should be wiped down with disinfecting wipe after each use?
   a. spatula
   b. wax pot
   c. headband
   d. facial chair

8. To ensure client care and safety during a waxing service, do not:
   a. re-dip spatula
   b. dispose of spatula
   c. wear single-use gloves
   d. test wax temperature

9. Which of the following is a guideline to be followed when waxing?
   a. do not wax tan skin
   b. do not wax clean skin
   c. do not wax over a mole
   d. do not wax over a freckle

10. A furrowed brow might be an example of a:
    a. verbal cue
    b. nonverbal cue
    c. loyal, return client
    d. very satisfied client

LESSON CHALLENGE REFERENCES

Check your answers. Place a check mark next to the page number for any incorrect answer. On the lines, jot down topics that you still need to review.

1. PAGE 67 _____
2. PAGE 67 _____
3. PAGE 67 _____
4. PAGE 67 _____
5. PAGE 68 _____

6. PAGE 69 _____
7. PAGE 69 _____
8. PAGE 70 _____
9. PAGE 70 _____
10. PAGE 70 _____

▶ GROW WHAT YOU KNOW

Reflect on what you have learned and predict how this information will be used in the future.

112ᶜ.10 //

MAKEUP THEORY

ACHIEVE //

Following this lesson on *Makeup Theory*, you'll be able to:

» Describe the law of color as it applies to makeup

» Identify the seven face shapes and the steps used to create the illusion of the oval shape

» Explain how makeup can visually alter facial features

FOCUS //

MAKEUP THEORY

Color Theory

Face Shapes

Facial Features

COLOR THEORY

CHIAROSCURO

LIGHTER COLORS	DARKER COLORS
Stand out	
	Minimize
Highlight attractive features	
	Shadow areas that you wish the minimize

The law of color: Out of all the colors in the universe, only three are pure.

3 PRIMARY COLORS

Mixing two primaries in varying proportions creates the three

_____ _____:

SECONDARY COLORS

Mixing primary and secondary colors in varying proportions creates

_____ _____:

TERTIARY COLORS

Yellow - _____	Red - _____	Blue - _____
Yellow - _____	Red - _____	Blue - _____

COMPLEMENTARY COLORS

- Red and _____
- Blue and _____
- Yellow and _____

Complementary colors will neutralize each other when mixed together.

Hue: _____

_____: Hue with white added

Shade: _____

_____: Lightness or darkness of color

Intensity: _____

_____: Warmth or coolness of color

COLOR SCHEMES

Same color with variations in value and intensity = _____

Three colors adjacent on the color wheel = _____

Three colors in a triangular position on the color wheel = _____

Colors across from each other on the color wheel = _____

Warm colors have red or yellow tones within them and cool colors have more blue tones within them.

Keep in mind:

Dark colors deminish. Light colors advance.

FACE SHAPES

7 BASIC FACE SHAPES

Shape:
Oval

Shape:

Shape:

Shape:

Shape:

Shape:

Shape:

FACIAL FEATURES

Using a pencil, sketch in the proper technique to correct the corresponding facial features.

Wide Nose

_____
_____
_____
_____

Long Nose/Prominent Chin

_____
_____
_____
_____

Undefined Cheekbones

_____
_____
_____
_____

Receding Chin

_____
_____
_____
_____

Pointed Chin

_____
_____
_____
_____

"Double" Chin

_____
_____
_____
_____

Broad or Square Jaw/High
or Broad Forehead

_____
_____
_____
_____

EYES

The eyes can be divided into 3 areas:

-
-
-

Ideal proportions:

Area between base of lashes and crease line of the eye = _____

Area between crease line and eyebrow makes up the remaining _____

- Well-spaced eyes have the width of one eye between them

EYEBROWS

Brow design and placement of lights and darks can visually alter the position of the eyes on the face.

To make eyes appear close-set:

-

-

To make eyes appear wide-set:

-

-

EYE SHAPES

Label each eye shape and use a pencil to create the illusion of the desired eye design.

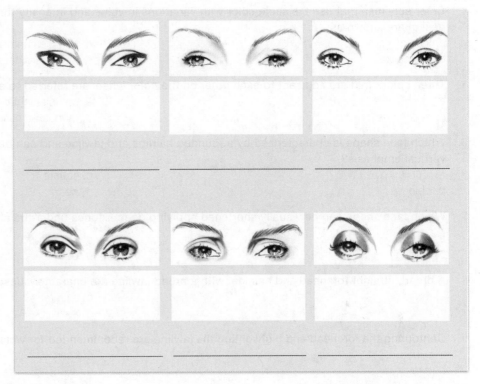

LIPS

Label each lip shape and use a pencil to create the desired correction.

LESSON CHALLENGE
Multiple choice. Indicate one correct answer for each question.

1. What colors seem to diminish or minimize the appearance of facial features?
   a. lighter colors
   b. darker colors
   c. primary colors
   d. complementary

2. What is another term for color?
   a. hue
   b. tint
   c. shade
   d. intensity

3. The vibrancy of a color is referred to as:
   a. hue
   b. shade
   c. value
   d. intensity

4. Color schemes that use the same color with variations in value and intensity throughout the makeup design are known as:
   a. triadic
   b. analogous
   c. complementary
   d. monochromatic

5. Three colors that are adjacent to each other on the color wheel are referred to as:
   a. triadic
   b. analogous
   c. complementary
   d. monochromatic

6. Which face shape is characterized by a rounded hairline and jawline and can be slenderized by adding vertical emphasis?
   a. round
   b. oblong
   c. square
   d. pear

7. Which face shape can be visually shortened applying deeper tones under the chin and horizontally at the hairline?
   a. round
   b. oblong
   c. square
   d. pear

8. A broad, straight forehead and hairline, with a broad jawline are characteristics of which face shape?
   a. round
   b. oblong
   c. square
   d. pear

9. Contouring the forehead and highlighting the jawline are recommended for which face shape?
   a. square
   b. pear
   c. heart
   d. diamond

10. What face shape is characterized by a narrow forehead and jaw area with predominant width in the cheekbone area?
    a. oval
    b. round
    c. square
    d. diamond

LESSON CHALLENGE REFERENCES

Check your answers. Place a check mark next to the page number for any incorrect answer. On the lines, jot down topics that you still need to review.

1. PAGE 88 _____
2. PAGE 89 _____
3. PAGE 89 _____
4. PAGE 89 _____
5. PAGE 89 _____
6. PAGE 90 _____
7. PAGE 91 _____
8. PAGE 91 _____
9. PAGE 91 _____
10. PAGE 91 _____

GROW WHAT YOU KNOW

Reflect on what you have learned and predict how this information will be used in the future.

112ᶜ.11 //
MAKEUP
PRODUCTS AND DESIGN

ACHIEVE //

Following this lesson on *Makeup Products and Design*, you'll be able to:

» Identify the products used to create makeup designs

» List the most common applications related to makeup design

FOCUS //

MAKEUP PRODUCTS AND DESIGN

Makeup Products

Makeup Design

MAKEUP PRODUCTS

The foundation for all makeup design begins with learning about basic products.

PRODUCTS FOR:	PRODUCT EXAMPLES	WHAT PRODUCT CAN DO
Skin	• • •	Even out skin tone
Eyes	• Eyeliner • Mascara	
Cheeks	• •	Add color to the face
Lips	• Lipliner • Lip color	

SKIN PREPARATION

Preparing the skin involves cleansing, toning, moisturizing and
_____.

SKIN

With makeup design, it's important to create an even _____ _____.

SKIN COLOR	TONE
	Light Creamy
Yellow cast; light	
	Pink
Carmel-colored to brown; light to dark with red or yellow undertones	
Yellowish-green; medium to dark	
	Brown
Mahogany and/or blue undertones; dark to very dark	

CONCEALER

TYPES OF CONCEALERS	AMOUNT OF COVERAGE
Liquid	
Cream	
Stick	

Undertone:	Base to Use:
Yellow	
Red	Green
Green	
Blue/Purple	Yellow/Orange

FOUNDATION

PRIMARY USES OF FOUNDATION	
•	•

FORMS			

When used for coverage:

•

•

When used for correction:

•

•

To test a foundation shade to determine if you have chosen the correct color, blend a small amount of foundation on the client's _____.

FACIAL POWDER

Facial powders are designed to "set" other makeup products.

Two Types:

_____ – May be worn with any foundation shade

_____ – Used with matching foundations or for sheerest coverage

Contouring and Highlighting

The most common type of products to contour and highlight are powder, liquid and creams.

Lighter shades of foundation are used to _____.

Darker shades of foundation are used to _____.

EYES

The elements of eye design include eyebrow color, eyeliner, eye shadow, mascara and artificial lashes.

WHAT PRODUCT DOES

EYEBROW COLOR

EYELINER — Defines and emphasizes the shape and size of the eyes

EYE SHADOW

MASCARA — Defines, lengthens and thickens the eyelashes; enhances shadow color

ARTIFICIAL LASHES (OPTIONAL)

EYE TABBING — Application of individual or clusters of false lashes

MATCHING

Place the steps for applying artificial strip lashes in the correct order by numbering 1-5.

_____ Apply adhesive to base of upper lashes

_____ Bend upper lashes into horseshoe shape

_____ Apply upper lashes beginning with the shorter, or inside, lashes

_____ Measure upper lash

_____ Apply bottom lashes in the same manner as for the upper lashes

CHEEKS

The elements of cheek design include blush and bronzer.

BLUSH

Four Types:

-
-
-
-

BRONZER

Uses:

- Like blush, gives color to cheeks
- Gives skin the illusion of a _____
-

LIPS

The elements of lip design include lipliner and lip color.

LIPLINER

- Applied to outer edge of lips to define the _____
- Prevents lipstick from "_____"

LIP COLOR

- Completes the balance of _____
- Usually last cosmetic applied

PRIMARY TYPES

-
-

LIP SHAPE *Sketch your ideal lip shape.*

Identify key concepts for each makeup design.

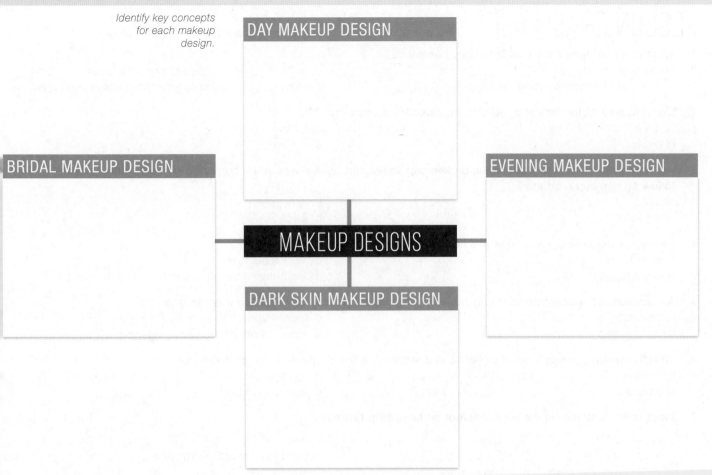

DAY MAKEUP DESIGN

BRIDAL MAKEUP DESIGN

MAKEUP DESIGNS

EVENING MAKEUP DESIGN

DARK SKIN MAKEUP DESIGN

MATCHING

Place the letter of the matching description below each item.

A. Contoured brush
B. Fan brush
C. Medium chisel brush
D. Large powder brush (dome)
E. Small chisel brush
F. Large blending brush
G. Medium fluff brush
H. Large camouflage brush
I. Angle brush
J. Detail angle brush
K. Latex sponge
L. Eyelash separator
M. Small fluff brush
N. Lip brush

LESSON CHALLENGE

Multiple choice. Indicate one correct answer for each question.

1. **What must be done before applying any cosmetics?**
   a. hair must be styled
   b. client must remove watches and rings
   c. client must be wrapped in a warm blanket
   d. skin must be cleansed, toned, moisturized and protected

2. **On what area of the face is a foundation tested for a color match?**
   a. nose
   b. eyelid
   c. jawline
   d. forehead

3. **Problems such as under-eye circles, broken capillaries and blemishes can be corrected by using which of the following makeup products?**
   a. blush
   b. mascara
   c. concealer
   d. facial powder

4. **Facial powders are primarily designed to:**
   a. reflect light
   b. produce odor
   c. reduce perspiration
   d. "set" other makeup products so they last longer

5. **A colorless, translucent powder may be worn with any foundation shade since it is designed to:**
   a. add color to the face
   b. conceal any blemishes on the skin
   c. frame the eyes and balance the face
   d. allow the skin/foundation shade to show through

6. **Which makeup product is used to define and emphasize the shape and size of the eyes?**
   a. eyeliner
   b. mascara
   c. eye shadow
   d. eyebrow pencil

7. **What is the first step in the application of artificial strip lashes?**
   a. apply lashes
   b. apply adhesive
   c. measure upper lash
   d. bend into horseshoe shape

8. **Blush is used to add color to the face, especially the cheek area, and it can also be used to enhance:**
   a. foundation
   b. facial contouring
   c. facial highlighting
   d. the color of the eye shadow

9. **Where in the course of a makeup appication does applying lip color usually occur?**
   a. last cosmetic to be applied
   b. first cosmetic to be applied
   c. third cosmetic to be applied
   d. second cosmetic to be applied

10. **The overall effect of an evening makeup application when compared to daytime could be described by all of the following EXCEPT:**
    a. more intense
    b. more dramatic
    c. less intense
    d. more definition

LESSON CHALLENGE REFERENCES

Check your answers. Place a check mark next to the page number for any incorrect answer. On the lines, jot down topics that you still need to review.

1. PAGE 100 _____
2. PAGE 101 _____
3. PAGE 101 _____
4. PAGE 102 _____
5. PAGE 102 _____

6. PAGE 103 _____
7. PAGE 104 _____
8. PAGE 105 _____
9. PAGE 106 _____
10. PAGE 111 _____

GROW WHAT YOU KNOW

Reflect on what you have learned and predict how this information will be used in the future.

112ᶜ.12 //

MAKEUP GUEST EXPERIENCE

ACHIEVE //

Following this lesson on *Makeup Guest Experience*, you'll be able to:

>> Identify the service essentials related to makeup

>> Provide examples of infection control and safety guidelines for makeup services

>> Explain the three areas of a makeup service

FOCUS //

MAKEUP GUEST EXPERIENCE

Makeup Service Essentials

Makeup, Infection Control and Safety

Makeup Service Overview

Makeup Rubric

SMART NOTES

MAKEUP SERVICE ESSENTIALS

CONNECT

Three guidelines for welcoming a client

1.

2.

3.

CONSULT

Ask client to determine:
•

Analyze client's:
•
•

Assess:
•
•

Explain:
•
•
•
•

Gain Feedback
•

CREATE

• Ensure client _____
• Stay focused on delivering the service to the best of your _____
• If explanations are needed, be clear and _____

COMPLETE

• Request satisfaction feedback from your _____
• Escort client to retail area and show _____
• Recommend products for _____ _____ _____
• Invite client to make a _____
• Ask client for referrals
• Suggest future appointment time and offer to _____
• Offer appreciation to client for visiting the school or salon
• Record recommended products on _____ _____ _____

MAKEUP INFECTION CONTROL AND SAFETY

Cleaning is a process of removing dirt and debris to aid in preventing the growth of _____.

Cleaning is performed prior to _____

Disinfection methods kill certain but not _____ _____.

Be sure to follow the manufacturer's directions for mixing disinfecting solutions and contact time if applicable.

CLEANING AND DISINFECTION GUIDELINES

Store disinfected tools and multi-use supplies in a clean, dry, covered container or cabinet.

TOOLS/SUPPLIES	FUNCTION	CLEANING GUIDELINES	DISINFECTION GUIDELINES
HEADBAND	• Holds client's hair out of the way during application	• Remove hair and debris • Wash in washing machine after each use	• Use an additive that _____ _____ _____
COTTON	• Removes _____	• Single-use item; Must be discarded	• Cannot be disinfected
TOWEL/ MAKEUP DRAPE	• Protects client's clothing	• Wash in washing machine after each use • Dry thoroughly	• Use an _____
TISSUE	• Blots the skin; removes excess _____	• _____ _____	• Cannot be disinfected
COTTON SWABS	• Clean up; correct errors	• _____ _____	• Cannot be disinfected
PALETTE	• Holds desired amount of product	• Preclean with soap and water	• Use an _____ _____ as directed
SPATULAS	• Remove product from _____	• If single-use item; discard	• If mulitple-use item, disinfect by complete immersion in an approved EPA-registered disinfectant solution
COSMETIC SPONGES	• Apply foundation and concealer; blending	• _____ _____	• Cannot be disinfected
TWEEZERS	• Shape eyebrows; remove stray hairs	• Remove hair and debris • Preclean with soap and water	• Immerse in _____ _____
BRUSHES	• Apply makeup; specific to needs	• Preclean with _____ _____ _____	• Immerse in an EPA-registered brush cleaner disinfectant
EYELASH CURLER	• Curls and enhances lashes	• Preclean with soap and water	• Immerse in _____ _____
DISPOSABLE MASCARA WANDS	• Apply mascara	• Single-use item; must be discarded	• Cannot be disinfected
LIP BRUSHES	• Apply lip color	• Preclean with _____ _____ _____	• Immerse in an EPA-registered disinfectant solution
LASH SEPARATOR	• Separates lashes after mascara application		• Immerse in an EPA-registered disinfectant solution

MAKEUP EQUIPMENT

EQUIPMENT	FUNCTION	CLEANING GUIDELINES	DISINFECTION GUIDELINES
MIRROR	• _____ _____		• Use an _____ _____
PROPER LIGHTING	• Allows artist to work accurately and gauge results	• As recommended by manufacturer	• Cannot be disinfected
MAKEUP CHAIR	• _____ _____		• Use an _____ _____

CARE AND SAFETY

Follow infection control procedures for personal care and client safety guidelines before and during the makeup design service to ensure your safety and the client's, while also contributing to the salon care.

PERSONAL CARE

- Check that your personal standards of hygiene minimize the spread of

  _____
- Wash hands and _____
- Keep your fingernails well-groomed to avoid _____ _____
- Disinfecting workstation
- Clean and disinfect tools appropriately
- Minimize fatigue by maintaining good _____
- Refer to your area's regulatory agency for proper mixing or handling of disinfectant solutions

CLIENT CARE PRIOR TO THE SERVICE

- Seat client in comfortable position for the service
- Use a fresh drape on _____ _____
- Cleanse, tone, moisturize and _____ _____ _____
- Read and follow manufacturer's instructions for tools, supplies, products and equipment
- Handle tools and products with care
- If any tools are dropped be sure to pick them up, then clean and

  _____

CLIENT CARE DURING THE SERVICE

- Be aware of any skin _____
- Remove product if you see signs of allergic reactions to cosmetic products such as redness, swelling or _____
- Work carefully around non-removable jewelry/piercings
- Avoid excess pressure in and around the _____ _____
- Avoid using products and makeup directly from containers
- Use spatulas to place the desired amount of product on your makeup palette. If more product is needed, remember to use a _____ _____
- Be aware of nonverbal cues the client may be conveying
- Store soiled towels in an appropriate _____

  _____
- Exercise extra precautions to avoid getting products or tools in the _____

CARE AND SAFETY (CONT'D)

SALON CARE

- Follow health and safety guidelines, including cleaning and disinfecting procedures
- Ensure equipment is clean and _____
- Promote a professional image by assuring your workstation is clean and tidy throughout the service
- Disinfect all tools after each use. Always use disinfected tools, supplies and equipment for _____
- Use disposable applicators whenever possible and _____
- Sharpen all pencils before and after each use

MAKEUP PRODUCTS

PRODUCTS	FUNCTION
Cleanser/Makeup Remover	Removes dirt, makeup and _____
Toner	Restores _____
Moisturizer	Replenishes moisture/oil; protects skin
Sunscreen	Protects client's skin from _____
Concealer	Eliminates _____

PRODUCTS	FUNCTION
Foundation	Creates an even skin _____
Blush/bronzer	Adds color or _____
Eyeliner	Accentuates and defines shape of eyes
Eye Shadow	Contours or highlights the eyes
Brow Pencil or Powder	Fills in; corrects shape of _____
Mascara	Defines, lengthens and _____
Lipliner	Defines natural or corrected shape of lips
Lip Color	Adds color and texture to the lips

MAKEUP SERVICE OVERVIEW

MAKEUP PREPARATION

- Clean and disinfect workstation.
- Arrange disinfected makeup tools and supplies including brushes, disposable applicators, spatula, headband and assorted makeup.
- Wash hands.
- Perform analysis of skin.
- Ask client to remove jewelry; store in a secure place.

MAKEUP PROCEDURE

- Drape client for the service (include headband and position chair).
- Use disposable applicators whenever possible and discard after each use.
- Use spatula to remove products from containers.
- Sharpen all pencils before and after each use.
- Avoid excess pressure in and around eye area.
- Exercise extra precautions to avoid getting products or tools in the eyes.

MAKEUP COMPLETION

- Reinforce client's satisfaction with overall salon experience.
- Make professional product recommendations.
- Prebook client's next appointment.
- End client's visit with warm and personal goodbye.
- Discard single-use supplies; disinfect tools and multi-use supplies; disinfect workstation and arrange in proper order.
- Complete client record card.
- Wash hands.

MATCHING

Place the following 10 steps in the correct order by placing the number of their order on the line to the left of each statement.

_____ Groom brows (brush and/or tweezer)

_____ Select blush color and apply to cheek bones

_____ Prepare the skin

_____ Select and apply appropriate lip color

_____ Shade brows (brush and fill in as needed)

_____ Apply eye shadow, eyeliner and mascara

_____ Check application for proper blending and overall symmetry

_____ Apply facial powder (tinted or translucent) to "set" other makeup products

_____ Remove product if signs of allergic reaction are visible (redness, swelling, inflammation)

_____ Select appropriate foundation and concealer color

LESSON CHALLENGE

Multiple choice. Indicate one correct answer for each question.

1. During which of the following makeup service essentials would you have the client fill out the makeup service record form?
   a. Create
   b. Consult
   c. Connect
   d. Complete

2. Analyzing your client's skin tone and type is performed during which of the following makeup service essentials?
   a. Create
   b. Consult
   c. Connect
   d. Complete

3. Assessing the facts and thoroughly thinking through your recommendations by visualizing the end result is achieved during which of the following makeup service essentials?
   a. Create
   b. Consult
   c. Connect
   d. Complete

4. Suggesting a future appointment time and offering to prebook your client's next visit occurs during which of the following makeup service essentials?
   a. Create
   b. Consult
   c. Connect
   d. Complete

5. Which of the following items is used to hold the desired amount of makeup products?
   a. tissue
   b. spatula
   c. palette
   d. cotton swabs

6. An infection control and safety guideline regarding eyeliner pencil or an eyebrow pencil is to:
   a. discard daily
   b. discard after use
   c. sharpen only before each use
   d. sharpen before and after each use

7. Which of the following products can be used to remove dirt and makeup?
   a. toner
   b. cleanser
   c. concealer
   d. moisturizer

8. A product that can restore the pH of the skin is called a:
   a. toner
   b. cleanser
   c. concealer
   d. moisturizer

9. Which of the following products replenishes moisture or oil to the skin?
   a. toner
   b. cleanser
   c. concealer
   d. moisturizer

10. Which of the following products is used to create an even skin tone and uniform surface for makeup application?
    a. toner
    b. cleanser
    c. foundation
    d. moisturizer

LESSON CHALLENGE REFERENCES

Check your answers. Place a check mark next to the page number for any incorrect answer. On the lines, jot down topics that you still need to review.

1. PAGE 117 _____
2. PAGE 117 _____
3. PAGE 117 _____
4. PAGE 117 _____
5. PAGE 119 _____

6. PAGE 122 _____
7. PAGE 123 _____
8. PAGE 123 _____
9. PAGE 123 _____
10. PAGE 123 _____

▶ GROW WHAT YOU KNOW

Reflect on what you have learned and predict how this information will be used in the future.

113^c.1 //
NAIL THEORY

ACHIEVE //

Following this lesson on *Nail Theory*, you'll be able to:

>> Identify the parts of the nail

>> Explain the growth of the nail

>> Recognize nail diseases that a salon professional may encounter during a skin and nail evaluation

>> Identify nail disorders that a salon professional may encounter in the salon

>> Give examples of nail conditions and available salon services that may help

FOCUS //

NAIL THEORY

Structure of the Nail

Growth of the Nail

Nail Diseases, Disorders and Conditions

STRUCTURE OF THE NAIL

The nail is an _____ of the skin. The technical name for the nail is _____.

The study of the structure and growth of the nails is _____.

MATCHING

Fill in the number next to the corresponding illustration of the nail anatomy.

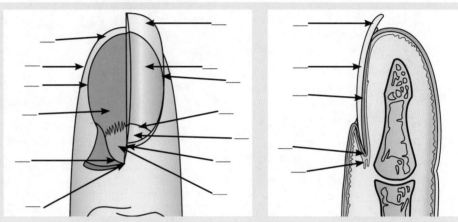

Fill in the blank with the correct component of the nail.

1. The _____ is the pocket-like structure that holds the root and matrix.

2. The _____ is the active tissue that generates cells, which harden as they move outward to form the nail plate.

3. The _____ is attached to the matrix at the base of the nail, under the skin and inside the mantle.

4. The _____ is the area of the nail where the nail body rests. Nerves and blood vessels found here supply nourishment.

5. The_____ (nail body) is the visible nail area from the nail root to the free edge.

6. The _____ is the half-moon shape at the base of the nail, which is the visible part of the matrix and appears lighter.

7. The _____ is the live tissue at the base of the nail.

8. The _____ is the overlapping dead tissue that is loose and pliable around the nail.

9. The _____ are the tracks on either side of the nail that the nail moves on as it grows.

10. The _____ are the folds of skin on either side of the nail groove.

11. The _____ is the living tissue that overlies the nail plate on the sides of the nail.

12. The _____ is the part of the nail that extends beyond the finger or toe and protects the tips of the fingers and toes.

13. The _____ is the living tissue underneath the free edge of the nail.

GROWTH OF THE NAIL

The nail is made up of _____ _____, like hair.

Nail growth originates in the _____.

The matrix contains:

- _____
- _____
- _____

Cells are created and pushed outward from the nail root. When the cells

_____ or harden as they reach the eponychium, they form the

_____ _____.

The thinness or thickness of a nail plate is determined by the rate of

_____ _____ in the matrix.

Average fingernail growth rate is _____ inch per month for adults

It takes _____

months on average for a new

fingernail to grow

It takes _____

months on average for a new toenail

to grow

Give an example of an instance when a permanent distortion may occur in the nail plate.

_____

_____

_____

_____

_____

_____

NAIL DISEASES, DISORDERS AND CONDITIONS

Onychosis is any _____, _____ or _____ of the nail.

_____ is the cause of the disease, disorder or condition:

-

-

-

SKIN AND NAIL EXAMINATION

6 SIGNS OF INFECTION

1.

2.

3.

4.

5.

6.

Temperature of skin:

- Cold may indicate =

  _____

- Hot may indicate =

  _____

Texture of skin indicates:

- _____ or _____

Inflammation/redness on skin or nails indicates:

- _____ or _____

Color/condition of nail bed indicates:

- Visible _____   • Disease   • Poor _____

Length and condition of free edge indicates:

- Nail _____

- _____ or _____ nails

Tenderness or stiff joints

Nail plate shape and thickness indicates:

- _____ or _____

NAIL DISEASES

As treatment for the following diseases, no service may be performed and client should be referred to a physician.

DISEASE

DESCRIPTION

_____

_____

Indicator: Ringworm of nail

_____

Indicator: Ringworm of hand

_____

Indicator: Ringworm of feet

_____

Indicator: Inflammation of skin around nail

_____

Indicator: Shedding or falling off of nails

_____

Indicator: Inflammation of nail matrix

_____

Indicator: Atrophy of nail or wasting away of nail

_____

Indicator: Loosening or separation of nail

NAIL DISORDERS

DISORDER	DESCRIPTION	TREATMENT
_____ _____ Indicator: Appear bluish in color		Manicure with caution.
_____ _____ Indicator: Very thin, soft		Polish to protect.
_____ _____ Indicator: Horizontal wavy ridges across nail		Lightly buff and apply a base coat.
_____ _____ Indicator: Nails with a concave shape		File carefully and polish to protect.
_____ _____ Indicator: Indented vertical lines down nail plate		Lightly buff and apply base coat to protect.
_____ _____ Indicator: Increased curvature of nails		Clean under free edge and file.
_____ _____ Indicator: Ingrown nails		Soften skin and trim nail.
_____ _____ Indicator: A brown or black darkening of nail		Make client aware of possible cause; suggest seeing physician.
_____ _____ Indicator: Thickening of nail plate or an abnormal outgrowth of nail		Lightly buff.

NAIL CONDITIONS

CONDITION	DESCRIPTION	TREATMENT
_____ _____ Indicator: Split cuticles; loose skin partially separated from cuticle		Trim hangnail and moisturize.
_____ _____ Indicator: Dark purplish discoloration under nail		No pressure on nail plate.
_____ _____ Indicator: White spots appearing in nail		Perform nail service as usual.
_____ _____ Indicator: Living skin that becomes attached to nail plate either at eponychium (dorsal pterygium) or hyponychium (inverse pterygium)		No service may be performed on affected nails.
_____ _____ Indicator: Indentations similar to horizontal corrugations that run across nail		Make client aware of possible cause; perform nail service as usual.
_____ _____ Indicator: Bitten nails		Perform nail service weekly.
_____ _____ Indicator: Split or brittle nails		Soften nails well before trimming; moisturizing treatment

LESSON CHALLENGE
Multiple choice. Indicate the correct answer for each question.

1. Which part of the nail serves as a watertight seal that protects the matrix against infection?
   a. eponychium
   b. lunula
   c. mantle
   d. hyponychium

2. The part of the nail plate that extends beyond the end of the finger is called the:
   a. sidewall
   b. free edge
   c. eponychium
   d. hyponychium

3. The living tissue that overlies the nail plate on the sides of the nail is known as the:
   a. mantle
   b. eponychium
   c. lunula
   d. perionychium

4. The nail plate rests on which area of the nail?
   a. sidewall
   b. free edge
   c. nail bed
   d. nail groove

5. The study of the structure and growth of the nails is called:
   a. onyx
   b. etiology
   c. onychology
   d. keratinization

6. A protein substance found in nails, skin and hair is:
   a. keratin
   b. cuticle
   c. lunula
   d. epithelium

7. Another term for tinea pedis is:
   a. athlete's foot
   b. hangnail
   c. tinea unguium
   d. contact dermatitis

8. A loosening or separation of the nail is referred to as:
   a. paronychia
   b. corrugations
   c. onycholysis
   d. onychocryptosis

9. Another name for split or brittle nails is:
   a. agnails
   b. onychophagy
   c. leukonychia
   d. onychorrhexis

10. Another term for bitten nails is:
    a. onychoptosis
    b. onychophagy
    c. onychogryposis
    d. onychorrhexis

LESSON CHALLENGE REFERENCES

Check your answers. Place a check mark next to the page number for any incorrect answer. On the lines, jot down topics that you still need to review.

1. PAGE 6 _____
2. PAGE 6 _____
3. PAGE 6 _____
4. PAGE 6 _____
5. PAGE 6 _____
6. PAGE 7 _____
7. PAGE 10 _____
8. PAGE 11 _____
9. PAGE 15 _____
10. PAGE 15 _____

▶ GROW WHAT YOU KNOW

Reflect on what you have learned and predict how this information will be used in the future.

113ᶜ.2 //
NATURAL NAILS

ACHIEVE //

Following this lesson on *Natural Nails*, you'll be able to:

» Describe a basic manicure in your own words

» Describe the basic pedicure in your own words

» Explain the different massage movements that are used during natural nail services

» Identify specialty services that can be combined with natural nail services

FOCUS //

NATURAL NAILS

Basic Manicure

Basic Pedicure

Massage

Specialty Nail Services

BASIC MANICURE

A manicure is the _____ _____ of the hands and fingernails.

The purpose of a manicure is to _____ the _____ of the _____ and, in particular, the _____.

FIVE BASIC NAIL SHAPES

MATCHING

Draw a line to identify the nail shape and fill in the blanks to the right.

Point

- Straight across at _____ _____ and squared at _____
- Full width at tip of nail provides _____
- Corners, though smooth, can _____ _____

Round

- Combination of square and _____
- _____ across at free edge with slightly _____ corners
- Also known as soft square or rounded square
- Sturdy due to width at _____ _____
- Typically kept shorter
- Good for _____ clients

Square

- Tapered and _____ at tip
- Typically worn _____

Oval

- Slightly _____ at tip
- Typically worn _____
- Most common shape for _____

Squoval

- Tapered to a slightly _____ tip
- Typically worn _____
- Tend to _____ more easily

BASIC PEDICURE

A pedicure is the _____ _____ of the _____ and _____.

MASSAGE

Benefits of massage include:

• Increased circulation of blood supply to _____

• Tighter, firmer _____

• Stimulation of _____ activities of skin

• Stronger _____ tissue

• Relief from _____

• Softer, improved _____ of skin

• Relief of emotional stress and _____ _____

MASSAGE CAUTIONS

Avoid massage on clients with:

• Skin _____

• Heart _____/
high blood pressure

• Stroke

• Pregnancy

Use caution on clients with:

• Prominent _____ veins

• Arthritis

FIVE BASIC MASSAGE TECHNIQUES

EFFLEURAGE

• Light stroking/_____ movement

• _____, smooth and gentle

• Performed with pads of the _____ and palms of the _____

• Often used to _____ and _____ massage

PETRISSAGE

• Light or heavy _____, pinching and rolling of the muscles

• Stimulates _____, nerves and skin glands

• Increases circulation of _____ and _____

FRICTION

• Circular or _____ movement with no _____

• Stimulates and _____ the muscles

• _____ circulation

TAPOTEMENT OR PERCUSSION

• Light _____ or slapping movement

• Increases blood circulation, stimulates nerves and promotes _____ contraction

• Helps skin release _____ _____ and waste material

• Most _____ massage movement

VIBRATION

• _____ movement

• Very _____

• Only done for a _____ amount of time

IMPORTANT MASSAGE POINTS

1. Check for _____

2. Avoid massage that is too deep, _____ or lengthy

3. Provide an even _____ or _____ to ensure relaxation

4. Avoid _____ hands from body once massage has begun

5. Use _____ - _____ movements to remove the hands

SPECIALTY NAIL SERVICES

REFLEXOLOGY

A massage method that uses _____ on specific points on hands, _____ and sometimes the ears to relieve tension and influence certain body _____.

AROMATHERAPY

The controlled use of _____ _____ that are highly fragranced for specific outcomes.

Write the effect of each essential oil in the space below.

OIL	EFFECT
Bergamot	
Chamomile	
Eucalyptus	
Geranium	
Lavender	
Peppermint	
Rosemary	
Tea Tree	

PARAFFIN TREATMENT

Paraffin is a type of wax used for _____ and

_____ services. Paraffin wax is _____ and

then placed on the client's hands or feet.

Paraffin helps _____ and _____ the skin,

leaving it soft and smooth.

FRENCH MANICURE

French polish is a style used to polish the nails creating a

_____-_____ effect.

NO-CHIP POLISH

• Referred to as _____ _____

• Typically lasts _____ weeks

• Uses an _____ or _____ light to cure each layer

No-chip polish is removed by soaking the client's nails in an

_____-based product.

NAIL DESIGN

Nail design is a way to add a _____ touch.

LESSON CHALLENGE *Multiple choice. Indicate the correct answer for each question.*

1. Manicure refers to the cosmetic care of the:
   a. hands and fingernails
   b. feet and toenails
   c. fingernails only
   d. toenails only

2. The most common nail shape worn by men is:
   a. squoval
   b. oval
   c. square
   d. round

3. A benefit of massage is:
   a. decreased circulation
   b. stimulation of glandular activity
   c. muscle soreness
   d. decreased blood supply

4. A stroking or circular massage movement that is soothing and relaxing is:
   a. tapotement
   b. friction
   c. effleurage
   d. petrissage

5. A type of massage method that uses pressure on specific points of the hands and feet is known as:
   a. aromatherapy
   b. exfoliation
   c. reflexology
   d. friction

6. An essential oil that is soothing and healing is:
   a. eucalyptus
   b. tea tree
   c. rosemary
   d. chamomile

7. What treatment soothes and moisturizes the skin?
   a. reflexology
   b. massage
   c. paraffin
   d. aromatherapy

8. A polish technique that creates a natural-looking effect on nails is called:
   a. no-chip polish
   b. French polish
   c. marbeling
   d. striping

9. What type of light does no-chip polish utilize to cure?
   a. halogen
   b. infrared
   c. IPL
   d. LED

10. A service that involves adding designs or accents to manicured nails is:
    a. nail design
    b. paraffin
    c. tapotement
    d. no-chip polish

LESSON CHALLENGE REFERENCES

Check your answers. Place a check mark next to the page number for any incorrect answer. On the lines, jot down topics that you still need to review.

1. PAGE 20 _____
2. PAGE 21 _____
3. PAGE 24 _____
4. PAGE 25 _____
5. PAGE 26 _____

6. PAGE 26 _____
7. PAGE 26 _____
8. PAGE 27 _____
9. PAGE 27 _____
10. PAGE 27 _____

▶ GROW WHAT YOU KNOW

Reflect on what you have learned and predict how this information will be used in the future.

113ᶜ.3 //
NATURAL NAIL PRODUCTS
AND ESSENTIALS

ACHIEVE //

Following this lesson on *Natural Nail Products and Essentials*, you'll be able to:

>> Identify products, tools or implements, supplies and equipment used for natural nail services

>> Describe the purpose they serve while performing natural nail services

FOCUS //

NATURAL NAIL PRODUCTS AND ESSENTIALS

Natural Nail Products

Natural Nail Essentials

NATURAL NAIL PRODUCTS

Safety Data Sheets (SDS) for all _____ used in the salon must be available.

PRODUCTS	DESCRIPTION	FUNCTION
Disinfectant	Chemical product	
Antiseptic		Reduces microbes on the skin
Styptic Product	Liquid or spray	
_____	Acetone or non-acetone	Dissolves polish
Cuticle Remover Cream		Loosens dead skin
_____	Lightener or high-percent hydrogen peroxide	Removes stains and whitens nails
Soaking Solution	Liquid soap used with warm water in finger bowl or pedicure basin	
_____	Moisturizer	Softens cuticle skin, moisturizes brittle nails
Lotion or Massage Cream/Oil	Lubricant	
Nail Preparation Solution		Removes oil and product to help polish adhere to the nail plate; dehydrating product
_____	Colorless polish that dries quickly; contains cellulose chemicals to create a tacky layer for polish to adhere to	Evens out nail plate, holds nail color to nail, prevents pigments from penetrating nail plate
Top Coat or Sealer	Colorless, clear polish that dries to a high shine; contains nitrocellulose, which contributes to the shine	
Colored Polish	Polish containing pigments to give color, enamel	Creates a colored effect
_____	Drying agent; spray, drops or polish applied over top coat	Aids in fast drying of polish; protects from stickiness
Nail Strengthener (Nail Hardener)	Usually a colorless, clear polish applied prior to the base coat; may contain strengthening fibers, moisturizers or proteins	
Exfoliant		Removes dead skin cells on the hands and feet

NATURAL NAIL ESSENTIALS

Nail service tools must be _____ or _____ after every use.

TOOLS/IMPLEMENTS	DESCRIPTION	FUNCTION
Nail Clippers	2 types – Fingernail (smaller) and toenail (larger); curved or straight blades	
_____	3 types available: Disposable, glass, metal The higher number in grit the softer it is; 240 or higher should be used on fingernails to prevent damage.	Shortens and shapes nails
Cuticle Pusher	Curved shape is designed to follow the natural curve of the nail	
Cuticle Nippers		Trim hangnails; check with your area's regulatory agency regarding usage
_____	Metal instrument with a spoon-shaped end	Removes debris from the nail margins/sidewalls; typically used on toenails
Nail Rasp	Metal tool with a file on the end designed to file in only one direction like a cheese grater	
Foot File (Foot Paddle)		Removes dry, flaky skin and smooths calluses
Nail Brush	Synthetic bristles	
Buffer	Several types available: 3-way buffer, block buffer, chamois buffer, buffing blocks, finishing buffers Follow regulatory guidelines on whether to dispose or disinfect buffers	

SUPPLIES	DESCRIPTION	FUNCTION
Cosmetic Spatula		Removes product from jars; ensures infection control
_____	Thin round wooden stick with a flat end and sometimes a pointed end	Loosens and pushes back cuticles; applies cosmetics; cleans under free edge, removes polish from sidewalls
Cotton or Lint-Free Wipes	Absorbent disposable material	
Toe Separators		Placed between toes before polish application
_____	Open-toed sandals worn instead of shoes while polish dries	Allows polish to dry
Towels		Dry hands and feet; can be folded into a cushion

NATURAL NAIL EQUIPMENT

Nail service equipment is _____ to provide a _____ nail service.

EQUIPMENT	DESCRIPTION	FUNCTION
_____	Most tables will have drawers for storing products, supplies and implements	Provides a flat, nonporous area to perform services on the hands
Technician Chair		Allows easy access to all tools and the client
Client Chair	Stationary chair; no wheels or swivel	
Client Cushion		Used to rest client's arm or foot during service
Disinfection Container	Needs to be large enough to allow complete immersion of implements	
_____	Space-saving container used to prevent cross contamination	Holds absorbent cotton, cotton swabs and other accessories
Lamp		Lights the area for close detail work
Finger Bowl	Large enough to immerse the fingernails	
_____	Considered an "all-in-one" area designed specifically for pedicures	Provides a comfortable seat with arm rests, pedicure basin, foot rest and technician stool for pedicure services
Pedicure Basin or Bath		Serves as a water container used to soak client's feet during a pedicure service

MATCHING

Draw a line from each item pictured below to its corresponding label.

Nail Rasp

Foot File

Cuticle Nippers

Orangewood Sticks

LESSON CHALLENGE
Multiple choice. Indicate the correct answer for each question.

1. Which of the following products helps prevent nails from splitting?
   - a. cuticle cream
   - b. polish remover
   - c. nail preparation solution
   - d. nail strengthener

2. An example of an exfoliant is:
   - a. sloughing lotion
   - b. foot soak
   - c. lotion
   - d. styptic product

3. Which implement is used to smooth out ridges on the nail plate?
   - a. cuticle pusher
   - b. cuticle nippers
   - c. buffer
   - d. file

4. To smooth dry, flaky skin or calluses on the feet, use a:
   - a. foot file
   - b. nail rasp
   - c. curette
   - d. nail brush

5. Cuticles can be softened by soaking fingernails in a:
   - a. speed dry
   - b. finger bowl
   - c. disinfection container
   - d. polish remover

LESSON CHALLENGE REFERENCES

Check your answers. Place a check mark next to the page number for any incorrect answer. On the lines, jot down topics that you still need to review.

1. PAGE 33 _____
2. PAGE 33 _____
3. PAGE 35 _____
4. PAGE 35 _____
5. PAGE 38 _____

▶ GROW WHAT YOU KNOW

Reflect on what you have learned and predict how this information will be used in the future.

113ᶜ.4 //
NAILS GUEST EXPERIENCE

ACHIEVE //

Following this lesson on *Nails Guest Experience*, you'll be able to:

» Summarize the service essentials related to nail care

» Provide examples of infection control and safety guidelines for a nail service

FOCUS //

NAILS GUEST EXPERIENCE

Nail Service Essentials

Nail Service Infection Control and Safety

NAIL SERVICE ESSENTIALS

CONNECT

Guidelines for welcoming a client:

-
-

CONSULT

Ask client about:

-
-
-
-

Analyze client's:

-
-

Assess:

-
-
-

Gain Feedback:

-

CREATE

- Ensure client _____ throughout service.
- Stay focused on _____ nail service to best of ability.
- Produce a _____, _____ and _____ result.

Teach client:

-
-

COMPLETE

Request feedback and look for cues:

-
-

Escort client to the retail area:

-
-
-
-

NAIL SERVICE INFECTION CONTROL AND SAFETY

CLEANING

·

·

·

·

·

DISINFECTION

·

·

·

·

·

Single-use items must be _____ after each use.

CLEANING AND DISINFECTION GUIDELINES

	METAL TOOLS	MANICURE STATION	PEDICURE STATION
CLEAN	· · ·	·	·
DISINFECT (with approved EPA-registered disinfectant)	·	·	·

CARE AND SAFETY

PERSONAL CARE

- Ensure personal standards of _____ and _____ to minimize spread of _____.
- Wash hands and dry thoroughly with a _____ towel.
- _____ workstation.
- Clean and disinfect _____ appropriately.
- Wear single-use _____ as required.
- Minimize _____ by maintaining good _____ during service.
- Refer to your area's _____ _____ for proper mixing/handling of disinfection solutions.

CLIENT CARE PRIOR TO THE SERVICE

- Check the skin and nails for any _____ or _____. If any are evident, refer client to _____ and do not proceed with service.
- Protect the client's skin and _____ from water with a freshly _____ _____ if necessary.
- Handle _____ with care to ensure your safety and that of your clients.
- If any tools are dropped on the floor be sure to pick them up, then _____ and _____.

CLIENT CARE DURING THE SERVICE

- If you injure the client or yourself, immediately apply _____ procedures. If wound is severe, seek _____ _____ _____.
- Be aware of any _____ while massaging.
- Work carefully around _____ _____ / _____.
- Update client record noting nail or skin _____ and _____ provided.
- Be aware of _____ cues the client may be conveying.
- Store soiled towels in a _____, _____ receptacle until laundered.

CARE AND SAFETY (CONT'D)

SALON CARE

- Follow _____ and _____ guidelines, including _____ and _____ procedures.
- Ensure equipment, including the _____, is clean and _____.
- Promote professional image by ensuring your _____ is clean and tidy throughout service.
- _____ all tools after _____ use. Always use disinfected tools for _____ client.
- Ensure _____ _____ are properly positioned to avoid accidental falls.
- Ensure _____ _____, plugs and _____ are in good condition and remember to turn _____ after use.
- Sweep or _____ and dispose of _____ _____ at end of service.
- Report malfunctioning furniture/equipment to _____.
- Clean/mop water spillage from floor to avoid accidental _____.

MATCHING

Match the service essential to the appropriate descriptor.

1. **CONNECT**

2. **CONSULT**

3. **CREATE**

4. **COMPLETE**

_____ Show the client how to use cuticle oil to maintain cuticle health.

_____ Offer sincere appreciation to your client for visiting the school or salon.

_____ Meet and greet the client with a firm handshake and a pleasant tone of voice.

_____ Ask your client to describe what they are expecting; listen for details.

_____ Stay focused on delivering the nail service to the best of your ability.

_____ Assess the facts and thoroughly think through your recommendations.

_____ Ask questions to discover client needs.

_____ Escort client to the retail area and show the products you used.

_____ Analyze your client's skin and nails.

_____ Ask questions and look for verbal and nonverbal cues to determine your client's level of satisfaction.

_____ Communicate to build rapport and develop a connection with the client.

_____ Ensure client comfort throughout the service.

LESSON CHALLENGE *Multiple choice. Indicate the correct answer for each question.*

1. Communicating with your client prior to and during the nail service will help you avoid misunderstandings and ensure:
   a. predictable results
   b. a proper massage
   c. their friends will give them compliments
   d. the polish is dried in a timely manner

2. Each of the following is a guideline to follow during the Connect nail service essential EXCEPT:
   a. build rapport
   b. greet client with a firm handshake
   c. explain recommended solutions
   d. greet client with a pleasant tone of voice

3. Which of the following is a guideline to be followed during the Complete nail service essential?
   a. meet and greet the client with a firm handshake
   b. teach the client how to use a top coat if necessary
   c. ask specific questions such as, "What type of impression would you like to convey?"
   d. ask questions and look for verbal and nonverbal cues to determine your client's level of satisfaction

4. Ensuring your client's comfort during the service is important during which nail service essential?
   a. Create
   b. Consult
   c. Connect
   d. Complete

5. In order to determine your client's level of satisfaction look for verbal and nonverbal cues and:
   a. ask for referrals
   b. request feedback
   c. recommend products for purchase
   d. seek approval from staff members

6. Which is NOT a method used to disinfect tools and equipment?
   a. heat
   b. spray
   c. immersion
   d. disinfectant wipes

7. To clean metal tools, begin by:
   a. rinsing with hot water
   b. removing debris
   c. immersing in soap and water
   d. immersing in a disinfectant solution

8. Which of the following items must be discarded after use on a nail service client?
   a. nail clippers
   b. glass nail file
   c. cuticle pusher
   d. single-use item

9. All of the following are personal care guidelines for the salon EXCEPT:
   a. disinfect workstation
   b. wear single-use gloves as required
   c. clean and disinfect tools appropriately
   d. store soiled towels in a dry, covered receptacle until laundered

10. When completing the client record after a nail service, which of the following is NOT necessary to note?
    a. nail condition
    b. skin condition
    c. weather conditions
    d. services provided

LESSON CHALLENGE REFERENCES

Check your answers. Place a check mark next to the page number for any incorrect answer. On the lines, jot down topics that you still need to review.

1. PAGE 42 _____
2. PAGE 43 _____
3. PAGE 43 _____
4. PAGE 43 _____
5. PAGE 43 _____
6. PAGE 44 _____
7. PAGE 45 _____
8. PAGE 45 _____
9. PAGE 47 _____
10. PAGE 47 _____

▶ GROW WHAT YOU KNOW

Reflect on what you have learned and predict how this information will be used in the future.

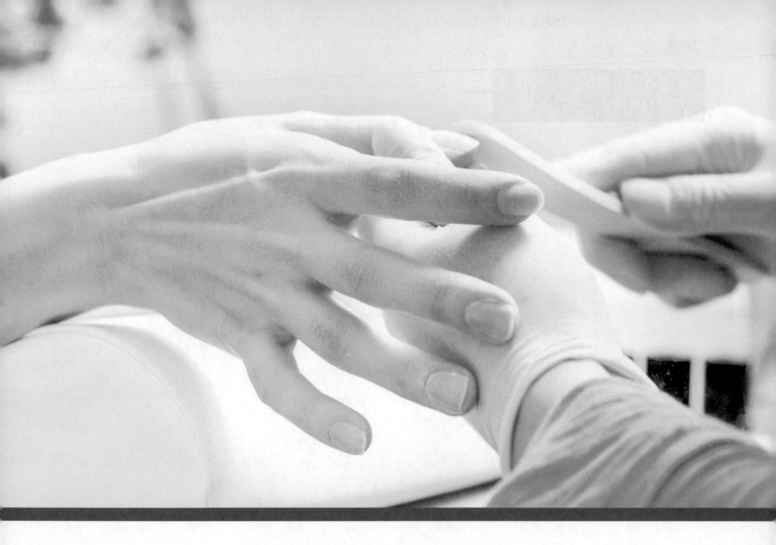

113ᶜ.8 //
ARTIFICIAL NAIL SYSTEM PRODUCTS AND ESSENTIALS

ACHIEVE //

Following this lesson on *Artificial Nail System Products and Essentials*, you'll be able to:

» Identify the two types of artificial nail systems

» Describe artificial nail preparation and why it is important

» Identify the different artificial nail basics and describe them in your own words

» Describe the different artificial removal methods in your own words

FOCUS //

ARTIFICIAL NAIL SYSTEM PRODUCTS AND ESSENTIALS

Artificial Nail Systems

Artificial Nail Preparation

Artificial Nail Basics

Artificial Nail Removal

ARTIFICIAL NAIL SYSYTEMS

There are 2 main types of artificial nail systems used today:

1. _____

2. _____

ACRYLIC NAILS

Monomer and polymer are common terms referring to acrylic _____

and acrylic _____ .

LIQUID MONOMER

Acrylic _____

_____ is the primary monomer in acrylic liquid.

Other additives found in liquid monomer include:

-
-
-
-
-
-

POWDER POLYMER

Acrylic _____

Contain:

-
-
-
-

ACRYLIC PRODUCTS		DESCRIPTION	FUNCTION
Monomer		Liquid in form	
Polymer			Mixes with the monomer to form an acrylic nail
_____ _____		Liquid in form; either contains methacrylic acid or is considered acid free	Ensures adhesion of acrylic product to nail

IMPLEMENTS/ TOOLS		DESCRIPTION	FUNCTION
Dappen Dish		Small glass container	
Acrylic Brush			Used to hold the monomer and polymer to build the acrylic nail; used to manipulate the product to the desired location

SUPPLIES		DESCRIPTION	FUNCTION
_____ _____		An abrasive in a variety of different grits, number of abrasive granules per square inch	Shortens, files and shapes artificial nails

Identify the file grit across from its corresponding purpose.

_____	Remove length on enhancements; removes excess product for artificial nail maintenance
_____	Shaping any nail and refining surface of enhancements
_____	Shaping and refining surface of any nail
_____	Smoothing surface imperfections on any nail; shining nails

SUPPLIES		DESCRIPTION	FUNCTION
Buffer		Extra-fine file	
Eyedropper			Used to move acrylic liquid from container to dappen dish
_____ _____		Lint-free single-use towel	Used to protect the table and used for cleaning and removing excess product from brushes

LIGHT-CURED GEL NAILS

Gel systems _____ exposure to a _____

_____ to cure.

Gels are mainly made of _____ _____ ;

other ingredients are dependent on the gels used:

- Base gels contain _____ molecules

- Gel sealer may contain _____ for thinning and speeding up

  the curing process

- _____ / _____ _____ may

  contain silica or polymers to thicken the gel

GEL PRODUCTS		DESCRIPTION	FUNCTION
Gel		Gel in form, comes in many colors and different viscosities (thicknesses)	
Gel Bonder or Primer			Ensures adhesion of gel product to nail
_____ _____		Thin gel product	Creates a high-shine finish and seals product

TOOLS/ IMPLEMENTS		DESCRIPTION	FUNCTION
Gel Brush		Made from synthetic fibers; can be many different shapes and sizes	

SUPPLIES		DESCRIPTION	FUNCTION
Nail File			Shortens, files and shapes artificial nails
		Extra-fine file	Smooths nails; shines surface of nail
Disposable Towel		Lint-free single-use towel	

MATCHING

Draw lines to identify the file grit with its corresponding purpose.

FINE 250-900   Shaping any nail and refining surface
                                              of enhancements

EXTRA-FINE   Shaping and refining surface of any nail

COARSE 80-120   Smoothing surface imperfections on any nail;
                                              shining nails

MEDIUM 130-240   Remove length on enhancements; removes
                                              excess product for artificial nail maintenance

ADHESIVES

- Create a _____ between two _____ surfaces

- Nail adhesives are created to be compatible with _____ and common materials found in _____ _____ _____.

ARTIFICIAL NAIL PREPARATION

Artificial nail preparation consists of a _____ manicure followed by the removal of shine, _____ and _____.

CUTICLE CARE

Perform a basic manicure without

_____ nails or

_____ hands

-

-

-

FILE

File the free edge as well as the

_____ _____

to remove shine

-

-

-

ARTIFICIAL NAIL BASICS

Areas of the nail:

Product application:

Zone 1.

Zone 2.

Zone 3.

OVERLAY

Product is applied over _____ _____ or

_____ _____ for added length.

NAIL TIPS

_____ the length of the nails

1. _____ _____: The area that adheres to the natural

   nail plate

2. _____ _____: A ridge underneath the nail tip

   where the free edge of the natural nail fits into place

SCULPTURED NAILS

Created over a _____ - _____ rather than

using a _____ for added _____

The form fits snugly _____ the _____ _____.

ARTIFICIAL NAIL MAINTENANCE

All artificial nail services require _____, or a _____,

to keep them healthy.

Maintenance is recommended every _____-_____ days.

2-WEEK MAINTENANCE

Apply acrylic or gel to the natural

nail exposed in Zone _____, the

_____ _____.

4-WEEK MAINTENANCE

Applies to _____-_____

acrylic or gel nails.

Reposition the _____

_____, Zone 1, as well

as fill in the new growth, Zone 3.

ARTIFICIAL NAIL REMOVAL

ACRYLIC NAIL REMOVAL

Most widely used solvent to remove acrylic nails is _____.

GEL NAIL REMOVAL

Traditional gel nails are removed by _____ the product off.

LESSON CHALLENGE *Multiple choice. Indicate the correct answer for each question.*

1. Another name for acrylic monomer is:
   a. acrylic liquid
   b. catalyst
   c. polymer
   d. acrylic oligomer

2. When moisture is trapped between an artificial nail and the natural nail, what can form?
   a. bacterial infection
   b. mold
   c. fungal infection
   d. yeast

3. Which of the following ingredients is the powder used to form an acrylic nail?
   a. polymer
   b. methacrylate
   c. methacrylic
   d. monomer

4. What grit of nail file is used to remove excess artificial nail product?
   a. 0-70
   b. 80-120
   c. 130-240
   d. 250-900

5. An acrylic brush is made of what type of hair?
   a. nylon
   b. plastic
   c. acrylic
   d. natural

6. Gels are mostly made up of what type of polymers?
   a. cyanoacrylates
   b. cross-linking monomers
   c. oligomers
   d. monomers

7. The type of product that causes a nail tip to stick to a nail plate is known as:
   a. adhesive
   b. bonder gel
   c. methacrylate
   d. primer

8. The type of artificial nail service that requires the use of a form is referred to as:
   a. light-cured gels
   b. sculptured nails
   c. overlay
   d. nail wraps

9. Artificial nail product remover contains:
   a. no acetone
   b. methacrylic
   c. acetone
   d. methacrylate

10. The most widely used solvent in the nail industry is:
    a. catalyst
    b. acetone
    c. monomer
    d. polymer

LESSON CHALLENGE REFERENCES

Check your answers. Place a check mark next to the page number for any incorrect answer. On the lines, jot down topics that you still need to review.

1. PAGE 74 _____
2. PAGE 75 _____
3. PAGE 75 _____
4. PAGE 76 _____
5. PAGE 76 _____
6. PAGE 77 _____
7. PAGE 78 _____
8. PAGE 80 _____
9. PAGE 84 _____
10. PAGE 84 _____

▶ # GROW WHAT YOU KNOW

Reflect on what you have learned and predict how this information will be used in the future.

PIVOT POINT

ACKNOWLEDGMENTS

Pivot Point Fundamentals is designed to provide education to undergraduate students to help prepare them for licensure and an entry-level position in the cosmetology field. An undertaking of this magnitude requires the expertise and cooperation of many people who are experts in their field. Pivot Point takes pride in our internal team of educators who develop cosmetology, esthetics and nails education, along with our print and digital experts, designers, editors, illustrators and video producers. Pivot Point would like to express our many thanks to these talented individuals who have devoted themselves to the business of beauty, lifelong learning and especially for help raising the bar for future professionals in our industry.

EDUCATION DEVELOPMENT | **Janet Fisher // Sabine Held-Perez // Vasiliki A. Stavrakis**
Markel Artwell
Eileen Dubelbeis
Brian Fallon
Melissa Holmes
Lisa Luppino
Paul Suttles
Amy Gallagher
Lisa Kersting
Jamie Nabielec
Vic Piccolotto
Ericka Thelin
Jane Wegner

EDITORIAL | **Maureen Spurr // Wm. Bullion // Deidre Glover**
Liz Bagby
Jack Bernin
Lori Chapman

DESIGN & PRODUCTION | **Jennifer Eckstein // Rick Russell // Danya Shaikh**
Joanna Jakubowicz
Denise Podlin
Annette Baase
Agnieszka Hansen
Kristine Palmer
Tiffany Wu

PROJECT MANAGEMENT | **Jenny Allen // Ken Wegrzyn**

DIGITAL DEVELOPMENT | John Bernin
Javed Fouch
Anna Fehr
Matt McCarthy
Marcia Noriega
Corey Passage
Herb Potzus

Pivot Point also wishes to take this opportunity to acknowledge the many contributors and product concept testers who helped make this program possible.

INDUSTRY CONTRIBUTORS

Linda Burmeister
Esthetics

**Jeanne Braa Foster,
Dr. Dean Foster**
Eyes on Cancer

Mandy Gross
Nails

Andrea D. Kelly, MA, MSW
University of Delaware

Rosanne Kinley
*Infection Control
National Interstate Council*

Lynn Maestro
Cirépil by Perron Rigot, Paris

Andrzej Matracki
*World and European
Men's Champion*

MODERN SALON

Rachel Molepske
*Look Good Feel Better, PBA
CUT IT OUT, PBA*

Peggy Moon
Liaison to Regulatory and Testing

Robert Richards
Fashion Illustrations

Clif St. Germain, Ph.D
Educational Consultant

Andis Company

International Dermal Institute

HairUWear Inc.

Lock & Loaded Men's Grooming

PRODUCT CONCEPT TESTING

**Central Carolina
Community College**
Millington, North Carolina

Gateway Community Colleges
Phoenix, Arizona

MC College
Edmonton, Alberta

Metro Beauty Academy
Allentown, Pennsylvania

**Rowan Cabarrus
Community College**
Kannapolis, North Carolina

**Sunstate Academy of
Cosmetology and Massage**
Ft. Myers, Florida

Summit Salon Academy
Kokomo, Indiana

TONI&GUY Hairdressing Academy
*Costa Mesa, California
Plano, Texas*

Xenon Academy
*Omaha, NE
Grand Island, NE*

LEADERSHIP TEAM

Robert Passage
Chairman and CEO

Robert J. Sieh
*Senior Vice President,
Finance and Operations*

Judy Rambert
Vice President, Education

Kevin Cameron
*Senior Vice President,
Education and Marketing*

R.W. Miller
*Vice President, Domestic Sales
and Field Education*

Jan Laan
*Vice President, International
Business Development*

Katy O'Mahony
Director, Human Resources

In addition, we give special thanks to the North American Regulating agencies whose careful work protects us as well as our clients enhancing the high quality of our work. These agencies include Occupational Health and Safety Agency (OSHA) and the U.S. Environmental Protection Agency (EPA). *Pivot Point Fundamentals* promotes use of their policies and procedures.

Pivot Point International would like to express our SPECIAL THANKS to the inspired visual artisans of Creative Commons, without whose talents this book of beauty would not be possible.